THE BOYS' AND GIRLS' HANDBOOK

This edition first published in 1985
exclusively for Marylebone Books

Text and illustrations © 1981, 1985
Octopus Books Ltd.

Editor: Fiona Hellowell
Art Editor: Ronnie Wilkinson
Jacket Designer: Ian Butterworth
Designed by: Design 23

ISBN 0 86178 339 5

Printed in Great Britain by
Richard Clay (The Chaucer Press)
Limited, Bungay, Suffolk

THE
BOYS'
AND
GIRLS'
HANDBOOK

CONTENTS

THE UNIVERSE

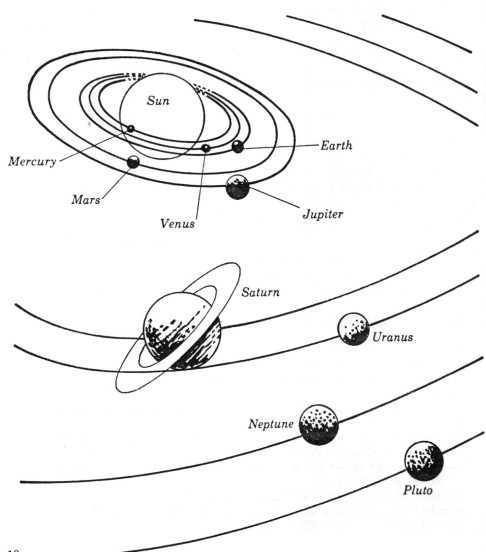

The Scale of the Universe

If we imagine that our Sun is only 1 m (3.27 ft) in diameter, on that scale the planet Pluto, the most distant of the nine known planets, would be about 4.6 km (nearly 3 miles) away at its average distance. The nearest star would be about 26,000 km (16,000 miles) away.

Our Sun is just one of many millions of stars in the Milky Way, the name for our galaxy. The Milky Way is a spiral galaxy and almost all the stars we see at night lie in one of the spirals or 'arms'. Compared to the other stars, the Sun is unremarkable in either size or brightness. It lies about two-thirds of the way to one edge from the centre. On the scale we have adopted, the Milky Way would be about 1,300 million km (800 million miles) across. But even on that scale distances become quite impossible to visualize.

Outside our galaxy are hundreds of millions of other galaxies. One of the largest and nearest of these, visible to the naked eye in the northern hemisphere, is the great spiral galaxy in the constellation Andromeda. If the Milky Way were a mere 1,000 km (620 miles) across, it would be about 13,000 km (8,000 miles) away from us. The world's greatest telescopes have photographed galaxies more than 1,000 times farther away than this!

The mean distance between the Earth and the Sun, 150,000,000 km (93,000,000 miles), is known as an *astronomical unit*. But when we go beyond the solar system, kilometres and astronomical units are both inconveniently small for reckoning distances. The unit used is the *light-year*, the distance light travels in one year. Light travels at 2,997,925 km (186,282 miles) per second, so in a year it covers 9,470,000,000,000 km – nearly 6,000,000,000,000 miles.

Here are some facts and figures on the planets and the stars:

Number of stars in the Milky Way galaxy: 100,000 million (10^{11}) approx.
Distance across Milky Way galaxy: 100,000 light-years approx.
Distance of Sun from centre of Milky Way: 32,000 light-years approx.
Distance of Sun from most distant star in Milky Way: 75,000 light-years approx.
Distance to Magellanic Clouds (the two small galaxies which are nearest to ours): 160,000 light-years approx.
Distance to Great Spiral galaxy in Andromeda (limit of naked eye vision): 2,200,000 light-years
Distance of the most distant galaxies detectable by radio telescope: 17,500,000,000 light-years
Number of stars visible to the naked eye: 5,776
Number of galaxies in the detectable universe: 10^{11} to 10^{12} (100,000,000,000 to 1,000,000,000,000)

Facts and figures on the planets and stars (cont'd)
Total number of stars in detectable universe: 10^{22} to 10^{23}
(10,000,000,000,000,000,000,000 to 100,000,000,000,000,000,000,000)
Estimated age of the universe: between 17,500 million and 21,500
million years
Estimated age of the Sun: 4,600,000,000 years

THE TWENTY BRIGHTEST STARS

NAME	VISUAL MAGNITUDE	DISTANCE IN LIGHT-YEARS
Sirius	−1.43	8.6
Canopus	−0.72	98
Alpha Centauri	−0.27	4.3
Arcturus	−0.06	36
Vega	+0.04	26
Capella	+0.05	45
Rigel	+0.08	600
Procyon	+0.37	11.4
Betelgeuse	+0.41 (variable)	600
Archernar	+0.47	65
Beta Centauri	+0.63	300
Altair	+0.77	16.6
Aldebaran	+0.86 (variable)	52
Alpha Crucis	+0.87	390
Spica	+0.91 (variable)	274
Antares	+0.92 (variable)	420
Pollux	+1.16	37
Fomalhaut	+1.19	22.6
Beta Crucis	+1.24	490
Deneb	+1.26	1,400

The brightest stars

The stars in the night sky differ in apparent brightness, and these differences are measured on the scale of stellar magnitudes. Roughly speaking, the brightest stars in the sky are of the first magnitude. All the other stars visible to the naked eye on a clear night are divided into five lower magnitudes, the very faintest belonging to the sixth. The stars of each magnitude are 2.5 times as bright as those of the next lower magnitude. Negative magnitudes are brightest. A star that has a magnitude of -1 is ten times brighter than one of $+1.5$.

THE NEAREST STARS

STAR	DISTANCE IN LIGHT-YEARS	APPARENT MAGNITUDE
Proxima Centauri	4.28	$+11.0$
Alpha Centauri	4.38	-0.27
Barnard's Star	5.91	$+9.5$
Wolf 359	7.60	$+13.3$
Lalande 21185	8.13	$+7.5$
Sirius	8.65	-1.43

The Constellations

In ancient times the stars were divided into groups, each of which was named after a mythological character or common object. One of the great astronomers, Ptolemy (*fl.* AD 140), drew up a star catalogue containing 48 constellations. Since then the list has been extended because many star groups can only be seen from the southern hemisphere and therefore remained unknown to classical astronomers.

There are now 88 constellations recognized internationally; these are listed below in alphabetical order. N indicates the northernmost and S the southernmost star groups.

ALPHABETICAL LIST OF CONSTELLATIONS

NAME	MEANING	NAME	MEANING
Andromeda	Daughter of King Cepheus	Caelum	Chisel
		Camelopardalis	Giraffe
Antlia	Pump	Cancer	Crab
Apus (S)	Bird of Paradise	Canes Venatici	Hunting Dogs
Aquarius	Water Carrier	Canis Major	Greater Dog
Aquila	Eagle	Canis Minor	Lesser Dog
Ara (S)	Altar	Capricornus	Goat
Aries	Ram	Carina	Ship's Keel
Auriga	Charioteer	Cassiopeia (N)	Mother of Andromeda
Boötes	Herdsman		

Constellations of the northern hemisphere

NAME	MEANING	NAME	MEANING
Centaurus	Centaur	**Fornax**	Furnace
Cepheus (N)	King of Ethiopia	**Gemini**	Twins
Cetus	Whale	**Grus**	Crane
Chamaeleon (S)	Chameleon	**Hercules**	Hercules
Circinus (S)	Dividers	**Horologium**	Clock
Columba	Dove	**Hydra**	Water Serpent
Coma Berenices	Berenice's Hair	**Hydrus (S)**	Water Snake
Corona Australis	Southern Crown	**Indus (S)**	Indian
Corona Borealis	Northern Crown	**Lacerta**	Lizard
Corvus	Crow	**Leo**	Lion
Crater	Cup	**Leo Minor**	Lion Cub
Crux (S)	Southern Cross	**Lepus**	Hare
Cygnus	Swan	**Libra**	Scales
Delphinus	Dolphin	**Lupus**	Wolf
Dorado (S)	Swordfish	**Lynx**	Lynx
Draco (N)	Dragon	**Lyra**	Lyre
Equuleus	Foal	**Mensa (S)**	Table
Eridanus	River Eridanus	**Microscopium**	Microscope

Constellations of the southern hemisphere

NAME	MEANING	NAME	MEANING
Monoceros	Unicorn	**Scorpius**	Scorpion
Musca (S)	Fly	**Sculptor**	Sculptor
Norma	Rule	**Scutum**	Shield
Octans (S)	Octant	**Serpens**	Serpent
Ophiuchus	Serpent Holder	**Sextans**	Sextant
Orion	The Hunter	**Taurus**	Bull
Pavo (S)	Peacock	**Telescopium**	Telescope
Pegasus	Winged Horse	**Triangulum**	Triangle
Perseus	Son of Zeus	**Triangulum**	
Phoenix	Phoenix	**Australe (S)**	Southern Triangle
Pictor (S)	Easel	**Tucana (S)**	Toucan
Pisces	Fishes	**Ursa Major**	Greater Bear,
Piscis Austrinus	Southern Fish		Plough
Puppis	Ship's Poop	**Ursa Minor (N)**	Lesser Bear
Pyxis	Ship's Compass	**Vela**	Ship's Sail
Reticulum (S)	Net	**Virgo**	Virgin
Sagitta	Arrow	**Volans (S)**	Flying Fish
Sagittarius	Archer	**Vulpecula**	Little Fox

15

The Solar System

THE PLANETS (in order of distance from the Sun)

PLANET	EQUATORIAL DIAMETER KM	MILES	LENGTH OF YEAR (SIDEREAL PERIOD) IN EARTH YEARS OR DAYS	ROTATION PERIOD
Mercury	4,878	3,031	88 days	58 days
Venus	12,100	7,519	225 days	243 days
Earth	12,756	7,926	365 days	24 hours
Mars	6,793	4,221	687 days	24½ hours
Jupiter	142,880	88,780	12 years	10 hours
Saturn	120,000	74,600	29½ years	10 hours
Uranus	50,800	31,600	84 years	10¾ hours
Neptune	48,600	30,200	165 years	15¾ hours
Pluto	5,500	3,400	248½ years	6½ days

Our Sun
Mean distance from the Earth: 150,000,000 km (93,000,000 miles)
Time light takes to travel from Sun to Earth: 8⅓ minutes
Diameter: 139,000,000 km (865,000 miles)
Volume: more than one million times that of the Earth
Mass: more than 300,000 times that of the Earth
Mean density: about 1½ times that of water
Rotation period: equator, once every 25 days; poles, once every 34 days
(the Sun does not rotate as a solid body)
Surface temperature: 6,000 °C
Temperature of interior: 20,000,000°C approx.
Power output: 3.8×10^{23} kilowatts

The natural satellites
Satellites are small planets orbiting larger ones. The Earth has only one satellite, the Moon, which is an exceptionally large one in proportion to the size of the Earth. Jupiter and Saturn have bigger moons than ours, but these are smaller in proportion to the size of their planets.

The Moon is 3,476 km (2,172 miles) in diameter and revolves around the Earth at a distance of 382,000 km (239,000 miles). It rotates on its axis in the same time that it revolves round the Earth; that is why we always see the same face of the Moon.

16

SURFACE TEMPERATURE °C	SURFACE GRAVITY COMPARED TO THAT OF THE EARTH	MEAN DISTANCE FROM SUN KM	MILES
−180 to +420	0.38	58,000,000	36,000,000
+500	0.90	108,200,000	67,200,000
−88 to +58	1.00	149,600,000	93,000,000
−125 to +30	0.38	228,000,000	141,000,000
−25	2.64	778,000,000	484,000,000
−110	1.16	1,427,000,000	887,000,000
−160	0.94	2,870,000,000	1,780,000,000
−160	1.20	4,497,000,000	2,794,000,000
−220	0.24	5,900,000,000	3,658,000,000

SATELLITES OF THE PLANETS

Planet/ Satellite	Mean distance from planet 1000s OF KM	1000s OF MILES	Diameter KM	MILES
MARS				
Phobos	9.3	5.8	23	14
Deimos	23.4	14.6	11	7
JUPITER				
Amalthea	181	113	200	124
Io	419	262	3,650	2,268
Europa	667	417	2,900	1,802
Ganymede	1,066	666	5,000	3,107
Callisto	1,872	1,170	4,500	2,796
Himalia	11,392	7,120	100	62
Leda	11,115	6,910	?	?
Lysithea	11,664	7,290	20	12

SATELLITES OF THE PLANETS (Jupiter continued)

Planet/ Satellite	Mean distance from planet 1000s OF KM	1000s OF MILES	Diameter KM	MILES
Elara	11,680	7,300	30	19
Ananke	20,800	13,000	20	12
Carme	22,400	14,000	20	12
Pasiphae	23,360	14,600	20	12
Sinope	23,520	14,700	20	12

14th satellite (unnamed): details not fully established yet

SATURN

Janus	157	98	300	186
Mimas	181	113	500	310
Encelades	238	149	600	373
Tethys	293	183	1,040	646
Dione	376	235	820	510
Rhea	525	328	1,580	982
Titan	1,216	760	5,830	3,623
Hyperion	1,472	920	500	311
Iapetus	3,520	2,200	1,600	994
Phoebe	12,880	8,050	200	124

URANUS

Miranda	122	76	300	186
Ariel	190	119	800	498
Umbria	266	166	600	373
Titania	435	272	1,100	684
Oberon	582	364	1,000	621

NEPTUNE

Triton	352	220	3,700	2,300
Nereid	5,600	3,500	300	186

THE EARTH

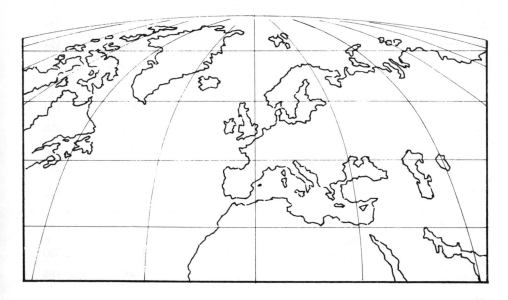

Features of the Earth

SOME FACTS ABOUT THE EARTH
Estimated age of the Earth: over 4,500 million years
Diameter of Earth at Equator: 12,757 km (7,927 miles)
Diameter of Earth at Poles: 12,714 km (7,900 miles)
Equatorial circumference: 64,496 km (24,902 miles)
Meridianal circumference: 64,387 km (24,860 miles)
Total surface area: 510,100,000 sq km (196,950,000 sq miles)
Land area: 148,950,000 sq km (57,510,000 sq miles)
Sea area: 361,150,000 sq km (139,440 sq miles)

PRINCIPAL OCEANS AND SEAS OF THE WORLD

NAME	AREA SQ KM	AREA SQ MILES	AVERAGE DEPTH METRES	AVERAGE DEPTH FEET	GREATEST DEPTH METRES	GREATEST DEPTH FEET
Pacific Ocean	160,000,000	63,986,000	4,280	14,040	11,033	36,198
Atlantic Ocean	81,663,000	31,530,000	3,926	12,880	9,188	30,143
Indian Ocean	73,427,000	28,350,000	3,962	13,000	7,000	22,968
Arctic Ocean	14,353,000	5,541,500	1,280	4,200	5,440	17,850
Mediterranean Sea	2,851,000	1,145,000	1,372	4,500	4,400	14,435
South China Sea	2,318,000	895,000	1,645	5,400	5,016	16,456
Bering Sea	2,274,000	878,000	507	1,665	4,091	13,422
Caribbean Sea	1,942,500	750,000	2,560	8,400	7,239	23,750
Gulf of Mexico	1,813,000	700,000	1,433	4,700	3,787	12,426
Sea of Okhotsk	1,507,000	582,000	914	3,000	3,847	12,621
East China Sea	1,243,000	480,000	186	610	3,200	10,500
Yellow Sea	1,243,000	480,000	49	160	106	348
Hudson Bay	1,222,500	472,000	134	440	457	1,500
Sea of Japan	1,049,000	405,000	1,474	4,835	3,109	10,200
North Sea	572,500	221,000	55	180	609	1,998
Red Sea	461,000	178,000	454	1,490	2,211	7,254
Black Sea	436,415	168,500	1,311	4,300	2,244	7,362
Baltic Sea	409,000	158,000	67	221	396	1,300

CONTINENTS OF THE WORLD

CONTINENT	AREA SQ KM	SQ MILES
Africa	30,259,000	11,683,000
Antarctica	16,000,000	6,178,000
Asia	43,250,000	16,699,000
Europe	10,360,000	4,000,000
America: North America	21,500,000	8,301,000
South America	17,793,000	6,870,000
Central America	2,750,000	1,062,000
Oceania (Australia, New Zealand and the Pacific islands – Polynesia, Melanesia and Micronesia)	8,935,000	3,450,000

THE WORLD'S GREATEST MOUNTAIN RANGES

RANGE	LENGTH KILO-METRES	MILES	HIGHEST MOUNTAIN	HEIGHT METRES	FEET
Himalaya-Karakoram-Hindu Kush-Pamir	3,800	2,400	Mount Everest	8,847	29,028
Andes	7,200	4,500	Aconcagua	6,960	22,834
Rocky Mountains	6,000	3,750	Mt Elbert	4,399	14,431
Trans-Antarctic Mountains	3,500	2,200	Mt Kirkpatrick	4,529	14,860
Great Dividing Range (E. Australia)	3,600	2,250	Kosciusko	2,228	7,310
Brazilian Atlantic Coast Range	3,000	1,900	Pico da Bandeira	2,890	9,482
West Sumatran-Javan Range	2,900	1,800	Kerintji	3,805	12,484
Tien Shan (S. Central Asia)	2,250	1,400	Pik Pobeda	7,439	24,406

The world's highest mountains
The Himalaya-Karakoram-Hindu Kush-Pamir Range of Asia includes the highest mountains of the world, with 104 peaks over 7,315 m (24,000 ft) above sea level. One of these, Mount Everest, in the Himalayas, reaches a height of 8,847 m (29,028 ft). The Andes Range, the second greatest, has 54 peaks over 6,096 m (20,000 ft).

OTHER NOTABLE MOUNTAIN PEAKS

	MOUNTAIN	HEIGHT METRES	FEET	LOCATION
Highest mountain in USSR	Communism Peak	7,495	24,590	Tadzhik
Highest mountain in USA	Mt McKinley	6,194	20,320	Alaska
Highest mountain in Canada	Mt Logan	6,050	19,850	Yukon
Highest active volcano	Cotopaxi	5,897	19,347	Ecuador
Highest mountain in Africa	Kilimanjaro	5,895	19,340	Tanzania
Highest mountain in western Europe	Mont Blanc	4,807	15,771	France/Italy

GREAT DESERTS OF THE WORLD

DESERT	APPROX. AREA SQ KM	SQ MILES	TERRITORIES
Sahara	16,835,000	6,500,000	Algeria, Chad, Libya, Mali, Mauritania, Niger, Sudan, Tunisia, Egypt, Morocco
Australian	1,550,000	600,000	Australia
Arabian	1,300,000	500,000	Saudi Arabia, Syria, Yemen
Gobi	1,040,000	400,000	Mongolia, Inner Mongolia
Kalahari	520,000	200,000	Botswana
Kara-Kum	350,000	135,000	Turkmen SSR
Taklamakan	320,000	125,000	Sinkiang (region of China)
Sonoran	310,000	120,000	Arizona, California, Mexico
Namib	310,000	120,000	Namibia
Thar	260,000	100,000	N.W. India, Pakistan
Somali	260,000	100,000	Somalia

THE WORLD'S LARGEST LAKES

LAKE	AREA SQ KM	SQ MILES	LOCATION
Caspian Sea (salt)	371,800	143,550	USSR and Iran
Superior	82,350	31,800	Canada and USA
Victoria	69,500	26,830	Kenya, Uganda and Tanzania
Aral Sea (salt)	65,500	25,300	USSR
Huron	59,600	23,010	Canada and USA
Michigan	58,000	22,400	USA
Tanganyika	32,900	12,700	Tanzania, Zaire and Zambia
Great Bear	31,800	12,275	Canada
Baykal	30,500	11,780	USSR
Malawi	29,600	11,430	Malawi, Mozambique and Tanzania
Great Slave	28,500	10,980	Canada
Erie	25,700	9,930	Canada and USA
Winnipeg	24,500	9,465	Canada
Ontario	19,500	7,520	Canada and USA
Ladoga (Ladozhskoye)	17,700	6,835	USSR
Balkhash	17,400	6,720	USSR
Chad	16,300	6,300	Chad, Cameroon, Niger and Nigeria
Onega	9,840	3,800	USSR
Eyre (salt)	9,585	3,700	Australia
Rudolf (salt)	9,065	3,500	Kenya
Titicaca	8,290	3,200	Peru-Bolivia
Athabasca	7,920	3,058	Canada
Nicaragua	7,770	3,000	Nicaragua
Reindeer	6,320	2,440	Canada
Torrens (salt)	6,215	2,400	Australia
Koko Nor (salt)	5,960	2,300	China
Issyk-Kul	5,895	2,276	USSR
Vänern	5,570	2,150	Sweden

THE WORLD'S LARGEST ISLANDS

ISLAND	AREA SQ KM	SQ MILES	LOCATION
Greenland	2,175,600	840,000	Arctic Ocean
New Guinea	831,390	321,000	W. Pacific
Borneo	738,150	285,000	Indian Ocean
Madagascar	590,002	227,800	Indian Ocean
Baffin Island	476,065	183,810	Arctic Ocean
Sumatra	473,607	182,860	Indian Ocean
Honshu	230,300	88,920	N.W. Pacific
Great Britain	218,041	84,186	N. Atlantic
Victoria Island	212,197	81,930	Arctic Ocean
Ellesmere Island	196,236	75,770	Arctic Ocean
Sulawesi (Celebes)	189,484	73,160	Indian Ocean
South Island, New Zealand	150,460	58,093	S.W. Pacific
Java	130,510	50,390	Indian Ocean
North Island, New Zealand	114,687	44,281	S.W. Pacific
Cuba	114,494	44,206	Caribbean Sea
Newfoundland	112,300	43,359	N. Atlantic
Luzon	104,688	40,420	W. Pacific
Iceland	102,846	39,709	N. Atlantic
Mindanao	94,628	36,536	W. Pacific
Hokkaido	88,775	34,276	N.W. Pacific
Ireland	82,460	31,839	N. Atlantic
Hispaniola	76,498	29,536	Caribbean Sea
Tasmania	67,897	26,215	S.W. Pacific
Sri Lanka	65,610	25,332	Indian Ocean

THE WORLD'S LONGEST RIVERS

RIVER	MAIN LOCATION	LENGTH KILO-METRES	MILES	OUTFLOW
Nile	Egypt	6,650	4,132	Mediterranean Sea
Amazon	Peru, Brazil	6,437	4,000	Atlantic Ocean
Mississippi-Missouri	USA	6,020	3,741	Gulf of Mexico
Yenisey	Siberia	5,540	3,442	Arctic Ocean
Yangtze	Tibet, China	5,494	3,434	East China Sea
Ob-Irtysh	W. Siberia	5,410	3,362	Gulf of Ob, Arctic Ocean
Zaire	Equatorial Africa	4,700	2,914	South Atlantic Ocean
Hwang-ho (Yellow River)	China	4,640	2,883	Gulf of Pohai
Lena	Siberia	4,400	2,734	Arctic Ocean
Mackenzie	Canada	4,241	2,635	Beaufort Sea
Niger	W. Africa	4,180	2,600	Gulf of Guinea
St Lawrence-Great Lakes	Canada	4,023	2,500	Gulf of St Lawrence
Rio de la Plata-Paraná	Brazil, Argentina, Uruguay	4,000	2,485	South Atlantic Ocean
Mekong	Tibet, China, Laos, Kampuchea, Vietnam	4,000	2,485	China Sea
Murray-Darling	Australia	3,780	2,350	Indian Ocean
Volga	USSR	3,690	2,293	Caspian Sea
Zambezi	S.E. Africa	3,540	2,200	Indian Ocean
Yukon	Canada, Alaska	3,200	1,988	Bering Strait
Madeira	Brazil	3,200	1,988	Amazon River
Rio Grande	USA, Mexico	3,040	1,885	Gulf of Mexico
Ganges-Brahmaputra	India	2,897	1,800	Bay of Bengal
São Francisco	E. Brazil	2,897	1,800	Atlantic Ocean
Salween	Tibet, Burma	2,880	1,790	Gulf of Martaban
Indus	Pakistan	2,880	1,790	Arabian Sea

Salween	Tibet, Burma	2,880	1,790	Gulf of Martaban
Danube	Europe	2,850	1,770	Black Sea
Amur	Mongolia, China, Siberia	2,824	1,755	Pacific Ocean
Tigris-Euphrates	Syria, Iraq	2,740	1,700	Persian Gulf
Nelson	Canada	2,570	1,600	Hudson Bay
Kolyma	N.E. Siberia	2,560	1,591	Arctic Ocean
Tocantins	Brazil	2,560	1,591	Atlantic Ocean
Orinoco	Venezuela	2,368	1,471	Atlantic Ocean
Colorado	W. USA	2,320	1,441	Gulf of California

THE WORLD'S DEEPEST-KNOWN CAVERNS

CAVE	DEPTH Metres	DEPTH Feet	LOCATION
Gouffre de la Pierre Martin	1,332	4,370	Basses-Pyrénées, France-Spain
Gouffre Jean Bernard	1,298	4,258	Savoy Alps, France
Gouffre Berger	1,141	3,743	Vercors, France
Kievskaya	1,080	3,543	USSR
Chourun des Aguilles	980	3,214	Dauphine Alps, France
Sumidero de Cellagua	970	3,182	Cantabria, Spain
Gouffre André Touya	950	3,116	W. pyrénées, France
Grotta di Monte Cuco	922	3,025	Perugia, Italy
Abisso Michele Gortani	920	3,018	Julian Alps, Italy

The largest-known cavern is the Big Room in the Carlsbad Caverns, New Mexico, USA. It is 1,438 m (4,720 ft) long, 100 m (328 ft) high and 200 m (656 ft) across. The most extensive known cave system is the Mammoth Cave-Flint Ridge system in Kentucky, USA, with a length of 292 km (181 miles). There may, of course, be larger, undiscovered caverns

THE WORLD'S HIGHEST WATERFALLS

NAME	TOTAL DROP Metres	Feet	RIVER	LOCATION
Angel (highest fall 807 m, 2,648 ft)	979	3,212	Carrao	Venezuela
Tugela (5 falls, the highest being 410 m, 1,350 ft)	947	3,110	Tugela	Natal, S. Africa
Utigârd (highest fall 600 m, 1,970 ft)	800	2,625	Jostedal Glacier	Norway
Mongefossen	774	2,540	Monge	Norway
Yosemite (upper section 205 m, 1,430 ft; middle, Cascades, section 205 m, 675 ft; lower section 97 m, 320 ft)	739	2,425	Yosemite Creek	Yosemite National Park, Cal., USA
Østre Mardøla Foss (highest fall 296 m, 974 ft)	656	2,154	Mardals	Norway
Tyssestrengane (highest fall 289 m, 948 ft)	646	2,120	Tysso	Norway
Sutherland (highest fall 248 m, 815 ft)	580	1,904	Arthur	S. Island, New Zealand

THE WORLD'S GREATEST WATERFALLS BY VOLUME

NAME	TOTAL HEIGHT Metres	Feet	WIDTH Metres	Feet	RIVER	LOCATION
Boyoma (7 cascades)	60	200	730	2,400	Upper Zaire	Zaire
Guaira	114	374	4,846	15,900	Parana	Brazil-Paraguay border
Khône	21	70	10,670	35,000	Mekong	Laos
Niagara (in two sections) American	50	167	300	1,000	Niagara	USA-Canada border
Canadian	48	160	760	2,500	Niagara	USA-Canada border

Inside the Earth

If it were possible to drill a hole from the surface all the way to the Earth's centre (6,378 km, 3,986 miles), it would be found that the Earth is composed of a number of layers. Although the deepest hole ever drilled reached only 10 km (6.25 miles), scientists have obtained information about the interior of the Earth by studying seismic waves produced by earthquakes.

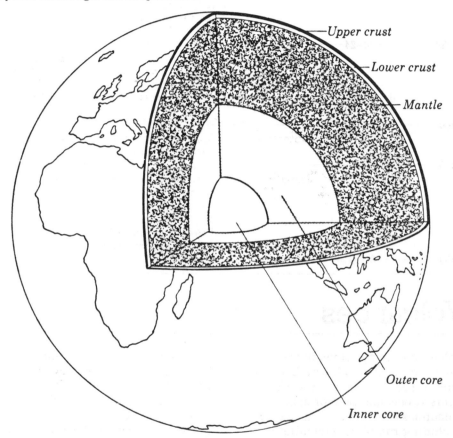

Structure of the Earth

STRUCTURE OF THE EARTH

DEPTH KM	MILES	LAYER	COMPOSITION	STATE
		Upper crust	Granite. Rich in silica and alumina.	Solid
17–25	10–15			
		Lower crust	Basalt. Rich in silica and magnesium. Temperature: 400–1,000°C	Solid
32–38	20–24			
		Mantle	Compressed iron and magnesium silicates. Temperature: 1,000–5,000°C	Probably solid to a depth of 725 km (450 miles)
2,900	1,800			
		Outer core	Mainly iron, probably with some nickel.	Fluid
5,000	3,100			
		Inner core	Mainly iron, probably with some nickel. Temperature: 4–10,000°C. Pressure: about 3.5 million atmospheres.	Solid
6,350	3,950			

Volcanoes

Volcanoes are openings in the Earth's crust through which magma (molten rock) reaches the surface, where it becomes lava or ash. Volcanoes are classified as active (including rumbling, steaming and erupting), dormant or extinct. It is estimated that there are about 535 active volcanoes on Earth, and 80 of these are submarine.

There are various types of volcanic eruption. Some are relatively quiet, although large amounts of lava may stream out. Others are quite violent, and some very violent – such as the eruption of Mt Pelée which destroyed the city of St Pierre in Martinique in 1902. An eruption can occur under the sea as well as on land, but if the depth is below 2,400 m (7,900 ft) there will be no sign of it on the surface of the water, and the lava simply spreads out over the ocean floor.

Many of the tallest mountains are volcanoes. Aconcagua, an

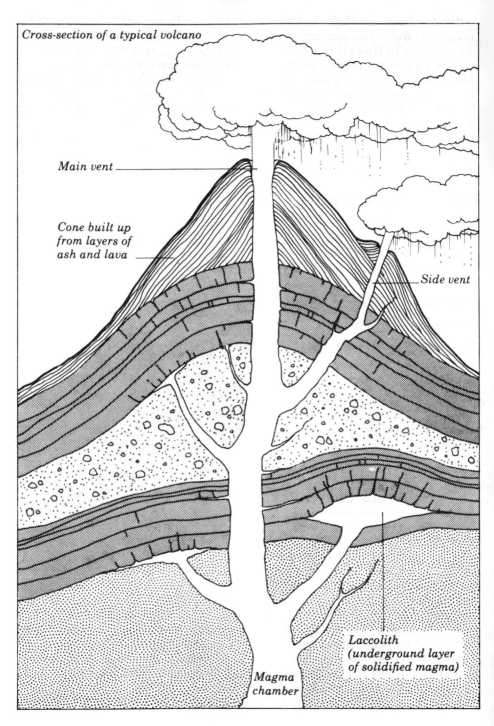

Cross-section of a typical volcano

Main vent

Cone built up
from layers of
ash and lava

Side vent

Laccolith
(underground layer
of solidified magma)

Magma
chamber

extinct volcano in Chile, is 6,960 m (22,834 ft) high. The summit of Mauna Loa in Hawaii is 4,200 m (13,780 ft) above the sea's surface. Measured from the sea floor, however, this active volcano reaches a height of 9,000 m (29,500 ft), rivalling Mt Everest.

New volcanoes have arisen in historic times, and have reached great heights in a short period.

Izalco in El Salvador has reached a height of 2,000 m (6,560 ft) in the 200 years since it first appeared. More recently, in 1943, Paracutin suddenly made its appearance in a quiet field in Mexico, building up a cone of cinders 150 m (490 ft) high in one week. In 1963, a new volcanic island, Surtsey, appeared near the coast of Iceland.

THE GREATEST VOLCANIC ERUPTIONS KNOWN

VOLCANO	COUNTRY	DATE OF ERUPTION	VOLUME OF LAVA, ASH, ETC. IN CUBIC KILOMETRES
Tambora	Indonesia	1815	150
Veidivatna	Iceland	before 870	43
Katmai	Alaska	1912	30
Krakatoa	Indonesia	1883	18
Laki	Iceland	1783	12
Eldgja	Iceland	930	9
Bezymianny	Kamchatka, USSR	1956	3
Bandaisan	Japan	1888	1

The Earth's Crust

Composition of the earth's crust
The outer shell or crust of the Earth is composed of a great variety of rocks. These rocks include relatively soft and loosely compacted materials such as clay, sand and gravel. There are also hard ones such as sandstone, limestone and granite. Rocks can be classified into three groups: igneous, sedimentary and metamorphic rocks.

Igneous rocks are those which have solidified out of hot, molten material (magma), e.g. basalt. *Sedimentary* rocks may be formed from the breakdown of existing rocks, from the shells of marine organisms or by chemical precipitation. These substances are deposited on land, or on sea or river beds. Sedimentary rocks cover most of the Earth's surface but constitute only about five per

The form of a perfect quartz crystal

cent of the crust. Examples are sandstone, shale, limestone and chalk. *Metamorphic* rocks are formed from igneous or sedimentary rocks by the action of heat and pressure, e.g. marble, slate and schist.

Rocks are composed of minerals. About 2,000 different minerals are found on the Earth, and each mineral is composed of chemical elements. A few elements, such as gold, are found in a free, uncombined state but most minerals are composed of a combination of elements. The commonest elements found in the Earth's crust are shown in the table.

Minerals composed of silicates (compounds of silicon and oxygen) make up more than 95 per cent of the Earth's crust and are usually combined with one or more of the metallic elements such as aluminium, calcium, iron, magnesium, potassium and sodium. One of the commonest of all silicates is the mineral quartz (SiO_2).

With few exceptions, minerals are crystalline, though the crystals are often microscopically small, or so bunched up that they have lost their perfect form. The regular external form characteristic of crystals is caused by the orderly arrangement of their atoms.

Gemstones

Some 120 minerals have been classified as gemstones, but only about 25 are in common use in jewellery. Those classified as precious stones are diamond, emerald, ruby, sapphire, black opal and pearl. Among those classified as semi-precious are amethyst, topaz, aquamarine, garnet, turquoise, jade and amber. There are other stones, less valued, which can be classified as ornamental stones.

Most gems occur as natural minerals. Many are found in igneous rocks, e.g. beryl, topaz and tourmaline. There are others which are found in metamorphic rocks, e.g. emerald, garnet and diamond. Quite often gemstones, including diamonds, are found in the gravels of river beds. There are some substances of organic origin that are classed as gems. Amber is a fossilized resin. Jet is a hard, shiny black fossilized wood. Coral is made by small sea animals, and pearls form inside oysters.

A gem is valued for its beauty and rarity, and for its size. Opaque and cloudy gems, such as opals, are valued for their colour. Transparent gems are valued for their brilliance, as well as their durability and colour. Many gems are composed of the colourful oxides of aluminium, beryllium and magnesium, sometimes with silica. Others are coloured by metal

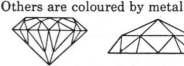
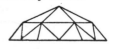

A diamond is cut so that slight movement of the stone produces scintillating flashes of rainbow colours.

oxides that are only present as impurities.

Diamond is the hardest of all minerals. It also refracts light more than any other precious stone. Variation in refraction for different colours (dispersion) accounts for the brilliant flashes of colour – the 'fire' – of a faceted diamond.

Diamonds are the most valued of all gems, apart from the deepest-red rubies. The largest diamond in the world was the Cullinan diamond, found in 1905 in the Premier mine in Transvaal, South Africa. It was purchased by the Transvaal government and presented to the reigning king, Edward VII. Originally weighing 3,106 carats (a carat is equal to 200 milligrams), the diamond was cut into 2 large stones, 7 medium and 96 smaller ones. The largest of the stones, weighing 530 carats, is the pear-shaped gem set in the English sceptre called the Star of Africa. It is also the largest cut diamond in the world. The second largest, the Cullinan II, is set in the Imperial State Crown.

Very few precious stones are set just as they are found. They are seldom perfect enough. To show their colour and sparkle to the full, they have to be polished and cut. Stones may be cut with a curved surface (a cabochon) or in facets. There are various names for different kinds of faceting. For example, a brilliant is usually cut with 58 facets, 33 above and 25 below, with a band running between the two halves which is the part gripped by the setting. Diamonds are generally cut this way.

Another very large diamond in the British Crown Jewels collection is the Indian diamond Koh-i-noor (Mountain of Light), which was given to Queen Victoria in 1850 by the East India Company. The largest coloured diamond is also from India; it is the vivid blue Hope Diamond (44·4 carats) belonging to the Smithsonian Institution in Washington D.C.

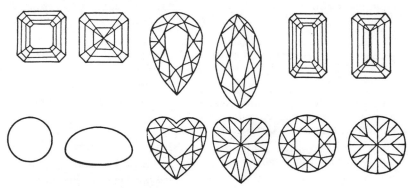

A selection of precious stone faceting

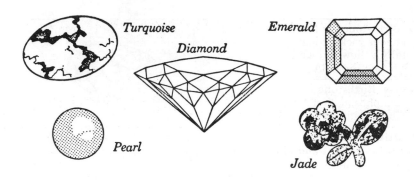

Turquoise

Diamond

Emerald

Pearl

Jade

GEMSTONES IN COMMON USE

Garnet Birthstone for January – symbolizes faithfulness. Garnets are silicates of various minerals (calcium, magnesium, titanium, iron, aluminium). The blood-red variety is an important gemstone.

Amethyst Birthstone for February – symbolizes sincerity. It is a violet-coloured quartz. The best specimens come from Brazil and the USSR.

Aquamarine Birthstone for March – symbolizes courage. A light blue-green form of beryl. (Beryl is composed of beryllium and aluminium silicates.) The best ones are from Brazil and the USSR.

Diamond Birthstone for April – symbolizes innocence. Diamonds are a crystallized form of carbon, the most prized ones being colourless. Principal source is South Africa.

Emerald Birthstone for May – symbolizes love. A rare green variety of beryl. The finest occur in Colombia, South America.

Pearl Birthstone for June – symbolizes health. Found mainly in oysters. Pearls are believed to be formed from secretions built up around specks of foreign matter in the shell.

Ruby Birthstone for July – symbolizes contentment. The ruby is a red variety of the aluminium oxide mineral, corundum. The best are deep red in colour and come from Burma.

Peridot Birthstone for August – symbolizes married happiness. A transparent variety of the green mineral olivine (a magnesium-iron silicate). The finest come from Australia, Brazil, Burma, Norway and Thailand.

Sapphire Birthstone for September – symbolizes clear thinking. A variety of corundum, sapphires are commonly deep blue, but they can occur in other colours. The finest come from Burma and Thailand.

Opal Birthstone for October – symbolizes hope. Opals are a non-crystalline form of quartz containing varying amounts of water. The most valuable types are called 'black opals' which, despite their name, flash with several different colours; they come from the Australian continent.

Topaz Birthstone for November – symbolizes fidelity. Found in granites and other igneous rocks, topaz is a silicate of aluminium and fluorine. The crystals are usually yellow, brown or, when heated, pink. Topaz is found mainly in Brazil, the USSR and the USA.

Turquoise Birthstone for December – symbolizes prosperity. A copper and aluminium phosphate mineral, blue or greenish-blue in colour. It is found in Iran, India, Tibet, Poland and the USA.

Alexandrite (Chrysoberyl) An oxide of beryllium and aluminium, alexandrite is dull green in daylight and blood-red in artificial light. It is found in Brazil, the USA, the USSR and Czechoslovakia.

Chalcedony A mixture of quartz and opal, often white and creamy with a waxy lustre. The orange-red variety is called cornelian (also called carnelian), the brown is sard. Chrysoprase is apple-green and is an alternative May birthstone to emerald. Bloodstone, which is green with red spots, is an alternative to Aquamarine for the March birthstone. Jasper is a red, brown or yellow variety of chalcedony, and sometimes a mixture of all three colours. Onyx and agate, two other varieties, are characterized by parallel bands of colour. Sardonyx, a reddish-brown and white banded agate, is an alternative to peridot, the August birthstone.

Jade An opaque, waxy or pearly mineral, it is usually green but can be white, yellow or pink. There are two kinds of jade. The rarer *jadeite* (a sodium aluminium silicate) comes from Burma, Tibet and China. *Nephrite* (a calcium magnesium silicate) is found in New Zealand, China and the USSR.

Lapis lazuli A rock rich in lazurite, an opaque, deep-blue mineral. It consists of a silicate of sodium and aluminium. Lapis lazuli has been used as an ornamental stone and as a gemstone since ancient times. When it is ground, the pigment ultramarine is obtained. Lapis lazuli is an alternative to sapphire, the September birthstone.

Moonstone Composed of albite, a form of feldspar, moonstone is white with a bluish sheen. It is an alternative to pearl which is June's birthstone.

Obsidian A volcanic glass, green or yellowish in colour.

Quartz gems Quartz is a common and usually colourless mineral. When found in pure, hexagonal crystals it is called rock crystals. It is an alternative to diamond for April's birthstone. Other varieties of quartz include amethyst (violet), citrine (yellow), rose quartz (pink), milky quartz and smoky quartz. Cat's eye and tiger's eye contain asbestos fibres.

Spinel An oxide of magnesium and aluminium, it sometimes reaches gem quality. The best red spinels come from Sri Lanka. Brown, green and blue ones also occur.

Tourmaline A double silicate of aluminium and boron, tourmaline is commonly black but when it occurs in other colours (green, red or blue) it is a gemstone. It forms long crystals, sometimes varicoloured. Chief sources are Brazil, Sri Lanka and the USSR.

Zircon An oxide of zirconium and silicon, zircon is found in igneous rocks. The clear brown crystals turn blue when heated and thereby make better gems.

Life on Earth

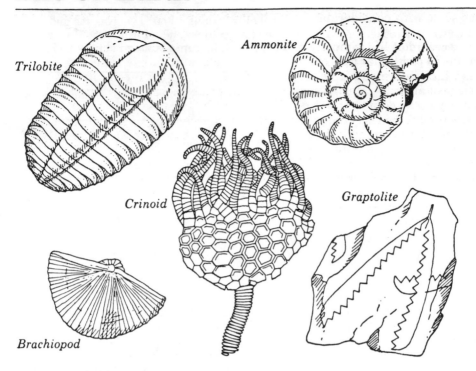

Trilobite

Ammonite

Crinoid

Graptolite

Brachiopod

Life is believed to have originated some 3,000 million years ago. All the major groups of animals and plants subsequently developed from the first few relatively primitive forms. Ever-increasing numbers of species later evolved, but those that did not adapt to changing Earth conditions, or were not as successful as rival species, dwindled and became extinct.

Palaeontology (the study of fossils) traces the evolutionary paths of various animals and plants, some of which were the ancestors of present-day species. The development of modern life is rather difficult to trace, however, because the fossil record is incomplete.

Most fossils are found in sedimentary rocks formed long ago from mud, sand or clay, and even by microscopic sea organisms (limestone and chalk). The sediments were deposited in seas, lakes, deserts and river valleys, sometimes covering the remains of dead animals or plants and thereby preserving their forms.

In general, the older the fossil the deeper it lies in the beds or strata of any particular rock formation – a fact which allows events to be related in chronological order. The occurrence of a certain type of fossil which existed for a limited time only in beds of rock several miles apart proves that these rocks were formed at the same time. Some rocks can also be dated by the radioactive minerals they contain, enabling geologists to calibrate a time scale with considerable accuracy.

The record of life is mostly one of sea life, in particular that of shallow seas which swarmed with a large variety of animals. Marine sedimentary rocks containing these fossils tend to be less eroded than those deposited on land; they are thicker and display more complete sequences.

If you find a fossil, it will most likely be that of a sea animal – many areas that are now dry land were once under the sea. If you wish to see fossil land animals, such as dinosaurs, probably the best place to look is in a museum, because they are quite rare. The rarest fossils of all are those of man. Fragments of bone found in Africa indicate that humans, or near-humans, date back to nearly 1,750,000 years ago.

Coal and oil are known as *fossil fuels*, because they are the remains of ancient living organisms.

A fossil is the remains of a prehistoric animal or plant, or some other evidence that it existed. Hard parts, such as bone, teeth or shells, have been found preserved with little alteration, but often the original material has been replaced by dissolved mineral matter, or it may simply have disappeared and left a cast showing where it had been. Soft parts have rarely been preserved, but impressions made in soft mud which subsequently hardened into shale are occasionally found.

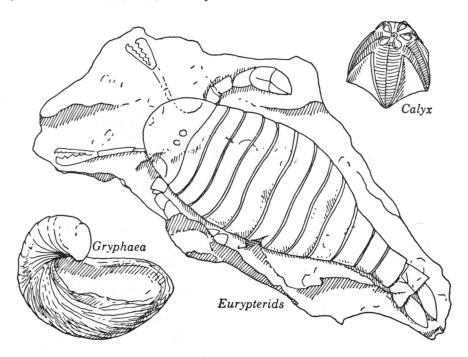

Calyx

Gryphaea

Eurypterids

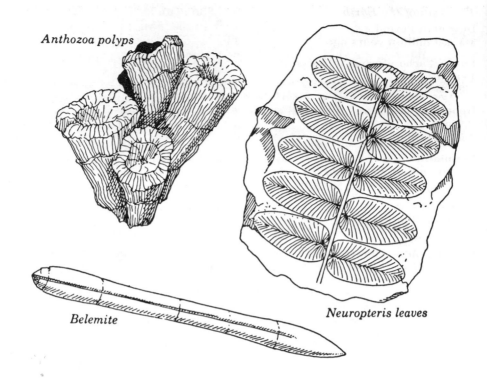

Anthozoa polyps

Belemite

Neuropteris leaves

THE AGES OF THE EARTH

STEPS IN THE EVOLUTION OF LIFE

Pre-Cambrian Period	Algae, worms, jellyfish and other simple
Earlier than 600 million years ago	soft-bodied life forms

LOWER PALAEOZOIC ERA ('ANCIENT LIFE')

Cambrian Period	Abundant marine invertebrates
500–600 million years ago	
Ordovician Period	Earliest fish and molluscs
425–500 million years ago	

UPPER PALAEOZOIC ERA

Silurian Period	Earliest land plants
400–425 million years ago	

The Ages of the Earth

Devonian Period
345–400 million years ago

Earliest insects; the first bony fishes

Lower Carboniferous (Mississippian) Period
320–345 million years ago

Earliest conifers (the great coal forests), tree ferns and club mosses

Upper Carboniferous (Pennsylvanian) Period
280–320 million years ago

Earliest quadruped (*Ichthyostega*); earliest spiders; giant trees abundant

Permian Period
230–280 million years ago

Earliest land reptiles (*Seymouria*)

MESOZOIC ERA ('MIDDLE ERA OF LIFE')
Triassic Period
180–230 million years ago

Earliest dinosaurs

Jurassic Period
130–180 million years ago

Earliest flying reptiles; first bird (*Archaeopteryx*); earliest mammals

Cretaceous Period (period of chalk formation)
64–130 million years ago

Dinosaurs were abundant during the early part of this period but declined at its close; first flowering plants appeared, and hardwood trees were abundant, including many now familiar to us (beech, holly, ivy, oak, maple, poplar, magnolia, laurel)

CENOZOIC ERA ('RECENT LIFE')
Tertiary Period
Palaeocene Epoch (earliest recent forms)
54–64 million years ago

Tremendous increase in mammals; forerunners of carnivores and hoofed mammals

Eocene Epoch
38–54 million years ago

First true rodents; types of rhinoceros; *Hyracotherium*, a tiny, four-toed ancester of the horse, 30 cm (12 in) in height; appearance of deer, camels, pigs, cattle; ancestors of tapirs and elephants; sabre-toothed tiger

Oligocene Epoch
26–38 million years ago

Mesohippus, a three-toed ancestor of the horse, 60 cm (24 in) in height

Miocene Epoch
7–26 million years ago

Continued rise of modern mammals; *Merychippus*, a three-toed ancestor of the horse, 100 cm (40 in) in height

Pliocene Epoch
2–7 million years ago

Ancestors of elephants, camels, rhinoceroses, and dogs abounded; *Pliohippus*, an ancestor of the horse, 150 cm (60 in) high, with one toe

QUATERNARY PERIOD
Pleistocene Epoch
1,750,000–50,000 BC

Man first appeared; the period of the Ice Ages; animal species included the woolly mammoth, 39·5 m (12 ft) high, and a woolly type of rhinoceros, *Coelodonta*, 19·7 m (6 ft) high, as well as most of the modern animals.

Holocene Epoch
50,000 BC–Present

All recent forms

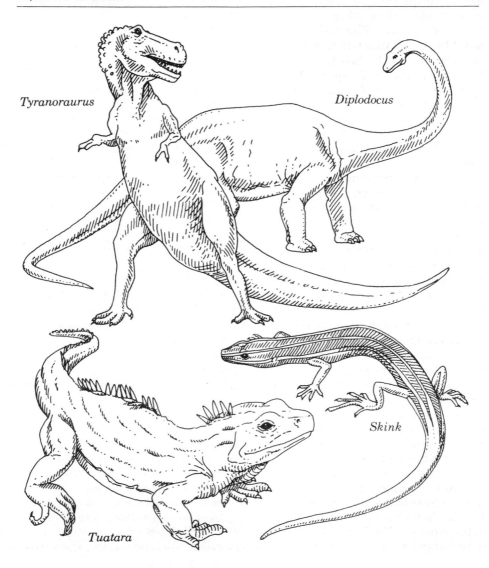

Tyranoraurus

Diplodocus

Skink

Tuatara

Wildlife in Danger

Largely as a result of man's activities, it has been estimated that as many as 100,000 species of animals and plants may be in danger of extinction. Some species are declining because they are not as well adapted as others in the fight for survival. The majority of animals and plants which have become rare in the last few hundred years are disappearing, however, because of man's greed or thoughtlessness.

Man has always hunted wild animals for food and skins but, in the past, traditional hunting methods probably did not cause many species to die out. Modern technology, however, has produced such things as guns with telescopic sights, the repeating rifle and the snowmobile which make it much easier for the hunter to kill. At the same time the human population has greatly increased. Demand for skins has also considerably increased and the prices that they can fetch has consequently gone up. These factors weigh very heavily against the chances of survival of many species of animals. Some have already become extinct, such as the Quagga, a kind of zebra which was once numerous in southern Africa. Excessive hunting led to its extermination by 1883.

Several species of whale, for example the blue whale (the largest animal ever to have lived on the Earth), have been almost exterminated. The blue whale didn't stand much of a chance against the great Russian and Japanese factory ships which slaughtered them with explosive harpoons for their oil and meat. Since 1963 the blue whale has had complete protection in all oceans and is slowly increasing in numbers.

The greatest danger to wildlife is the destruction of their natural habitats. Vast areas of tropical forest are being felled and burned, and the animals that once lived in them have vanished. The drainage of wetlands for industry, agriculture or housing has led to the disappearance of many animals and birds that were once quite common.

In the United States, the great prairies that once existed have been largely ploughed and turned over to grain and cattle. Once these prairies were roamed by vast herds of bison (sometimes incorrectly called 'buffalo'). The bison were hunted by the Indians for food and clothing, but that did not seriously affect their numbers. When the white man came, however, the bison were slaughtered in large numbers. Now only a few remain in reservations.

The introduction by man of alien species is a common cause of the extinction of many animals. The egg-laying mammals (monotremes) of Australia have suffered from the introduction of the dingo, which the Aborigines brought with them 10,000 years ago. Domestic livestock such as the goat, a voracious eater, may also threaten

THE NUMBER OF ANIMAL SPECIES IN THE WORLD

Arthropods	900,000
Chordates	45,000
Molluscs	45,000
Protozoans	30,000
Worms	38,000
Other invertebrates	21,000
Total:	approximately 1,000,000

Species of mammals in danger of extinction: approx. 120
Species and subspecies of birds in danger of extinction: approx. 350

The American bison was once numbered in millions, now there are just a few.

Hunted for its eggs, meat and shell, the green turtle has been greatly reduced in numbers.

THE NUMBER OF PLANT SPECIES IN THE WORLD

Algae, fungi, etc.	60,000
Ferns, conifers, etc.	10,000
Flowering plants	250,000
Mosses and liverworts	23,000
Total:	approximately 350,000

Species of plants which may be threatened: approx 20,000

the food supplies of native animals. Many plants, too, are threatened with extinction where once-lush areas have been eaten bare by grazing livestock.

What can be done to help endangered species? The International Union for Conservation of Nature and Natural Resources (IUCN), a scientific organization with headquarters in Switzerland, studies threatened animals and birds, and some reptiles, amphibians, fish and plants, too. Its experts decide what must be done to save each species and also consult with the authorities in the countries concerned. The World Wildlife Fund (WWF), another international organization based in Switzerland, raises funds and works hard at persuading national governments to take the necessary action to save wildlife.

Reserves have been set up for a few endangered animals and plants. In India, the tiger would soon be extinct were it not for the special sanctuaries established by the Indian government. Zoos, too, can play an important part by breeding rare animals in captivity and so giving them a chance of survival.

Reserves have been established in India to save the tiger from extinction.

One of the world's rarest birds, the King of Saxony bird of paradise, is from New Guinea. Although trading in its plumes was banned in 1924, illegal trading continues. Destruction of its forest habitat further threatens its survival.

The leopard and other spotted cats are threatened by the fashion for fur coats.

The Quagga of southern Africa was hunted to extinction.

The blue whale was nearly exterminated for its meat and oil.

THE WORLD
AND ITS PEOPLE

North
America

Europe

Asia

South
America

Africa

Oceania

Countries of the World

Population figures in the following list cannot be absolutely accurate as there are many areas of the world where no census is taken. Furthermore, some countries have not been fully surveyed, so the areas given here may in some cases be only approximate.

An asterisk (*) denotes that the country is a member of the British Commonwealth.

AFGHANISTAN, Democratic Republic of   population: 18,598,000
Capital: Kabul
Land area: 636,270 sq km (245,664 sq miles)
Principal languages: Pushtu, Dari (Persian), Turki
Currency: 100 puls = 1 afghani

ALBANIA   population: 3,135,000
Capital: Tirana
Land area: 28,748 sq km (11,099 sq miles)
Principal languages: Gheg, Tosk
Currency: 100 qintars = 1 lek

ALGERIA   population: 22,541,000
Capital: Algiers
Land area: 2,381,000 sq km (919,592 sq miles)
Principal languages: Arabic, French
Currency: 100 centimes = 1 dinar

ANDORRA   population: 40,000
Capital: Andorra la Vella
Land area: 466 sq km (180 sq miles)
Principal languages: Catalan, French, Spanish
Currency: French and Spanish currency both in use

ANGOLA   population: 8,837,000
Capital: Luanda
Land area: 1,246,700 sq km (481,351 sq miles)
Principal languages: Portuguese, tribal languages
Currency: 100 lwei = 1 kwanza

ARGENTINA   population: 29,920,000
Capital: Buenos Aires
Land area: 2,777,815 sq km (1,072, 514 sq miles)
Principal language: Spanish
Currency: 100 centavos = 1 peso

*AUSTRALIA, Commonwealth of   population: 16,036,000
Capital: Canberra
Land area: 7,686,884 sq km (2,967,906 sq miles)
Principal language: English
Currency: 100 cents = 1 Australian dollar

AUSTRIA
Capital: Vienna
Land area: 83,853 sq km (32,376 sq miles)
Principal language: German
Currency: 100 groschen = 1 schilling

population: 7,606,000

*BAHAMAS, Commonwealth of the
Capital: Nassau
Land area: 13,864 sq km (5,353 sq miles)
Principal language: English
Currency: 100 cents = 1 Bahamas dollar

population: 230,000

BAHRAIN
Capital: Manama
Land area: 570 sq km (220 sq miles)
Principal languages: Arabic, Urdu
Currency: 1,000 fils = 1 dinar

population: 458,000

*BANGLADESH (formerly the eastern province of
Pakistan)
Capital: Dhaka
Land area: 144,020 sq km (55,606 sq miles)
Principal language: Bengali
Currency: 100 paise = 1 taka

population: 102,124,000

*BARBADOS
Capital: Bridgetown
Land area: 430 sq km (166 sq miles)
Principal language: English
Currency: 100 cents = 1 Barbados dollar

population: 263,000

BELGIUM
Capital: Brussels
Land area: 30,513 sq km (11,781 sq miles)
Principal languages: Dutch (Flemish), French, German
Currency: 100 centimes = 1 franc

population: 9,917,000

BENIN, People's Republic of (formerly Dahomey)
Capital: Porto Novo
Land area: 112,622 sq km (43,483 sq miles)
Principal languages: French, local languages
Currency: 100 centimes = 1 franc CFA

population: 4,137,000

*BERMUDA
Capital: Hamilton
Land area: 53 sq km (20 sq miles)
Principal language: English
Currency: 100 cents = 1 Bermuda dollar

population: 65,000

BHUTAN
Capital: Thimphu
Land area: 46,600 sq km (18,000 sq miles)
Principal language: Dzongkha
Currency: 100 paise = 1 rupee (Ngultrum)

population: 1,268,000

BOLIVIA population: 6,344,000
Capital: La Paz
Land area: 1,098,580 sq km (424,160 sq miles)
Principal languages: Spanish, Quechua, Aymara
Currency: 100 centavos = 1 Bolivian peso

*BOTSWANA (formerly Bechuanaland Protectorate) population: 1,142,000
Capital: Gaborone
Land area: 575,000 sq km (222,000 sq miles)
Principal languages: English, Setswana
Currency: 100 thebe = 1 pula

BRAZIL, Federative Republic of population: 138,813,000
Capital: Brasilia
Land area: 8,511,965 sq km (3,286,470 sq miles)
Principal language: Portuguese
Currency: 100 centavos = 1 cruzeiro

*BRUNEI population: 232,000
Capital: Bandar Seri Begawan
Land area: 5,800 sq km (2,226 sq miles)
Principal languages: Malay, English
Currency: 100 sen = 1 Brunei dollar

BULGARIA, People's Republic of population: 9,053,000
Capital: Sofia
Land area: 110,912 sq km (42,823 sq miles)
Principal languages: Bulgarian, Turkish
Currency: 100 stotinki = 1 lev

BURKINA FASO (formerly Upper Volta) population: 7,094,000
Capital: Ouagadougou
Land area: 274,200 sq km (105,900 sq miles)
Principal languages: French, local languages
Currency: franc CFA

BURMA, Socialist Republic of the Union of population: 38,108,000
Capital: Rangoon
Land area: 678,000 sq km (262,000 sq miles)
Principal language: Burmese
Currency: 100 pyas = 1 kyat

BURUNDI (formerly part of Ruanda-Urundi) population: 4,753,000
Capital: Bujumbura
Land area: 27,834 sq km (10,747 sq miles)
Principal languages: Kirundi, French
Currency: 100 centimes = 1 Burundi franc

CAMBODIA *see* Kampuchea

CAMEROON, United Republic of population: 10,479,000
Capital: Yaoundé
Land area: 474,000 sq km (183,000 sq miles)
Principal languages: French, English
Currency: franc CFA

47

*CANADA, Dominion of   population: 25,936,000
Capital: Ottawa
Land area: 9,220,975 sq km (3,560,218 sq miles)
Principal languages: English, French
Currency: 100 cents = 1 Canadian dollar

CAPE VERDE   population: 317,000
Capital: Praia
Land area: 4,033 sq km (1,557 sq miles)
Principal language: Portuguese
Currency: 100 centavos = 1 escudo

CENTRAL AFRICAN REPUBLIC(formerly   population: 2,644,000
Central African Empire)
Capital: Bangui
Land area: 625,000 sq km (241,000 sq miles)
Principal languages: French, Sangho
Currency: franc CFA

CEYLON *see* Sri Lanka

CHAD   population: 5,037,000
Capital: N'djamena
Land area: 1,284,000 sq km (496,000 sq miles)
Principal languages: French, Arabic, African languages
Currency: franc CFA

CHILE   population: 12,252,000
Capital: Santiago
Land area: 741,767 sq km (286,396 sq miles)
Principal language: Spanish
Currency: 1,000 escudos = 1 new peso

CHINA, People's Republic of   population: 1,058,851,000
Capital: Peking (Beijing)
Land area: 9,597,000 sq km (3,705,000 sq miles)
Principal language: Chinese (especially Mandarin and
Cantonese dialects)
Currency: 100 fens = 1 yuan (renminbi)

COLOMBIA   population: 29,114,000
Capital: Bogotá
Land area: 1,138,914 sq km (439,735 sq miles)
Principal language: Spanish
Currency: 100 centavos = 1 peso

COMOROS (Comoro Republic)   population: 408,000
Capital: Moroni
Land area: 1,862 sq km (719 sq miles)
Principal languages: Comoran, French, Arabic
Currency: franc CFA

CONGO, People's Republic of the   population: 1,937,000
Capital: Brazzaville
Land area: 342,000 sq km (132,000 sq miles)

Principal languages: French, Bantu languages
Currency: franc CFA

COSTA RICA
population: 2,560,000
Capital: San José
Land area: 51,100 sq km (19,730 sq miles)
Principal language: Spanish
Currency: 100 centimos = 1 colon

CUBA
population: 10,115,000
Capital: Havana
Land area: 114,524 sq km (44,218 sq miles)
Principal language: Spanish
Currency: 100 centavos = 1 Cuban peso

*CYPRUS
population: 665,000
Capital: Nicosia
Land area: 9,251 sq km (3,572 sq miles)
Principal languages: Greek, Turkish
Currency: 1,000 mils = 1 Cyprus pound

CZECHOSLOVAKIA (Czechoslovak Socialist Republic)
population: 15,697,000
Capital: Prague
Land area: 127,877 sq km (49,373 sq miles)
Principal languages: Czech, Slovak
Currency: 100 halers = 1 koruna

DENMARK
population 5,150,000
Capital: Copenhagen
Land area: 43,075 sq km (16,631 sq miles)
Principal language: Danish
Currency: 100 öre = 1 krone

DJIBOUTI (formerly French Somaliland; Afars and Issas)
population: 484,000
Capital: Djibouti
Land area: 23,000 sq km (9,000 sq miles)
Principal languages: French, Somali, Danakil, Arabic
Currency: 100 centimes = 1 Djibouti franc

*DOMINICA
population: 84,000
Capital: Roseau
Land area: 751 sq km (290 sq miles)
Principal language: English
Currency: The French franc, pound sterling and East Caribbean dollar are all legal tender

DOMINICAN REPUBLIC
population: 6,437,000
Capital: Santo Domingo
Land area: 48,442 sq km (18,700 sq miles)
Principal language: Spanish
Currency: 100 centavos = 1 peso

ECUADOR population: 8,848,000
Capital: Quito
Land area: 276,000 sq km (106,508 sq miles)
Principal languages: Spanish, Quechua and other
Amerindian languages
Currency: 100 centavos = 1 sucre

EGYPT, Arab Republic of (formerly United Arab population: 48,995,000
Republic)
Capital: Cairo
Land area: 1,000,000 sq km (386,000 sq miles)
Principal language: Arabic
Currency: 100 piastres = 1 Egyptian pound

EQUATORIAL GUINEA population: 379,000
Capital: Malabo
Land area: 28,050 sq km (10,830 sq miles)
Principal languages: Spanish, Arabic
Currency: 100 centimos = 1 ekuele

ETHIOPIA population: 35,877,000
Capital: Addis Ababa
Land area: 1,023,000 sq km (395,000 sq miles)
Principal language: Amharic
Currency: 100 cents = 1 birr

*FIJI population: 708,000
Capital: Suva
Land area: 18,272 sq km (7,055 sq miles)
Principal languages: English, Melanesian languages
Currency: 100 cents = 1 Fiji dollar

FINLAND population: 4,901,000
Capital: Helsinki
Land area: 305,475 sq km (118,000 sq miles)
Principal languages: Finnish, Swedish
Currency: 100 pennia = 1 markka

FRANCE population: 55,411,000
Capital: Paris
Land area: 550,634 sq km (212,600 sq miles)
Principal language: French
Currency: 100 centimes = 1 franc

GABON population: 724,000
Capital: Libreville
Land area: 267,667 sq km (103,346 sq miles)
Principal languages: French, Bantu languages
Currency: franc CFA

*GAMBIA, The population: 777,000
Capital: Banjul
Land area: 10,368 sq km (4,003 sq miles)
Principal languages: English, African languages

Currency: 100 bututs = 1 dalasi

GERMAN DEMOCRATIC REPUBLIC (DDR)
population: 16,734,000
Capital: Berlin (East)
Land area: 108,179 sq km (41,768 sq miles)
Principal language: German
Currency: 100 pfennig = 1 mark of the GDR

GERMANY, Federal Republic of
population: 61,506,000
Capital: Bonn
Land area: 248,630 sq km (95,996 sq miles)
Principal language: German
Currency: 100 pfennig = 1 Deutsche mark

*GHANA
population: 13,368,000
Capital: Accra
Land area: 238,305 sq km (92,010 sq miles)
Principal languages: English, African languages
Currency: 100 pesewa = 1 cedi

GILBERT ISLANDS see Kiribati

GREECE
population: 10,209,000
Capital: Athens
Land area: 131,986 sq km (50,960 sq miles)
Principal language: Greek
Currency: 100 lepta = 1 drachma

*GRENADA
population: 117,000
Capital: St George's
Land area: 344 sq km (133 sq miles)
Principal language: English
Currency: 100 cents = 1 East Caribbean dollar

GUATEMALA
population: 8,692,000
Capital: Guatemala City
Land area: 108,889 sq km (42,042 sq miles)
Principal languages: Spanish, Amerindian languages
Currency: 100 centavos = 1 quetzal

GUINEA
population: 6,206,000
Capital: Conakry
Land area: 245,857 sq km (95,000 sq miles)
Principal languages: French, African languages
Currency: 100 cauris = 1 syli

GUINEA-BISSAU (formerly Portuguese Guinea)
population: 991,000
Capital: Bissau
Land area: 36,125 sq km (13,948 sq miles)
Principal languages: Portuguese, African languages
Currency: 100 centavos = 1 escudo

*GUYANA (formerly British Guiana)
population: 820,000
Capital: Georgetown
Land area: 210,000 sq km (81,000 sq miles)

Principal languages: English, Amerindian languages
Currency: 100 cents = 1 Guyana dollar

HAITI   population: 5,591,000
Capital: Port-au-Prince
Land area: 27,750 sq km (10,700 sq miles)
Principal languages: French, Creole
Currency: 100 centimes = 1 gourde

HONDURAS   population: 4,542,000
Capital: Tegucigalpa
Land area: 112,088 sq km (43,227 sq miles)
Principal languages: Spanish, tribal languages
Currency: 100 centavos = 1 lempira

HUNGARY   population: 10,795,000
Capital: Budapest
Land area: 93,032 sq km (35,920 sq miles)
Principal language: Hungarian (Magyar)
Currency: 100 filler = 1 forint

ICELAND   population: 244,000
Capital: Reykjavik
Land area: 103,000 sq km (39,768 sq miles)
Principal language: Icelandic
Currency: 100 aurar = 1 krona

*INDIA   population: 785,000,000
Capital: New Delhi
Land area: 3,166,828 sq km (1,222,712 sq miles)
Principal languages: Spanish, Amerindian languages
Gondi, English and many others.
Currency: 100 paise = 1 rupee

INDONESIA   population: 166,825,000
Capital: Djakarta
Land area: 1,903,650 sq km (735,000 sq miles)
Principal language: Bahasa Indonesia
Currency: 100 sen = 1 rupiah

IRAN, Islamic Republic of   population: 46,585,000
(formerly Persia)
Capital: Teheran
Land area: 1,648,000 sq km (636,000 sq miles)
Principal languages: Persian (Farsi), Kurdish
Currency: 100 dinars = 1 rial

IRAQ   population: 16,300,000
Capital: Baghdad
Land area: 438,446 sq km (169,284 sq miles)
Principal languages: Arabic, Kurdish
Currency: 1,000 fils = 1 dinar

IRELAND, Republic of   population: 3,677,000

Capital: Dublin
Land area: 68,893 sq km (26,600 sq miles)
Principal languages: English, Irish (Gaelic)
Currency: 100 pence = 1 Irish pound

ISRAEL
population: 4,390,000

Capital: Jerusalem
Land area: 20,700 sq km (8,000 sq miles)
Principal languages: Hebrew, Yiddish, Arabic and
several European languages
Currency: 100 new agorot = 1 shekel

ITALY
population: 57,000,000

Capital: Rome
Land area: 301,245 sq km (116,300 sq miles)
Principal language: Italian
Currency: 100 centesimi = 1 lira

IVORY COAST
population: 10,575,000

Capital: Abidjan
Land area: 322,500 sq km (124,500 sq miles)
Principal languages: French, African languages
Currency: franc CFA

*JAMAICA
population: 2,360,000

Capital: Kingston
Land area: 10,991 sq km (4,244 sq miles)
Principal language: English
Currency: 100 cents = 1 Jamaican dollar

JAPAN
population: 122,872,000

Capital: Tokyo
Land area: 370,370 sq km (143,000 sq miles)
Principal language: Japanese
Currency: 100 sen = 1 yen

JORDAN
population: 3,489,000

Capital: Amman
Land area: 101,140 sq km (39,050 sq miles)
Principal language: Arabic
Currency: 1,000 fils = 1 dinar

KAMPUCHEA, Democratic (formerly Cambodia and
population: 6,682,000

Khmer Republic)
Capital: Phnom Penh
Land area: 181,000 sq km (70,000 sq miles)
Principal language: Khmer
Currency: money was abolished in 1978; its use
was restored in 1980

*KENYA
population: 21,259,000

Capital: Nairobi
Land area: 582,600 sq km (224,960 sq miles)

Principal languages: Arabic, Swahili, Kikuyu and other tribal languages
Currency: 100 cents = 1 Kenya shilling

*KIRIBATI (formerly Gilbert Islands)   population: **63,000**
Capital: Tarawa
Land area: 956 sq km (369 sq miles)
Principal languages: English, Gilbertese
Currency: 100 cents = 1 Australian dollar

KOREA, Democratic People's Republic of (North Korea)   population: 20,660,000
Capital: Pyongyang
Land area: 122,370 sq km (47,250 sq miles)
Principal language: Korean
Currency: 100 chon = 1 won

KOREA, Republic of (South Korea)   population: 41,254,000
Capital: Seoul
Land area: 98,447 sq km (38,002 sq miles)
Principal language: Korean
Currency: 100 jeon = 1 won

KUWAIT   population: 1,667,000
Capital: Kuwait
Land area: 24,280 sq km (9,375 sq miles)
Principal language: Arabic
Currency: 1,000 fils = 1 dinar

LAOS (Lao People's Democratic Republic)   population: 3,892,000
Capital: Vientiane
Land area: 235,700 sq km (91,000 sq miles)
Principal languages: Lao, French
Currency: 100 ats = 1 kip

LEBANON   population: 2,624,000
Capital: Beirut
Land area: 10,400 sq km (4,000 sq miles)
Principal language: Arabic
Currency: 100 piastres = 1 Lebanese pound

*LESOTHO (formerly Basutoland)   population: 1,542,000
Capital: Maseru
Land area: 30,340 sq km (11,715 sq miles)
Principal languages: English, Sesotho
Currency: 100 lisente = 1 loti

LIBERIA   population: 2,317,000
Capital: Monrovia
Land area: 112,600 sq km (43,500 sq miles)
Principal languages: English, African languages
Currency: 100 cents = 1 Liberian dollar

LIBYA (Socialist People's Libyan Arab Jamahiriyah)   population: 3,772,000

Capital: Tripoli
Land area: 1,759,540 sq km (679,358 sq miles)
Principal language: Arabic
Currency: 1,000 dirhams = 1 dinar

LIECHTENSTEIN   population: 26,000
Capital: Vaduz
Land area: 160 sq km (62 sq miles)
Principal language: German
Currency: 100 centimes = 1 Swiss franc

LUXEMBOURG   population: 371,000
Capital: Luxembourg
Land area: 2,586 sq km (998 sq miles)
Principal languages: Letzeburgesch; French, German
and English are widely used
Currency: 100 centimes = 1 Luxembourg franc

MADAGASCAR, Democratic Republic of   population: 10,220,000
Capital: Antananarivo
Land area: 594,180 sq km (229,400 sq miles)
Principal languages: Malagasy, French, English
Currency: 100 centimes = 1 Malagasy franc

*MALAWI, Republic of (formerly Nyasaland)   population: 7,310,000
Capital: Lilongwe
Land area: 117,614 sq km (45,411 sq miles)
Principal languages: English, Nyanja-Chewa,
Tumbuka, Yao
Currency: 100 tambala = 1 kwacha

*MALAYSIA   population: 15,959,000
Capital: Kuala Lumpur
Land area: 334,110 sq km (129,000 sq miles)
Principal languages: Malay, English, Chinese, Tamil
Currency: 100 cents = 1 Malaysian dollar (ringgit)

MALDIVES, Republic of   population: 184,000
Capital: Malé
Land area: 298 sq km (115 sq miles)
Principal language: Divehi
Currency: 100 laris = 1 rupee

MALI   population: 7,882,000
Capital: Bamako
Land area: 1,204,021 sq km (464,873 sq miles)
Principal languages: French, Bambara
Currency: 100 centimes = 1 Mali franc

*MALTA   population: 371,000
Capital: Valletta
Land area: 246 sq km (95 sq miles)
Principal languages: Maltese, English
Currency: 100 cents = 1 Maltese pound

MAURITANIA (Mauritanian Islamic Republic) population: 1,752,000
Capital: Nouakchott
Land area: 1,030,700 sq km (398,000 sq miles)
Principal languages: Arabic, French
Currency: 5 khoums = 1 ouguiya

*MAURITIUS population: 1,047,000
Capital: Port Louis
Land area: 1,865 sq km (720 sq miles)
Principal languages: English, French, Creole, Hindi
Currency: 100 cents = 1 rupee

MEXICO (United Mexican States) population: 81,828,000
Capital: Mexico City
Land area: 1,967,183 sq km (759,530 sq miles)
Principal languages: Spanish, Amerindian languages
Currency: 100 centavos = 1 peso

MONACO population: 28,000
Capital: Monaco
Land area: 190 hectares (467 acres)
Principal languages: French, Monegasque
Currency: 100 centimes = 1 French franc

MONGOLIA (Mongolian People's Republic) population: 1,974,000
Capital: Ulan Bator
Land area: 1,565,000 sq km (604,247 sq miles)
Principal language: Mongol
Currency: 100 möngö = 1 tugrik

MOROCCO population: 22,466,000
Capital: Rabat
Land area: 659,970 sq km (254,814 sq miles)
Principal languages: Arabic, Berber, French, Spanish
Currency: 100 francs = 1 dirham

MOZAMBIQUE, People's Republic of population: 15,404,000
Capital: Maputo
Land area: 784,961 sq km (303,073 sq miles)
Principal language: Portuguese
Currency: 100 centavos = metical

*NAURU population: 8,400
Capital: Nairu
Land area: 2,130 hectares (5,263 acres)
Principal language: English
Currency: 100 cents = 1 Australian dollar

NEPAL population: 17,155,000
Capital: Katmandu
Land area: 141,400 sq km (54,600 sq miles)
Principal languages: Nepali, Maithir, Bhojpuri
Currency: 100 pice (paisa) = 1 Nepalese rupee

NETHERLANDS, The population: 14,677,000
Seat of government: The Hague
Capital: Amsterdam
Land area: 41,160 sq km (15,892 sq miles)
Principal language: Dutch
Currency: 100 cents = 1 guilder (florin)

*NEW ZEALAND population: 3,315,000
Capital: Wellington
Land area: 268,704 sq km (103,747 sq miles)
Principal language: English
Currency: 100 cents = 1 NZ dollar

NICARAGUA population: 3,363,000
Capital: Managua
Land area: 148,000 sq km (57,000 sq miles)
Principal language: Spanish
Currency: 100 centavos = 1 cordoba

NIGER population: 6,657,000
Capital: Niamey
Land area: 1,187,000 sq km (458,300 sq miles)
Principal languages: French, Arabic, African languages
Currency: Franc CFA

*NIGERIA, Federal Republic of population: 101,137,000
Capital: Lagos
Land area: 923,770 sq km (356,670 sq miles)
Principal languages: English, Hausa, Ibo, Yoruba
Currency: 100 kobo = 1 naira

NORWAY population: 4,179,000
Capital: Oslo
Land area: 323,895 sq km (125,056 sq miles)
Principal language: Norwegian
Currency: 100 öre = 1 krone

OMAN (formerly Muscat and Oman) population: 1,304,000
Capital: Muscat
Land area: 212,380 sq km (82,000 sq miles)
Principal language: Arabic
Currency: 100 baiza = 1 riyal

PAKISTAN population: 98,160,000
Capital: Islamabad
Land area: 803,943 sq km (310,403 sq miles)
Principal languages: Urdu, Punjabi, Sindhi, Pushtu,
Baluchi, Brahvi
Currency: 100 paisa = 1 rupee

PANAMA population: 2,102,000
Capital: Panama City
Land area: 75,650 sq km (29,210 miles)
Principal language: Spanish

Currency: 100 centesimos = 1 balboa

*PAPUA NEW GUINEA   population: 3,402,000
Capital: Port Moresby
Land area: 462,840 sq km (178,700 sq miles)
Principal language: English
Currency: 100 toea = 1 kina

PARAGUAY   population: 3,457,000
Capital: Asuncion
Land areas: 406,752 sq km (157,047 sq miles)
Principal languages: Spanish, Guarani
Currency: 100 centimos = 1 guarani

PERU   population: 19,195,000
Capital: Lima
Land area: 1,285,215 sq km (496,223 sq miles)
Principal languages: Spanish, Quechua, Aymara
Currency: 100 centavos = 1 sol

PHILIPPINES, The   population: 56,469,000
Capital: Manila
Land area: 300,000 sq km (115,830 sq miles)
Principal languages: Pilipino, English, Spanish and
over 70 Malayo-Polynesian languages
Currency: 100 centavos = 1 peso

POLAND   population: 37,550,000
Capital: Warsaw
Land area: 312,683 sq km (120,727 sq miles)
Principal language: Polish
Currency: 100 groszy = 1 zloty

PORTUGAL   population: 10,539,000
Capital: Lisbon
Land area: 91,631 sq km (35,379 sq miles)
Principal language: Portuguese
Currency: 100 centavos = 1 escudo

QATAR   population: 282,000
Capital: Doha
Land area: 11,000 sq km (4,247 sq miles)
Principal language: Arabic
Currency: 100 dirham = 1 riyal

ROMANIA   population: 23,219,000
Capital: Bucharest
Land area: 237,500 sq km (91,700 sq miles)
Principal language: Romanian
Currency: 100 bani = 1 leu

RWANDA   population: 6,323,000
Capital: Kigali
Land area: 26,330 sq km (10,170 sq miles)

Principal languages: Kinyarwanda, French
Currency: 100 centimes = 1 Rwanda franc

*ST LUCIA population: 128,000
Capital: Castries
Land area: 616 sq km (238 sq miles)
Principal language: English
Currency: 100 cents = 1 East Caribbean dollar

SALVADOR, EL population: 5,717,000
Capital: San Salvador
Land area: 21,393 sq km (8,260 sq miles)
Principal language: Spanish
Currency: 100 centavos = 1 colon

SAN MARINO population: 21,600
Capital: San Marino
Land area: 61 sq km (24 sq miles)
Principal language: Italian
Currency: Italian and Vatican City currencies are in
general use

SÃO TOMÉ AND PRINCIPE population: 109,000
Capital: São Tomè
Land area: 964 sq km (372 sq miles)
Principal language: Portuguese
Currency: 100 centavos = 1 dobra

SAUDI ARABIA population: 10,437,000
Capital: Riyadh
Land area: 2,400,000 sq km (927,000 sq miles)
Principal language: Arabic
Currency: 100 halalas = 1 riyal

SENEGAL population: 6,710,000
Capital: Dakar
Land area: 197,720 sq km (76,340 sq miles)
Principal language: French
Currency: franc CFA

*SEYCHELLES population: 67,000
Capital: Victoria (on island of Mahé)
Land area: 404 sq km (156 sq miles)
Principal languages: English, French, Creole
Currency: 100 cents = 1 rupee

*SIERRA LEONE population: 3,475,000
Capital: Freetown
Land area: 73,326 sq km (28,311 sq miles)
Principal languages: English, African languages
Currency: 100 cents = 1 leone

*SINGAPORE population: 2,599,000
Capital: Singapore

Land area: 616 sq km (238 sq miles)
Principal languages: Malay, Chinese, Tamil, English
Currency: 100 cents = 1 Singapore dollar

*SOLOMON ISLANDS   population: 280,000
Capital: Honiara (on Guadalcanal Island)
Land area: 29,785 sq km (11,500 sq miles)
Principal languages: English, Melanesian languages
Currency: Australian dollar, Solomon Islands dollar

SOMALIA (Somali Democratic Republic)   population: 5,041,000
Capital: Mogadishu
Land area: 630,000 sq km (243,000 sq miles)
Principal languages: Somali, Arabic, Italian, English
Currency: 100 cents = 1 Somali shilling

SOUTH AFRICA, Republic of   population: 34,052,000
Administrative capital: Pretoria
Legislative capital: Cape Town
Judicial capital: Bloemfontein
Land area: 1,140,519 sq km (440,354 sq miles)
Principal languages: Afrikaans, English, Xhosa,
Zulu, Sesotho
Currency: 100 cents = 1 rand

SPAIN   population: 39,223,000
Capital: Madrid
Land area: 504,879 sq km (194,934 sq miles)
Principal languages: Spanish (Castilian), Catalan,
Galician, Basque
Currency: 100 centimos = 1 peseta

*SRI LANKA (formerly Ceylon)   population: 16,218,000
Capital: Colombo
Land area: 65,610 sq km (25,332 sq miles)
Principal languages: Sinhala, Tamil
Currency: 100 cents = 1 rupee

SUDAN   population: 22,869,000
Capital: Khartoum
Land area: 2,500,000 sq km (967,500 sq miles)
Principal language: Arabic
Currency: 100 piastres = 1 Sudan pound

SURINAM   population: 363,000
Capital: Paramaribo
Land area: 163,000 sq km (63,000 sq miles)
Principal languages: Sranan (Taki Taki), Dutch,
English, Spanish, Hindi, Javanese, Chinese
Currency: 100 cents = 1 Surinam guilder

*SWAZILAND   population: 762,000
Capital: Mbabane
Land area: 17,400 sq km (6,700 sq miles)

Principal languages: English, Siswati
Currency: 100 cents = 1 lilangeni (plural, emalangeni);
South African rand also in use

SWEDEN population: 8,402,000
Capital: Stockholm
Land area: 411,479 sq km (158,872 sq miles)
Principal language: Swedish
Currency: 100 öre = 1 krona

SWITZERLAND population: 6,441,000
Capital: Bern
Land area: 41,288 sq km (15,941 sq miles)
Principal languages: German, French, Italian,
Romansch
Currency: 100 centimes = 1 franc

SYRIA (Syrian Arab Republic) population: 10,876,000
Capital: Damascus
Land area: 185,680 sq km (71,690 sq miles)
Principal language: Arabic
Currency: 100 piastres = 1 Syrian pound

TAIWAN (formerly Formosa) population: 18,700,000
Capital: Taipei
Land area: 35,989 sq km (13,895 sq miles)
Principal language: Chinese (Mandarin and Amoy
dialects)
Currency: 100 cents = 1 new Taiwan dollar

*TANZANIA (a union formed in 1964 between population: 22,498,000
Tanganyika, Zanzibar and Pemba)
Capital: Dodoma
Land area: 939,706 sq km (363,708 sq miles)
Principal languages: Swahili, English
Currency: 100 cents = 1 Tanzanian shilling

THAILAND population: 53,223,000
Capital: Bangkok
Land area: 514,000 sq km (198,500 sq miles)
Principal language: Thai
Currency: 100 satang = 1 baht (tical)

TOGO population: 3,074,000
Capital: Lomé
Land area: 56,000 sq km (22,000 sq miles)
Principal languages: French, Ewe, Mina, Dajomba,
Tim, Cabrais
Currency: franc CFA

*TONGA (Friendly Islands) population: 108,000
Capital: Nuku'alofa (on the island of Tongatapu)
Land area: 700 sq km (270 sq miles)
Principal languages: Polynesian, English

Currency: 100 seniti = 1 pa'anga

*TRINIDAD AND TOBAGO population: 1,150,000
Capital: Port-of-Spain
Land area: 4,828 sq km (1,864 sq miles)
Principal language: English
Currency: 100 cents = 1 Trinidad and Tobago dollar

TUNISIA population: 7,350,000
Capital: Tunis
Land area: 164,150 sq km (63,380 sq miles)
Principal languages: Arabic, French
Currency: 1,000 millimes = 1 dinar

TURKEY population: 50,673,000
Capital: Ankara
Land area: 779,452 sq km (300,946 sq miles)
Principal language: Turkish
Currency: 100 kurus = 1 Turkish pound (lira)

*UGANDA population: 15,035,000
Capital: Kampala
Land area: 236,860 sq km (91,430 sq miles)
Principal languages: English, Bantu languages,
including Swahili
Currency: 100 cents = 1 Uganda shilling

USSR (Union of Soviet Socialist Republics) population: 279,729,000
Capital: Moscow
Land area: 22,400,000 sq km (8,650,000 sq miles)
Principal languages: Russian, Ukrainian, Uzbek and
several others
Currency: 100 kopeks = 1 rouble

UNITED ARAB EMIRATES (a federation consisting population: 1,208,000
of the former Trucial States; Abu Dhabi, Dubai,
Sharjah, Ajman, Umm al Qawain and Fujairah joined
in 1971, Ras al Khaimah joined in 1972)
Capital: Abu Dhabi
Land area: 92,100 sq km (35,560 sq miles)
Principal language: Arabic
Currency: 100 fils = 1 dirham

UNITED KINGDOM OF GREAT BRITAIN AND population: 55,893,000
NORTHERN IRELAND
Capital: London
Land area:
  England: 130,362 sq km (50,333 sq miles)
  Wales: 20,761 sq km (8,016 sq miles)
  Scotland: 78,772 sq km (30,414 sq miles)
  Northern Ireland: 14,121 sq km (5,452 sq miles)
Total land area: 244,016 sq km (94,205 sq miles)
Principal languages: English, Welsh, Gaelic
Currency: 100 pence = 1 pound sterling

USA (United States of America)   population: 240,083,000
Capital: Washington DC
Land area: 9,363,169 sq km (3,615,120 sq miles)
Principal language: English
Currency: 100 cents = 1 dollar

URUGUAY   population: 3,013,000
Capital: Montevideo
Land area: 177,508 sq km (68,536 sq miles)
Principal language: Spanish
Currency: 100 centesimos = 1 new peso

VATICAN CITY STATE   population: 1,000
Land area: 44 hectares (108.7 acres)
Principal language: Italian
Currency: 100 centesimi = 1 lira

VENEZUELA   population: 19,133,000
Capital: Caracas
Land area: 912,050 sq km (352,143 sq miles)
Principal language: Spanish
Currency: 100 centimos = 1 bolivar

VIETNAM, Socialist Republic of   population: 63,408,000
Capital: Hanoi
Land area: 329,566 sq km (127,245 sq miles)
Principal language: Vietnamese
Currency: 100 xu = 1 dong

***WESTERN SAMOA**   population: 164,000
Capital: Apia (on island of Upolu)
Land area: 2,842 sq km (1,097 sq miles)
Principal languages: English, Samoan
Currency: 100 sene = 1 tala (dollar)

YEMEN ARAB REPUBLIC (North Yemen)   population: 8,409,000
Capital: San'a
Land area: 195,000 sq km (75,000 sq miles)
Principal language: Arabic
Currency: 100 fils = 1 riyal

YEMEN, The People's Democratic Republic of (South   population: 2,150,000
Yemen)
Capital: Aden
Land area: 336,700 sq km (130,000 sq miles)
Principal language: Arabic
Currency: 1,000 fils = 1 dinar

YUGOSLAVIA   population: 23,397,000
Capital: Belgrade
Land area: 255,804 sq km (98,766 sq miles)
Principal languages: Serbo-Croat, Slovene,
Macedonian
Currency: 100 paras = 1 dinar

ZAIRE (formerly Congo Democratic Republic) population: 34,559,000
Capital: Kinshasa
Land area: 2,345,500 sq km (905,600 sq miles)
Principal languages: French, Lingala, Swahili,
Luba, Kongo
Currency: 100 makuta = 1 zaire

*ZAMBIA population: 5,140,000
Capital: Lusaka
Land area: 752,620 sq km (290,590 sq miles)
Principal languages: English, Bantu languages
Currency: 100 ngwee = 1 kwacha

*ZIMBABWE (formerly Rhodesia) population: 8,622,000
Capital: Harare
Land area: 390,622 sq km (150,820 sq miles)
Principal languages: English, Shona, Ndebele
Currency: 100 cents = 1 Zimbabwe dollar

Internal Political Boundaries

THE STATES OF AUSTRALIA

STATE	AREA SQ KM	POPULATION	CAPITAL
Australian Capital Territory	2,432	233,200	Canberra
New South Wales	801,431	5,332,200	Sydney
Northern Territory	1,356,176	131,400	Darwin
Queensland	1,736,595	2,449,900	Brisbane
South Australia	984,381	1,334,100	Adelaide
Tasmania	67,897	430,600	Hobart
Victoria	227,516	4,013,200	Melbourne
Western Australia	2,527,633	1,351,400	Perth

COUNTIES OF WALES	AREA SQ KM	POPULATION	ADMINISTRATIVE HEADQUARTERS
Clwyd	2,425	394,500	Mold
Dyfed	5,765	333,500	Carmarthen
Gwent	1,376	440,200	Cwmbran
Gwynedd	3,868	231,900	Caernarfon
Mid-Glamorgan	1,019	539,300	Cardiff
Powys	5,077	110,500	Llandrindod Wells
South Glamorgan	416	389,800	Cardiff
West Glamorgan	815	368,500	Swansea

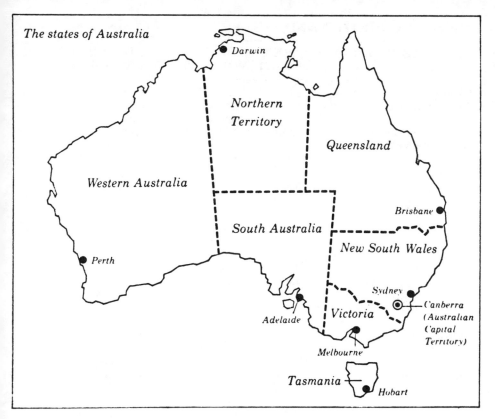

The states of Australia

Darwin

Northern Territory

Queensland

Western Australia

Brisbane

South Australia

New South Wales

Perth

Sydney

Adelaide

Victoria

Canberra (Australian Capital Territory)

Melbourne

Tasmania

Hobart

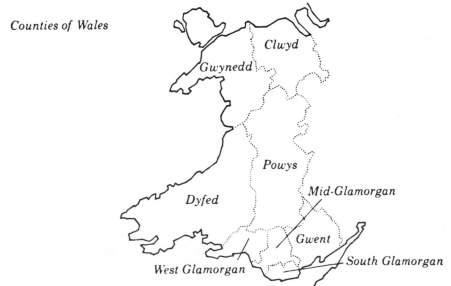

Counties of Wales

Clwyd

Gwynedd

Powys

Mid-Glamorgan

Dyfed

Gwent

West Glamorgan

South Glamorgan

65

ENGLISH COUNTIES AND SHIRES

NON-METROPOLITAN COUNTIES	AREA SQ KM	POPULATION	ADMINISTRATIVE HEADQUARTERS
Avon (1)	1,338	930,900	Bristol
Bedfordshire (2)	1,235	511,900	Bedford
Berkshire (3)	1,256	699,500	Reading
Buckinghamshire (4)	1,883	580,800	Aylesbury
Cambridgeshire (5)	3,409	596,600	Cambridge
Cheshire (6)	2,322	931,900	Chester
Cleveland (7)	583	566,900	Middlesbrough
Cornwall and Scilly Isles (8)	3,546	429,600	Truro
Cumbria (9)	6,809	482,500	Carlisle
Derbyshire (10)	2,631	910,900	Matlock
Devon (11)	6,715	966,200	Exeter
Dorset (12)	2,654	604,600	Dorchester
Durham (13)	2,436	608,100	Durham
Essex (14)	3,674	1,484,100	Chelmsford
Gloucestershire (15)	2,638	505,500	Gloucester
Hampshire (16)	3,772	1,486,300	Winchester
Hereford and Worcester (17)	3,927	638,500	Worcester
Hertfordshire (18)	1,634	967,500	Hertford
Humberside (19)	3,512	855,800	Hull
Kent (20)	3,732	1,485,000	Maidstone
Lancashire (21)	3,043	1,384,100	Preston
Leicestershire (22)	2,553	860,700	Leicester
Lincolnshire (23)	5,884	551,800	Lincoln
Norfolk (24)	5,355	704,900	Norwich
Northamptonshire (25)	2,367	537,000	Northampton
Northumberland (26)	5,033	299,700	Newcastle-upon-Tyne
Nottinghamshire (27)	2,164	991,400	Nottingham
Oxfordshire (28)	2,611	547,600	Oxford
Shropshire (29)	3,490	380,400	Shrewsbury
Somerset (30)	3,458	432,300	Taunton
Staffordshire (31)	2,716	1,019,000	Stafford
Suffolk (32)	3,800	611,200	Ipswich
Surrey (33)	1,655	1,013,900	Kingston-upon-Thames
Sussex, East (34)	1,795	670,600	Lewes
Sussex, West (35)	2,016	672,500	Chichester
Warwickshire (36)	1,981	477,300	Warwick
Wight, Isle of (37)	381	119,000	Newport, IOW
Wiltshire (38)	3,481	527,500	Trowbridge
Yorkshire, North (39)	8,317	678,100	Northallerton

(Numbers and letters in brackets refer to map position)

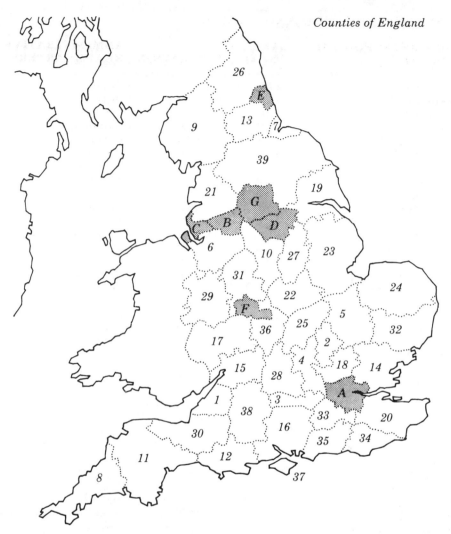

Counties of England

METROPOLITAN COUNTIES	AREA SQ KM	POPULATION	ADMINISTRATIVE HEADQUARTERS
Greater London (A)	1,580	6,765,100	London
Greater Manchester (B)	1,286	2,605,000	Manchester
Merseyside (C)	652	1,511,000	Liverpool
South Yorkshire (D)	1,560	1,312,800	Barnsley
Tyne and Wear (E)	540	1,149,600	Newcastle-upon-Tyne
West Midlands (F)	899	2,667,000	Birmingham
West Yorkshire (G)	2,039	2,063,100	Wakefield

THE SCOTTISH REGIONS

REGION OR ISLAND AUTHORITIES	AREA SQ KM	POPULATION	ADMINISTRATIVE HEADQUARTERS
Borders	4,670	99,784	Newtown St Boswells
Central	2,621	273,391	Stirling
Dumfries and Galloway	6,369	145,139	Dumfries
Fife	1,305	327,362	Glenrothes, Fife
Grampian	8,702	471,942	Aberdeen
Highland	25,141	200,150	Inverness
Lothian	1,753	738,372	Edinburgh
Orkney	905	19,056	Kirkwall
Shetland	1,429	27,277	Lerwick
Strathclyde	13,849	2,404,532	Glasgow
Tayside	7,501	391,846	Dundee
Western Isles	2,898	31,884	Stornoway

THE PROVINCES OF IRELAND

PROVINCE	AREA SQ KM	POPULATION	COUNTIES AND COUNTY BOROUGHS
Connacht	17,775	424,410	Galway, Leitrim, Mayo, Roscommon, Sligo
Leinster	19,736	1,790,521	Carlow, Dublin County Borough, Dublin, Dun Laoghaire Borough, Kildare, Kilkenny, Laoighis, Longford, Louth, Meath, Offaly, Westmeath, Wexford, Wicklow
Munster	24,540	998,315	Clare, Cork County Borough, Cork, Kerry, Limerick County Borough, Limerick, Tipperary – North Riding, Tipperary – South Riding, Waterford County Borough, Waterford
Ulster (part of)	8,011	239,159	Cavan, Donegal, Monaghan

NORTHERN IRELAND

Northern Ireland consists of the major portion of the province of Ulster and is part of the United Kingdom. It is divided into 26 district and borough councils: Antrim, Ards, Armagh, Ballymena, Ballymoney, Banbridge, Belfast City, Carrickfergus, Castlereagh, Coleraine, Cookstown, Craigavon, Down, Dungannon, Fermanagh, Larne, Limavady, Lisburn, Londonderry City, Magherafelt, Moyle, Newry and Mourne, Newtownabbey, North Down, Omagh, Strabane.

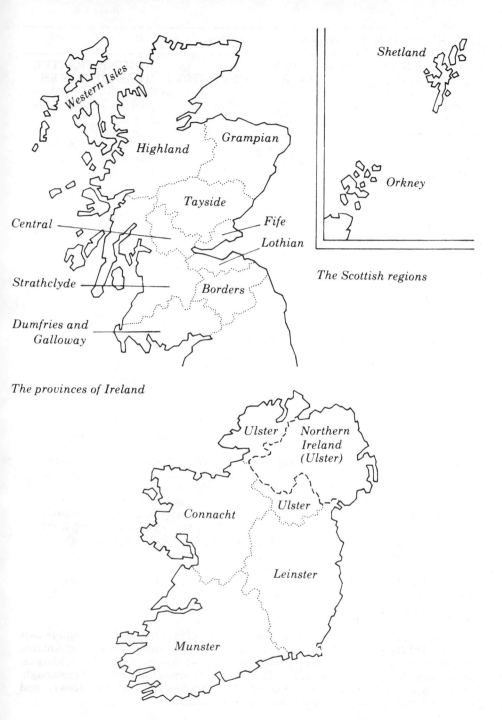

The Scottish regions

The provinces of Ireland

69

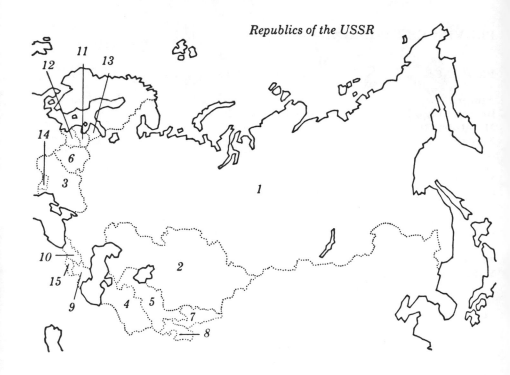

Republics of the USSR

THE 15 UNION REPUBLICS OF THE USSR

REPUBLIC	AREA SQ KM	POPULATION	CAPITAL
Russian Socialist Federal Soviet Republic (RSFSR) (1)	16,838,885	141,000,000	Moscow
Kazakhstan (2)	2,778,544	15,500,000	Alma-Ata
Ukraine (3)	582,750	50,500,000	Kiev
Turkmenistan (4)	491,072	3,000,000	Ashkhabad
Uzbekistan (5)	412,250	17,000,000	Tashkent
Belorussia (6)	209,790	9,800,000	Minsk
Kirghizia (7)	196,581	3,800,000	Frunze
Tadzhikistan (8)	144,263	4,200,000	Dushanbe
Azerbaijan (9)	86,661	6,400,000	Baku
Georgia (10)	69,671	5,100,000	Tbilisi
Latvia (11)	66,278	2,600,000	Riga
Lithuania (12)	65,201	3,500,000	Vilnius
Estonia (13)	45,610	1,500,000	Tallinn
Moldavia (14)	34,188	4,100,000	Kishinev
Armenia (15)	30,821	3,200,000	Erevan

PROVINCES OF CANADA

PROVINCE	AREA SQ KM	POPULATION	CAPITAL
Alberta (1)	661,188	2,237,724	Edmonton
British Columbia (2)	948,600	2,744,467	Victoria
Manitoba (3)	650,000	1,026,241	Winnipeg
New Brunswick (4)	72,481	696,403	Fredericton
Newfoundland and Labrador (5)	404,519	567,681	St John's
Nova Scotia (6)	54,556	847,442	Halifax
Ontario (7)	1,068,587	8,625,107	Toronto
Prince Edward Island (8)	5,657	122,506	Charlottetown
Quebec (9)	1,540,687	6,438,403	Quebec
Saskatchewan (10)	651,903	968,313	Regina

TERRITORY			
Yukon Territory (11)	536,327	22,135	Whitehorse
Northwest Territories (12)	3,379,711	45,471	Yellowknife

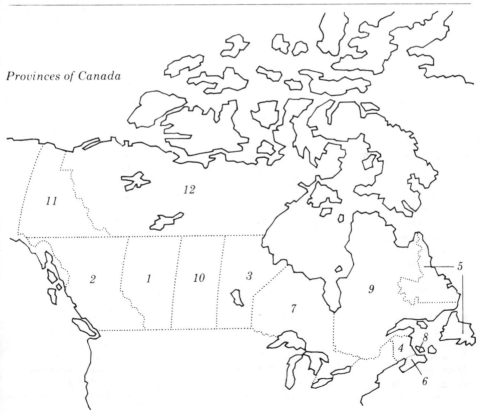

Provinces of Canada

THE UNITED STATES OF AMERICA

STATE	AREA SQ KM	POPULATION	CAPITAL
Alabama (1)	133,667	3,893,888	Montgomery
Alaska (2)	1,518,776	401,851	Juneau
Arizona (3)	295,024	2,718,215	Phoenix
Arkansas (4)	137,534	2,286,435	Little Rock
California (5)	411,014	23,667,902	Sacramento
Colorado (6)	270,000	2,889,964	Denver
Connecticut (7)	12,973	3,107,567	Hartford
Delaware (8)	6,138	594,338	Dover
Florida (9)	151,670	9,746,324	Tallahassee
Georgia (10)	152,489	5,463,105	Atlanta
Hawaii (11)	16,638	964,691	Honolulu
Idaho (12)	216,413	943,935	Boise
Illinois (13)	146,076	11,426,518	Springfield
Indiana (14)	93,994	5,490,224	Indianapolis
Iowa (15)	2,789,893	2,913,808	Des Moines
Kansas (16)	213,095	2,363,679	Topeka
Kentucky (17)	104,623	3,660,777	Frankfort
Louisiana (18)	125,675	4,205,900	Baton Rouge
Maine (19)	86,027	1,124,660	Augusta
Maryland (20)	27,394	4,216,975	Annapolis
Massachusetts (21)	21,386	5,737,037	Boston
Michigan (22)	150,779	9,262,078	Lansing
Minnesota (23)	217,736	4,075,970	St Paul
Mississippi (24)	123,584	2,520,638	Jackson
Missouri (25)	180,456	4,916,686	Jefferson City
Montana (26)	377,456	786,690	Helena
Nebraska (27)	200,147	1,569,825	Lincoln
Nevada (28)	286,299	800,493	Carson City
New Hampshire (29)	24,097	920,610	Concord
New Jersey (30)	20,295	7,364,823	Trenton
New Mexico (31)	315,115	1,302,894	Santa Fé
New York (32)	128,402	17,558,072	Albany
North Carolina (33)	136,524	5,881,766	Raleigh
North Dakota (34)	183,022	652,717	Bismarck
Ohio (35)	106,608	10,797,630	Columbus
Oklahoma (36)	181,090	3,025,290	Oklahoma City
Oregon (37)	250,948	2,633,105	Salem
Pennsylvania (38)	117,412	11,863,895	Harrisburg
Rhode Island (39)	3,144	947,154	Providence
South Carolina (40)	80,432	3,121,820	Columbia
South Dakota (41)	199,552	690,768	Pierre
Tennessee (42)	109,412	4,591,120	Nashville
Texas (43)	692,408	14,229,191	Austin
Utah (44)	219,932	1,461,037	Salt Lake City
Vermont (45)	24,887	511,456	Montpelier
Virginia (46)	105,711	5,346,818	Richmond

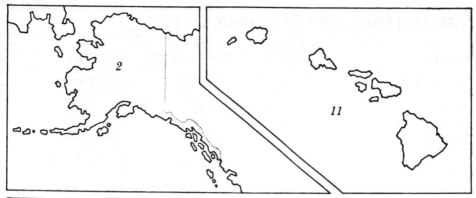

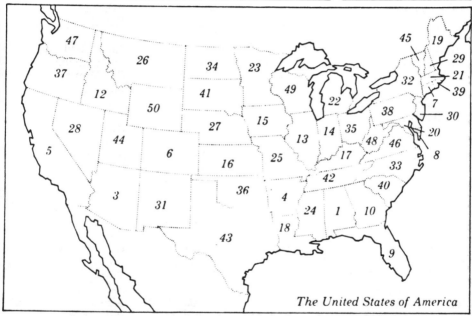

The United States of America

STATE	AREA SQ KM	POPULATION	CAPITAL
Washington (47)	176,617	4,132,156	Olympia
West Virginia (48)	62,629	1,949,644	Charleston
Wisconsin (49)	145,439	4,705,767	Madison
Wyoming (50)	253,597	469,557	Cheyenne
Dist. of Columbia (D.C.)	179	638,333	The capital territory is governed by Congress through a Commissioner and City Council

Languages of the World

PRINCIPAL LANGUAGES OF THE WORLD

LANGUAGE	NUMBER OF SPEAKERS	LANGUAGE FAMILY
Northern Chinese (Mandarin, Guoyu, or Beifanghira)	740,000,000	Sino-Tibetan
English	403,000,000	Indo-European
Russian	277,000,000	Indo-European
Hindustani (a combination of Hindi and Urdu	339,000,000	Indo-European
Spanish	266,000,000	Indo-European
Arabic	160,000,000	Hamito-Semitic
Bengali	155,000,000	Indo-European
Portuguese	154,000,000	Indo-European
Japanese	120,000,000	Inrelated to any known language
Malay-Indonesian	119,000,000	Malayo-Polynesian
German	118,000,000	Indo-European
French	109,000,000	Indo-European
Punjabi (spoken in Punjab region and Pakistan)	67,000,000	Indo-European
Italian	62,000,000	Indo-European
Korean	62,000,000	Unrelated to any known language
Telugu (spoken in south India)	60,000,000	Dravidian
Tamil (spoken in Sri Lanka, south India and Malaysia)	59,000,000	Dravidian
Marathi (spoken in west and central India)	58,000,000	Indo-European
Cantonese (a dialect of Chinese spoken in the Kwang-tung area)	56,000,000	Sino-Tibetan
Javanese (spoken in Indonesia)	49,000,000	Malayo-Polynesian

Over 4,000 languages – living or dead – have been identified and more than 2,000 are spoken today. They are classified into families. One of the largest families is known as the Indo-European group

The Population of the World

Between 1750 and 1850 the world's population increased from 750,000,000 to well over 1,000,000,000. This was largely the result of technological progress. An English clergyman, Thomas Malthus (1766–1834), noted in his famous *Essay on Population* that the rate of growth of food production could not keep pace with the rate of increase of population. Ultimately, he wrote, disease and malnutrition among the poorer peoples was the only foreseeable check on population growth.

Since Malthus's time, great advances in medical science have further reduced the death rate (which used to roughly balance the birth rate), swelling the world's population to an even greater degree. At the same time there has been enormous progress in technology and greater use of resources. But it is now becoming increasingly clear that the world's resources are not limitless. As the human population increases, new ways have to be devised to support the growing numbers.

Many millions are undernourished and living in extremely poor conditions. In the developing countries of Africa, Asia and Latin America the birthrate is far higher than in the industrialized countries of Europe, North America, the USSR, parts of South America, Japan, Australia and New Zealand. Unfortunately, the countries where the population growth is highest are the least able to provide enough food for the many extra mouths.

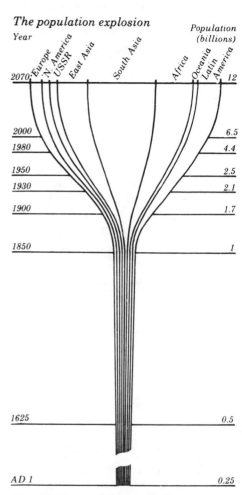

The population explosion

In 1850, the world's population was over 1,000,000,000. By 1930 the figure had doubled. Only 30 years later, another 1,000,000,000 were added. By the end of this century, if the present pattern of growth continues, a population of more than 6,000 million will be reached. But recently, the rate of growth has declined and deaths are now expected to balance births in the year 2100, when there will be about 10,200 million people.

Monarchies

COUNTRY	RULER	DATE OF ACCESSION
Belgium	King Baudouin (married Dõna Fabiola de Mora y Aragòn in 1960)	1951
Bhutan	King Jigme Singye Wangchuck	1972
Denmark	Queen Margrethe II (married Count Henri de Monpezat [Prince Henrik of Denmark] in 1967)	1972
Japan	Emperor Hirohito (married Princess Nagako in 1924)	1926
Jordan	King Hussein	1952
Liechtenstein	Prince Franz Josef II (married Countess Gina von Wilczek in 1943)	1938
Luxembourg	Grand Duke Jean (married Princess Joséphine Charlotte of Belgium in 1953)	1964
Monaco	Prince Rainier III (married Miss Grace Kelly in 1956)	1949
Morocco	King Hassan II	1961
Nepal	King Birendra Bir Bikam Shah Deva	1972
Netherlands	Queen Beatrix (married Prince Claus George Willem Otto Frederik Geert of the Netherlands, Jonkheer van Amsberg, in 1966)	1980
Norway	King Olav V (married Princess Märthe of Sweden in 1929)	1957
Saudi Arabia	King Fahd bin Abdulaziz	1982
Spain	King Juan Carlos I de Borbón y Borbón (married Princess Sophia of Greece, 1962)	1975
Sweden	King Carl XVI Gustav (married Fraulein Silvia Renate Sommerlath in 1976)	1973
Thailand	King Bhumibol Adulyadej (married Princess Sirikit Kityakara in 1950)	1946
Tonga	King Taufa' ahau Tupou IV	1965
UK	Queen Elizabeth II (married Prince Philip, Duke of Edinburgh, in 1947)	1952

The World's Principal Political, Economic and Military Organizations

United Nations Organization
This worldwide association of almost all independent countries came into being on 26 June 1945 with the signing of the UN Charter – as World War II drew to its close – with the primary aim of ensuring that no further global conflicts ever take place. With the exception of a small number of countries which are not fully independent, or whose status is in dispute, the organization includes every sovereign state, although Switzerland has not become a member in order to preserve her neutrality.

The United Nations has four main purposes: the preservation of security, the administration of justice, the provision of welfare and the guardianship of human rights. Members pledge themselves to settle their disputes without resort to force, and to support the Charter's terms at all times.

Six major organs are contained within the UN:
1 **The General Assembly** Meeting annually, the representatives of all the member countries consider matters concerned with world peace and security and make recommendations to the Security Council. The Assembly also elects the Economic and Social Council and supervises its work, besides controlling the financial affairs of the UN.

2 **The Security Council** The Security Council, which sits continuously, has the responsibility of arranging peaceful settlement of international disputes, and of stopping wars when they occur. Five of the Council's 15 seats are held permanently by Britain, China, France, the USSR and the USA. The other ten are occupied, temporarily, by countries elected periodically in the General Assembly. The Council can take no action in an emergency, however, if any one of its permanent members uses the veto (the right to forbid the Council taking action).

3 **The Economic and Social Council** The purpose of this body is to help raise the standards of life all over the world. The Council concerns itself with matters of health, education, employment, human rights and all the economic and social problems to be found everywhere, but more particularly in the underdeveloped, and often poverty-stricken, areas of the world. Regional and functional commissions have been set up to deal with these affairs, plus four special bodies: UN Children's Fund (UNICEF), Commissioner for Refugees (UNHCR), Conference on Trade and Development (UNCTAD) and Industrial Development Organization (UNIDO). In addition, the Council has fifteen intergovern-

ment agencies for special purposes as follows: International Atomic Energy Agency (IAEA), International Labour Organization (ILO), Food and Agriculture Organization (FAO), UN Educational, Scientific and Cultural Organization (UNESCO), World Health Organization (WHO), World Bank, International Finance Corporation (IFC), International Monetary Fund (IMF), International Development Association (IDA), International Civil Aviation Organization (ICAO), Universal Postal Union (UPU), International Telecommunications Union (ITU), World Meteorological Organization (WMO), Intergovernmental Maritime Consultative Organization (IMCO) and General Agreement on Tariffs and Trade (GATT).

4 **The Trusteeship Council**
5 **The International Court of Justice**
6 **The Secretariat**

Since 1945 the United Nations Organization has stationed military peace forces, composed of detachments from various member countries, in a number of places where fighting has either broken out or is threatened. These have helped to keep warring nations apart, and have given time for peace talks and negotiations to be arranged.

The Commonwealth
The British Commonwealth of Nations is composed of fully independent countries from all over the world. It arose out of the former British Empire and was legalized

SECRETARY-GENERALS OF THE UNITED NATIONS

1946 Trygve Lie (Norway)

1951 Trygve Lie (resigned in 1952)

1953 Dag Hammarskjöld (Sweden)

1957 Dag Hammarskjöld (killed in an air crash in 1961)

1961 Sithu U Thant (Burma)

1966 Sithu U Thant

1972 Kurt Waldheim (Austria)

1977 Kurt Waldheim

1982 Javier Perez de Cuellar

by the Statute of Westminster (1931) by Australia, Canada, New Zealand and the United Kingdom. Member nations of this organization and their dependencies associate freely together in the work of the Commonwealth. They attend conferences, co-operating to promote the best interests of the countries concerned, and also try to help the causes of peace and development in the world at large. The members all regard Queen Elizabeth II of the United Kingdom as Head of the Commonwealth, and many of them acknowledge her as Head of State also. The Commonwealth countries, in order of joining, are as follows: United Kingdom, Canada, Australia, New Zealand, India, Sri Lanka, Ghana, Nigeria, Cyprus, Sierra Leone, Jamaica, Trinidad and Tobago, Uganda, Kenya, Malaysia, Malawi, Malta, Tanzania, Zambia, Gambia, Singapore, Barbados, Botswana, Guyana, Lesotho, Mauritius, Nauru (limited membership), Swaziland,

Fiji, Tonga, Western Samoa, Bangladesh, Bahamas, Grenada, Papua New Guinea, Seychelles, Solomon Islands, Tuvalu (special member), Dominica, St Lucia, Kiribati. St Vincent (special member), Zimbabwe, Vanuatu, Belize, Antigua and Barbuda, Maldives, St Christopher and Nevis, Brunei.

Caribbean Community (CARICOM)

The Caribbean Community was set up in 1973 by Barbados, Guyana, Jamaica, and Trinidad and Tobago. Antigua, Belize, Dominica, Grenada, Montserrat, St Lucia, St Christopher and Nevis, and St Vincent joined in 1974. The Bahamas also became a member of the Community, but not of the Caribbean Common Market established by the Community. CARICOM aims at economic integration through the Common Market, the operation of some common services, and the co-ordination of foreign policies.

Organization of American States (OAS)

A pan-American regional alliance, founded in 1948, to assist American nations towards greater under-standing and co-operation. Its members are:
Antigua and Barbuda, Argentina, Bahamas, Barbados, Bolivia, Brazil, Chile, Colombia, Costa Rica, Cuba, Dominica, Dominican Republic, Ecuador, El Salvador, Grenada, Guatemala, Haiti, Honduras, Jamaica, Mexico, Nicaragua, Panama, Paraguay, Peru, St Christopher and Nevis, St

Lucia, St Vincent and the Grenadines, Surinam, Trinidad and Tobago, USA, Uruguay, Venezuela.

Organization of African Unity (OAU)

Another regional alliance, covering Africa, and embracing all fully independent countries in that continent with the exception of the Republic of South Africa. Founded at Addis Ababa in 1963, OAU seeks to bring member countries together for the mutual advantage of all concerned, and to solve disputes among them or with nations outside the organization.

League of Arab States (Arab League)

An association of Arab countries in North Africa and Southwest Asia, founded in 1945. The Arab League includes in its membership: Algeria, Bahrain, Djibouti, Iraq, Jordan, Kuwait, Lebanon, Libya, Mauritania, Morocco, Oman, Palestine, Qatar, Saudi Arabia, Somalia, Sudan, Syria, Tunisia, United Arab Emirates, Yemen Arab Republic, South Yemen. Disagreements between members have caused problems and the membership of Egypt (a founder member) was suspended in 1979.

Council of Europe

The Council comprises a Consultative Assembly and a Committee of Ministers. Founded in 1949, it comprises 19 member nations and has its headquarters at Strasbourg. The Council of Europe is greatly concerned with human rights and the growth of international co-operation in areas such as social

European Economic Community (EEC)

Created by the Treaty of Rome in 1957, the EEC, or 'Common Market', originally comprised six members – Belgium, France, Italy, Luxembourg, the Netherlands and West Germany. It was enlarged in 1973 when Denmark, the Republic of Ireland and the United Kingdom joined. Greece became the tenth member on 1 January 1981 and Portugal and Spain became members on 1 January 1986.

The EEC consists of a Commission, Council of Ministers, Parliament (Assembly) and Court of Justice. It was founded to create a common market by gradually adjusting all aspects of the economies of the member countries until they operate as a whole, with no great economic differences between one country and the next. At the same time, social and commercial activities are to be harmonized, and 'closer relations established between its member states' in every sphere.

The EEC has its headquarters in Brussels. The Assembly, made up of elected members from constituencies in the nine countries, meets regularly to debate major policy issues, study legislation and control part of the Community's budget.

European Free Trade Association (EFTA)

Although Britain and Denmark left EFTA on joining the EEC, the other EFTA members have continued to operate the free trade area created since 1958 while, at the same time, concluding co-operative agreements with the Community. The EFTA countries are: Austria, Iceland, Norway, Portugal, Sweden, Switzerland and Finland (an associated member). EFTA objectives include an end to tariff restrictions. Industrial customs barriers between EFTA and the EEC were removed in 1976.

Council for Mutual Economic Assistance (COMECON)

Established in 1949, Comecon represents the East European counterpart to the EEC. It brings together, through economic co-operation, Bulgaria, Cuba, Czechoslovakia, East Germany, Hungary, Mongolia, Poland, Romania, the USSR and Vietnam. Afghanistan, Angola, Ethiopia, Laos, Mozambique and South Yemen send observers to COMECON meetings.

Association of Southeast Asian Nations (ASEAN)

This organization was formed in 1967 to promote economic and political co-operation amongst the non-Communist countries of Southeast Asia: Indonesia, Malaysia, the Philippines, Singapore and Thailand. Brunei became a member in 1984.

Latin American Free Trade Association (LAFTA)

Comprising 11 nations, LAFTA was set up in 1960 to bring about closer economic association among its members: Argentina, Bolivia, Brazil, Chile, Colombia, Ecuador, Mexico, Paraguay, Peru, Uruguay and Venezuela.

Organization for Economic Co-operation and Development (OECD)

Stemming from the OEEC (Organization for European Economic Co-operation), this body was formed in 1961. Its member nations are Australia, Austria, Belgium, Canada, Denmark, West Germany, Finland, France, Greece, Iceland, Ireland, Italy, Japan, Luxembourg, the Netherlands, New Zealand, Norway, Portugal, Spain, Sweden, Switzerland, Turkey, the UK and the USA. The OECD works to promote economic growth and development, and in expanding world trade. It has recently been particularly concerned with the worldwide energy crisis and in helping to ease its effects.

Organization of Petroleum Exporting Countries (OPEC)

This association of countries concerned with large-scale petroleum exports was founded in Caracas, the capital of Venezuela, in 1961. Member nations from various parts of the world meet regularly to agree upon the price and quantities of oil to be made available for sale to importing countries. The power and import-ance of OPEC have grown enormously recently, with the development of the world's energy crisis.

North Atlantic Treaty Organization (NATO)

NATO represents a defensive alliance covering Europe, the North Atlantic and North America. It arose from a pact, made in 1949, between Belgium, Canada,

Denmark, France, Iceland, Italy, Luxembourg, the Netherlands, Norway, Portugal, the United Kingdom and the USA. Greece and Turkey were admitted to the treaty in 1952, West Germany in 1955, and Spain in 1982. France withdrew militarily in 1966, though it remained a member of the alliance.

Warsaw Treaty Organization (Warsaw Pact)

In effect, the Warsaw Pact is the East European equivalent of NATO in the West. Formed in 1955, it is a military mutual assistance organization. Its members are Bulgaria, Czechoslovakia, East Germany, Hungary, Poland, Romania and the USSR. From 1962, Albania, a founder member, was no longer invited to Warsaw Pact meetings, though it was not formally expelled from the organization.

Anzus Pact

Also known as the Pacific Security Treaty, this tripartite alliance dates from 1951, when Australia, New Zealand and the USA agreed to align themselves to preserve the security of the Pacific area and to seek peaceful settlement of disputes arising in that region.

Southeast Asia Treaty Organization (SEATO)

Another regional defensive organization, set up in 1954 for the better security of Southeast Asia. The eight members of this alliance are Australia, France, New Zealand, Pakistan, the Philippines, Thailand, the United Kingdom and the USA.

Man-made Structures

LARGEST CITIES OF THE WORLD

The following cities are ranked according to the size of population in their metropolitan areas. The figures are taken from the most recent censuses or estimates.

CITY	POPULATION
Mexico City	16,000,000
Shanghai	11,859,000
Tokyo	11,806,729
Cairo	11,000,000
Paris	10,073,059
Buenos Aires	9,677,200
Peking (Beijing)	9,230,687
Calcutta	9,200,000
Mowcow	8,546,000
Sao Paulo	8,490,763
Seoul	8,367,000
Bombay	8,300,000
Tientsin (Tianjin)	7,390,000
New York City	7,071,030
Surabaya	7,027,913
London	6,776,000
Djakarta	6,503,449
Ch'ungch'ing (Chongqing)	6,200,000
Teheran	6,200,000
Delhi	6,196,000

THE WORLD'S TALLEST INHABITED BUILDINGS

BUILDING	HEIGHT METRES	FEET	NUMBER OF STOREYS	WHEN BUILT	LOCATION
Sears Tower	443	1,454	110	1974	Chicago, Illinois
World Trade Center	411	1,350	110	1973	New York City
Empire State Building	381	1,250	102	1930	New York City
Standard Oil Building	346	1,136	80	1973	Chicago, Illinois
John Hancock Center	343	1,127	100	1968	Chicago, Illinois
Chrysler Building	319	1,046	77	1930	New York City

The tallest man-made structure in the world is the Warsaw Radio Mast, 646 m (2,120 ft) high.

83

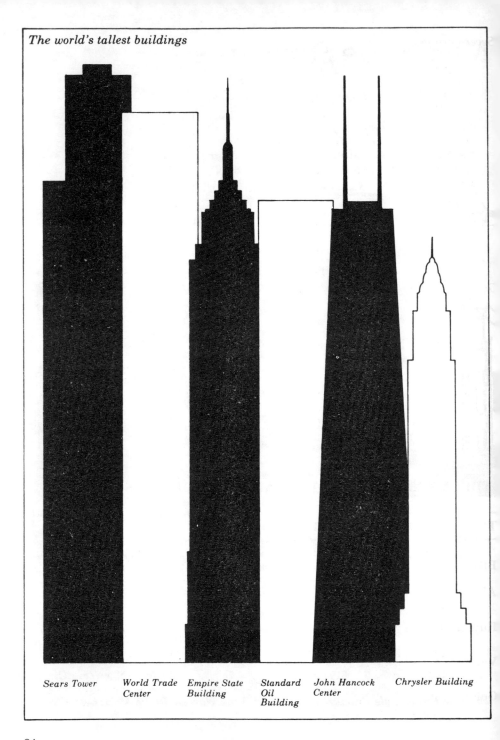

The world's tallest buildings

Sears Tower

World Trade Center

Empire State Building

Standard Oil Building

John Hancock Center

Chrysler Building

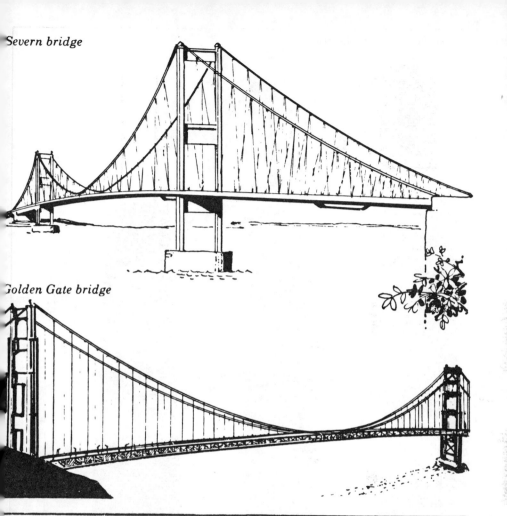

Severn bridge

Golden Gate bridge

THE WORLD'S LONGEST SUSPENSION BRIDGES

BRIDGE	LENGTH METRES	FEET	YEAR OF COMPLETION	LOCATION
Akashi-Kaikyo	1,780	5,840	Under construction	Honshu–Shikoku, Japan
Humber Estuary	1,410	4,626	1981	Humber, England
Verrazano Narrows	1,298	4,260	1964	Brooklyn–Staten Island, USA
Golden Gate	1,280	4,200	1937	San Francisco Bay, USA

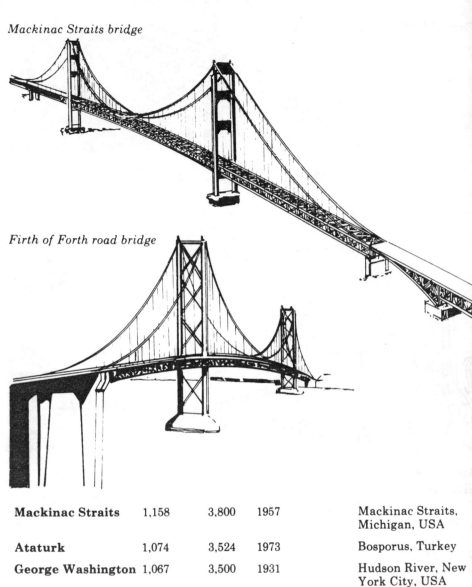

Mackinac Straits bridge

Firth of Forth road bridge

Mackinac Straits	1,158	3,800	1957	Mackinac Straits, Michigan, USA
Ataturk	1,074	3,524	1973	Bosporus, Turkey
George Washington	1,067	3,500	1931	Hudson River, New York City, USA
Ponto do 25 Abril	1,013	3,323	1966	Tagus River, Lisbon, Portugal
Firth of Forth (road bridge)	1,006	3,300	1964	Firth of Forth, Scotland
Severn	988	3,240	1966	Severn Estuary, England

Firth of Forth railway bridge

THE WORLD'S LONGEST CANTILEVER BRIDGES

BRIDGE	LENGTH METRES	FEET	YEAR OF COMPLETION	LOCATION
Quebec (railway bridge)	549	1,800	1917	St Lawrence River, Canada
Firth of Forth (railway bridge)	521	1,710	1889	Firth of Forth, Scotland
Delaware River	501	1,644	1971	Chester, Pennsylvania, USA
Greater New Orleans	480	1,575	1958	Algiers, Mississippi River, Louisiana, USA

THE WORLD'S GREATEST STEEL ARCH BRIDGES

BRIDGE	LENGTH METRES	FEET	YEAR OF COMPLETION	LOCATION
New River Gorge	518	1,700	1977	Fayetteville, West Virginia, USA
Bayonne	504	1,652	1931	Bayonne, New Jersey–Staten Island, New York, USA
Sydney Harbour	503	1,650	1932	Sydney, Australia
Fremont	383	1,255	1971	Portland, Oregon, USA

Sydney Harbour bridge

THE WORLD'S LONGEST RAIL TUNNELS

TUNNEL	LENGTH KM	MILES	LOCATION	DATE OF CONSTRUCTION
Seikan	54	33.5	Tsugaru Channel, Japan	1972–
Northern Line – Morden to East Finchley (underground)	28	17	London, England	1939
Simplon II	20	12	Brig, Switzerland, to Iselle, Italy	1918–22
Simplon I	20	12	Brig, Switzerland, to Iselle, Italy	1898–1906
Great Apennine	18.5	11.5	Vernio, Italy	1923–34

GREAT SHIP CANALS OF THE WORLD

CANAL	COUNTRY	LENGTH KM	MILES	DEPTH METRES	FEET	YEAR OPENED
Amsterdam	Netherlands	26.5	16.5	7	23	1876
Corinth	Greece	6.5	4	8	26	1893
Elbe and Trave	Germany	66	41	3	10	1900
Gota	Sweden	185	115	3	10	1832
Houston (Texas)	USA	92	57	10	34	1940
Kiel	Germany	98	61	13.5	45	1895
Manchester	England	57	35.5	8.5	28	1894
Panama	Panama	81	50.5	13.5	45	1914
Princess Juliana	Netherlands	32	20	5	16	1935
Saulte Ste Marie	Canada	1.8	1.1	7	22	1895
Saulte Ste Marie	USA	2.6	1.6	7	22	1855
Suez	Egypt	162.5	101	12	39	1869
V.I. Lenin Volga–Don	USSR	100	62	—	—	1952
Welland	Canada	43.5	27	7.5	25	1887
White Sea–Baltic (formerly Stalin Canal)	USSR	227	141	5	16.5	1933

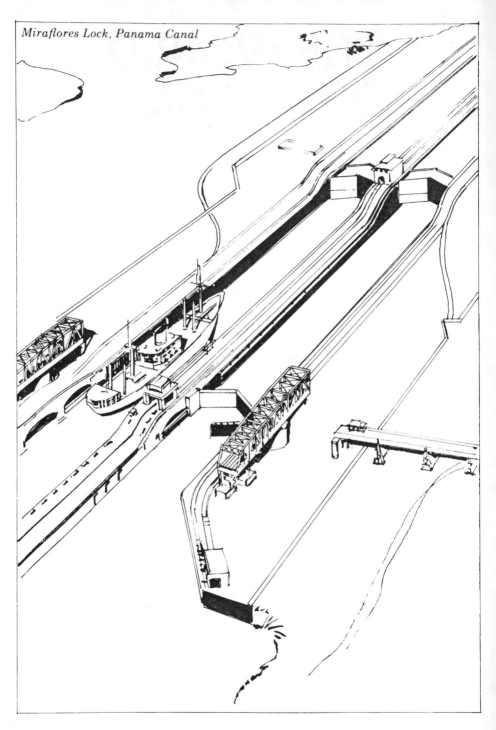

Miraflores Lock, Panama Canal

THE WORLD OF SCIENCE

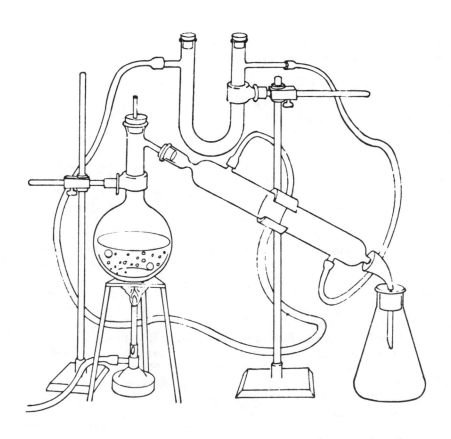

Recent Developments in Science and Technology

In 18th-century England, machinery was invented to perform various kinds of work which, until then, people had always done by hand. The goods manufactured with the use of machines were produced faster and were often better in quality than those hitherto made by country craftsmen. This was the beginning of what is known as the Industrial Revolution. Today there are machines that can do what people cannot do mentally (at least, not without an enormous amount of effort). We might call this development the Electronics Revolution.

Electronics

Electronics is a branch of science and engineering closely related to the science of electricity. It started with the discovery of the electron by Sir J. J. Thomson in 1897. Every atom has one or more electrons, particles which carry an electric charge. In materials called conductors (which include most metals) the atoms have electrons that can flow freely from atom to atom. Such a flow forms an electric current. An electric current is utilized in all electrical equipment, such as electric lights and electric motors. Electric power is controlled by varying the voltage or the current. Electronic equipment, such as TV sets and computers, on the other hand, mostly uses minute voltages and current from specialized devices producing pulses of

Transistor

electrons. One such device is the transistor.

Transistors can perform many of the functions of thermionic valves, which they have largely replaced. They can be made very small and are more reliable than valves. Both valves and transistors amplify (increase) small voltages and currents to control a much larger one. The transistor is made of a solid, semiconductor material. A semiconductor is neither a good conductor of electricity nor a good insulator. The materials commonly used in transistors are germanium or silicon. When 'doped', i.e. treated with impurities such as arsenic or phosphorus, they can conduct electricity.

The invention of the transistor in 1949 led immediately to the transistor radio. It also marked the beginning of the computer industry as computers could at last be made cheaper and less prone to breaking down. However, transistors were to be replaced by even more amazing devices called integrated circuits. The weakness of the transistor system was the circuit of wires joining the individual transistors, resistors and other components. As electronic circuits became more complicated, this wiring took more and more time to assemble. During the 1950s the problem was overcome by the use of printed circuits.

A printed circuit is made from an insulating board with a layer of copper on one side. The copper is dissolved away except along the paths which connect the components mounted on the board. These conducting pathways are thus chemically 'printed'. The basic principles underlying the printed circuit were used in the development of integrated circuits. The wires and components of integrated circuits are manufactured as a single unit by the treatment of different areas of the material.

Microelectronics

Most integrated circuits consist of an entire electronic circuit fitted on to a minute sliver of silicon. In its pure state, silicon does not conduct electricity but when slightly contaminated it becomes a semiconductor. Part of the tiny 'chip' of pure silicon is made electrically positive and therefore capable of conducting signals. This is achieved by 'doping' pathways in the silicon with impurities. Negative areas are created by charging the rest of the silicon with electrons. How is such an

intricate job done? A full-scale circuit diagram is drawn and then photo-reduced to the size of the chip. This is then used as a photo-mask. It is placed over the chip and the network is etched into it by exposure to ultra-violet light. The areas shielded from the rays remain soft and are washed away with acid. The areas exposed to the rays, on the other hand, harden and resist the acid.

The techniques of silicon chip manufacture are still being developed. Electron and laser beams may be used as alternative means of making the masks. Some factories now 'shoot' atoms of impurity directly into the silicon. Although the development and machinery costs of silicon chip production are extremely high, the cost of the raw materials used in making a chip is almost negligible. Furthermore, the density of the circuits that can be placed on a chip is increasing all the time. A 3mm by 3mm chip (or microprocessor) can perform all the calculations that a large computer can do, just as fast and at much less cost. Data (information) can be stored in microelectronics memory circuits, just as in a computer. And just as our brain can store up past experiences, electronic machines are able to call upon stored data in their 'memory' when it is needed.

Since the mid-1970s microprocessors have been used in pocket calculators, digital watches, video games and some household appliances. They are so reliable that they are used in the flight control devices on aircraft. Soon we can expect to see many more gadgets and machines under the control of microprocessors. For example, microcircuits that are sensitive to temperature will be placed between the panes of double-glazed windows or in strategic parts of a room to feed back information on temperature and humidity. The information will be processed by a microcomputer which will calculate what the rate of heat production of the central heating system should be to make up for the heat loss if it is a cold day. On hot days the cooling rate will be calculated.

Similar circuits can be used to control the amount of lighting in a room. Light-sensitive microcircuits can cause blinds to open and close and electric lights to switch on and off as needed. Mechanical door locks may become old-fashioned as electronic ones take over. Microprocessors programmed to recognize magnetically coded patterns on keys will cause the door to be opened. Even control by voice is a possibility. Simple as the action of opening or closing a door is, microprocessors will be cheap enough to make their use feasible for this function.

Tasks involving calculations of great complexity can only be carried out by microprocessors that work with *digital* instructions and are linked to a more powerful memory. This is the type of microprocessor used in a computer.

Computers

There are two kinds of computer. Analogue computers are normally used to monitor and control changes in quantity or conditions, in an industrial process for example. Essentially, they deal with quantities of things, measured in terms of other quantities rather than numbers – just as a bathroom scale indicates your weight by the distance the dial moves.

Digital computers solve problems by counting with numbers, using what is called a *binary* code. Ordinary, or decimal, numbers have the symbols 0, 1, 2, 3, 4, 5, 6, 7, 8 and 9, i.e. the base is 10. Binary numbers have the base 2. There are only two symbols, or *bits*: 0 and 1. They correspond with the only two positions an electrical switch can have: 'on' or 'off'.

Before a digital computer can solve a problem it must have a set of instructions called a *program* that tells it what to do with the facts and figures put into it by a human operator. The programmer writes a program in a special computer language consisting of certain words or symbols. The language used depends on what sort of job has to be done and the particular computer that is being used. One computer language is called COBOL (*CO*mmon *B*usiness *O*rientated *L*anguage). It is used for processing business data. Another language is FORTRAN (*FOR*mula *TRAN*slation) which is used in solving algebraical problems. Both these languages use words for the instructions but the computer can only deal with the instructions by changing the words into numbers.

The information put into a computer is often in the form of tiny magnetic spots on a plastic tape. A machine 'reads' the tape and sends the information into

BINARY CONVERSION SCALE

DECIMAL (OR DENARY) NUMBERS	BINARY NUMBERS	DECIMAL (OR DENARY) NUMBERS	BINARY NUMBERS
1	1	16	10000
2	10	17	10001
3	11	18	10010
4	100	19	10011
5	101	20	10100
6	110	32	100000
7	111	64	1000000
8	1000	100	1100100
9	1001	128	10000000
10	1010	144	10010000
11	1011	150	10010110
12	1100	200	11001000
13	1101	250	11111111
14	1110	500	111110100
15	1111	1,000	1111101000

the computer in the form of electric signals. Automatic typewriters and printing machines electrically connected to computers record the information they produce at high speed. Computers can work at a speed only a little less than the speed of light and can perform about one million operations in one second.

All sorts of people use computers for all kinds of purposes. Scientists have many uses for them. For example, computers keep spacecraft on course during interplanetary missions. Business people use computers for bookkeeping and accounting, for keeping track of sales, payments by customers and the amount of stock in warehouses. Home computers have become very popular in recent years and schools run computer courses. Many people use their PC ('personal computer') for playing games although some are used in small businesses.

Word processors

A time can be foreseen when few people need go to an office to do their work because office services will be computerized. The time-consuming tasks of dictating, drafting, typing and mailing letters

Integrated circuit (actual size)

Computer terminal and print-out

Pocket calculator

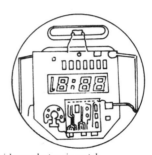

Inside an electronic watch.
The integrated circuit can be seen at the bottom

may be eliminated. Electronic machines called word processors take a good deal of work out of these processes. The text of standard letters is stored in the memory of a word processor. A draft of this may go to the business executive from a normal typewriter, or it may be shown on a visual display screen where it can be altered as required. Any words, lines or paragraphs that have to be altered, deleted or moved on the draft can be marked. The operator then types the instructions to the microprocessor. The letter is printed by a high-speed automatic printer that prints at the rate of 60 characters a second. As many copies as the boss needs can be produced, each with minor alterations if necessary.

What about the labour of mailing all those letters? 'Electronic mail' can now handle them. This is how it's done. A machine reduces the image on the printed page into digital code, then transmits that code down the telephone line to anyone with a suitable receiver at the end of their phone. This produces a facsimile (exact copy) of the original letter. Even facsimile transmission may become outdated if everyone has a computer receiver-transmitter in their home. There would be no need to put the message on paper at all. The text would be shown directly on a video screen. Think of all the paper that would be saved!

Telecommunications

Telegraph, telephone, radio, television and radar are all means of sending messages over a long distance. In other words, they are all forms of telecommunications. New developments in tele-communications have followed developments in electronic computer control.

The means of transmitting telephone calls is generally through copper cables. This involves unsightly pylons and the digging of holes to bury the cables under-ground. However, a new way of transmitting telephone calls without the use of cables has been adopted. This is by means of microwaves, beamed from the tops of tall towers.

There are some problems in microwave transmission, however. The expense of building the towers, which must be no more than 25 km (15½ miles) apart, offsets the savings made in not having to install cables. Furthermore, all radio transmissions are affected by bad weather and various kinds of interference.

Yet another means of telephone transmission is now being developed by the use of cables of glass fibres. An optical fibre will be able to carry 10,000 simultaneous telephone conversations in less space than is taken today by a copper cable whose limit is 5,000.

How can telephone conversations

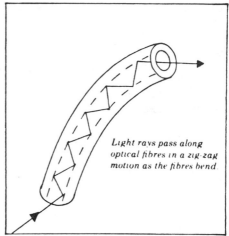

Light rays pass along optical fibres in a zig-zag motion as the fibres bend

be transmitted by a filament of glass? Optical fibres (they may be glass or plastic) are so-called because they transfer light. Rays of light are reflected on the inner surface of the glass instead of passing through it. In other words, the light in the centre core cannot break out to the outer layer but bounces along it in zig-zag fashion as the fibre bends and turns. Signals are sent along the fibres by a light source flashing on and off. Each flash represents a pulse in the digital code. The light source is a laser, which produces an intense narrow beam of light.

Television programmes can also be transmitted through glass cables. A receiver at the end of the fibres changes the light signals into copies of the original sounds and pictures.

Teletext

People in Britain and America (and soon many other countries) can link up their telephones and television sets to certain computers to obtain all kinds of information. For

Teletext system

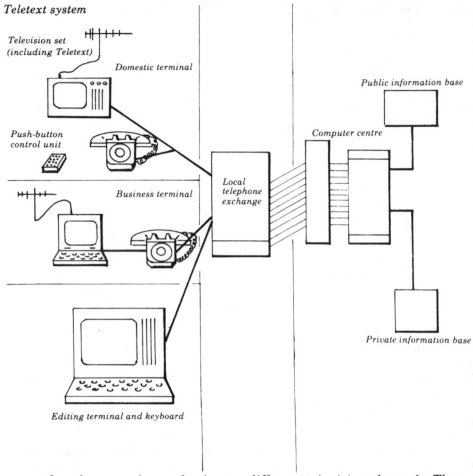

Television set (including Teletext)

Domestic terminal

Public information base

Push-button control unit

Computer centre

Business terminal

Local telephone exchange

Private information base

Editing terminal and keyboard

example, a horse-racing enthusiast does not need to wait for the day's racing results to appear in the newspapers if he has a teletext system in his home. With a push-button control unit about the size of a pocket calculator he can call up the information, which has been stored on a computer, and have it immediately displayed in words and simple diagrams on his television screen.

There are numerous other kinds of information available on different television channels. These cover national and international news, weather, sports, finance, travel information, entertainment, recipes and a multitude of other items.

In the future it may be commonplace for people to have direct contact with a public computer linked to their telephone. They will be able to ask the computer for advice on various matters and, if they wish, play games with it.

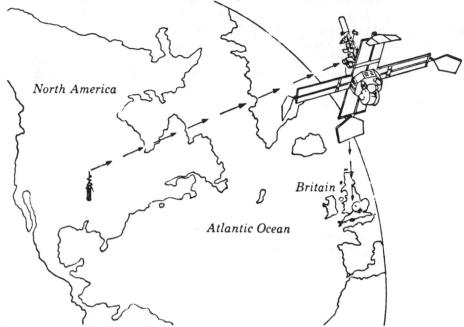

An active communications satellite linking North America and Britain

North America

Britain

Atlantic Ocean

Communications satellites

When we receive immediate television pictures of events that are occurring in far distant countries, these pictures are beamed to us by artificial satellite. How is this possible?

A communications satellite is either passive or active, depending on the way it sends signals back to Earth. A passive satellite reflects signals, just as a mirror reflects light. The first passive communications satellite, launched in 1960, was *Echo 1*, a huge 30 m (100 ft) plastic balloon coated with a thin layer of metal. Signals sent to passive satellites must be strong because radio waves weaken as they travel to the satellite and back to Earth. The satellite must be large, too, so that it can reflect the radio waves back to ground stations.

Active communications satellites carry a radio receiver and transmitter. The signals received from transmitting stations on Earth are amplified (strengthened) and retransmitted to Earth. The electronic equipment is powered by solar cells (batteries) which harness energy from the Sun.

Because a single satellite can serve less than a third of the Earth's surface, a series of satellites is necessary to provide global coverage. Usually a communications satellite is launched to a height of 35,890 km (22,340 miles). At this altitude it takes 24 hours to complete an orbit round the Earth. Because the Earth takes 24 hours to rotate once, the satellite appears to be staying in the same place. *Telstar*, the first active telecommunications satellite (launched in

99

1962) took a mere 2½ hours to complete an orbit. It was therefore within range of the ground stations in Europe and North America for very short periods. In 1964 the International Telecommunications Satellite Organization (Intelsat) was founded to create an international system. By 1978 over 100 countries had joined.

Theoretically, three satellites only, properly placed, can now link stations in any two parts of the world. For example, television pictures are sent to Britain from the USA through a satellite over the Atlantic Ocean. The other two satellites to complete the system are positioned over the Indian Ocean and the Pacific Ocean. Sending and receiving stations must point their antennae at the satellites.

Communications satellites carry a wider range of wave lengths than ordinary short-wave radio and the quality of reception is better. With advancing technology, satellites have been developed to carry telephone, telex and computer data as well as television.

The Earth's dwindling resources
All the exciting technological achievements mentioned above, and many others, may well encourage us to look towards the future with cheerful optimism. Given time, science seems to come up with the answers to a good many problems. Nevertheless, there are mounting world problems that present a great challenge to scientists and technologists, and time is not on our side. For example, millions of people in the world today do not have enough to eat. Will we have to find new kinds of food?

Many of our raw materials are in short supply. How will we manage when the fossil fuels (petroleum, coal and natural gas) run out? Already there is great concern about the shortage of oil. At the present rate of consumption, the world's fossil fuels and the radioactive materials used in the present types of nuclear power station will be exhausted within a few decades. Public anxiety about possible accidents at nuclear power stations, and the dangers from their radioactive byproducts, has furthermore led to a virtual halt in the building of new power stations.

Many people hope that we shall soon find a means to obtain energy by atomic fusion, the same process that makes the Sun burn. Scientists have achieved nuclear fusion, in an uncontrolled way, in hydrogen bombs. The problem they now face is to achieve fusion in a controlled way. To bring about a fusion reaction, very light atomic nuclei, such as those of hydrogen, deuterium and tritium, must be brought together and fused into a single nucleus. This would release a great quantity of nuclear energy. To achieve fusion of the nuclei, they would have to be forced together for long periods of time at an extremely high temperature – about one million degrees centigrade. Even if the necessary requirements for fusion can be met, it would still take many years for a commercial reactor to be designed and built.

The great advantage of nuclear

fusion is that the materials for making the reaction possible, heavy hydrogen, deuterium and tritium, are all readily obtainable. The environmental hazards from these materials if an accident should occur are considerably less than in the case of plutonium, the byproduct of the fast breeder type of reactor.

What alternatives are there to nuclear energy? Solar energy is one. It is used already in many small devices. Solar cells, made from thin slices of semiconductor materials, convert light into electricity. They have been used in artificial satellites. Another solar device is the flat-plate collector which is used to heat houses. It consists of a metal plate painted black which is placed where it faces the Sun. (Black absorbs sunlight more than any other colour.) The plate absorbs sunlight and becomes hot. The heat is kept in by one or more layers of glass that cover the plate. A system of pipes is used to distribute the heat through the house. Solar energy could produce a clean and almost limitless supply of power but unfortunately it is spread so thinly that a huge land area would be required to harness it on a large scale.

Wind power can turn windmills to produce energy but they are practicable only on a very small scale. Tidal energy can be utilized wherever there happens to be a high tide in a bay that can be closed by a dam. During high tide the bay fills with water. At low tide the level of the sea drops below the level of the water held behind the

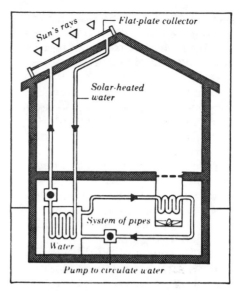

dam. When the water is released it drives turbines that generate power. A disadvantage of tidal power is that it can produce electricity only at certain times and for rather short periods. Another disadvantage is that there are very few places where such plants can be built.

Capturing the heat trapped in the core of the Earth may be one of the answers to our energy needs. When water comes into contact with hot underground rocks it turns to steam. The steam can be directed against the blades of a steam turbine to produce electricity.

Fuel cells are kinds of battery in which gas or liquid fuels combine chemically to generate electricity. Their disadvantage is that they are expensive to make. Garbage in the form of plant or animal waste can be a quite valuable source of energy. It can be burnt to produce electrical power, or converted to a fuel such as methanol.

A great deal of money will be

101

spent in the future on research into new ways of obtaining energy. As oil becomes scarcer and more expensive, the schemes mentioned above and many others, such as wave power and energy from fast-growing plants, will have to be considered seriously.

Progress in Space Research

The 1960s and 1970s will be famous for centuries to come as a time when tremendous advances were made in space technology, and exciting discoveries about the Moon and planets took place.

The V2 rocket of World War II was the direct ancestor of modern space probes. But rocket speeds many times faster than that of the V2 had to be developed before a satellite could be placed in orbit. The Soviet *Sputnik 1*, whose launch in 1957 surprised the world, marked the beginning of the Space Age.

While a satellite needs a launching speed of about 29,000 km/h to place it in orbit several hundred kilometres above the Earth, a rocket must travel at over 40,000 km/h to escape from the Earth's gravitational pull and set course for the planets.

Before human beings were risked on space missions, unmanned crafts containing instruments were used, and sometimes animals were sent into space. The design of manned spacecraft incorporates control systems to regulate cabin tempera-ture, pressure and atmospheric conditions, food and waste-handling equipment, and other equipment needed by the crew to sustain them during periods of rapid acceleration on the one hand and weightlessness on the other. There are guidance and navigation systems for keeping on course and making manoeuvres, and communications receivers and transmitters. Some of the hazards of space travel proved not to be as great as had been feared. The effects of weightlessness were not as severe as had been first thought, and the risks of collision with meteorites not high.

Space exploration reached a climax when man first landed on the Moon in 1969. However, almost all of the really significant scientific discoveries have been obtained through the use of robot spacecraft. Some of these discoveries have been most astonishing. On Mars there are huge volcanoes and canyons which dwarf any on Earth, even though Mars is a smaller planet. There are also sandstorms approaching the speed of sound. The chemistry of the soil is so puzzling that the presence of micro-organisms in it has not been discounted.

Surprisingly, Jupiter is now known to have a thin flat ring encircling it. Two of its moons, Europa and Ganymede, show remarkable networks of straight and curved surface markings, while on Io active volcanoes have been seen. Titan's clouds containing organic substances are another extraordinary sight. It seems, though, that manned flight to Jupiter is unlikely because of the belts of high radiation found there.

Equally inhospitable is Venus, with its clouds of sulphuric acid and high surface temperatures. Probes have revealed continuous thunder and lightning and strange chemical fires on the planet.

IMPORTANT DATES IN SPACE RESEARCH

1957	October 4	*Sputnik 1* put in orbit (USSR).
	November 3	*Sputnik 2* launched carrying dog, Laika (USSR).
1958	January	*Explorer 1* put into orbit. Provided first information about radiation zones around the Earth now known as the Van Allen belts (USA).
1959	January	*Luna 1* bypassed Moon at 6,400 km (4,000 miles) (USSR).
	September	*Luna 2* crash-landed on Moon (USSR).
	October	*Luna 3* made first circumlunar flight; first pictures of hidden side of Moon (USSR).
1960	March	*Pioneer 5* measured solar system and returned data on solar wind (USA).
	August	*Discoverer 13* launched. First successful recovery of a capsule from orbit (USA).
		Echo 1 launched. First successful voice and picture transmission by reflection off satellite (USA).
		Sputnik 5 launched. Two dogs, six mice and insects returned safely (USSR).
1961	April 12	Yuri Gagarin made full circuit of Earth in *Vostok 1* (USSR).
	May 5	Alan Shepard became first American in space in *Freedom 7*; the suborbital flight lasted about 15 minutes.
	August	Gherman Titov made 17 orbits (USSR).
1962	February	John Glenn made three orbits in *Friendship 7* (USA).
	December	*Mariner 2*, first successful planetary probe, bypassed Venus at 35,000 km (22,000 miles); sent back valuable data (USA).
1963	June 16	Valentina Tereshkova became first woman in space. She made 48 orbits in *Vostok 6* (USSR).
1964	July	*Ranger 7*, first of three successful Ranger probes, took close-range pictures of the Moon's surface before crash-landing (USA).

1965	March	Alexei Leonov became the first man to venture outside an orbiting space capsule, the two-man *Voskhod 2* (USSR).
	June	Edward White walked in space during Gemini programme (USA).
	July	*Mariner 4* bypassed Mars and transmitted close-range pictures of the surface (USA).
	December	Manned spacecraft *Gemini 6* and *Gemini 7* met in space, coming within 30 cm (1 ft) of each other. This was a rehearsal of the docking procedure to be used in future Moon landings (USA).
1966	January	*Luna 9* made first successful soft landing on Moon; several pictures of the surface (USA).
	February	*Venera 2*, first successful Soviet planetary probe, bypassed Venus at 24,000 km (15,000 miles).
	March	*Venera 3* soft-landed on Venus (USSR). *Luna 10* became first spacecraft to orbit Moon (USSR).
	May	*Surveyor 1* made first American soft landing on Moon; transmitted pictures of surface.
1966–7		*Orbiters 1* to *5* put into orbit round Moon. Thousands of pictures transmitted, enabling whole lunar surface to be mapped (USA).
1967	October	*Venera 4* soft-landed on Venus; transmitted data during descent (USSR). *Mariner 5* bypassed Venus at 4,000 km (2,500 miles) and sent back data (USA).
1968	January	*Surveyor 7* soft-landed on Moon near crater Tycho; sent back high-quality pictures of crater wall (USA).
	October	*Soyuz 2* used in docking manoeuvres with *Soyuz 3* (USSR).
	December	*Apollo 8* made ten orbits of the Moon with crew: Frank Borman, James Lovell and William Anders (USA).
1969	May	*Veneras 5* and *6* soft-landed on Venus; data transmitted from surface (USSR).
	July 20	*Apollo 11* Moon mission. Neil Armstrong was the first man to set foot on the Moon; with him was Edwin Aldrin. Michael Collins piloted the command module orbiting above (USA). *Mariners 6* and *7* bypassed Mars. High-quality pictures transmitted (USA).
	November	*Apollo 12* Moon mission. Landed close to an earlier probe, *Surveyor 3*. Astronauts Charles Conrad and Alan Bean brought parts of it back together with rock samples (USA).
1970	September	*Luna 16* landed on Moon. Sample of Moon rocks gathered

by robot and returned to Earth (USSR).

	November	*Luna 17* landed on Moon in Mare Imbrium. Automated machine 'Lunokhod' crawled along for months sending back information to Earth (USSR).
	December	*Apollo 13* Moon mission was unlucky. An explosion on the outward journey put the main propulsion unit out of action and the Moon landing was called off. Astronauts used motors of lunar module to pass around Moon and return to Earth (USA).
1971	February	*Apollo 14* Moon mission; landing by astronauts Shepard and Mitchell; Roosa was in the command module. Rock samples brought back (USA).
	June	*Soyuz 10* docked with *Salyut* space station. Three Russian cosmonauts became the first crew to transfer from an orbiting spacecraft to an orbiting space station.
	July	First joint US–USSR space project; crews of *Soyuz* craft and specially modified *Apollo* capsule were able to enter each others' craft after docking in space.
	August	*Apollo 15* Moon landing with lunar rover vehicle; rock samples brought back (USA).
	November	*Mariner 9* put into orbit around Mars. Thousands of high-quality pictures transmitted of Mars and its satellites (USA). *Mars 2* put in orbit around Mars (USSR).
	December	*Mars 3* made soft landing on Mars (USSR).
1972	February	*Luna 20* soft-landed on Mars and returned to Earth with rock samples (USSR).
	March	*Pioneer 10*, first Jupiter probe, launched (USA).
	April	*Apollo 16* Moon mission; landing by Young and Duke, with Mattingly in command module (USA).
	July	*Venera 8* landed on Venus (USSR).
	December	*Apollo 17* Moon mission; landing by Cernan and Schmitt with Evans in command module (USA).
1973	January	*Luna 21* Moon landing; 'Lunokhod 2' gathered and analyzed specimens (USSR).
	March	*Pioneer 11* launched towards Jupiter (USA).
	May	*Skylab*, first American space station, was launched. Three successive crews spent a total of 171 days on the craft.
	December	*Pioneer 10* reached Jupiter, passing within 132,000 km (182,000 miles). It then moved away to begin a journey without end into space (USA).

1974	February	*Mariner 10* bypassed Venus before swinging towards Mercury; sent back data and photographs (USA).
	March	*Mariner 10* made close contact with Mercury (USA)
	May	*Luna 22* soft-landed on the Moon (USSR).
	September	*Mariner 10* made second contact with Mercury after orbiting the Sun (USA).
	October	*Luna 23* soft-landed on Moon (USSR).
	December	*Pioneer 11* reached Jupiter; further data obtained. Afterwards it flicked away towards Saturn, when it was renamed *Pioneer Saturn* (USA).
1975	March	*Mariner 10* bypassed Mercury for third time (USA).
	October	*Venera 9* soft-landed on Venus. Pictures transmitted for about one hour, after which the cameras were put out of action by extreme heat and pressure on planet. *Venera 10* followed shortly afterwards, but cameras again soon ceased functioning (USSR).
1976	July	*Viking 1* landed on Mars. Soil analyzed (USA).
	August	*Luna 24* landed on Moon. Soil samples taken and returned to Earth (USSR).
	September	*Viking 2* landed on Mars (USA).
1977	August	*Voyager 2* launched towards Jupiter (USA).
	September	*Voyager 1* launched. On the way to Jupiter, it overtook *Voyager 2* which was launched 16 days earlier (USA).
1978	December	Two space probes which had been launched close together, *Pioneer Venus 1* and *2*, reached the atmosphere of Venus. The first probe went into orbit round the planet. The other, consisting of a battery of probes, crash-landed two probes which continued to send data for a short time (USA). *Veneras 11* and *12* reached Venus (USSR).
1979	February	*Voyager 1* reached Jupiter (USA).
	July	*Voyager 2* reached Jupiter (USA).
	September	*Pioneer Saturn* reached Saturn. Afterwards it drifted off into the solar system (USA).
1980	November	*Voyager 1* flew past Saturn, sending back pictures showing that Saturn's rings consist of over 100 thin discs (USA).
1981	April	The flight of Space Shuttle *Columbia* was the first space mission to employ a reusable space vehicle (USA).
	August	*Voyager 2* passed Saturn, sending back many pictures before flying on towards Uranus (USA).

1982	December	Two cosmonauts, Anatoly Berezovnoy and Valentin Lebedev, who had manned the *Salut 7* orbiting station, returned to Earth, completed a record flight of 211 days, 9 hours, 4 minutes and 32 seconds (USSR).
1983	June	The Space Shuttle *Challenger* took Sally Ride, the first American woman astronaut into space (USA).
1984	February	Bruce McCandless, using a jet propulsion backpack of his own design, became the first astronaut to make an untethered flight in space. This occurred during the fourth *Challenger* Space Shuttle mission (USA).
	April	The fifth *Challenger* Space Shuttle mission was the first to repair a damaged satellite in space.

The Elements

An element is a substance which cannot be split up into simpler substances by chemical means. There are 92 naturally occurring elements. Some elements have been made artificially in nuclear reactors or machines called cyclotrons; these are known as the *transuranic* elements.

The smallest whole unit of an element which cannot be subdivided by chemical means is the atom. An atom of any element consists of a positively charged nucleus orbited by electrons. The electrons have a negative charge which exactly balances that of the nucleus. The nucleus is composed of two types of particle – protons and neutrons. The proton is positively charged; the neutron has no charge but it has slightly more mass than that of a proton. The simplest atom is that of hydrogen, consisting of one proton and one electron only. A carbon atom has six orbiting electrons, six protons and six neutrons.

The *atomic number* of an element indicates the number of protons in the nucleus of an atom, which is also equivalent to the number of orbiting electrons.

The atomic weight is the weight of an element compared with that of a carbon atom whose weight is taken as exactly 12.

The atoms of the various elements differ only in the number and arrangement of their protons, neutrons and electrons. Atoms of the same element, i.e. of identical atomic number, but differing in the number of neutrons present in the nucleus, are called *isotopes*. If the number of outer electrons of an atom is altered then it becomes an *ion*. The addition of electrons creates negative ions; the removal of electrons creates positive ions. Chemical combination takes place by the transfer or sharing of electrons between combining atoms.

THE NATURAL ELEMENTS

ATOMIC NUMBER	ELEMENT	SYMBOL	ATOMIC WEIGHT
1	Hydrogen	H	1.008
2	Helium	He	4.003
3	Lithium	Li	6.939
4	Beryllium	Be	9.012
5	Boron	B	10.811
6	Carbon	C	12.011
7	Nitrogen	N	14.007
8	Oxygen	O	15.999
9	Fluorine	F	18.998
10	Neon	Ne	20.183
11	Sodium	Na	22.990
12	Magnesium	Mg	24.312
13	Aluminium	Al	26.982
14	Silicon	Si	28.086
15	Phosphorus	P	30.974
16	Sulphur	S	32.064
17	Chlorine	Cl	35.453
18	Argon	A	39.948
19	Potassium	K	39.102
20	Calcium	Ca	40·08
21	Scandium	Sc	44.956
22	Titanium	Ti	47.90
23	Vanadium	V	50.94
24	Chromium	Cr	52.00
25	Manganese	Mn	54.94
26	Iron	Fe	55.85
27	Cobalt	Co	58.93
28	Nickel	Ni	58.71
29	Copper	Cu	63.54
30	Zinc	Zn	65.37
31	Gallium	Ga	69.72
32	Germanium	Ge	72.59
33	Arsenic	As	74.92
34	Selenium	Se	78.96
35	Bromine	Br	79.909
36	Krypton	Kr	83·80
37	Rubidium	Rb	85.47
38	Strontium	Sr	87.62
39	Yttrium	Y	88.905
40	Zirconium	Zr	91.22
41	Niobium	Nb	92.906
42	Molybdenum	Mo	95.94
43	Technetium	Tc	99.00
44	Ruthenium	Ru	101.07
45	Rhodium	Rh	102.91

ATOMIC NUMBER	ELEMENT	SYMBOL	ATOMIC WEIGHT
46	Palladium	Pd	106.4
47	Silver	Ag	107.87
48	Cadmium	Cd	112.40
49	Indium	In	114.82
50	Tin	Sn	118.69
51	Antimony	Sb	121·75
52	Tellurium	Te	127.60
53	Iodine	I	126.904
54	Xenon	Xe	131.30
55	Caesium	Cs	132.905
56	Barium	Ba	137.34
57	Lanthanum	La	138.91
58	Cerium	Ce	140.12
59	Praseodymium	Pr	140.907
60	Neodymium	Nd	144.24
61	Prometheum	Pm	147
62	Samarium	Sm	150.35
63	Europium	Eu	151.96
64	Gadolinium	Gd	157.25
65	Terbium	Tb	158.92
66	Dysprosium	Dy	162.50
67	Holnium	Ho	164.93
68	Erbium	Er	167.26
69	Thulium	Tm	168.93
70	Ytterbium	Yb	173.04
71	Lutecium	Lu	174.97
72	Hafmium	Hf	178.49
73	Tantalum	Ta	180.95
74	Wolfram	W	183.85
75	Rhenium	Re	186.2
76	Osmium	Os	190.2
77	Iridium	Ir	192.2
78	Platinum	Pt	195.09
79	Gold	Au	196.97
80	Mercury	Hg	200.59
81	Thallium	Tl	204.37
82	Lead	Pb	207.19
83	Bismuth	Bi	208.98
84	Polonium	Po	210
85	Astatine	At	211
86	Radon	Rn	222
87	Francium	Fr	223
88	Radium	Ra	226.05
89	Actinium	Ac	227.05
90	Thorium	Th	232.12
91	Protactinium	Pa	231.05
92	Uranium	U	238.07

THE TRANSURANIC ELEMENTS

ATOMIC NUMBER	ELEMENT	SYMBOL	ATOMIC WEIGHT
93	Neptunium	Np	237
94	Plutonium	Pu	239
95	Americum	Am	241
96	Curium	Cm	242
97	Berkelium	Bk	243–250
98	Californium	Cf	251
99	Einsteinium	Es	246, 247
100	Fermium	Fm	250, 252–256
101	Mendelevium	Md	256
102	Nobelium	No	254
103	Lawrencium	Lr	257
*104	—	—	—
*105	—	—	—
*106	—	—	—

*Names proposed for elements 104, 105 and 106 have been Kurchatovium, Rutherfordium (and Hahnium) and Nielsbohrium respectively.

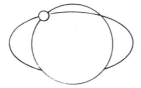

Hydrogen atom

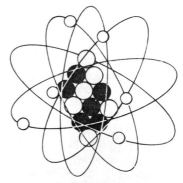

Carbon atom

Inventors and Inventions

INVENTION	YEAR	INVENTOR
Adding machine	1642	Blaise Pascal (France)
Airplane	1903	Orville and Wilbur Wright (USA)
Airship (non-rigid)	1852	Henri Giffard (France)
(rigid)	1900	Graf Ferdinand von Zeppelin (Germany)
Aspirin	1899	Herman Dreser (Germany)
Autogyro	1923	Juan de la Cierva (Spain)
Bakelite	1907	Leo H. Backeland (Belgium/USA)
Ballpoint pen	1888	John J. Loud (USA)
Barometer	1644	Evangelista Torricelli (Italy)
Bathysphere	1930	William Beebe (USA)
Bicycle	1839	Kirkpatrick Macmillan (Britain)
Bicycle tyre (pneumatic)	1888	John Boyd Dunlop (Britain)
Bifocal lens	1780	Benjamin Franklin (USA)
Bunsen burner	1855	Robert Wilhelm von Bunsen (Germany)
Burglar alarm	1858	Edwin T. Holmes (USA)
Calculating machine	1823	Charles Babbage (Britain)
Carburettor	1876	Gottlieb Daimler (Germany)
Carpet sweeper	1876	Melville R. Bissell (USA)
Cash register	1879	James Ritty (USA)
Cellophane	1908	Dr Jacques Brandenberger (Switzerland)
Celluloid	1861	Alexander Parkes (Britain)
Cement	1824	Joseph Aspdin (Britain)
Chronometer	1735	John Harrison (Britain)
Clock (pendulum)	1656	Christiaan Huygens (Netherlands)
Electric battery	1800	Alessandro Volta (Italy)
Electric iron	1882	H. W. Seeley (USA)
Electric generator (DC)	1831	Michael Faraday (Britain)
Electric light	1878	Thomas Alva Edison (USA)
Electric motor (DC)	1873	Zénobe Gramme (Belgium)
(AC)	1888	Nikola Tesla (USA)
Electromagnet	1824	William Sturgeon (Britain)
Engine, Diesel	1890–2	Herbert Akroyd Stuart (Britain) and Rudolf Diesel (Germany)
Engine, Internal combustion (gas)	1860	Etienne Lenoir (France)
Engine, Jet	1930	Frank Whittle (Britain)
Engine, Steam (condenser)	1765	James Watt (Britain)
(piston)	1712	Thomas Newcomen (Britain)
Fountain pen	1884	Lewis E. Waterman (USA)
Gas lighting	1792	William Murdock (Britain)
Glider	1853	Sir George Cayley (Britain)
Gramophone (cylinder phonograph)	1877	Thomas Alva Edison (USA)
(disc)	1887	Emile Berliner (USA)
Gyrocompass	1911	Elmer A. Sperry (USA)

Gyroscope	1852	Jean Foucault (France)
Hot-air balloon	1783	Jacques and Joseph Montgolfier (France)
Hovercraft	1955	C. S. Cockerell (Britain)
Laser	1960	Dr Charles H. Townes (Britain)
Lift	1852	Elisha G. Otis (USA)
Lightning conductor	1752	Benjamin Franklin (USA)
Linoleum	1860	Frederick Walton (USA)
Locomotive, Steam	1804	Richard Trevithick (Britain)
Loudspeaker	1900	Horace Short (Britain)
Machine gun	1718	James Puckle (Britain)
Margarine	1869	Hippolyte Mège-Mouries (France)
Match	1827	John Walker (Britain)
Match (safety)	1855	J. E. Lundstrom (Sweden)
Microphone	1876	Alexander Graham Bell (USA)
Microscope, Compound	1590	Zacharies Janssen (Netherlands)
Miners' safety lamp	1816	Sir Humphry Davy (Britain)
Morphine	1806	Friederich Sertürner (Germany)
Motion-picture camera	1888	William Friese-Greene (Britain)
Motor car	1885	Karl Benz (German)
Motorcycle	1885	Gottlieb Daimler (German)
Neon lamp	1910	Georges Claude (France)
Nylon	1937	Dr Wallace H. Carothers (USA)
Parachute	1797	André-Jacques Garnerin (France)
Penicillin	1929	Sir Alexander Fleming (Britain)
Photography (on metal)	1826	J. Nicéphore Niépce (France)
(on paper)	1835	W. H. Fox Talbot (Britain)
(on film)	1888	John Carbutt (USA)
Pianoforte	1709	Bartolommeo Cristofou (Italy)
Pneumatic tyre	1845	Robert Thompson (Britain)
Power loom	1785	Edmund Cartwright (Britain)
Printing press	c.1455	Johann Gutenberg (Germany)
Propellor, Ship's	1837	Francis Smith (Britain)
Radar	1935	Sir Robert Watson-Watt (Britain)
Radio telescope	1931	Karl Jansky (USA)
Radio valve	1904	Sir Ambrose Fleming (Britain)
Rayon	1883	Sir Joseph Swan (Britain)
Razor, Electric	1931	Col. Jacob Schick (USA)
Record, Long Playing	1948	Dr Peter Goldmark (USA)
Refrigerator	1850	James Harrison (Britain) and Alexander Catlin (USA)
Safety pin	1849	William Hunt (USA)
Sewing machine (domestic)	1851	Isaac M. Singer (USA)
Sextant	1730	John Hadley (Britain)
Slide rule	1621	William Oughtred (Britain)
Spinning frame	1769	Sir Richard Arkwright (Britain)
Spinning jenny	1764	James Hargreaves (Britain)
Spinning mule	1779	Samuel Crompton (Britain)
Stainless steel	1913	Harry Brearly (Britain)
Steam ship	1775	J. C. Périer (France)
Steam turbine	1894	Sir Charles A. Parsons (Britain)

Stethoscope	1816	René Laennec (France)
Submarine	1776	David Bushnell (USA)
Tank	1914	Sir Ernest Swinton (Britain)
Telegraph	1837	W. F. Cooke and Sir Charles Wheatstone (Britain)
Telephone	1876	Alexander Graham Bell (USA)
Telescope (refracting)	1608	Hans Lippershey (Netherlands)
(reflecting)	1669	Isaac Newton (Britain)
Television	1926	John Logie Baird (Britain)
Terylene	1941	J. R. Whinfield and J. T. Dickson (Britain)
Thermometer	1593	Galileo Galilei (Italy)
Torpedo	1868	Robert Whitehead (Britain)
Transistor	1948	John Bardeen, William Shockley and Walter Brattain (USA)
Typewriter	1808	Pellegrine Tarri (Italy)
Vaccination	1796	Edward Jenner (Britain)
Vacuum flask	1892	Sir James Dewar (Britain)
Welder, Electric	1877	Elisha Thomson (USA)
Wireless telegraphy	1895	Guglielmo Marconi (Italy)
X-ray	1895	Wilhelm von Röntgen (Germany)
Zip fastener	1891	Whitcomb L. Judson (USA)

Weather Forecasting

Meteorology concerns the study of all things which have a direct bearing on the world's weather, and the forecasting of what can be expected in the immediate future in any given area.

Worldwide observation stations keep a constant watch on all the atmospheric factors and weather movements, relying upon instrument readings of pressure, temperature, humidity, wind speeds and directions, clouds and so on. Earth satellites such as *Tiros* and *Nimbus* relay information, collected by special instruments, about atmospheric conditions all around the world. Computers are employed to assist in analyzing this information so that forecasts can be compiled and issued for the benefit of farmers, sailors, airmen and people in general. Modern forecasts have become very accurate, and even long-term analyses have a high degree of success.

Observations are also made locally. By recording temperature readings and using simple instruments such as the barometer, individuals can become reasonably accurate forecasters of the weather within their own immediate area. There is no reason to scorn all the traditional methods of weather-forecasting. Countrymen and seamen still use many of them quite successfully for short-term local forecasting. They watch the behaviour and movement of birds, look at the appearance of the sky and clouds (remember the saying 'a red sky at night is the shepherd's delight, a red sky in the morning is the shepherd's warning'), consider visibility (how clear and close, for example, a range of hills appears to be), measure the air's moisture content with seaweed, and study flowers (sensitive flowers will close up when it is dull, for instance).

The ordinary household barometer indicates broadly what is happening in the atmosphere and what can be expected of the weather. It measures the weight, or pressure, of the atmosphere. This is determined by changes in temperature, wind variations, and height above sea-level. The atmosphere is heavier in fine weather than it is in bad weather, and it is also heavier at sea-level than on a hill top. Aneroid barometers (from the Greek *a* and *neros* meaning 'without wet') are the most usual and useful; wet barometers use a liquid known as quicksilver (mercury).

Cyclones and anticyclones
As cyclones and anticyclones play such an important role in the

---

CLOUDS AND THE WEATHER
There are ten distinct types of cloud, as you can see in the accompanying illustration:

1 **Cirrus** Usually white and feathery. They are composed of ice-crystals and occur at a height of 6,100–7,600 m (20,000–25,000 ft).

2 **Cirrocumulus** Layers of small flaked or rounded clouds (a 'mackerel sky'), at 3,050–5,500 m (10,000–18,000 ft).

3 **Cirrostratus** A fine, whitish veil, forming haloes around the Sun or Moon, some 3,650 m (12,000 ft) high.

4 **Altocumulus** Grey or white flakes, or flattened round masses at 1,800–4,600 m (6,000–15,000 ft).

5 **Altostratus** A grey veil across the sky, sometimes thick enough to hide the Sun or Moon, at a height of 1,800–3,650 m (6,000–12,000 ft).

6 **Stratocumulus** Thick and dark, at 900–1,800 m (3,000–6,000 ft).

7 **Cumulus** Huge, rounded masses, with their lower surfaces almost level, at 760–900 m (2,500–3,000 ft).

8 **Cumulonimbus** Very big, rounded and towering masses, black or dark grey, often 300–1,370 m (1,000–4,500 ft) in height. They possess powerful up-currents and are a sign of bad weather and possibly thunderstorms.

9 **Nimbostratus** Grey, often dark, layers of clouds usually thousands of metres thick. They are composed of mixtures of ice crystals, raindrops and snowflakes, and occur below 2,000 m (6,500 ft).

10 **Stratus** Horizontal layers sometimes resting on higher ground as mist, but also up to 610 m (2,000 ft) in height.

Cumulus clouds

WIND FORCES – THE BEAUFORT SCALE

FORCE NO.	WIND DESCRIPTION	VISIBLE EFFECTS	SPEED km/h(mph)
0	Calm	Smoke rises vertically	Below 1·5 (1)
1	Light air	Smoke shows wind direction	1·5–5 (1–3)
2	Light breeze	Wind is felt on face, leaves rustle and wind-vanes move	6·5–11 (4–7)
3	Gentle breeze	Leaves and twigs move; light flag is extended	13–18 (8–12)
4	Moderate breeze	Dust and loose paper rise; small branches move	21–29 (13–18)
5	Fresh breeze	Small trees sway	30·5–38·5 (19–24)
6	Strong breeze	Large branches move and telegraph wires whistle	40–49·5 (25–31)
7	Moderate gale	Whole trees move; it is difficult to walk against the wind	51–61 (32–38)
8	Fresh gale	Tree twigs break off	62·5–73·5 (39–46)
9	Strong gale	Slight damage takes place; slates and chimney-pots can be blown down	75–86·5 (47–54)
10	Whole gale	Trees may be uprooted and considerable structural damage is done	88–101 (55–63)
11	Storm	Widespread damage occurs	102·5–120 (64–75)
12	Hurricane	A wind-force experienced in tropical revolving storms	Over 120 (75)

weather, it is essential for forecasters to recognize and understand them, as shown in Map A and Map B.

Winds, tempests and hurricanes
The Beaufort Scale table describes the various wind forces, and their speeds and effects.

Winds blowing toward the equator, from north and south, are deflected, because of the Earth's rotation, so that they become northeast and southeast winds respectively. These are called Trade Winds.

People living in certain regions of the world suffer from two forms of particularly violent wind – hurricanes and tornadoes. Formed by the violent entry of a large mass of cold air into a region of hot, moist air, a hurricane proceeds with a whirling movement. The wind races round in circles which frequently have a diameter of several hundred miles. Moving at a colossal speed, the hurricane tears across the ocean, leaving a trail of shipwreck and damage to coastal areas and islands in its wake.

Tornadoes occur on land and often can be even worse than hurricanes. A tornado is produced when cold air descends and hot air rises. This forms a spiral which contains a partial vacuum and moves at frightening speed across the country, destroying almost everything in its path.

Rain, blizzards and thunderstorms
When warm air, charged with water vapour collected from the sea, lakes and rivers, enters a cooler zone, some of the vapour is

Cyclone
Isobar 760 (760 mm of mercury) indicates areas of high-pressure air. These flow inward in the direction of low pressure, encircled by isobar 735 (735 mm of mercury), but are deflected by the Earth's rotation. They become a swirling wind, represented by the anticlockwise arrow.

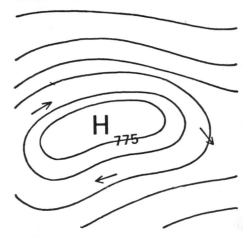

Anticyclone
In this case, the wind blows outwards from the centre of high pressure (isobar 775). It, also, is deflected but in this case in a clockwise direction, as indicated by the arrow.

116

forced out of the air and forms minute particles of water or ice. Many millions of these particles form a cloud and, if the process continues, the tiny drops join together and become rain.

If the condensation of the water vapour occurs at a temperature below freezing, a cloud of ice-particles is formed. Falling slowly towards the ground, the frozen droplets form into snowflakes and cover the earth with snow, if the temperature of the land is low enough.

When a snowfall is accompanied by strong winds, blizzard conditions prevail. The snowflakes are driven blindingly across the land, blanketing everything.

Thunderstorms take place when there is a great difference between electrical pressure either at the top and bottom of a cloud or between a cloud and the ground. Raindrops become electrically charged when they are formed, break up or evaporate. All of these processes take place in a thundercloud. Whenever the drops become charged, the air around the raindrops becomes oppositely charged. The charge in the raindrops is carried downwards, while the charge in the air rises. The difference in pressure created becomes unbearable and is stabilized by a flash of lightning.

The power of a big flash has been calculated at 10,000 million volts but it lasts only for approximately one thousandth of a second. The thunderous noise is produced by the lightning flash itself as the air rushes in to fill the gap and the sound echoes among the clouds.

Fog and mist

On land, fog is generally formed in valleys where the ground is cold and moist, and the air comparatively warm and windless. Often it takes the form of a ground mist, particularly in autumn, but thickens into fog during the winter months. The introduction of smokeless zones has reduced the frequency and degree of fog in many cities. This is particularly true of London where smoke-laden fogs of the past (referred to as 'pea-soupers') have virtually disappeared.

Fogs and mists at sea are formed like clouds. Warm air carrying moisture meets the cold sea and the water condenses into tiny drops which are too small to fall as rain. At sea, fog can be accompanied by some wind.

Special climatic features

There are a number of outstanding or unusual climatic features around the world which have a profound effect on the weather over vast areas.

In south and east Asia, for example, monsoons occur. They arise out of the great changes of temperature which take place over the land mass between summer and winter. Monsoons are regular and persistent winds which, for example, bring India heavy rainfall from June to October each year, after their long journey across the sea. The wet southwest monsoon is replaced by the dry and cold northeast monsoon during the October to March period, when the wind switches round to the opposite direction.

Another important feature is the Gulf Stream, which flows out of the warm Gulf of Mexico in a 'river' more than 48 km (30 miles) in width and almost 300 m (1,000 ft) in depth. The Gulf Stream flows towards the northeast and then divides, one part going towards Greenland, and the other to the Azores. In the mid-Atlantic it splits again. One part continues to the African coast, before swinging round to return to the Gulf of Mexico, while the other moves northeast past the coast of northwestern Europe.

The effect on northwestern Europe's weather is considerable. The warmth of the Gulf Stream helps to keep winter temperatures much higher, on average, than they would otherwise be. It is also responsible for sea fogs, however, when its warmth meets cold air from the north.

CHEMICAL NAMES FOR SOME COMMON SUBSTANCES

SUBSTANCE	CHEMICAL NAME
Alcohol	Ethyl alcohol (ethanol)
Alum	Aluminium potassium sulphate
Baking powder	Sodium bicarbonate
Black lead	Graphite (a form of carbon)
Boracic acid	Boric acid
Borax	Sodium borate
Brimstone	Sulphur
Caustic soda	Sodium hydroxide
Chalk	Sodium carbonate
Common salt	Sodium chloride
Cream of tartar	Potassium bitartrate
DDT	Dichlor-diphenyl-trichlorethane
Epsom salts	Magnesium sulphate
Glauber salts	Sodium sulphate
Hypo	Sodium Thiosulphate
Magnesia	Magnesium oxide

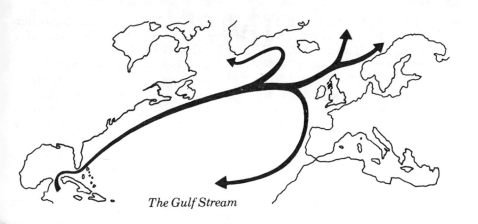

The Gulf Stream

Marsh gas	Methane
Plaster of Paris	Calcium sulphate
Plumbago	Graphite (a form of carbon)
Potash	Potassium carbonate
Quick-lime	Calcium oxide
Quicksilver	Mercury
Red lead	Triplumbic tetroxide
Sal-ammoniac	Ammonium chloride
Saltpetre (nitre)	Potassium nitrate
Salts of lemon	Potassium quadroxalate
Sal volatile	Ammonium carbonate
Spirits of salts	Hydrochloric acid
TNT	Trinitrotoluene
Vinegar	Dilute acetic acid
Washing soda	Crystalline sodium carbonate
White lead	Basic lead carbonate
Wood spirit	Methyl alcohol (methanol)

TIME

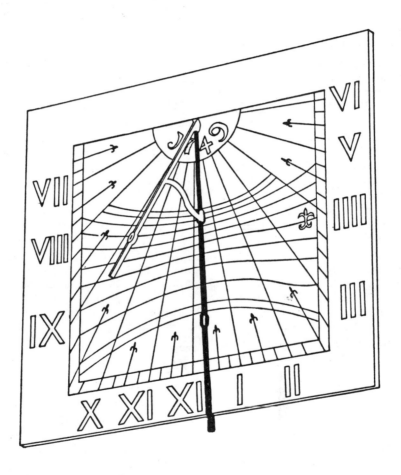

Time, Clocks and Calendars

The measurement of time owes its origin to early man's observation of the heavens – chiefly the movements of the Sun and the Moon, together with regular seasonal changes noted over long periods.

Clocks

Gradually, with the advance of knowledge over many centuries, man developed the means of calculating and measuring time on a more accurate basis, and early forms of clocks were invented. The earliest of these was the shadow clock introduced by the ancient Egyptians some 3,500 years ago. This eventually gave rise to the sundial but these devices were useless at night or when clouds obscured the Sun. The clepsydra (water clock) was used at these times, and sand clocks were helpful for the calculation of short intervals.

On one of the islands of the Nile, in those ancient times, 360 vessels were tended by 360 priests at a temple to the Egyptian god Osiris. Each of these vessels had a hole in the bottom, just the right size to allow milk, poured in to fill the container, to empty out in precisely 24 hours. The priests did this to each vessel in turn, day after day, throughout the year!

Before the invention of mechanical clocks, people frequently used candles and simple oil lamps, often marked in divisions to show how much time had elapsed, particularly during the night. Although the date of the invention of the first mechanical clock is not known, a device driven by water was certainly constructed in Peking in 1090.

The pendulum clock was invented in the 17th century by Christiaan Huygens, and the first watches appeared as early as 1500 in Nuremberg, Germany.

Modern quartz-crystal clocks have achieved an accuracy of one-thousandth of a second a day. The latest development in the measurement of time, an atomic clock using natural vibrations of the caesium atom, is considered to achieve accuracy to one second in 300 years.

Of all the many different kinds of interesting and elaborate clocks, one of the most famous is in the cathedral at Strasbourg, in France. The structure of this clock is, in fact, a model of the cathedral and on its tower there are three dials. The lowest, a revolving circle, is divided into the 365 days of the year. The figure of Apollo, on one side of the dial, points to the correct day of the year with an arrow.

The ingenious maker of the clock, Schwilgué, so built this mechanical calendar that, at midnight on the last day of each year, all the days of the week adopt new positions. An extra day is added each leap year, and the movable holiday of Easter is shown appropriately year by year. The middle dial on Schwilguè's clock is a normal one for telling the hours, but the top one indicates the position of each of the seven planets then known, as seen in the heavens from Earth (Neptune and Pluto had not been discovered when the clock was made).

There are two galleries on the upper part of the tower. Each quarter of an hour, a tiny human figure moves along the lower gallery and rings out the quarter: first quarter, a child; second quarter, a young man; third quarter, a middle-aged man; and, at the hour, an old man carrying Death and his scythe. At noon, the figures of 12 little monks proceed along the upper gallery, and a tiny cock cries out 'cock-a-doodle-doo!'

Another clock of world fame is London's Big Ben, although that is actually the name of the bell, not the clock itself. One of the sights of the city, if only because of its great size, Big Ben became well-known all over the world as a result of its chimes being broadcast regularly by the BBC during the days of World War II. Each of the clock's four dials is 7 metres (23 feet) in diameter and the bell weighs more than 13 tonnes.

Calendars
The Sun was responsible, in the first place, for man's measurement of the days and hours, but the Moon played its part in the calculation of weeks and months – and also of tides and their effects – in conjunction with the Sun. A period of 29 days, 12 hours, 44 minutes, 2·87 seconds represents the mean time taken from full Moon to full Moon, and this is known as the lunar month. Since

1926, however, a month is *legally* considered to be a calendar month.

Calendars of a sort were in use before the birth of Christ in many different parts of the world. There is, for instance, a 50-tonne Aztec monolith, found in Mexico in 1790, which is thought to be an early form of calendar inscribed on stone.

Julius Caesar introduced the Julian Calendar just over 2,000 years ago. This, being based on a year of $365\frac{1}{4}$ days, included the principle of the leap year. Despite its accuracy over a comparatively short period, the Julian Calendar was approximately 11 minutes out of true in the course of each year, because the Earth orbits the Sun in 365 days, 5 hours, 48 minutes, 46 seconds (mean solar time).

Over the centuries, the error accumulated until, in 1582, Italy introduced the Gregorian Calendar to rectify the miscalculation and adjust the passing of months and years precisely. This was done by counting century years as leap years only when they are divisible by 400, as will happen when we reach the year 2000. The Gregorian or New Style Calendar, named after Pope Gregory III who introduced it, is still in use today.

TIMES AROUND THE WORLD

When it is 1200 hrs (noon), Greenwich Mean Time,* clocks and watches around the world will normally show times as listed.

CITY	TIME	CITY	TIME
Adelaide	21.30	Melbourne	22.00
Amsterdam	13.00	Montreal	07.00
Ankara	14.00	Moscow	15.00
Athens	14.00	Nairobi	15.00
Auckland	24.00	New York	07.00
Belgrade	13.00	Oslo	13.00
Berlin	13.00	Ottawa	07.00
Bombay	17.30	Panama	07.00
Brisbane	22.00	Paris	13.00
Brussels	13.00	Peking	20.00
Budapest	13.00	Perth	20.00
Buenos Aires	09.00	Prague	13.00
Cairo	14.00	Quebec	07.00
Calcutta	17.30	Rangoon	18.30
Cape Town	14.00	Rio de Janeiro	09.00
Chicago	06.00	Rome	13.00
Copenhagen	13.00	San Francisco	04.00
Gibraltar	13.00	St John's (N.F.)	08.30
Helsinki	14.00	Singapore	19.30
Hobart	22.00	Stockholm	13.00
Hong Kong	20.00	Sydney	22.00
Istanbul	14.00	Teheran	15.30
Jerusalem	14.00	Tokyo	21.00
London	12.00	Toronto	07.00
Madeira	12.00	Vancouver	04.00
Madrid	13.00	Vienna	13.00
Malta	13.00	Winnipeg	06.00
Mauritius	16.00	Yokohama	21.00

*Greenwich Mean Time is based on the meridian at Greenwich, London. It dates, in practice, from the building of a clock, in 1852 and still in existence, at the Greenwich Observatory. GMT was adopted all over the world in 1884 and became Universal Time.

WEDDING ANNIVERSARIES

1st	Cotton	25th	Silver
5th	Wood	40th	Ruby
10th	Tin	50th	Gold
15th	Crystal	60th	Diamond
20th	China	70th	Platinum

DAYS OF THE WEEK

ENGLISH	LATIN	ANGLO-SAXON
Monday	Dies Lunae	Moon's Day
Tuesday	Dies Martis	Tiu's Day
Wednesday	Dies Mercurii	Woden's Day
Thursday	Dies Jovis	Thor's Day
Friday	Dies Veneris	Frigg's (or Freyja's) Day
Saturday	Dies Saturni	Saturn's Day
Sunday	Dies Solis	Sun's Day

DAYS OF THE MONTH

'Thirty days hath September,
April, June, and November.
All the rest have thirty-one,
Excepting February alone,
That has 28 days clear,
And 29 each leap year.'

ANIMALS
AND PETS

Scottish wild cat

Lion

Domestic cat

Cats

There is something very cosy and homely about the cat, one of the most popular of household pets. This cosiness is the reason why for some time certain cats were bred especially to be nursed by ladies to keep their laps warm. This same popularity reveals itself in the old nursery rhyme 'I love little pussy, her coat is so warm'. Though, amusingly, there follows the immediate warning about, 'If you don't tease her, she'll do you no harm'. A very timely reminder!

The history of the cat family can be traced back to prehistoric times, over millions of years, but there is still an uncertainty as to the exact ancestry of the domestic species.

According to one source, the cat originated in Persia. The very nickname 'puss' is possibly a corruption of 'pers'. It is more likely, however, that puss's true ancestor was the cat tamed and then worshipped by the ancient Egyptians, the African wildcat, *Felis ocreata*. This was very different from the striped tabby wildcat of Europe, considered by others to be the true ancestor. Argument over which came first still goes on today.

The wild and large cats
In the same general family as the cat (Felidae) are the lion, tiger, lynx, leopard, jaguar and many

Panther

Lynx

Cheetah

others you will be able to name. The word 'Cat' is usually applied only to the smaller species, but there are similarities in all members of the family. The mouth of puss has characteristics of a jungle hunter. It is perfectly created for cutting and eating meat and the rough tongue, like a rasp, is used to draw out the juices. The same speed and stealth are used to capture and destroy prey – always that same springing movement to bring down or bowl-over the victim. This helps to explain why some people consider cats cruel and are not among cat-lovers, though what better way is there of keeping down rats and mice? Factories and farms rely heavily on puss's hunting ability. A most useful pet indeed.

Their agility
Since the cat is more of a jumper than a runner, its legs are light and delicate. The power comes from its very muscular and strongly developed hips. While running it draws in its claws, which no longer act as a protection for the feet – unlike those of the dog. Of course, those same claws help it to climb and descend, apart from their very formidable use in fighting or capturing prey.

The looseness of the skin permits the cat's rippling, muscular grace of movement. This, combined with the small head and strong, supple spine, enhances the cat's agility and speed. In the middle of each foot is a large springy ball or pad divided into five parts, with a similar pad at the base of each toe.

(Look closely at the tracks of any cat in soft mud to examine the distinct pattern.) These are specially designed to break the force of a fall, rather like landing on sponge rubber or elastic. As you know, a cat, however dropped, almost always manages to land on its feet.

The whiskers, set above and at the sides of the mouth, are also an aid for survival. Each is connected to a delicate nerve. These whiskers enable a cat to tell whether or not a hole or gap is wide enough to admit the width of its body, and are particularly useful when the cat is crossing difficult terrain or moving through undergrowth. They act as an important sensory organ at night as well.

From the above description it is easy to see why the cat is often referred to as having 'nine lives'. Its great powers of resistance tend to make it a natural survivor. Its supersensitive hearing and awareness of even distant vibration account for what sometimes appears to be a 'sixth sense'.

Legends and myths

The cat has many unusual and mysterious features. Its eyes are particularly interesting, for they are specially adapted for seeing well in the dark. This is made possible because of a reflecting surface at the back of the eye that catches and makes the most of every single bit of light. The brilliant and rather glaring green colour is due to this reflection of the light. During daylight the pupils narrow down to mere slits. It is no wonder then that the cat was once regarded as an emblem of the moon and, from time immemorial, has always been associated with witches.

Witches were thought to have the power to change into cats. In Greek mythology the Fates changed Galinthia into one, and the goddess Hecate chose a cat form when Typhon compelled all gods and goddesses to disguise themselves in animal form.

Unfortunately these beliefs, particularly in olden days, resulted in cats being feared and treated cruelly in various counties of England. The old saying 'not enough room to swing a cat' referred to one of these cruel actions. It was even mentioned by Shakespeare. When the fear of witches disappeared, the other fears and the cruelty disappeared also. It is interesting, however, that it is only in Britain that black cats are thought to be lucky!

Breeds of cats

The domestic short-haired cats have interbred over many years to produce more varieties than any other breed. Cats produced from selected breeding are much sought after and can be very expensive.

The Persian cat is probably the most fancied. Championships generally go to a blue furred variety with deep orange or amber eyes. It is a dignified, 'soft-voiced' cat with short and compact legs and body.

The Siamese cat probably first came to Europe a little more than 50 or so years ago. Generally the body is sandy or fawn-coloured and the slanted eyes are deep blue. It is often regarded as rather difficult to train and inclined to be treacherous, though some would prefer the word 'mischievous'. These cats have great acrobatic agility and will quite naturally do tricks which other breeds could not perform without training.

In all there are many popular breeds of show cats, though the Persian and Siamese are probably the most popular.

The Manx cat does not have a tail and originated from the Isle of Man. Even so, it is sometimes called the Cornish cat and one source gives its origin as Japan. It is unlikely, however, that any Manxman would agree with this. It is a gentle pet, very easy to train and manage, and naturally trusting.

The Scottish Wildcat deserves a special mention because it is totally wild. For sheer ferocity and savagery, per pound of weight, it is unequalled. It resembles a large and rather powerfully built tabby cat, and is about 0·6 m (2 ft) long, with the tail adding another 0·3 m (1 ft). The wild cat lives on game, rabbits, hares, small birds and watercourses. It is untamable and can travel at such a speed that few of its victims ever escape. It is on record that a Scottish Wildcat once attacked and killed a man. Both were found dead, still gripping each other, on the porch of a church. It is generally known as the European Wild Cat, *Felis silvestris.*

Interesting facts
Cats are generally clean and fastidious and have an incredible

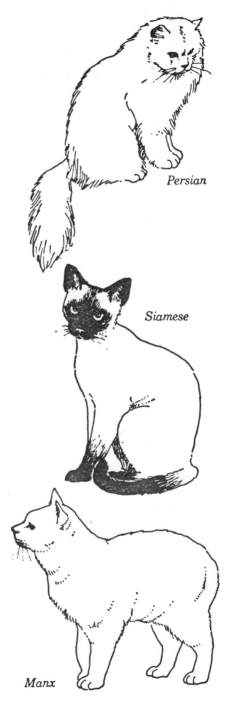

Persian

Siamese

Manx

'homing' instinct. Unlike that other favourite pet, the dog, they can return to the wild with comparative ease. Their attachment to a particular owner is not as great. It is often said that no one owns a cat but that a cat owns people.

In the past the fur of cats was used for the trimmings of coats and cloaks. Its skin was also highly desirable. Catgut was used, then, for the finer strings of violins and also for the strings of tennis rackets. A smaller kind of fiddle was consequently known as a 'kit'. Another link with the violin is that cats were once trained to dance and perform to its music, but this died out in the 19th century. The old nursery rhyme, 'Hey diddle diddle, the cat and the fiddle . . .' probably stems from that source. Though white cats with blue eyes were wrongly considered to be deaf.

'Making someone a cat's-paw'
This originated from the old fable about the artful monkey who retrieved roasted chestnuts from the embers of a fire by using the paw of a luckless cat which happened to be nearby. It appears to have some foundation in fact, for a similar situation is on record in Dr John Careri's book *A Voyage Round the World* (1695). In this case, the nut was a coconut, but the artful monkey's part was the same.

'Letting the cat out of the bag'
A favourite old trick of countrymen going to market in former times was to offer for sale a sucking-pig carried in a tied sack or, as it was called, poke. An unwary buyer, talked into a quick 'bargain', would purchase the sack before opening it – when he would find a very angry cat inside, instead of a pig. By that time the sharp-witted salesman would be elsewhere. So the saying, 'letting the cat out of the bag', came to mean an unlucky or premature disclosure. It also explains why one should never buy 'a pig in a poke', meaning that you should always investigate first before making a purchase.

Dogs

The dog is such a popular pet that almost from the beginning of time it seems to have been linked with man. It is almost as if some strange chemical attraction drew them together. One can almost imagine a wild, rather wolflike creature approaching a cave where primitive man sat, and gazing at him not with attack in mind but rather with an instinctive desire to make friends. Perhaps, on the other hand, some early man found a litter of wild dog pups, took them home and carefully reared them, producing the first domesticated dogs. One way or another, a kind of affinity does seem to exist.

Generally speaking, the dog was used for companionship, in various working roles and quite often as an object of adoration. The loyalty and affection it returns are accepted as unparalleled in the animal kingdom. The early Egyptians and Syrians revered and worshipped the dog. Their sculptures and images of it have been found dating from the beginning of history. Red Indian tribes regarded the dog as one of the sacred forms of their deities. So it is perhaps not surprising that in world folklore dogs have often been credited with mysterious knowledge and an insight into the spiritual realm. For example, the German philosopher and occultist Cornelius Agrippa, regarded as a magician, had a dog companion suspected of being a spirit incarnate.

Origin of the dog
Charles Darwin believed that the domestic dog originated from two species of wolf as well as various canine species and the jackal. The wolf-descent theory was widespread but it is now generally accepted that both wolf and dog may have had a common ancestor many millions of years ago and that the four earliest breeds of dog descended from this ancestor.

The term, dog, referring to our domestic pet, may also be extended to cover foxes, wolves, jackals and other allied species. However, certain differences are apparent, particularly in the shape of the pupil of the eye.

Uses of the dog
The range of activities is wide. The ancient Greeks used dogs on the battlefields as well as in hunting.

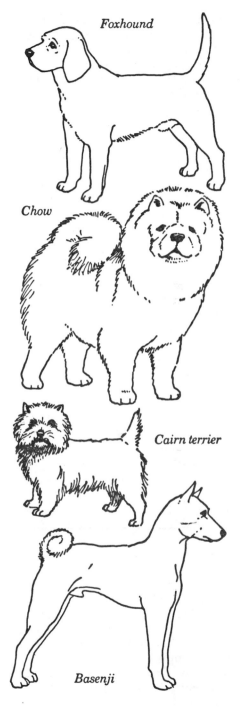

Foxhound

Chow

Cairn terrier

Basenji

131

Corgi

Poodle

Chihuahua

Dalmatian

Aerdale

The Romans classified theirs into three types: guard-dogs, hunting-dogs and sheep-dogs. In England, during the Middle Ages, dogs were used chiefly for sport, some of it, unfortunately, cruel. Bulldogs, then known as butcher's hounds, were used for bull-baiting as well as for catching cattle. Earlier still, Britain was renowned for her mastiffs. According to one source they played a significant part in the Gallic Wars. Dogs have been used constantly in exploration, Columbus took dogs with him when he discovered America and several polar expeditions used dog teams to tow sleds.

On the European continent, not too long ago, dogs were commonly used to pull small carts of various kinds; while in England, 'turnspit' dogs were used to turn the spits used for roasting meat. A kind of treadmill was specially designed for this purpose. There is a humorous story of how cne dog refused to work the spit when he decided it was another dog's turn, and such instances are actually on record. Many folk would agree that, as well as being intelligent, dogs have a sense of humour.

Dogs have been used in war, have been known to save people from drowning, and have been used as trackers and as guides for the blind. One famous St Bernard named 'Barry' is recorded as having saved 40 lives.

Much depends on the keen natural senses of the dog. He is a sniffer, relying on air and ground scents as much as on keen sight and hearing. The wet nose is particularly sensitive in this

Dachshund

Spaniel

Bulldog

Scots terrier

respect. The dog learns a great deal from a scent – whether he likes or dislikes a person, whether that person is afraid. So his nose is often more important than his eyes when he is seeking something. Special breeds can follow a scent trail several hours old. The dogs used by police and custom officials come in this group. In contrast, the greyhound hunts by sight, perhaps because of its amazing speed.

Breeds of dog
The Kennel Club lists over 100 breeds but, across the world, the total must be around 400. Those imported into the U.K. include the Dachshund, Doberman Pinscher, Rottweiler, Boxer and the Alsation from Germany, poodles from France, the Japanese Spaniel and others too numerous to mention.

Certain breeds tend to be used for particular working tasks. Alsatians are generally chosen as police dogs and as guide dogs for the blind. This is because they are not only excellent 'seeing' dogs but have a reasoning power along with their natural intelligence. Such an ability can never be substituted by even the very best training. For example, the French Poodle is highly intelligent and can be trained easily, yet it lacks this ability to reason. It would obey the order of a blind master equally blindly and might lead him straight in front of a bus. A particular breed of dog is chosen and sometimes specially bred for a particular task.

Wild dogs
We have already mentioned the

wolf, fox and jackal. The other types of dog may be divided into four main groups: American (North and South), African, Asiatic and Australian. From the Americas come the coyote (North), the Crab-eating dog (South) and the Bushdog of Brazil. The African group includes the hyena and Cape hunting-dog; the Asiatic includes the pariah dog, the dhole and the Raccoon dog of North China and Japan. The Australian wild dog is also known as the dingo, being unique in that it is the only wild carnivore living there today. It is found nowhere else in the world. All wild dogs belong to the general family of Canidae, one section of flesh-eating mammals.

Dogs in literature
Dogs are named and characterized in the works of Marlowe, Shakespeare, Chaucer, Sir Walter Scott, Homer, Sir Isaac Newton and others. The same interest in dogs applies to famous owners who revered their special pets to such an extent that the names of the cherished dogs are still recorded today with the names of their owners. In song, story and painting, owners sought to immortalize them. Two French dramas were based on dogs: *Le Chien de Montargris* by Guilbert de Pixérécourt, and *Le Chien D'Aubry*.

Superstitions and legends
The dog, as an omen of death or disaster, crops up in folklore under several different names and in varying places. The dreaded 'Black Shuck' of Britain, a kind of Hell Hound, goes back at least to Anglo-Saxon times. Even today, though not always black, a similar creature is mentioned and feared in rural areas. Conan Doyle's *The Hound of the Baskervilles* seems almost certainly inspired by such a legend. The Devil was sometimes depicted as hunting with a pack of grisly hounds.

From Biblical times it was believed that the howling of a dog signified death; the ancient Gaels believed that the victim would be the dog's master. The Chinese say that the blood of a dog will reveal a person who has made himself invisible. An old Latin quotation states: 'When dogs wallow in dust, expect foul weather.' Even today, we say of a sullen or sulky person, 'He has the Black Dog on his shoulder.' The guardian of Hades, in Greek mythology, was the terrible many-headed dog monster, Cerberus.

Interesting facts
In view of the fact that the dog is generally considered man's best friend, it is surprising that many unfavourable expressions (some intended as insults) are linked with this favourite pet. For instance, we have: you dog!, you cur!, whelp, insolent puppy, a dog's trick, a dog's life, dog sick, dog cheap, and many more. Perhaps the reason for this is that, particularly in the East, dogs are street scavengers.

In contrast, many wayside plants and flowers have 'dog' as part of their more common names. A glance through a dictionary will give some idea of the number. We also have 'Dog-days', referring to that period when the Dogstar (Sirius) rises and sets with the Sun.

Sizes of dogs
These vary greatly. The heaviest is the St Bernard, which can weigh around 113 kg (250 lb). The tallest are the Great Dane and Irish Wolfhound, both reaching 1 m (39 in) at the shoulder. The smallest breeds are the short-haired Chihuahua, Toy Poodle and Yorkshire Terrier. The fastest dogs are the Greyhound and Arabian Saluki.

Horses

The horse, like the dog, is sometimes called man's best friend. Horses have been helping man for 4,000 years. Before that they were hunted for food by the primitive tribes of Europe and Asia. Then, gradually, man began to capture and tame them. They were trained to work and carry riders.

The horse has played a very important part in our history. Just think how this noble beast has served us by pulling chariots and ploughs, bearing knights and soldiers into battle, and opening up the Wild West with cowboys. Horses are also used for sports such as racing, jumping and polo. And there are many other ways in which man's best friend earns his title.

Most of the 65 million horses in the world today are kept for riding – everything from police horses to children's ponies. The 300 breeds range from the tiny Falabella, an Argentine pony no bigger than a St Bernard dog and usually kept as a pet, to the mighty English Shire horse which is so powerful that only an elephant is stronger.

The first horses
The horse's earliest ancestors, *Eohippus*, lived 55 million years ago. He was a strange, striped animal standing just 20 cm (8 in) high. *Eohippus* made his home in

Eohippus   *Mesohippus*

swampy forests and ate leaves, not grass. Each of his front feet had four toes and his hind feet three.

This little creature was replaced, 15 million years later, by *Mesohippus*. As the earth's climate became drier and the prehistoric forests shrank, *Mesohippus* moved on to the plains. He had three toes on each foot and ate grass.

Then, after another 15 million years, came *Merychippus*. He was bigger than the other two and had a longer neck. To help him escape danger in the open, he had long legs, strong muscles and could run fast on his middle toes. The side toes became less and less important and eventually disappeared. *Pliohippus* was the first horse with only one toe, and the toe was protected by a hard nail, or hoof.

Pliohippus evolved about five million years ago and is the direct ancestor of *Equus caballus* – the horse we all know.

Running wild

Nowadays, there are very few wild horses left in the world. One type, named Przewalski's Horse after the explorer who discovered it in 1881, can still be found in Mongolia. The famous and beautiful white horses that roam the Camargue in southern France are only half wild; as are the black Mérens mountain ponies of southwest France.

Britain's Welsh Mountain and Exmoor ponies are also semi-wild. The Exmoor is a particularly ancient breed and was used by Queen Boadicea when she fought against the Roman army.

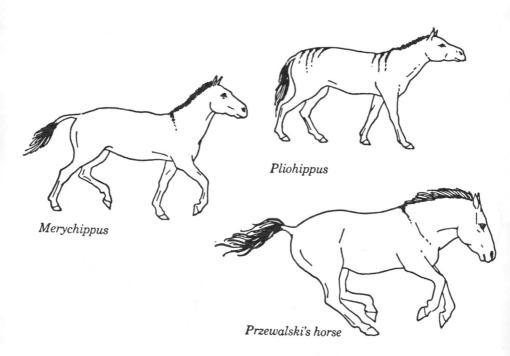

Pliohippus

Merychippus

Przewalski's horse

There are, however, other members of the horse family that still live in the wild. The black and white striped zebra lives free in the African savannahs, and the donkey is another wild species that is related to the horse.

Kings of horses

If horses had a king, he would be an Arab. This handsome horse is one of the world's oldest and purest breeds. He is a very fast animal. All racehorses which can run at up to 69 km/h (43 mph) have some of his blood in their veins. Indeed, most modern breeds, including circus, rodeo and jumping horses, are related to the Arab.

Four-footed giants

The world's biggest and strongest horses are draught horses. They are descended from the great horses of the Middle Ages which used to carry armoured knights into battle. During the 18th and 19th centuries, draught horses hauled ploughs across fields, barges along canals and heavy loads of timber or coal on roads. Today, however, machines have taken over and few of the four-footed giants are still working. At times you can see them pulling British brewery drays (carts) stacked with barrels of beer for public houses. They are also a popular attraction at horse shows.

Britain is lucky enough to have three fine breeds of draught horse. They are the Shire (tallest of all horses), the Suffolk Punch and the Clydesdale. France has the Breton

Equus Caballus

Pony

Donkey

Zebra

137

Draught and the Percherons, Holland has the Dutch Draught, Denmark has the Jutland (once ridden by Vikings), Sweden has the Ardennes and Italy has the Italian Draught. It would be a sad day if these magnificent creatures ever died out.

Ponies

After the giants, let's look at the pygmies of the horse family – the ponies. These small horses stand no higher than 1·4 m (4 ft 8 in). Some are much shorter. The much-loved Shetland pony from Scotland is only 0·9 m (3 ft) tall, while the Argentine Fallabella, mentioned earlier, stands less than 0·7 m (2 ft 4 in) high. Ponies are used as working animals in many countries because they are strong and hardy. In Norway, for example, the Fjord pony pulls heavy loads up the snowy mountains, while on the great cattle ranges of South America the sturdy Criollo is a cowboy's pony. Furthermore, as ponies are intelligent, good-natured and small, they are ideal for children to ride.

Among the best-known breeds are the Pony of the Americas, the Australian pony, England's friendly New Forest pony, South Africa's tough Basuto, Japan's fast Hocaido, Austria's long-living Haflinger and the Iceland pony which has been kept for work and food since the days of the Vikings.

Points of a horse

The following diagram shows the various parts of the horse. These parts are called points. The points of a horse add up to its

conformation, the way it is put together. A horse may have a good or bad conformation. Features such as an extra-large head or a hollow back would give the creature a bad conformation.

Colours and markings

What colour was the last horse you saw? Compare your answer with the descriptions below, which give the correct names for different coloured horses.

● **Cream** – Creamy coat, mane and tail with pinkish eyes
● **Chestnut** – Reddish-brown body, mane and tail
● **Strawberry Roan** – Chestnut mixed with white hairs
● **Palomino** – Golden with pale mane and tail
● **Dun** – Sandy with black mane and tail
● **Piebald** – Large patches of black and white
● **Skewbald** – Brown and white patches
● **Grey** – Mixed black and white hairs
● **Brown** – Dark brown with dark brown mane and tail
● **Bay** – Brown body with black mane, tail and legs
● **Black** – All black

Many horses have what are called markings. These may be white marks on the head, body or legs. The following illustration shows some of them. A horse with no markings is known as whole-coloured.

Coaches and carriages

Horse-drawn vehicles existed as

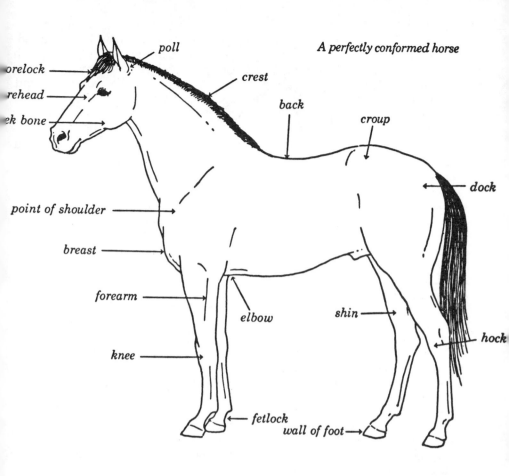

A perfectly conformed horse

forelock

forehead

cheek bone

poll

crest

back

croup

dock

point of shoulder

breast

forearm

elbow

shin

hock

knee

fetlock

wall of foot

Scenes such as these are no longer as common as they were in pre-motor days.

long ago as 2000 BC. It was, however, much later, during the 18th century, that coaches and carriages became popular. Then, there were state coaches for royalty, mail coaches for letters, stagecoaches for travellers, and carriages for the gentry. All were drawn by special horses such as the English Cleveland Bay, the Czechoslovakian Kladruber and the Dutch Gelderland.

Today, coaches and carriages are hardly ever seen in the street except on ceremonial occasions or as tourist attractions. On the other hand they are still widely used for sporting events. An event called driving involves different kinds of vehicles and different numbers of horses. There can be one, a pair, or a team of four or six horses. Another exciting event is trotting.

The horses race round a track pulling light carriages known as gigs or sulkies. In this race the horse is not allowed to gallop.

Riding and jumping

Riding is fun. There are lots of things to learn before you start. For example, you must know how to mount, dismount, sit, balance and hold the reins. An expert at a riding school will teach you. Later, when you can control your horse as it walks, trots, canters and gallops (the four different paces), you may decide you want to learn jumping.

Many people, as they get better at riding and jumping, go in for competitions such as show-jumping and eventing. Eventing consists of three tests: dressage, cross-country and, of course, show-jumping.

The saddle is kept in place by the girth, a strap which fastens round the horse's belly.

More about horses

'Don't look a gift horse in the mouth.' Perhaps you have heard this saying. It means that when you are given a surprise present, you should not question its worth and should be grateful for your luck. By examining a horse's teeth you can tell its age and decide whether it is a healthy horse or not. Soon after a horse is born, it develops small, white milk (baby) teeth. Large adult teeth start growing at three years. By the time a horse is five, it has a full mouth of permanent teeth. The older a horse is the more worn its teeth become.

To protect their feet from hard surfaces such as roads, horses are fitted with metal shoes. Horses need new shoes after six to eight weeks. This is not because the old ones are worn out but because the outside, or wall, of the hoof is continually growing. The wall grows fast and can easily outgrow the shoe, causing lameness. So a blacksmith takes off the old shoe, cuts away the extra growth and attaches a new shoe. The horse feels no pain.

When the rider is seated in the saddle, the left-hand side of the horse is the nearside and the right-hand side is the offside.

Horses of different ages and sexes have special names as you can see from this list:

● **Stallion** – A male horse over four years of age, used for breeding
● **Mare** – A female over four
● **Colt** – A male between one and four
● **Filly** – A female between one and four
● **Foal** – A horse up to one year

The awkward one

Like people, horses can be either easy or difficult to get along with. There is, however, one of our four-footed friends which is noted for its extreme stubbornness. It is the mule, which is a cross between a horse and a donkey. Mules are sterile and cannot breed. So every mule that is born has a horse and a donkey for parents. Mules are agile animals that can carry heavy packs through rugged terrain such as mountains. If a mule decides not to move, however, there is nothing you can do to change its mind!

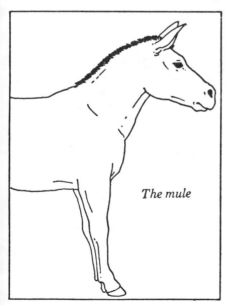

The mule

RELIGION

Main Religions of the World

Many world religions are in the process of rapid growth, perhaps as a response to the challenge of the technological revolution which is rapidly changing the face of the Earth.

Hinduism

This is the religion of the great majority of people in India. It has a number of religious books containing its main beliefs, especially the *Veda*, the *Brahmanas*, the *Upanishads* and the *Bhagavad-gita*.

Hinduism's two main doctrines are *karma* and reincarnation, or rebirth. A person's destiny is shaped by his deeds (*karma*). He can seek release from an endless succession of lives by living a hard, ascetic life, or through the discipline of yoga. If he fails to attain release, the person is reincarnated to a higher or lower form of life after he dies. Hinduism absorbs other beliefs into its system, no matter how contradictory they are.

Buddhism

Buddhism is a widespread religion of the Orient which grew out of a Hindu background. It takes its name from its founder, the Hindu prince Siddhartha Gautama, known as the Buddha ('the enlightened one'), who lived around the 6th century BC.

The Buddha was dissatisfied with Hinduism as he contemplated the human problem of suffering. His meditations fall into 'four noble truths' which are the basis of Buddhism:

1 Existence is a nightmare of unhappiness

2 Unhappiness is the result of selfish desire or craving

3 Selfish desire can be destroyed

4 It is destroyed by following an Eightfold Path involving morality and discipline

Islam

This is the religion of one out of every six people in the world, and today it is undergoing a great revival. It comes out of a Judaistic and Christian background, with prophets and a belief in one God who created the universe.

Islam's two main divisions are between the conservative Shi'ites and the Sunnis. The Shi'ites wish for a distinct Muslim culture based on the *Sharia*, the strict Muslim law. The Sunnis are more prepared to Westernize. Present-day Islam is a major world influence and its power is likely to increase in the future as an alternative to both Western values and Communism.

The importance of law and good behaviour is clear from the 'five pillars of Islam':

1 The confession: 'There is no God but Allah, and Muhammad is his prophet'

2 The ritual prayers

3 Ritual alms and offerings

4 The month-long annual fast of Ramadan

5 The pilgrimage to Mecca

Christianity

This religion is centred on Jesus of Nazareth, son of God and Messiah. Its beliefs are based upon the Bible, in particular the teachings of Jesus which are recorded in the New Testament. Christianity is statistically the world's largest religion, but there are many different branches within it.

Judaism

Judaism shares with Christianity the Old Testament but it rejects the Christian interpretation given by the New Testament. Nevertheless, Jews and Christians have much in common in their belief in a personal creator God. Jewish belief adds other sacred books to the Old Testament.

There is a special 'covenant' relationship between God and his chosen people, the Jews. Judaism is a social and family religion and its observances concern every aspect of ordinary daily life.

THE TEN COMMANDMENTS

Jesus Christ summarized the Ten Commandments – central to Old Testament teaching – as loving God with all your heart, soul, mind and strength, and loving your neighbour as you love yourself. Christianity teaches that a person's relationship with God determines his relationship with other people.

The commandments may be simplified as follows:

1 Worship only the true God
2 Worship no idols
3 Don't misuse God's name
4 Keep the seventh day as a day of rest from work
5 Respect your parents
6 Don't murder
7 Don't commit adultery
8 Don't steal
9 Don't falsely accuse anybody
10 Don't desire someone else's possessions

THE TWELVE APOSTLES

These people were specially chosen by Jesus Christ to spread his message

Andrew, brother of Peter

Peter

Bartholomew, also called Nathanael

Philip

James the Elder, son of Zebedee, and brother of John

John

James the Younger, son of Alphaeus

Judas, also called Thaddeus or Lebbaeus

Matthew, also called Levi

Simon the Zealot

Thomas

Judas Iscariot, the betrayer of Jesus

Mathias

MAIN CHRISTIAN FESTIVALS

Advent	The fourth Sunday before Christmas
Christmas Day	25 December, celebrating Jesus' birth
Ash Wednesday	The first day of Lent
Lent	The fast of forty days before Easter
Palm Sunday	Celebrating Christ's triumphant entry into Jerusalem a few days before he died
Good Friday	The day of Christ's death (originally probably called God's Friday)
Easter	Celebrating the resurrection of Christ. The date varies annually between 22 March and 25 April
Ascension Day	The withdrawal of Christ to Heaven. Celebrated on the sixth Thursday (the fortieth day) after Easter
Whitsunday	The second Sunday after Ascension Day, celebrating the coming of the Holy Spirit to the Church at Pentecost
Trinity Sunday	The first Sunday after Whitsunday, celebrating the Holy Trinity.

Most of the festivals depend upon the date of Easter for their timing each year. Easter is the Christian Passover, as Christ's death and resurrection occurred during the Jewish Passover. In fact, Christ celebrated the Passover before he died. There was much controversy within the Church over when Easter's date should be fixed but finally agreement was reached.

Britain, for example, followed the practice of the rest of Europe after the Synod of Whitby in 664. Easter falls on one of 35 days between 22 March and 25 April. Throughout Christendom various Easter celebrations take place such as lighting fires and giving Easter eggs – eggs being symbols of resurrection, life and fruitfulness.

Events in the Bible

The Bible is a collection of 66 books spanning thousands of years. It claims to give a true picture of human history from beginning to end. This is from the start of mankind in the deep past to some-time in our future when Christ, the true king of men, will return.

The religion of the Bible is based upon a God who made the entire universe. This God is a person who deals with man in history, and who himself became a man – Jesus Christ. Christians long ago divided

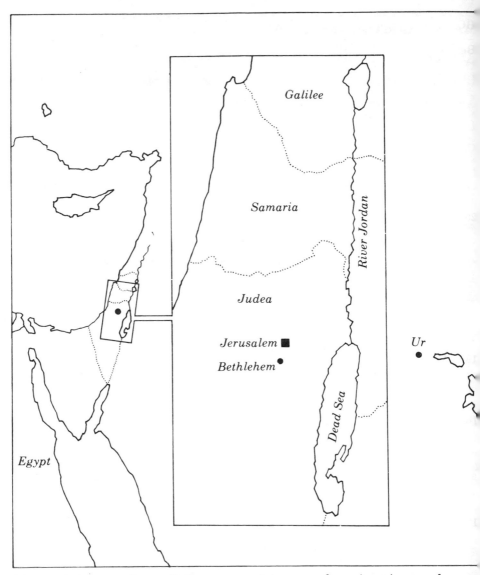

history into BC and AD – *Before
Christ* and *Anno Domini* (literally,
'in the year of the Lord') referring
to the years since his birth. A slight
computing error was made; Christ
in fact was born several years BC,
probably 6 BC.

In the following chronology,

dates are often given in round
figures, or are approximate. When
speaking of very ancient times, this
doesn't usually mean that the
record of events is inaccurate. The
main Bible books which relate to
each period appear in brackets at
the end of each entry.

Before 2000	The early history of man from his beginnings. Man disobeys God and brings a curse upon himself and upon his environment. This is called 'the fall of man'. From early times the twin themes of history's pattern begin to work out – man's quest for salvation (and God's provision for this) and his cruelty as the result of his disobedience to God. These are seen in the murder of Abel by his brother Cain, in catastrophic judgement (as the early civilization is destroyed by the great flood) and in the breaking up of society (after Babel, standing for man's pride). The world then increasingly takes the form of a variety of nations and civilizations. (The Book of Genesis, which means 'beginning' or 'origin')
2000	The Age of the Patriarchs begins (the age of Abraham, his son Isaac, Isaac's son Jacob and Jacob's son Joseph). Abraham migrates from the civilized centre, Ur of Sumeria, to Canaan. He is called by God to forsake polytheism (the worship of many gods) and return to the original monotheism (worship of one god) of the human race. Abraham is chosen to be the founder of a new nation, which God promises will one day have the blessing of his salvation. The new nation is promised the land of Palestine as its eventual home. During this time Palestine, in its Bronze Age, is inhabited by the Canaanites. (Genesis)
1900–1750	Isaac, Abraham's son, long promised by God, is born when his parents are old. When Abraham is about to sacrifice the young Isaac, God provides a substitute – a ram – to die in his place. (Genesis)
1800–1700	Jacob, Isaac's son. Traditionally, the family inheritance is passed to the eldest son, but Jacob tricks his big brother into selling his birthright for a bowl of lentils one day when he is very hungry. Jacob is notorious for his trickery, and this leads him into a lot of trouble. He is eventually renamed 'Israel' by God. His new name is passed down to his descendants and finally the new nation. (Genesis)
1750–1650	Joseph. Jacob's favourite son, Joseph, is secretly sold as a slave in Egypt because of his brothers' jealousy. In a classic case of 'rags to riches', he rises to the top of Egyptian society. Joseph is reunited with his family after many years, and they settle in Egypt. (Genesis)
1700–1280	Israel in Egypt. During Egypt's New Kingdom, the Israelites stay several centuries. Finally, increasing oppression forces them to leave as refugees. Permission for their exodus is not granted until after a series of ten increasingly fearful plagues. (Exodus)
1280	The exodus from Egypt is led by Moses, a great leader. This is the central event of the Old Testament. The leaving of Egypt and migration to Palestine is an act of faith that God will fulfil his

promise of a national territory for the growing body of Israelite people. (Exodus, Numbers, Deuteronomy)

1240 After many years in the desert, the Israelites cross the River Jordan. This is the natural geographical boundary of Palestine to the east. The nation is now led by Moses' successor, Joshua. This is the beginning of the gradual occupation of Palestine. The time roughly corresponds with the beginning of the Iron Age in Palestine. (Joshua)

1220?–1050/45? The period of the 'judges'. These are military leaders, usually local, who lead the resistance – both physical and spiritual – to the Philistines and other warlike neighbouring nations. The 'judges' include Samson, who has a disastrous affair with the beautiful Philistine, Delilah. The final 'judge' is Samuel, under whom the nation has its first king. (Judges, Ruth, 1 Samuel)

1050/45?–931/30 The New Kingdom. In this period there are three kings, all of them national heroes – Saul, David and Solomon. This is the time of Israel's Golden Age, and Solomon builds a magnificent temple in the capital, Jerusalem. It is dedicated to the one, true, unseen God. Loving dedication to God is seen as the basis of a good national life which provides peace, security and quality of living. (1 and 2 Samuel, 1 Kings, 1 Chronicles, 2 Chronicles)

From 931/30 The nation falls into disunity and rivalry. The kingdom is divided into a Northern Kingdom and the Southern Kingdom of Judah. In both kingdoms prophets appear, interpreting political and historical events in terms of God's blessing and judgement upon nations, depending upon whether they obey or disobey Him. The greatest judgement prophesied upon the Jews is the loss of their national territory. In 722 Samaria, the northern capital, falls to the Assyrians. This marks the end of the Northern Kingdom. Many of the inhabitants are taken into captivity. In 587 a similar fate overtakes Jerusalem, the capital of Judah, this time by Assyria's successors, the Babylonians. In this and earlier conquests a great number of Judeans are taken into exile in Babylon. (1 Kings, 2 Kings, 2 Chronicles)

539 Babylon falls to the Persians.

538 Zerubbabel and other Jews return to Jerusalem. He helps lay the foundations of a new temple to replace the destroyed one. (Ezra)

520 Temple rebuilding is resumed after hindrances.

516 The temple is completed.

458 The scribe Ezra goes to Jerusalem, leading a party from captivity. (Ezra)

445–433 Nehemiah is given permission by the Persian king to go to Jerusalem to rebuild the walls and set up new gates. He is appointed governor of Judah. (Nehemiah)

The period from this time up to the birth of Jesus Christ is not recorded in the Old Testament. But full historical records of much of the period are to be found in apocryphal (non-canonical) books such as 1 and 2 Maccabees, which are included in many editions of the Bible. During this period Greece, Egypt, Syria and finally Rome are dominant influences upon Palestine.

331–323	Alexander the Great conquers many lands and founds the Egyptian city of Alexandria where many Jews settle. His empire includes Palestine.
323–63	The Age of the Ptolemies and Seleucids. After Alexander's sudden death his empire is divided up. Ptolemy, one of his generals, rules Egypt, while Seleucus, another general, seizes Babylonia and Asia Minor. The Ptolemies of Egypt rule Palestine for a hundred years. Then in 198 Antiochus the Great, a Seleucid, occupies it for Syria until Roman rule is established in 63.
68	Antiochus Epiphanes, son of Antiochus, marches against Jerusalem, killing and looting. The temple is desecrated and is replaced by a statue of Zeus, outraging the Jews.
67	The Maccabean revolt begins in the tiny village of Modein, near Jerusalem. One of the greatest leaders of the revolt is Judas Maccabeus. The rebels conduct a successful guerrilla war.
64	Rededication of the temple.
63	Pompey establishes a Roman protectorate in Palestine.
40	Herod the Great is appointed king of Judea by Rome.
5?	Jesus Christ is born in Bethlehem in Judea. (Matthew, Luke)
4	Herod the Great dies.

AD

14–37	Reign of Tiberius Caesar.
26–36	Pontius Pilate is Roman Procurator, based in Jerusalem.
29?	Baptism of Jesus and the beginning of his public life as a travelling preacher and teacher. (the Gospels)
30	During the annual Passover, Jesus is in Jerusalem.
30–31	Jesus is in Samaria, a province lying between Judea and Galilee – Jesus' home area.
31	During the annual Feast of Tabernacles Jesus is in Jerusalem.
32	At the time of the Passover, Jesus feeds the five thousand.
32	During both the Feast of Tabernacles and the Feast of Dedication Jesus is in Jerusalem.

33	The annual Passover becomes the prelude for the first Christian Easter when Jesus is executed by crucifixion and rises from the dead on the third day.
34–5	Paul's conversion. (The Acts of the Apostles)
37–8	Paul's first visit to Jerusalem as a Christian.
37–41	Reign of Caligula Caesar.
41–54	Reign of Claudius Caesar.
45–6	The Church in Antioch makes a collection for a great famine.
46–7	Paul's first missionary journey.
48	The apostles hold a council in Jerusalem.
48–51	Paul's second missionary journey.
50	Paul reaches Corinth, the largest seaport in Greece.
53	The third missionary journey begins.
54–68	Reign of Nero Caesar.
54–7	Paul stays in Ephesus.
57	Departure for Troas.
58–9	Paul is in Macedonia and Achaia.
59	Paul returns to Jerusalem.
59–61	He is imprisoned in Caesarea.
61	He appeals directly to Nero Caesar and leaves for Rome.
62	Paul arrives at Rome after being shipwrecked.
62–4	Imprisonment in Rome. (His death there by execution is not recorded in the Bible)
62?	The martyrdom of James, brother of Jesus.
70	The fall of Jerusalem.
81–96	Persecution of Christians under Domitian Caesar.
c. 100	Death of John the apostle.

HISTORY

Major Historical Events

A world chronology of major events
Prehistory spans the time from when the world was formed until man
began to write. Rocks, fossils and artifacts alone tell the story of these
early times, until someone between 5000 to 4000 BC when recorded history
began.

4000–3000 BC	Foundation of Susa (today called Sousse, in Tunisia). Civilization well established in Sumeria. Cuneiform writing introduced. Start of civilization in Egypt, where some early pyramids are built and first calendar compiled.
3000–2000 BC	The great Egyptian Empire dominates this period, which includes the Great Pyramid age.
2000–1000 BC	Flourishing civilizations in Mesopotamia, Crete (the Minoans), Ugarit (North Syria), and the spread of the Phoenicians with their sea-power and trade. The Jews are in bondage in Egypt, followed by their exodus and invasion of Palestine.
1000–900 BC	Beginning of the Chou Dynasty in China. Kingdom of David and Solomon. Achaeans occupy Greece.
900–800 BC	The Greek city-states make their appearance. The Assyrians begin to record events chronologically.
800–700 BC	Rome founded. Period of the great Hebrew prophets. Southern Italy colonized by Greeks.
700–600 BC	The rise and fall of the Assyrian Empire. Destruction of Nineveh.
600–500 BC	The Athenians receive their laws from Solon. Buddha (died 480) teaches in India, and Confucius (died 479) in China.
500–400 BC	Great Age of Greece, with Pericles in power, the Parthenon under construction, and such outstanding figures as Aeschylus, Phidias, Herodotus, Euripides and Sophocles.
400–300 BC	The Gauls occupy Rome. Philip II of Macedon defeats the Greek city-states. After his assassination, he is succeeded by Alexander who defeats the Persians, captures Tyre, and occupies Egypt and the Punjab.
300–200 BC	Rise of Rome, with colonial expansion along the west coast of the Mediterranean. Hannibal challenges the power of Rome and is finally defeated in 207. The kingdom of Ch'in conquers all Chinese lands and, in 214, the Great Wall of China is completed, by joining together a number of existing walls.
200–100 BC	Roman Empire grows steadily across the eastern Mediterranean coast, and into Asia and Africa; Carthage is destroyed in 146. China also spreads her power and control.
100 BC–AD 1	Julius Caesar conquers Gaul and mounts expeditions to Britain in 55 and 54. Following the assassination of Caesar in 44, Octavian triumphs over all his adversaries and becomes Emperor Augustus

and supreme ruler of the Roman Empire. The birth of Jesus Christ marks the end of this century; the year 6 is often reckoned to be the actual year of His Nativity at Bethlehem.

AD 1–100 Crucifixion of Jesus Christ, circa 29, following which the Christian message is carried far afield in Europe. Roman expansion continues and includes the conquest of Britain. An eruption of Mt Vesuvius destroys Pompeii in 79. Expedition from China reaches the Persian Gulf in 97.

AD 100–200 The accession of Hadrian, in 197, sees the Roman Empire commanding more power and territory than at any other time; by the end of the century Rome's decline begins.

AD 200–300 In 212, Rome confers citizenship on every free inhabitant of its Empire. China suffers the first of many invasions which last over a period of 300 years and her power and control begin to decline.

AD 300–400 The decline of the Roman Empire gathers momentum until in 395, on the death of Emperor Theodosius the Great, it is divided into East and West.

AD 400–500 The collapse of Rome, in 476, follows the invasion of Spain by the Visigoths, raids into Gaul and Italy by Attila the Hun, and the pillaging of Rome itself by Vandals in 455.

AD 500–600 The Byzantines reconquer North Africa and, later in 552, Italy. Christianity continues to spread. A mission is founded at Iona by St Columba (543) and St Augustine crosses the sea to Kent (597). Muhammad is born in 570.

AD 600–700 The rise of the T'ang Dynasty in China introduces system of administration which is destined to last for some 1,300 years. Beginnings of Islamic expansion in 622; Arabia entirely Muslim by the time of Muhammad's death in 632, followed by the capture of Jerusalem (638), Persia (641), Alexandria (643) and Carthage (698). The Slavs completed their occupation of the Balkans by 650.

AD 700–800 Muslim occupation of southern Spain. Beginning of the wide-flung raids and settlements by the Vikings. At the century's end, Charlemagne is crowned as Holy Roman Emperor.

AD 800–900 Following the death of Charlemagne, in 814, and the break-up of his empire, the Muslims seize much of southern Italy. The Vikings scourge many lands, from England and France to Russia. In eastern Europe the first Bulgar Empire is founded and the Magyars reach Hungary, whilst in the west Alfred the Great brings stability to much of England.

AD 900–1000 The century starts with Ghana's powerful empire in west Africa. Norsemen continue to dominate the seas around Europe, and discover both Greenland and North America (Leif Ericsson in 1000). Many rulers of northern Europe accept Christianity, including kings of Denmark, Poland, Kiev and Sweden.

AD 1000–1100 Rise of Norman power in western Europe, particularly in Italy, and then in England, after the conquest in 1066; Domesday Book compiled in 1086. The Turks take Jerusalem in 1075 but the city falls again during the First Crusade in 1099.

AD 1100–1200 A century of crusades to Palestine. The third of these is led by the kings of England and France and the Holy Roman Emperor, Frederick Barbarossa. The Mediterranean becomes an important centre of trade. In 1161 explosives are used in battles during internal wars in China.

AD 1200–1300   The period of Mongol power across much of Asia, beginning with the proclamation of Temujin as Gengiz Khan in 1206; the Golden Horde sweep through Russia in 1237 and reach central Europe four years later. China ruled by Kublai Khan in 1260. The signing of the Magna Carta by King John, in England, leads to the establishment of the first real Parliament in 1265 by Simon de Montfort. Crusades to the Holy Land come to an end with the fall of Acre in 1291.

AD 1300–1400   Hundred Years' War, between England and France, begins in 1338. The Black Death appears in Europe in 1348 and sweeps westward from country to country.

AD 1400–1500   Joan of Arc inspires the French in their war with England. She is burnt at the stake in 1439. With the capture of Constantinople by the Turks the East Roman Empire comes to an end (1453). Printing from movable type is introduced in Germany (1454); Caxton operates his press in 1476 at Westminster. In 1492 the Spaniards finally oust the Muslims from their land. The age of great explorations and discoveries begins in 1488 with the rounding of the Cape of Good Hope by Diaz; Christopher Columbus discovers the West Indies in 1492; John Cabot finds Newfoundland in 1497; Amerigo Vespucci maps part of South America's coast in 1499; and Pedro Cabral discovers Brazil in 1500.

AD 1500–1600   Start of the Reformation in 1517, as Martin Luther openly renounces Roman Catholicism; Henry VIII of England breaks away in 1534. Another century of momentous seaborne discoveries and the foundation of trade and settlements all over the globe by such great navigators as Balboa, Magellan, Drake and Raleigh. Spain's threat to England is removed by the defeat of the Armada in 1588, and her hold over the Low Countries is broken by the rebellion of the Dutch people.

AD 1600–1700   Union of England and Scotland in 1603. Peak of Shakespeare's enormous contribution to world drama. Thirty Years' War commences in 1618. The Pilgrim Fathers colonize New England in 1620. English Civil War begins in 1642; Cromwell becomes Protector in 1653. Great advances in the field of science, dominated by such leading names as Galileo and Newton.

AD 1700–1800   A century of wars and revolutions, both in Europe and in other areas of the world which are being competitively colonized by the great European powers. In 1701 the War of the Spanish Succession breaks out; in 1756 the Seven Years' War begins; in 1775 the American War of Independence starts; and in 1789 the French Revolution starts, leading to the rise of Napoleon Bonaparte and the wars resulting from his military campaigns. Robert Clive succeeds in defeating Indian uprisings and finally establishes British rule throughout India. Industrial and commercial advances, particularly in textiles, take place in Britain; whilst in Europe outstanding philosophers include Spinoza, Descartes, Diderot, Voltaire, Kant and Goethe; and great composers such as J.S. Bach, Handel, Mozart and Beethoven.

AD 1800–1900   Early years of the century are dominated by the Napoleonic Wars,
ending with the French Emperor's defeat at Waterloo in 1815.
Later, Britain and her empire grow to an immense size and
strength, whilst many countries merge into their modern form,
such as Germany, Greece and Italy, and others become
independent, notably the South American republics. As well as a
series of colonial conflicts in Africa and Asia, three important
wars take place: the Crimea War (1854), the American Civil War
(1861–5), and the Franco-Prussian War (1870). The 19th century is
also noted for the industrial revolution and the development of
new kinds of machinery, equipment and methods of transport.
Towards the end of the century, major social reforms gradually
ease the misery and poverty of working people, and trade unions
are granted recognition. Culturally, the period sees the appearance
of a host of eminent composers and authors, many of the former
being German or Austrian, and of the latter British. Great
international undertakings include the building of important
canals: Suez (1869), Manchester (1894) and Kiel (1895).

AD 1900–   The pace of scientific investigation and technological advancement
accelerates enormously: motor-driven road transport; conquest of
the air and space; radio and television; modern methods of heating
and lighting; devices for the mass production of a vast range of
products – all these, and many more, are basically 20th century
achievements. Despite wonderful advances in medical knowledge
and skill human suffering has probably been on a greater scale
than in any previous century as a result of the two World Wars
(1914–18 and 1939–45), and the political upheavals and minor
conflicts arising out of them. Some particularly outstanding dates
in a variety of fields are: 1903, Orville and Wilbur Wright make the
first controlled flight in a machine heavier than air; 1909, Henry
Ford begins the era of low-price cars with his Model T chassis;
1917, revolution breaks out in Russia; 1926, General Strike in
Britain; 1933, Hitler appointed German Chancellor; 1945, atomic
bombs dropped on Hiroshima and Nagasaki, Japan; 1945, birth of
the United Nations; 1947, Independence of India and Pakistan;
1949, North Atlantic Treaty becomes effective, and the Chinese
People's Republic is established; 1969, landing of the first men on
the Moon by the Americans in Apollo rocket; 1970s and 1980s,
severe droughts in the Sahel region of North Africa led to great
suffering and the southward advance of the Sahara; the destruction
of natural habitats and studies of the dangers of pollution caused an
increasing awareness of the need for conservation.

Important Dates Through History

AD

306	Constantine the Great becomes Emperor.
354	St Augustine is born.
476	Fall of the Roman Empire in the West.
570	Mohammed is born in Mecca.
800	Pope Leo II crowns Charlemagne Emperor of the West.
1066	William, Duke of Normandy, conquers England.
1095	First Crusade.
1147	Second Crusade.
1189	Third Crusade.
1202	Fourth Crusade diverted to attack Constantinope; a Latin Empire is established there.
1215	Magna Carta is signed by King John in England.
1271	Marco Polo sets off on his travels.
1338	Hundred Years War between France and England begins.
1348	The Black Death sweeps Europe.
1452	Leonardo da Vinci is born.
1483	Martin Luther is born.
1492	Columbus discovers America. The Moors are driven from Spain.
1509	Henry VIII becomes King of England.
1534	Reformation in England.
1546	Death of Martin Luther.
1565	Shakespeare is born.
1618	The Thirty Years' War in Europe begins.
1649	*Mayflower* colonists land in New England.
1660	Execution of Charles I in England.
1665	Great Plague of London.
1666	Great Fire of London.
1745	Jacobite rebellion in England and Scotland led by Prince Charles Edward Stuart.
1775	Beginning of American War of Independence.
1776	American Declaration of Independence.
1789	French Revolution starts; Bastille is stormed.
1796	Napoleonic Wars begin.
1804	Napoleon becomes Emperor of France.
1812	Napoleon retreats from Moscow.
1815	Battle of Waterloo. Treaty of Vienna.
1825	First railway (Stockton to Darlington).
1837	Queen Victoria comes to the throne in Britain.
1840	Penny Post introduced in Britain.
1854–6	Crimean War.
1869	Suez Canal opened.

1899	Boer War begins in South Africa.
1903	First aeroplane flights by Wright brothers.
1912	China becomes a republic. Ocean liner *Titanic* sinks on its maiden voyage.
1914	World War I begins.
1917	Russian Revolution; Bolshevik regime established in Russia. USA enters World War.
1918	World War I ends.
1919	Treaty of Versailles between Allies and Germany. First trans-Atlantic flight made by Alcock and Brown.
1924	Death of Lenin.
1926	General Strike in Great Britain.
1933	Hitler comes to power in Germany.
1936–9	Spanish Civil War.
1938	Hitler annexes Austria.
1939	Germany invades Czechoslovakia, and later Poland. France, Britain and the Commonwealth declare war on Germany (World War II).
1940	Germany invades Denmark, Norway, the Netherlands, Belgium and Luxembourg. Fall of France. Evacuation of Dunkirk by British. Battle of Britain.
1941	Japanese attack Pearl Harbor. USA enters the War.
1943	Italy surrenders to the Allies.
1944	Allies liberate France.
1945	All German forces surrender. Atomic bombs dropped on Hiroshima and Nagasaki. End of World War II. United Nations established.
1949	People's Republic of China founded under leadership of Mao Tse-Tung.
1950–3	Korean War.
1963	Assassination of J. F. Kennedy, President of USA.
1969	First men on the moon (USA).
1975	Vietnam War ends.
1979	Islamic Revolution in Iran.
1982	Falklands conflict between Great Britain and Argentina.
1984–5	Widespread famine in many African countries.

Famous Queens

ADELAIDE (1792–1849) In 1818, Adelaide married the Duke of Clarence, later to reign as King William IV of Great Britain. She was a devoted wife and succeeded in raising standards of morality at Court to a considerable degree. All Queen Adelaide's children died as infants, and it was as a result of this that Victoria succeeded King William.

ALEXANDRA (of England) (1844–1826) A daughter of King Christian IX of Denmark, Alexandra married Queen Victoria's son Edward, then Prince of Wales, in 1863. She became Queen when her husband succeeded to the throne, as King Edward VII, in 1901. Greatly admired by her people, Alexandra devoted much of her time to charities and is well-known for the 'Rose Day' named after her. Her eldest son, the Duke of Clarence, died in 1892, and it was George, her second son, who eventually succeeded Edward VII to the throne.

ALEXANDRA (of Russia) (1872–1918) Married Tsar Nicholas II (Nikolai) in 1894 and became Tsarina. Alexandra had five children – Alexei, Olga, Tatiana, Maria and Anastasia. Aloof, withdrawn, stiff and haughty, she seldom carried out her public duties as empress, and was consequently unpopular. One reason for this was her constant anxiety about her son, Tsarevitch Alexei, who suffered from haemophilia and was often close to death. Alexandra befriended the mysterious and sinister 'holy man' Rasputin, who claimed to be able to cure Alexei's disease, inherited from his mother's side of the family. She perished with her husband and children, probably by being shot on the orders of Russia's revolutionary government in July, 1918.

ANNE (1665–1714) A daughter of King James II and cousin of King William III (of Orange), Anne became queen of Great Britain, in her own right, in 1702. Last of the Stuart monarchs, she was married to Prince George of Denmark, but all their children died young. Her reign is noted for the number of men of letters living at that time (sometimes termed Britain's Augustan Age), and also for the great victories won by the Duke of Marlborough (John Churchill) during the War of the Spanish Succession. Anne made the Duke's wife, Sarah, her friend and favourite for a long period; as the queen lacked self-confidence and seldom showed any initiative, Sarah Churchill wielded enormous influence at Court, until she eventually fell out of favour.

ANNE BOLEYN (1507–36) The second wife of King Henry VIII and mother of the future Queen Elizabeth I (q.v.). Formerly maid-in-waiting to Catherine of Aragon (q.v.), Anne enthusiastically supported her future husband's introduction of the Reformation, but her insolence caused a bitterly hostile faction to grow up. Henry eventually became disappointed at her inability to provide him with a male heir to the throne, and when her enemies accused Anne of adultery, she was beheaded on a charge of treason.

ANNE OF CLEVES (1515–57) King Henry VIII's fourth wife, Anne was chosen principally for political reasons because her brother, the Duke of Cleves, ruled a territory occupying a very important position on the lower Rhine. Henry, however, also looked forward to the marriage as he had been told that Anne was beautiful. Too late, he discovered that his new wife was exceedingly plain (she was sometimes

Queen Anne

Catherine II

referred to as 'the Flemish Mare'), and soon took steps to divorce her. Provided with a pension in 1540, Anne seems to have accepted the situation without rancour and settled down to a quiet life in England.

BEATRIX (1938–) Eldest daughter of ex-Queen Juliana (q.v.) and queen of the Netherlands since her mother's abdication, on retirement, in 1980. Born at Soestdijk Palace, she spent the war years abroad with her family, and then, as Crown Princess, married Claus von Amsberg in 1966. She has three sons, Willem-Alexander (1967), Johan Friss (1968) and Constantijn (1969).

BOADICEA (or BOUDICCA)
(AD 62) Queen of the Iceni, an East Anglian people, Boadicea led a revolt against Roman rule in England, largely because of the illtreatment of her family, following the death of her husband. The Celtic army, led by Queen Boadicea, stormed Camulodunum (Colchester), Verulamium (St Albans) and Londinium (London) in AD 61, reportedly killing some 70,000 Romans. The governor, Suetonius, however, soon brought up his trained Roman legions and defeated Boadicea's brave but ill-trained Britons. The queen

avoided being captured by the Romans by taking poison in AD 62.

CATHERINE OF ARAGON
(1485–1536) An attractive young lady of 24 when King Henry made her his first wife in 1509, Catherine of Aragon was described as being 'of a lively and gracious disposition'. Moreover, she proved to be a devoted wife, and an accomplished dancer, musician and English-speaker. After 18 years of marriage, however, Henry, already disturbed that Catherine's only living child was a girl – later to become Queen Mary I (q.v.) – and worried about the succession, became passionately fond of Anne Boleyn (q.v.), who, however, refused to be his mistress. Henry finally succeeded in divorcing Catherine in 1533.

CATHERINE THE GREAT (1729–96) Empress Catherine II of Russia was responsible for the considerable expansion of her country's boundaries as a result of the victories of her famous generals, Potemkin and Suvarov. By the treaty of Jassy, she obtained the fortress of Oczakov, and the region between the rivers Dnieper and Bug, on the Black Sea. She succeeded her husband, Peter III, when he was murdered and was a capable

Catherin de Medici

Elizabeth I

ruler for some time. Later, however, Catherine nearly·ruined Russia with the costs of her licentious excesses, and became known as the 'Semiramis of the North'.

CATHERINE HOWARD (?–1542) Unlucky fifth wife of King Henry VIII, whom he married in 1540 immediately following the divorce from Anne of Cleves (q.v.). Two years later, the king had Catherine beheaded.

CATHERINE DE MEDICI (1519–89) The wife of Henry II of France, Catherine was a woman who commanded great power and influence, particularly when acting as regent during the minority of Charles IX, her son. Two more of her sons became kings of France – Francis II and Henry III. Catherine had a great appreciation of literature and art, but she was a cruel woman. Her hostility to the French Protestants (or Huguenots) led to the infamous Bartholomew Massacre in Paris, on St Bartholomew's Day, 1572, when she organized the slaughter of a large number of them.

CATHERINE PARR (1512–48) King Henry VIII's sixth and last wife, whom he married in 1543. Catherine, the widow of Lord Latimer, made an

excellent wife for the king during his last four years.

CLEOPATRA (69–30 BC) The daughter of Ptolemy XII of Egypt, Cleopatra became joint ruler with a younger brother, Ptolemy XIII, at the age of 17. She later lost her authority and withdrew to Syria. Supported by Julius Caesar, Cleopatra succeeded in regaining the throne, Ptolemy XIII having been killed in the war and his successor, Ptolemy XIV, put to death by poisoning on her orders. Cleopatra then lived in Rome with Caesar until his assassination in 44 BC, when she returned to Egypt and declared her son by Caesar, Caesarion, joint monarch with her.

During the wars that followed Caesar's death, Cleopatra became the mistress of Mark Antony, but Octavian (later known as Augustus) declared war on them. After their naval defeat at Actium, in 31 BC, Antony committed suicide. Cleopatra failed to win Augustus over with her charms and, to avoid the ignominy of capture by the Romans, ended her life by poisoning, traditionally by means of an asp bite on her bosom. So, at only 39 years of age, this imperious, ambitious and intellectual queen died.

ELIZABETH I (1533–1603) Protestant Elizabeth followed her Roman Catholic half-sister Mary I (q.v.) to the throne of England in 1558. Intensely patriotic, courageous and strong-minded, she exerted a powerful influence on her country and, indeed, Europe generally. Elizabeth ruled well and presided over a period when England became a great power at sea, established colonies in the New World, and also shone in the literary sphere, notably because of the works of Shakespeare. Queen Elizabeth never married but had a number of Court favourites.

ELIZABETH II (1926–) The present queen of Great Britain and Northern Ireland – and monarch of several Commonwealth nations, besides acting as Head of the Commonwealth – Elizabeth came to the throne in 1952. She married her consort, Prince Philip, Duke of Edinburgh, in 1947; they have three sons, Charles, Prince of Wales (1948), Prince Andrew (1960) and Prince Edward (1964), and one daughter, Princess Anne (1950).

EUGENIE (1826–1920) As the wife of Napoleon III, Eugenie kept a brilliant Court but was forced to escape, in disguise, from Paris to England during the Franco–Prussian War. Joined by her husband, she lived in exile at Chislehurst, Kent, until his death, and then at Farnborough, in Hampshire.

ISABELLA OF CASTILE (1451–1504) She reigned over a united Spain jointly with her husband, Ferdinand V, and over a period of 30 years saw the country attain great power and authority. During their reign, Spaniards discovered America and began to establish an empire there. They also succeeded in ridding Spain of the Moors (Muslims).

JANE GREY (1537–54) The unfortunate daughter of the Duke of Suffolk and great-granddaughter of King Henry VII, Lady Jane Grey

became the tool of power-seekers. She was declared queen of England upon the death of Edward VI, to maintain the Protestant succession. Queen Mary I (q.v.), the rightful monarch, soon vanquished the Queen Jane faction by ousting her sixteen-year-old rival from the throne after a reign of only ten days. Jane and her husband, Lord Guildford Dudley, were executed some six months later.

JANE SEYMOUR (?–1537) Within a few days of the execution of Anne Boleyn (q.v.), King Henry VIII married Jane Seymour (1536), his third wife. She bore him his long-awaited son, Edward, in 1537 but unfortunately died within a few days of the birth.

JEZEBEL (died c.843 BC) The daughter of the priest-king Ethbaal, ruler of the cities of Tyre and Sidon, Jezebel married the ruler of Israel, King Ahab (ruled c.874–853 BC). She persuaded him to introduce the worship of the Tyrian god, Baal-Melkart, and tried to destroy anyone who opposed her. She had most of the prophets of Yahweh killed, and thus incurred the wrath of the prophet Elijah.

After Ahab had died in battle with the Syrians, Jezebel lived on for another ten years and her son Jehoram ruled. Elijah's successor, Elisha the prophet, had a military commander called Jehu anointed as king of Israel which led to a civil war. Jehu killed Jehoram and then went to Jezebel's palace. Jezebel, expecting him, adorned herself for the occasion and taunted him from a window. Jehu ordered her servants to throw her out of the window. Her body was never buried, as had been prophesied, because dogs devoured most of her remains.

JOSEPHINE (1763–1814) Napoleon Bonaparte married the widowed Josephine, formerly the wife of Vicomte Alexandre Beauharnais, in

Josephine

Maria Theresa

1796. She became empress when her husband was made Emperor Napoleon I of France in 1804. In 1809, however, Napoleon divorced Josephine, and it was her successor, Maria Louise, who bore him the son he desired to maintain the succession.

JULIANA (1909–) The daughter of Queen Wilhelmina (q.v.) of the Netherlands, Juliana succeeded her mother in 1948, when Wilhelmina decided to abdicate and retire from public life. Regarded with great affection by the Dutch people, Juliana helped her country enormously through the years of reconstruction after World War II. She followed the example of her mother by abdicating in 1980, in favour of her daughter Beatrix (q.v.), and went into well-earned retirement.

MARGRETHE II (1940–) She succeeded her father, King Frederick IX, in 1972, inheriting the throne of Denmark by virtue of a special act passed in 1953. It revised the country's law pertaining to royal succession and entitled her to become the first woman to reign over the country as monarch in her own right. Much travelled, Queen Margrethe was educated at Danish universities, Cambridge, the

London School of Economics and the Sorbonne, in Paris; her particular interest is archaeology.

MARIA THERESA (1717–80) This famous empress succeeded to the throne of Austria and its wide dominions in 1740 as a result of a special sanction executed by her father, Charles VI. Being a woman of remarkable ability and great strength of character, Maria Theresa succeeded, with the aid of allies such as Britain, in defeating those who challenged her right to rule during the War of the Austrian Succession. During her reign she did an enormous amount to enhance the prestige of the Austrian Empire.

MARIE ANTOINETTE (1755–93) The ill-fated daughter of Emperor Francis I of Austria, Marie Antoinette married King Louis XVI of France. She greatly enjoyed the gaiety of the French Court and became hated by the downtrodden mass of French people. Marie Antoinette was guillotined during the French Revolution which began in 1789.

MARY I (1516–58) Succeeding her half-brother, Edward VI, in 1553, this elder daughter of King Henry VIII reversed

her father's establishment of Protestantism in England. Almost a fanatical Roman Catholic, Queen Mary imprisoned, persecuted and burned at the stake hundreds of reformers whom she regarded as heretics. She married Philip of Spain in 1554 but had no children.

MARY II (1662–94) A daughter of King James II, Mary ruled Britain jointly with her husband and cousin, William IV (a Dutch prince known as William of Orange). She came to the throne in 1689 after her father fled into exile.

MARY STUART (1542–87) Mary, Queen of Scots, returned to Scotland after the death of her husband, the dauphin of France, and was recognized for some time as queen. Her marriage to Lord Darnley ended in his murder by Bothwell who then married Mary. The Scottish nobles were angered by these events and rebelled against the queen, who was forced to abdicate and eventually fled to England to seek Elizabeth I's (q.v.) protection. Elizabeth, however, imprisoned the exiled queen and, 19 years later, had her beheaded on a charge of conspiracy.

MATILDA (or Maud) (1102–67) After the death of her husband, Henry V

(Holy Roman Emperor), Matilda returned to England in 1125 and married Geoffrey of Anjou three years later. On the death of her father, King Henry I, in 1135, Matilda struggled to assert her claim to the throne, based upon the barons' pledge to recognize her as Henry's sole legitimate child. She lost the civil war to Stephen in 1142 and fled. Matilda's son, however, inherited the throne, as Henry II, on the death of King Stephen.

NEFERTITI (14th century BC) She was the wife of Pharaoh Akhnaton, 18th Dynasty King of Egypt. Akhnaton declared that the only god, Aton, was visible as the Sun's disk. He quarrelled with the priest of Amun, at Thebes, and then removed the capital to a new site, Tel-el-Amarna, and dedicated it to Aton. A fine sculptured head of Queen Nefertiti was discovered at Tel-el-Amarna and is now at the West Berlin Museum.

SHEBA, QUEEN OF (10th century BC) The Queen of Sheba ruled over a land in southern Arabia, now known as Yemen. It was rich by virtue of its control over an important trade route, particularly that of incense. The story of the Queen of Sheba's visit to King Solomon, the third king of Israel, is related in the Bible (1 Kings 10) and in the Koran. Known to Arab writers as Bilqis, she is reputed to have been the founder of the royal house of Ethiopia which was recently overthrown.

SOPHIA (or SOFIA) (1938–   ) The consort of King Juan Carlos I of Spain, whom she married in 1962. She has one son, Crown Prince Felipe (1968), and two daughters, Princess Elena (1963) and Princess Christina (1965). Sophia is the daughter of late King Paul of Greece and Queen Frederica; her brother is Constantine XII, ex-king of the Hellenes. A linguist, Queen Sophia has studied in Greece and Madrid, and at Salem College, Baden, in Germany.

VICTORIA (1819–1901) Queen of Great Britain and Ireland, and Empress of India, Victoria was only 18 when she came to the throne in 1837. She succeeded her uncle, King William IV. During her long and illustrious reign, the strength and power of Britain and the Empire increased enormously. Queen Victoria married Prince Albert of Saxe-Coburg-Gotha in 1840 and was criticized for virtually retiring from public life for many years after her consort's death in 1861. However, the Queen's influence and authority continued to be felt throughout the nation. Her closing years were marked with great public respect for her, and with the celebrations of her golden and diamond jubilees.

WILHELMINA (1880–1962) She became queen of the Netherlands in 1890 but her mother, Queen Emma, acted as regent until 1898. She reigned until 1948 (from overseas during World War II) and was held in great esteem by the Dutch people. After re-establishing the monarchy in the Netherlands following the war, Wilhelmina decided to abdicate and retired with the title of Princess of the Netherlands. She was succeeded by her daughter, Queen Juliana (q.v.).

Great Explorers

Amundsen, Roald ((1872-1928) The first explorer to sail through the Northwest Passage, and also to reach the South Pole. Aboard the *Gjoa*, this famous Norwegian navigated the Northwest Passage during the years 1903–6 and then, in 1911, beat his great rival, Scott, to the South Pole, arriving there on 14 December.
Baffin, William (1584-1622) English discoverer, in 1616, of the bay which bears his name. It lies between the northeast coast of Canada and Greenland.
Bering, Vitus (1680-1741) A Dane who entered into the service of Russia, Bering gave his name to the strait between the USSR and the USA's state of Alaska.
Cabot, John (1450-*c*. 1500) Born in Genoa, John Cabot went to live in Bristol, England. In 1497 he received letters-patent from King Henry VII to voyage westwards.
Burton, Sir Richard Francis (1821-90) Principally known for his exploration of Central Africa, this English linguist (he mastered 35 languages) discovered Lake Tanganyika in 1858. He also travelled from Afghanistan to Mecca in 1853, disguised as a pilgrim.

Columbus

Cook

He discovered Newfoundland and Nova Scotia, and possibly the American mainland ahead of Columbus – lands which he believed were part of eastern Asia.

Cabot, Sebastian (1474-1557) The son of John Cabot, Sebastian was born in Venice. He sailed as far as Hudson Bay, in search of a north-west passage to Asia, and then, in 1512, explored the Plate and Paraná rivers in South America for Spain. In the service of England, Sebastian Cabot sought a means of reaching India by way of a northeast passage, which opened up trade with Russia.

Cameron, Verney Lovett (1844-1894) An English explorer, Cameron was the first man to cross the continent of Africa from east to west. He also surveyed Lake Tanganyika and set out to look for Livingstone in 1872.

Cartier, Jacques (1494-1557) Born in St Malo, this French navigator was responsible for considerable exploration of Canada, particularly the St Lawrence gulf and river.

Columbus, Christopher (c.1451-1506) Christopher Columbus was born in Genoa. He set off on his famous voyage from Spain with the financial backing of King Ferdinand and Queen Isabella. He reached the Bahamas and Cuba in 1492, and the mainland of America in 1498.

Cook, James (1728-79) An English sailor and officer in the British Royal Navy, Cook commanded the *Endeavour, Resolution* and *Adventure* on Pacific Ocean voyages which led to the charting of a great deal of the coastlines of Australia and New Zealand. On his first expedition, in 1770, he found so many interesting plants in one area of Australia that he named it Botany Bay. Cook also surveyed the coast of Newfoundland and reached the Hawaiian Islands, where he met his death at the hands of the inhabitants.

Cortés, Hernando (1488-1547) Responsible for opening up the land of Mexico for his native Spain, Cortés conquered a vast region with a handful of men and destroyed the ancient Aztec civilization which existed there.

Dampier, William (1652-1715) This English seaman succeeded in sailing right round the world. He explored Australian waters and rescued Alexander Selkirk, the castaway who became the model for Defoe's character Robinson Crusoe.

Davis, John (*c.* 1550-1605) Discoverer of Davis Strait, between Canada's Baffin Island and Greenland. This Elizabethan sailor from Devonshire, in England, invented the backstaff, or Davis's quadrant, a nautical instrument for measuring the height of the Sun.

Diaz, Bartholomew (*c.* 1445-1500) A Portuguese navigator who explored the West African coast and then, during a storm, rounded the Cape of Good Hope.

Diemen, Anthony Van (1593-1645) As Dutch governor-general in the Far East, Van Diemen promoted exploration which led to Tasman's discovery of New Zealand and the naming of Van Diemen's Land, now known as Tasmania.

Drake, Sir Francis (*c.* 1540-96) The English seaman who, in 1577-1580, sailed round the world aboard the *Golden Hind.* Renowned for his exploits against the Spaniards, this Devon-born sailor died at sea off Panama.

Eric the Red (10th century) A leading Viking explorer, who is believed to have discovered and named Greenland, possibly in the year 982.

Ericsson, Leif (10th century) Credited with finding North America and landing on its coast, Leif Ericsson was another of the great sailor-explorers of this period from Scandinavia.

Flinders, Matthew (1774-1814) A navigator from England who made a number of discoveries in and around the continent of Australia. Bass Strait, through which Flinders sailed, was named in honour of his surgeon. His own name was given to the largest island in the Furneaux

Group off Tasmania, and also to a chain of mountains in South Australia.

Frobisher, Sir Martin (1535-94) An English seaman from Yorkshire, Frobisher made three voyages in search of the Northwest Passage, via Arctic waters, from the Atlantic Ocean to the Pacific. His great exploratory ventures are commemorated at Frobisher Bay, on Canada's Baffin Island.

Fuchs, Sir Vivian Ernest (1908-) Leader of the British Commonwealth Trans-Antarctic Expedition, 1957-8, Fuchs was the first explorer who succeeded in crossing the continent of Antarctica.

Gama, Vasco da (*c.* 1460-1524) A great Portuguese navigator who, by rounding the Cape of Good Hope in 1498, discovered and opened up the sea route to India.

Henry the Navigator (1394-1460) This famous prince was the son of King John I of Portugal. He organized important voyages of exploration, a result of which was the discovery of Madeira and the Azores, both of which remain Portuguese possessions to this day.

Hudson, Henry (died 1611) This English sailor, of whom nothing is known prior to 1607, discovered the Hudson River, Strait and Bay which are named after him. On his last voyage, Hudson's crew mutinied and set him adrift to die in the cold waters of northeast Canada.

Humboldt, Friedrich Heinrich Alexander, Baron Von (1769-1859) This German naturalist explored South America. He recorded his experiences in *Voyage de Humboldt* (1805-34) and *Kosmos* (1845).

Drake

Livingstone

Jansz, Willem (17th century) A Dutch Pacific explorer, Jansz unwittingly discovered Australia in 1606 while searching for New Guinea. He reached Torres Strait a few weeks before Torres himself.

Livingstone, David (1813-73) A renowned Scottish explorer and missionary who travelled widely in southern Africa. He discovered the course of the Zambezi River, the Victoria Falls and Lake Malawi (then named Lake Nyasa). Livingstone fought very hard against the slave trade. Believed lost on one of his expeditions, he was found by Stanley (q.v.) on 10 November 1871.

Magellan, Ferdinand (*c*. 1480-1521) In 1519, Magellan, a Portuguese sailor, became the first expedition commander to sail round the world. He successfully navigated the winding passage, 787 km (365 miles) in length and named after him, separating the tip of mainland South America and the island of Tierra del Fuego.

Mawson, Sir Douglas (1882-1958) A notable explorer of the Antarctic, Mawson took part in the Shackleton expedition, before leading the Australian Antarctic Expedition of

1911-14 and the British-Australian and New Zealand Expedition of 1929-31. In 1912, he was the only survivor of his party, which endured dreadful conditions and suffering.

Nansen, Fridijof (1861-1930) A Nobel peace-prize winner in 1922, this Norwegian explorer wrote an account of his north-polar expedition of 1893 in *Farthest North*. On that occasion, Nansen's party reached 86° 14′ – at that time the highest latitude achieved.

Oates, Lawrence Edward (1880-1912) The English Antarctic explorer who reached the South Pole with Scott (q.v.) and three others. On the return journey he deliberately left his companions in camp, to go out into a blizzard and meet his death, because his severe frost-bite was holding up the party's progress.

Park, Mungo (1771-1806) Author of *Travels in the Interior of Africa* (1799), Mungo Park was a Scottish explorer in the area of West Africa. He explored the course of the River Niger, in which he was drowned.

Parry, Sir William Edward (1790-1855) Rear-Admiral Parry, R.N., was an English commander of

167

Marco Polo

Raleigh

expeditions in the Arctic, where he made a number of important discoveries and attempted to reach the North Pole.

Peary, Robert Edwin (1856-1920) An American Rear-Admiral and Arctic explorer, Peary first conducted a sledging expedition towards the North Pole in 1891–2. Further expeditions took place in the Arctic in 1893, 1895, 1898, 1900–2 and 1906. Finally, on 6 April 1909, Peary succeeded in reaching the Pole.

Polo, Marco (1256-1323) Setting out from his native Venice, Marco Polo carried out amazing journeys – considered incredible in his day and age – through China, India and other eastern lands. He visited Kublai Khan, and wrote the story of his wonderful travels, experiences and discoveries.

Raleigh, Sir Walter (1552-1618) In 1584, this prominent English seaman started the colonization of Virginia, and he was responsible for the introduction of potatoes and tobacco to Europe. After a spell of 12 years as a prisoner in the Tower of London, Raleigh was released in 1615 by King James I to head an expedition to the region of the

Orinoco River, in northern South America, to search for gold. The failure of Raleigh's mission led to his execution.

Ross, Sir James Clark (1800-62) Accompanying his uncle, Sir John Ross (q.v.) on expeditions to the Arctic, Sir James Ross achieved distinction. He later commanded his own expedition (1839–43) to the Antarctic, during which he discovered the Ross ice barrier. Earlier, in 1831, he was responsible for discovering the North Magnetic Pole.

Ross, Sir John (1777-1856) A Rear-Admiral and eminent Scottish Polar explorer (the uncle of Sir James Ross), Sir John Ross searched for the Northwest Passage and found Boothia Peninsula, on the Arctic coast of Canada.

Scott, Robert Falcon (1868-1912) This English Antarctic explorer was the leader of two expeditions. The first, in 1901–4, resulted in the discovery of King Edward VII Land. The second expedition left in 1910 aboard the *Terra Nova* and reached the South Pole on 18 January 1912, only to find that Amundsen had already reached it on 14 December 1911. The party of five all perished

on their journey back to base.
**Shackleton, Sir Henry Ernest
(1874-1922)** Commander of the
Nimrod Farthest South expedition
of 1907–9, Shackleton reached a
point within 160 km (100 miles) of
the South Pole. On his fourth
expedition, a scientific voyage to
the Antarctic, the explorer died.
Smith, John (1580-1631) This noted
English seafarer and adventurer
carried out a colonizing and
pioneering expedition to Virginia
in 1605. During an expedition among
the Red Indians his life is said to
have been saved by Pocahontas, the
daughter of the Indian chief who
had captured him.
Soto, Hernando De (*c.* 1500-42)
A Spaniard, De Soto discovered
what is now Florida and Georgia in
southern USA, and also the
Mississippi River.
Speke, John Hanning (1827-64) A
British explorer, Captain Speke
first discovered Lake Victoria in
1858. Accompanied by Lt.-Col.
J. A. Grant, he then went on in
1860 to locate the River Nile
flowing out of the great lake.
**Stanley, Sir Henry Morton
(1841-1904)** Born at Denbigh, Wales,
Stanley went to the USA where he
fought on the Confederate side in
the American Civil War and then
became a *New York Herald*
correspondent. His newspaper
appointed Stanley to find the lost
explorer Livingstone (q.v.). He was
successful at Ujiji in 1871, and the
two men then explored Lake
Tanganyika. Stanley founded the
Congo Free State for Belgium in
1879.
**Stefansson, Vilhjalmur (1879-
1962)** Of Icelandic parentage, this
Canadian explorer carried out a lot
of valuable work in the Arctic
region, and recorded his findings in
Unsolved Mysteries of the Arctic.
**Tasman, Abel Janszoon (1603-
1659)** Sent on a voyage of discovery
by Van Diemen (q.v.), Tasman, a
Dutch navigator, reached the
Australian island of Tasmania
(formerly Van Diemen's Land) and
New Zealand in 1642.
Vespucci, Amerigo (1454-1512) A
Florentine merchant and explorer-
navigator, Vespucci went on
voyages across the Atlantic Ocean.
He travelled along the coast of
South America and discovered the
Rio de la Plata. The continent was
later called after his first name.

MYTHOLOGY

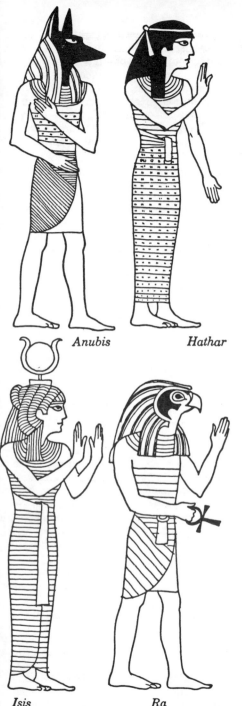

Anubis

Hathar

Isis

Ra

ANCIENT EGYPTIAN MYTHOLOGY

Ammon or **Amun** The chief god of upper Egypt, later identified with the Sun god Ra.

Anubis The son of Nephthys and Ra (or Osiris), his duty was to weigh the soul of a deceased person. If the soul was below standard it was eaten by a horrible monster. Anubis was represented with the head of a jackal.

Apis, or **Hapi** A sacred black bull worshipped at Memphis. The spirit of the god Osiris was thought to be living in the bull.

Atum Originally a local deity of Heliopolis, the Atum myth became merged with that of the Sun god Ra, giving rise to the deity Atum-Ra.

Bast or **Bastet**, Cat-headed goddess, the daughter of Isis. She was the goddess of the city of Bubastis in lower Egypt and of the kindly rays of the Sun as opposed to the fierce, harmful rays whose goddess was Sekhmet, Bast's sister.

Bes or **Bisu** God of recreation, represented as a dwarf with a large head, goggle eyes, protruding tongue, bow legs and bushy tail. Bes was often associated with children and childbirth.

Hathor or **Athor** Goddess of the sky and wife of Horus also considered to be the goddess of festivity, dance and love. She became identified with Isis. Hathor was sometimes represented with the head of a cow.

Horus The son of Osiris and Isis, the god of light who overcame darkness – he was believed to be the life-giving power of the Sun. A scorpion sent by the wicked god Set stung him to death, but he was revived by Isis with the help of the god Thoth.

Isis The sister-wife of Osiris and mother of Horus, Isis was the goddess of the Earth and of the Moon. She also

171

ruled in the underworld where she meted out rewards and punishments.

Keb or **Seb** A son of Shu and Tefnut (or of Ra), Keb was the god of the Earth and its vegetation. He was represented with the head of a goose.

Mut or **Maut** The wife of Ra or Amun and called the mother of the gods and mistress of the sky. Mut was represented with the head of a lioness or of a vulture (the symbol of maternity).

Nephthys or **Nebt-Het** A goddess of the dead, sister of Isis and wife of Isis' brother Set.

Nut Daughter of Shu and Tefnut, Nut was married to her own brother, Keb. She became the mother of Osiris, Isis, Set and Nephthys. Like Mut, she was called the mother of the gods, and was associated with childbirth and nursing.

Osiris Son of Keb and Nut, brother-husband of Isis and father of Horus, Osiris was the principle of Good. His foe was his brother Set, the god of evil and darkness who finally killed him and cut his body into 14 pieces. Isis collected all the pieces except one and buried them. According to one myth the pieces joined together again and the body became alive. Thus Osiris became the god of resurrection and life eternal, the lord of the underworld and judge of the dead.

Ptah, Neph, Num or **Nu** The maker of the Sun, the Moon and the Earth and everything in or on it including men and gods. He was represented as a potter at his wheel, often with a ram's head.

Ra or **Re** God of the Sun, Ra was represented as a hawk, or as a man with a hawk's head, on top of which was the red disc of the Sun or a snake (symbol of supreme power). His emblem was the scarab beetle.

Sekhmet or **Sekhet** Wife of Ptah and sister of Bast, Sekhmet was the fierce goddess of war and destroyer of the enemies of the Sun god, Ra. She was considered to be the eye of Ra and was placed as the uraeus serpent on Ra's head. Sekhmet was represented as a lioness or as a woman with a lioness' head on which was placed the solar disc and uraeus.

Set or **Seth** Regarded as either the brother or son of Osiris. Once a sky god, represented by a falcon he was both a partner and rival of Horus. When the cult of Osiris gained in popularity the myth developed that Seth was his murderer.

Shu Twin brother and husband of Tefnut, Shu was the god of light, air and the supporter of the sky.

Tefnut Twin sister of Shu and mother of Keb, Tefnut was the goddess of the waters above the heavens.

Thoth The god of learning, wisdom and of writing. In the underworld, Thoth kept accounts of the weight of souls, handing them to Osiris who judged them. Thoth was also god of the Moon, at which time he was represented with a crescent and disc. He was usually depicted with the head of an ibis.

CLASSICAL MYTHOLOGY

Acheron The river across which the dead are carried by Charon.

Achilles A strong and handsome Grecian hero of the Trojan war. One of the legends concerning him was that Thetis, his mother, dropped him in the river Styx as a baby to make him immortal, but she forgot to immerse his heel by which she was holding him. Achilles later died from a death-wound in the heel.

Actaeon A hunter, who was changed into a stag by Artemis because he had seen her bathing.

Adonis A beautiful youth beloved by Aphrodite. Jealous Hephaestus transformed himself into a boar which Adonis followed in the hunt, and the boar killed him.

Aesculapius or **Asclepius** The god of medicine.

Agamemnon Commander in chief of

he Greeks during the Trojan war.
Alcmene Wife of Amphitryon. Zeus,
disguised as her husband who was then
away on a journey, seduced her. To
Alcmene then was born Heracles.
Amazons A race of warlike females
said to have come from the Caucasus
and to have settled in Asia Minor.
Amphitrite Wife of Poseidon.
Andromeda Daughter of Cepheus,
king of Ethiopia, and Cassiopia. She
was offered as a sacrifice to a sea
monster that was sent by Poseidon to
lay waste to the country, but Perseus
slew the monster and saved her.
Antigone Daughter of Oedipus. She
accompanied her blind father when he
was forced to leave Thebes.
Aphrodite The goddess of love and
beauty, the daughter of Zeus and a
female Titan, Dione.
Apollo Son of Zeus and Leto, twin
brother of Artemis. Apollo was the god
of music, song and poetry, of
agriculture and the pastoral life.
Originally he was a god of light, who
thus made plants grow and fruits ripen.
Apollo never married.
Arachne A maiden who challenged
Athena in a test of weaving skill. The
girl's work was flawless and the angry
Athena changed her into a spider.
Ares The god of war. Ares was the son
of Zeus and Hera. He loved, and was
beloved by, Aphrodite.
Argonauts Sailors of the ship *Argo*
who were the heroes who sailed with
Jason to fetch the golden fleece.
Argus The 100-eyed guardian of the
cow into which Io, beloved of Zeus, had
been transformed by Zeus to escape the
wrath of Hera.
Ariadne Daughter of Minos, king of
Crete, who helped Theseus find his way
out of the maze known as the
Labyrinth after killing the Minotaur.
Artemis Unmarried daughter of Zeus
and Leto, twin-sister of Apollo, goddess
of hunting and the Moon. Artemis
often sent affliction and death to
mankind but sometimes cured or

Athena

alleviated suffering.
Atalanta The most swift-footed of
mortals. Atalanta required her suitors
to beat her in a foot-race and if they
failed they forfeited their lives. A
suitor, Melanion, dropped three golden
apples given to him by Aphrodite,
during his race with Atalanta.
Atalanta stopped to pick up the apples
and lost the race.
Athena, Athene or **Pallas Athena**
Unmarried daughter of Zeus and Metis.
Before birth Athena swallowed her
mother and afterwards sprang from the
head of Zeus in complete armour. She
was the goddess of wisdom and of war,
and the protector of Athens. She was
also the goddess of weaving and
agriculture.
Atlas A Titan who, along with the
other Titans, made war on Zeus. On
being conquered he was condemned to
hold up the heavens.
Bellerophon Son of the Corinthian
king Glaucus, he was sent to kill the
monster known as the Chimera, which
he did with the help of the winged
horse Pegasus.
Callisto A nymph beloved by Zeus who
changed her into a she-bear. During a
hunt, Hera caused Artemis to slay
Callisto whereupon Zeus placed her
among the stars.
Cassiopia The mother of Andromeda.

Diana

She also was placed among the stars.

Castor Brother of Pollux. *See* Dioscuri.

Centaurs Half men and half horses, they inhabited Mount Pelion in Thessaly.

Cepheus King of Ethiopia, husband of Cassiopia and father of Andromeda. He was placed among the stars after his death.

Cerberus A monstrous dog with several heads who guarded the entrance of Hades.

Chaos The empty space that existed prior to the creation of the world.

Charon The being usually described as an old man who conveyed the spirits of the dead across the rivers of the underworld in his boat. For this service he was paid with a coin placed in the mouth of every corpse.

Chimera A fire-breathing monster whose body consisted of the fore-parts of a lion, the middle part of a goat and the hind parts of a dragon. She was killed by Bellerophon.

Chiron The wisest of the Centaurs. Hercules accidentally killed Chiron with a poisoned arrow when Chiron was fighting with the other Centaurs. Zeus placed him among the stars as Sagittarius.

Clytemnestra The unfaithful wife of Agamemnon. She murdered her husband on his return from Troy and

was killed in revenge by her son Orestes.

Cronus Youngest of the Titans, a son of Ouranus (Heaven) and Gaea (Earth) Cronus dethroned his father and out of the drops of his blood sprang the Gigantes while from the foam gathering around his limbs in the sea Aphrodite was formed.

Cyclops A race of gigantic shepherds in Sicily each of whom had one eye in the centre of his forehead. They devoured human beings. The chief among them, Polyphemus, was blinded by Odysseus.

Daedalus To escape from Minos, king of Crete, Daedalus made wings for his son Icarus and himself which he fastened with wax. Unfortunately Icarus flew too close to the Sun, the wax melted and he fell to his death.

Danaë Daughter of Acrisius, king of Argos, and the mother of Perseus by Zeus. Zeus visited her in a shower of gold while she was imprisoned in a tower by her father.

Daphne A nymph who, pursued by Apollo, prayed for aid and as a result was transformed into a laurel tree.

Demeter or **Cores** A daughter of Cronus and Rhea, sister of Zeus and mother of Persephone. She was protectoress of agriculture and all the fruits of the earth. When her daughter was carried off by Hades she would not allow the earth to produce any fruits. Zeus sent Hermes to fetch Persephone back but she had eaten part of a pomegranate in the lower world and was therefore obliged to spend a third of each year in Hades.

Deucalion Son of Prometheus and king of Phthia in Thessaly. When Zeus decided to destroy mankind because of its iniquity Deucalion and his wife Pyrrha were saved on account of their piety. They built a ship which floated safely on the flood-waters which destroyed the rest of the human race.

Dione A female Titan, beloved by Zeus by whom she became the mother of the godess Aphrodite.

Dionysus The son of Zeus and a maiden, Semele. He was the god of wine.

Dioscuri The twin sons of Zeus, Castor and Pollux. Pollux was immortal but Castor was subject to old age and death. Pollux was allowed by Zeus to share his brother's fate. He lived alternately one day in the underworld and one day in the heavens with the gods. Castor and Pollux appear as stars in the constellation Gemini (The Twins).

Echo A nymph who used to engage Hera's attention by talking to her while Zeus sported with other nymphs. When Hera discovered the trick she punished her by changing her into an echo. Because of her unrequited love for Narcissus, Echo pined away, leaving nothing but her voice.

Electra Daughter of Agamemnon and Clytemnestra, sister of Iphigenia and Orestes. After her mother murdered her father Electra saved the life of Orestes. She incited him to avenge their father's death.

Elysium A happy land where favoured heroes went instead of going through death. Also part of the underworld where the shades of the blessed had their abode.

Endymion A youth of extraordinary beauty who perpetually slept.

Eos Goddess of the dawn.

Eros Son of Aphrodite, and the god of love. He is represented as a small boy, beautiful but wanton, with a bow and arrows.

Eumenides, Erinyes *see* the Furies.

Europa Daughter of a Phoenician king whose beauty caught the eye of Zeus. The god changed himself into a bull who was so tame that Europa was tempted to climb upon its back. The bull carried her off as far as Crete where she became the mother of Minos.

Eurydice The wife of Orpheus. He tried, without success, to rescue her from the underworld.

Fates (Moerae) The goddesses of fate, three in number. They are described either as old, hideous women or as grave maidens. One, sometimes all three, carry a spindle and they are said to cut off the thread of life when it comes to an end.

Furies, The (Eumenides, Erinyes) Three avenging deities represented as winged monsters with serpents twined in their hair and blood dripping from their eyes. The Furies lived in the depths of Tartarus. They punished the living and the dead for their crimes.

Gaea or **Ge** The personification of the Earth and the first being that sprang from Chaos. She gave birth to Ouranus (Heaven) and Pontus (Sea), and was the mother of the Titans by Cronus.

Galatea A sea nymph beloved by Polyphemus the Cyclops.

Ganymede The most beautiful of all mortals who was carried off by the gods to fill the cup of Zeus. Ganymede is placed among the stars as Aquarius.

Gigantes Giants who sprang from the blood of the mutilated Ouranus. They had legs like serpents and feet formed of reptiles' heads.

Gorgons Three frightful female creatures, Stheno, Euryale and Medusa. They had wings, claws, enormous teeth and serpents on their heads instead of hair. Medusa alone was mortal. She was once a maiden whom Athena had changed into a Gorgon. Anyone who looked at her was changed to stone.

Graces, The (Charites) Goddesses of fertility, charm and beauty they were daughters of Zeus and Hera. Three in number, their names were Aglaea (Brightness), Euphrosyne (Joyfulness) and Thalia (Bloom).

Hades Son of Cronus and Rhea, brother of Zeus and Poseidon, Hades was god of the underworld and of metals. His wife was Persephone, daughter of Demeter. He stole her from the upper world.

Harpies Wind spirits often represented

as winged maidens or as birdlike monsters with the heads of maidens. The Harpies were said to have snatched away people who had disappeared.

Hebe The goddess of youth, a daughter of Zeus and Hera. She married Heracles after he became a god.

Hecate A goddess of the Moon, the Earth and the underworld and one of the Titans. She is represented with three bodies and three heads. A teacher of sorcery and witchcraft, at night she sent forth phantoms from the underworld.

Helen Daughter of Zeus and Leda, sister of Castor and Pollux and a renowned beauty. She married Menelaus but was seduced by Paris who carried her off to Troy. The Trojan war was the result.

Helios God of the Sun, Helios was the son of Hyperion and Thea and brother of Selene (the Moon) and Eos (Dawn).

Hephaestus The god of fire and of the blacksmith's art, son of Zeus and Hera. He was born lame and weak and so was disliked by his mother who threw him down from Olympus.

Hera A daughter of Cronus and Rhea, sister and wife of Zeus, Hera was goddess of marriage and of the birth of children. Jealous and quarrelsome, she persecuted the children of Zeus born of mortal mothers and hence was the enemy of Dionysus and Heracles among others.

Heracles The most famous Greek legendary hero, Heracles was the son of Zeus and Alcmene and a descendant of Perseus. Zeus swore that the next son born in the line of Perseus should become ruler of Greece but by a trick of Hera another child, Eurystheus, was born first and became king. When Heracles grew up he had to serve him. Eurystheus imposed on Heracles the twelve famous labours, including slaying the Nemean lion, cleansing the Augean stables, fetching the golden apples of the Hesperides and bringing

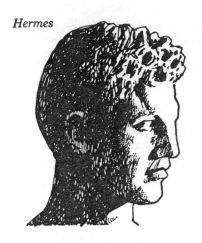
Hermes

back Cerberus from the underworld.

Hermes Son of Zeus and Maia, the daughter of Atlas, Hermes was the messenger of the gods. He himself was the god of prudence, cunning, trickery and theft, the alphabet, numbers, astronomy, music, gymnastics, weights and measures, commerce and riches, and of good luck. He also protected travellers. Hermes is represented with a winged hat, a staff bearing either ribbons or serpents and winged sandles.

Hesperides The guardians of the golden apples which Gaea gave to Hera at her marriage to Zeus.

Hestia A daughter of Cronus and Rhea who swore to remain a virgin. Hestia was the goddess of the fire burning on the hearth.

Horae Daughters of Zeus and Themis, the Horae were goddesses of the seasons.

Hyades Seven nymphs entrusted by Zeus to care for his infant son Dionysus. They were afterwards placed among the stars.

Hydra A gigantic monster with many heads, the centre one being immortal. The destruction of Hydra was one of the 12 labours of Heracles.

Hygiea Daughter or wife of Aesculapius and goddess of health.

Hymen God of marriage, represented

as an extremely handsome youth.

Hyperion A Titan, son of Ouranus and Gaea, father of Helios, Selene and Eos. He was sometimes identified with Helios himself.

Hypnus The god of sleep.

Iapetus A Titan, father of Atlas, Prometheus and Epimetheus.

Icarus The son of Daedalus (*q.v.*).

Io Daughter of the king of Argos. She was changed by Zeus, who loved her, into a cow to hide her from his jealous wife Hera. Hera, undeceived, put her in charge of Argus who was subsequently slain by Hermes at the command of Zeus. Hera then tormented Io with a gadfly which drove her from land to land. Eventually she found rest on the banks of the Nile and bore Zeus a son, Epaphus.

Iphigenia Daughter of Agamemnon and Clytemnestra. Her father killed a hart in a grove sacred to Artemis, angering the goddess who thereupon becalmed the Greek fleet which was about to sail for Troy. To placate Artemis, Iphigenia was offered as a sacrifice to her, but Artemis put a hart in Iphigenia's place and carried the maiden away.

Irene Goddess of peace, one of the Horae.

Iris Personfication of the rainbow, a sister of the Harpies.

Jason Leader of the Argonauts who set off to fetch the golden fleece in the possession of the king of Colchis and which was guarded by a dragon.

Leda Mother of Castor and Pullux, Clytemnestra and Helen. Zeus, the father, visited Leda in the guise of a swan.

Lethe A river in the underworld from which the dead drank to obtain forgetfulness.

Leto Daughter of the Titan Coeus and Phoebe, mother of Apollo and Artemis by Zeus.

Maia A daughter of Atlas and the eldest and most beautiful of the Pleiades sisters. She was the mother of

the god Hermes by Zeus.

Medea Daughter of the king of Colchis and skilled in magic. She assisted Jason in obtaining the golden fleece. Medea afterwards became Jason's wife but he deserted her and in revenge she murdered their two children.

Medusa *see* Gorgons.

Menelaus Younger brother of Agamemnon and husband of Helen.

Midas King of Phrygia, renowned for his riches. As a reward for his kindness a satyr agreed to grant him a wish. Midas wished that everything he touched should turn to gold.

Minos The son of Zeus and Europa, and king of Crete. Minos made war against the Athenians and ordered them to send a yearly tribute of seven youths and seven maidens to be fed to the Minotaur.

Minotaur Cretan monster, half man, half bull, kept in the maze called the Labyrinth.

Mnemosyne Memory, the daughter of Ouranus and mother of the Muses by Zeus.

Moerae *see* The Fates.

Morpheus The son of Hypnus and god of dreams.

Muses, The Nine daughters of Zeus and Mnemosyne, goddesses of the different arts and sciences. They were: Clio of history; Euterpe of lyric poetry; Thalia of humorous and idyllic poetry; Melpomene of tragedy; Terpsichore of dance and song; Erato of love poetry and mimicry; Polymnia of sacred poetry; Urania of astronomy, and Calliope of epic poetry.

Narcissus A beautiful youth who fell deeply in love with his own reflection in a pool and pined away. He was changed into the flower that bears his name.

Nemesis Goddess of fertility, and who meted out retribution to mortals for their wrongdoing.

Nymphs Lesser female divinities divided into groups according to the part of nature they were associated with: Oceanides, the oceans; Nereides, the Mediterranean sea; Naiades, fresh water (rivers, lakes and springs); Oreades, mountains and grottoes; Napaeae, glens; gryades and Hamadryades, trees.

Oceanus God of the water which was believed to surround the Earth. He was the husband of Tethys and father of the river gods and water nymphs.

Odysseus Grecian hero of the Trojan war. After the destruction of Troy he set off on a journey full of adventure which is related in Homer's Odyssey.

Oedipus Son of Laius, king of Thebes who, learning from an oracle that he would die by the hands of his own son, exposed Oedipus on a mountainside at birth. The baby, however, was found by a shepherd who reared him as his own son. Oedipus later killed his father and then married his mother not knowing that they were his real parents. When he discovered what he had done he put out his own eyes.

Olympus A high snow-covered peak which was the residence of the Grecian gods.

Orestes Son of Agamemnon and Clytemnestra.

Orion A giant and a hunter. He fell in love with a maiden, Merope, but her exasperated father deprived him of his sight with the help of Dionysus. Orion recovered his sight by exposing his eyes to the Sun's rays. On his death he was placed among the stars.

Orpheus A poet who received his lyre from Apollo and was instructed in its use by the Muses. Wild beasts, and even trees and rocks, were charmed by his music. When his wife Eurydice died from a serpent bite he followed her to Hades. He was allowed to have his wife back provided he did not look back upon her until they arrived in the upper world. To make sure she was following Orpheus did look behind him, and so lost her. His lyre can be found among the stars.

Ouranus Personification of Heaven.

Called the son, sometimes the husband, of Gaea (Earth). Ouranus hated his children and always confined them to Tartarus as soon as they were born. As a result, he was overthrown by his son Cronus.

Pan God of shepherds and their flocks, a son of Hermes. Pan is represented as a man with horns and a goat's hind legs, sometimes playing the syrinx.

Pandora The first woman on Earth. She had a jar, or box, containing every kind of evil. When it was opened the evils spread all over the world – only Hope remained.

Pegasus A winged horse which sprang from the blood of Medusa when her head was struck off by Perseus. He is found among the stars.

Penelope Wife of Odysseus, king of Ithaca.

Persephone The daughter of Zeus and Demeter, she was carried off by Hades who made her his wife.

Perseus The son of Zeus and Danaë, Perseus was the hero who cut off the head of the Gorgon Medusa.

Phaeton A son of Helios (the Sun). On being allowed to drive his father's chariot of the Sun across the sky he came too close to the earth and almost set it on fire. Zeus immediately killed him with a flash of lightning.

Phoebe Another name for Artemis as goddess of the Moon.

Phoebus Another name for Apollo as a Sun god.

Pleiades The daughters of Atlas and companions of Artemis. Pursued by Orion the hunter, they prayed to be rescued from him. The gods changed them into doves and set them among the stars.

Pollux Brother of Castor. *See* Dioscuri.

Polyphemus *see* Cyclops.

Poseidon A son of Cronus and Rhea, brother of Zeus and Hades, Poseidon was god of the sea.

Prometheus The son of the Titan Iapetus and a brother of Atlas, he stole fire from heaven and taught mortals all the useful arts. Zeus chained him to a rock where he was exposed to eternal torture. Every day an eagle fed on his liver which was always restored again during the nights.

Proteus An old man who could foretell the future. At midday he would rise from the sea and this was the only time he could be caught by anyone wanting to know the future. He would, however, cunningly change himself into all manner of different forms to avoid having to tell what he knew.

Psyche The personification of the human soul. Psyche was the daughter of a king. She aroused the jealousy of Aphrodite because of her beauty. The goddess ordered Cupid to cause Psyche to marry the most despicable of all men. But Cupid himself fell in love with her and visited her in the dark of night. One night she approached him carrying a lamp but, unfortunately, a drop of hot oil fell on Cupid who awoke and fled.

Rhea or **Cybele** Goddess of the Earth, daughter of Ouranus and Gaea. The wife of Cronus, she became the mother of Hestia, Demeter, Hera, Hades, Poseidon and Zeus.

Satyrs Beings, part man and part beast, associated with Dionysus. They represented the powers of nature.

Selene Moon goddess, sister of Helios (the Sun), and later identified with Artemis.

Semele A maiden beloved by Zeus, mother of Dionysus.

Styx The river which flows seven times around the underworld.

Tantalus A king who incurred the wrath of the gods. His punishment in the underworld was to suffer from a raging thirst whilst in the middle of a lake whose waters always receded from him when he tried to drink.

Tartarus Another name for Hades, or the lowest depth of Hades which was reserved for the rebel Titans.

Tethys Daughter of Ouranus and Gaea, wife of Oceanus and mother of

Zeus

the Oceanides.

Theseus Grecian hero who slew the Cretan Minotaur.

Titans Offspring of Ouranus (Heaven)

ROMAN EQUIVALENTS OF SOME CHARACTERS IN GREEK MYTHOLOGY

Aurora	=	Eos
Bacchus	=	Dionysus
Ceres	=	Demeter
Cupid	=	Eros
Diana	=	Artemis
Fauns	=	Satyrs
Fortuna	=	Tyche
Hercules	=	Heracles
Iuventas	=	Hebe
Juno	=	Hera
Jupiter	=	Zeus
Latona	=	Leto
Mars	=	Ares
Mercury	=	Hermes
Minerva	=	Athena
Neptune	=	Poseidon
Pax	=	Irene
Pluto	=	Hades
Proserpina	=	Persephone
Saturn	=	Cronus
Sol	=	Helios
Tellus	=	Gaea
Ulysses	=	Odysseus
Uranus	=	Ouranus
Vesta	=	Hestia
Vulcan	=	Hephaestus

and Gaea (Earth), 12 in number.
Triton Son of Poseidon and Amphitrite who dwelt in a golden palace on the sea floor.
Tyche Goddess of good luck.
Typhon A monster with 100 heads and terrible voices. The father of fierce winds, Typhon was struck by a thunderbolt from Zeus and was confined to Tartarus.
Zeus Son of Cronus and Rhea, brother of Poseidon, Hades, Hestia, Demeter and Hera (to whom he was married), and the greatest Olympian god.

TEUTONIC MYTHOLOGY
Aesir One of two main groups of deities which included Odin, Frigg, Tyr, Thor, Balder, Bragi, Idun, Jörd, Heimdall and Loki. The rival tribe of gods was the Vanir.
Asgard The land of the gods.
Balder A son of Odin and Frigg, Balder was beautiful and just, the favourite of the gods. The blind god Höd deceived by the evil god Loki, killed Balder with an arrow made of mistletoe, the only thing that could hurt him
Bifrost Bridge The rainbow bridge which was the only link between Midgard (the Middle Earth) and Asgard (the dwelling place of the gods).
Bragi A son of Odin, god of poetry and husband of the goddess Idun.
Donar *see* Thor
Fenrir A monstrous wolf, son of the evil god Loki and a giantess, Angerboda. The god Tyr bound Fenrir to a rock with magical chains. He would remain there until Doomsday when he would then break the bonds and fall upon the gods and, according to some myths, swallow the Sun.
Frey or **Freyr** Son of the fertility god Njord, ruler of rain and sunshine. His wife was Gerd, daughter of a giant.
Frigg, Freyja or **Frija** Wife of Odin, mother of Balder. Friday is derived from her name.
Heimdal The watchman of the gods.

Hel Goddess of Niflheim, the world of the dead.
Idun Wife of Bragi and guardian of the apples the gods ate to preserve their youth.
Jörd Goddess of the Earth, mother of Odin.
Loki Evil trickster god, who was punished by being bound to a rock. Loki was the father of the giantess Angerboda, bringer of distress, Hel, the goddess of death, Jörmungard, an evil serpent, and Fenrir the wolf.
Midgard The Middle Earth, the abode of mankind.
Niflheim The cold, misty world of the dead, ruled by the goddess Hel.
Njörd or **Nerthus** God of the sea, father of Frey and Frigg.
Norns Supernatural beings similar to the Fates of classical mythology. They were usually represented as three maidens spinning or weaving the fate of men.
Odin or **Woden** War god and protector of heroes. Fallen warriors joined him in Valhalla.
Thor Son of Odin, god of thunder and lightning.
Tyr or **Tiw** A powerful sky god, also associated with war, government and justice. His hand was bitten off by Fenrir the wolf when he was chaining him to a rock.
Valhalla Odin's palace for slain warriors.
Valkyries Maidens who served Odin. They went to the battlefields where they chose the slain worthy to join Odin in Valhalla.
Vanir A group of deities responsible for wealth, fertility and commerce, and rivals of the Aesir. In a war with the Vanir, the Aesir suffered many defeats before granting equality to the Vanir. The Vanir sent their gods Njörd and Frey to reside with the Aesir and took in exchange Hoenir and Mimir. The poet-god Kvasin was born as a result of the peace ritual in which the two races mingled their saliva in a vessel.

HOBBIES
AND PASTIMES

Outdoor Activities

Exercise in the fresh air, especially on a fine day, can be a very rewarding way to spend one's leisure time. Although some outdoor pursuits require special equipment, you need spend little or nothing to go for a walk in the country when the weather is good. If you live in a city you may have to find the bus or train fare to get to the country, but that is all.

For more strenuous hiking and hill walking, special boots and protective clothing are advisable. Walking boots are not only tough and flexible with a good, thick sole, but they also give support to your ankles when you walk on rocky, uneven surfaces.

In cold conditions it is better to wear several layers of thin woollen clothing than just one thick sweater. If you become too warm you can always take off one or two garments. Woollen trousers are warmer than denim jeans. When wet, wool dries more quickly than cotton. For added protection, take along some waterproof nylon overtrousers.

On mountains and the tops of high hills you will find that even on a beautiful summer's day temperatures can be icy, so be prepared. If you are too lightly dressed as well as wet, prolonged exposure to the cold can cause you to suffer from hypothermia. This is an inability to maintain adequate body temperature. The symptoms are uncontrollable shivering and slurred speech, leading to extreme sleepiness and, eventually, death.

A waterproof cagoule will help keep out the wind and rain, although one small snag is that it will tend to trap condensation inside, making you hot and sticky. A hooded anorak is another wind-proof garment. It should be large enough to cover your sweaters amply and long enough to reach well below your hips. The hood and hem should be fitted with draw strings and the sleeves should be elasticated so that in bad weather all the openings can be sealed up as much as possible.

On short hikes a small frameless rucksack is useful for carrying spare clothing and your maps, compass, first aid kit and a packed lunch. The rucksack will leave both your arms free and you will scarcely notice its weight when it is properly adjusted. For walking tours covering several days, when you might be camping at night or staying at youth hostels, you will want a larger rucksack for all your equipment. It is very important to choose one that is comfortable during long walks. Basically there are two types for this purpose. First there is the sort that is mounted on a metal frame which fits on your back with a curved waist support. The wide leather or webbing straps are adjustable and take the load. If you are thinking of getting a second-hand one beware of buying a badly designed, old-fashioned rucksack that tends to hang too low. This causes the wearer to lean forward. The better types are fairly narrow at the

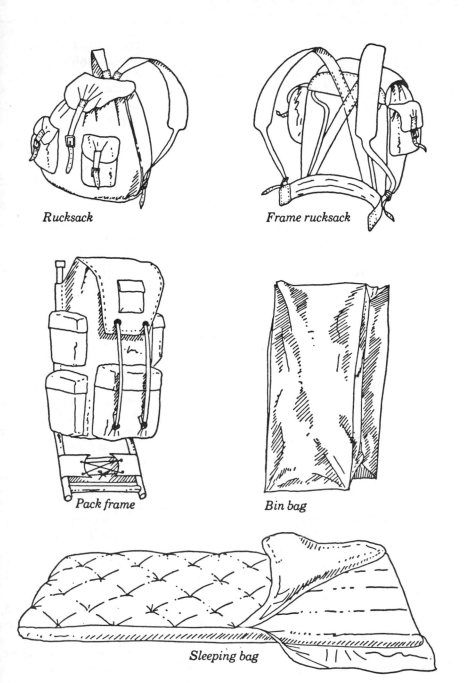

Rucksack

Frame rucksack

Pack frame

Bin bag

Sleeping bag

bottom and widen out at the top, fitting the contours of the back and shoulders.

Second, there is the pack frame and sack which is a most effective means of carrying a large load. The pack frame is made of a light alloy to which is attached two well-padded adjustable shoulder straps as well as the sack which is usually of nylon and has large external pockets.

Whatever type of carrier you use, the principles of packing are the same.

1 The heaviest items are packed at the top. It is easier to carry them high on the back.
2 Items that you may want to get at quickly should be readily available.
3 Light items and those which will be wanted last, such as a sleeping bag, should be packed first or wrapped in a polythene bag and strapped to the bottom of the frame below the sack.
4 Make sure that no hard object will dig into your back.
5 Never pack too heavy a load, it will spoil your trip. Take only the essentials.

Backpacking
If you like the idea of exploring remote areas on foot where there are no shops to obtain supplies, no hotels, not even youth hostels, then backpacking is the way to do it. Everything you need to survive for several days in the wild will have to be carried with you. This should include a tent, a sleeping bag, clothing, food and drink, and cooking utensils.

There are special lightweight tents for backpackers, some weighing 1.4 kg (3 lb) or less. They are made of nylon and have very little room inside, making them unsuitable for ordinary, leisurely camping. They are designed to give just sufficient protection for sleeping and often fit only one person.

An alternative to a tent is what is known as a bivibag. One type, made of polythene, gives cover for two people and is very cheap but it cannot be expected to last very long. Or you could rely on a waterproof sleeping bag with an improvised head cover made from a sheet of polythene tied to sturdy sticks. Various kinds of bivouac can be devised, but these are only a good idea if you can be certain that the weather will remain warm and dry.

Take care when choosing a sleeping bag for backpacking. The cheaper ones are rather heavy to carry and none too warm. The most expensive and the lightest in weight, are made of down. They can be rolled up into a very small bundle. There are now some polyester sleeping bags which are also very light and almost as warm as the down-filled sleeping bags, and much less expensive. These have the advantage that they do not attract the damp and if they happen to get wet they can be dried out easily.

Another way of exploring the country is by cycling. Long distances can be covered easily with a fair load carried in panniers and saddle-bag. There are many ways in which the load can be distributed. It is important, however, to spread it evenly and to keep it low, otherwise the bike will be difficult to handle and you could have an accident.

Types of lightweight camping tent

The most commonly used type of tent is the ridge tent. It has two poles, normally consisting of three sections of aluminium or wood. In some designs there is a third pole which lies horizontally, holding the two vertical poles apart. Guylines attached to the roof or walls of the tent run to pegs (usually made of metal) which are driven into the ground at an angle. These hold the tent down in windy conditions and. if properly fixed, ensure that it stands symmetrically. A sewn-in ground-sheet is an advantage as it reduces draughts and helps prevent rainwater getting into the tent. A flysheet gives added insulation by trapping air between it and the tent walls, especially if it is the type that stretches down to the ground. Furthermore it helps to keep the tent waterproof by taking the initial impact of rain drops which then run off the sloping edge.

You can choose a cotton canvas tent, or one made of nylon or terylene. Both have their advantages and disadvantages. The cotton fabric, which should be treated against rain and rot, will allow air to filter through the fine weave. As a result moisture will not tend to form inside. Nylon and terylene are lighter fabrics and do not shrink but condensation will form on the inner walls if there is

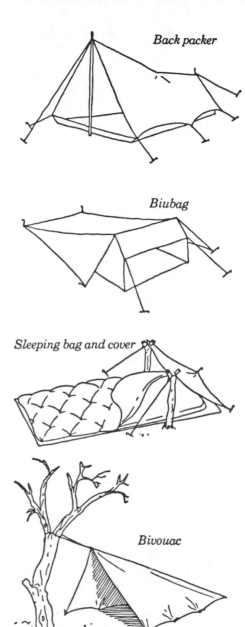

Back packer

Biubag

Sleeping bag and cover

Bivouac

185

Ridge tent

Mountain tent

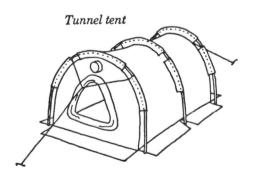
Tunnel tent

insufficient ventilation. An excellent compromise is to select a tent with cotton inner walls and a nylon flysheet.

There are various other kinds of tent on the market, some for special purposes such as the mountain tent which has a sleeve-like opening. Some tents are supported by A-frames (because they look like the letter A). Tents with an exterior frame have hangers to which the fabric is attached.

Selecting a camp spot
Finding a suitable spot at an organized camp site should present few problems. But suppose you wish to camp at a natural site where there are no laid-on facilities, with just a stream, perhaps, for water? First, obtain the permission of the landowner before you start pitching your tent. Make sure that the spot you choose is level, and free from lumps, rocks, tussocks, and thistles – and from too many flies. Be sure that any over-night rain will not cause you to be flooded out.

Don't pitch your tent under trees. In bad weather branches may break off and fall on you. Leaves tend to drip heavily long after a rain shower. Furthermore, it is dangerous to be at the foot of a tall, isolated tree during a thunderstorm. Long grass is also best avoided because it holds dew and will remain damp for a long time.

A site near a clear stream is a good one as you can use the water for personal washing and for washing up. You can use the water for drinking provided it is sterilized. Boil it for at least five minutes before drinking it. You can buy, at a chemist, water purifying tablets which you simply dissolve.

Camp cooking

There are several points to be borne in mind when planning meals for a lightweight camping expedition. The food you take should be light in weight and not so bulky that it takes up too much room in your rucksack. It should keep well. Fresh meat or fish won't last long in hot weather. Of course, you will need to produce balanced, nutritious meals, including carbohydrates, proteins and fats, and they should be as appetizing as possible. Fortunately fresh air and exercise tend to produce a terrific appetite and simple food cooked in a primitive manner will taste more delicious than it would if dished up on the dining room table. You also feel exhilarated with a sense of achievement when you have produced a meal from very basic resources.

There are various kinds of dried vegetables that you can buy beforehand that are very light to carry as well as reasonable in price and so ideal for campers. Types available include mashed potato, onions, peas, beans and mixed vegetables. Dried fruits such as apricots, apple-rings and prunes can be very handy, and don't forget packet soups. Remember, too, that some dehydrated fruits and vegetables need to be soaked for several hours before use, which is a drawback if food is wanted quickly.

You will not be able to carry a large amount of fuel, so food that needs a great deal of cooking should be left out. Aim for a hot breakfast and evening meal. During the day, cheese, nuts, raisins and chocolates can be eaten. They are quite sustaining and may be all you need until later in the evening. Instant coffee and tea-bags weigh next to nothing and a good brew-up revives the spirit and the body.

Porridge or muesli will make a nourishing breakfast. If you hanker after fried eggs and bacon, however, carry your eggs already cracked in a lidded container. Vacuum packed bacon will keep for several days in the cool.

Fresh vegetables, eggs and milk may be obtainable from a nearby farm. Fresh greens will certainly make a welcome change from the packaged or canned variety. Boil the water first before adding the vegetables to conserve the vitamins as much as possible.

Macaroni and spaghetti will provide a useful foundation for many dishes. Put it in salted water and boil until tender. Then mix with grated cheese, tinned meat or vegetables. For variety, a simple curry sauce may be made by frying a little onion, stirring in a few teaspoonfuls of curry powder and then adding water or gravy. A small quantity of lemon juice and sugar will improve the taste.

Bread is a bulky item which could be left out altogether. Crispbread could be taken instead. If you want jam on it, try mashing up soft wild fruit such as bilberries with sugar. You may even prefer it to cooked jam you use at home.

It is fun to make your own camp bread using self raising flour. Make a biscuit dough by mixing four parts of flour to a little over one part of water and a good pinch of salt. Having mixed the dough there are several ways you could cook it.

Dampers Pull off small balls of dough about the size of eggs and flatten them in your hands to make discs. Put them on a hot pan or in front of a reflector fire (*see* below). If you put them in a pan, shake them in the early stages to prevent them sticking. As soon as one side is brown, turn them over. The dampers should rise a little like a small cake. Cut the dampers in half and butter them.

Ember bread This is made on an open fire. Take a dollop of dough and slightly flatten it. Rake over your fire to expose the hot earth. Place the dough on the ground and rake the embers over it. Cook for about 15 minutes. The outside may be burnt but all you have to do is to scrape off the outside to get at the nicely cooked bread within.

Bread twist Cut a green stick about 2.5 cm (1 in.) thick, peel it and heat it until the sap bubbles out at the end. Now make the dough into a long sausage and twist it around the heated stick leaving a gap between the coils. Hold the stick over the embers, turning it frequently until the dough is golden brown. Be sure the stick is really hot before you put the dough on it otherwise the outside will be cooked and the inside uncooked. When baked it should easily slide off the stick and can be filled with cheese or jam.

When using sticks for cooking you need a fire of coals, not flames. Avoid resinous woods and willow because they have an unpleasant taste which can flavour the food. Any kind of food suitable for grilling can be cooked with the aid of sharpened sticks over a fire.

Cooking stoves

Several types of lightweight cooking stove are available from camping suppliers. They burn either solid fuel, methylated spirits, petrol, paraffin or camping gas.

One of the cheapest is a little picnic stove which houses the fuel container within the combined pot stand and windshield. Meths is poured into the centre of the hollow, cup-shaped container to a set level. A lighted match is then applied to the surface which produces a ring of fire. Although this stove is comparatively safe care must be taken not to pour in more meths when a flame is still left. The meths will flare up and could cause a serious accident. It is well to remember that meths burns with an almost invisible flame. One of the disadvantages of this stove is that it uses a fair amount of fuel.

The solid fuel stove is the lightest of all. It consists of a small steel box which when folded up is not much larger than a pack of playing cards. It opens out to form a pot stand and burner plate with supporting legs. The best results are obtained when lightweight cooking utensils are used. A disadvantage of the solid fuel stove is that it does not cook quickly.

The primus stove uses paraffin. It is a powerful cooker, burning for a

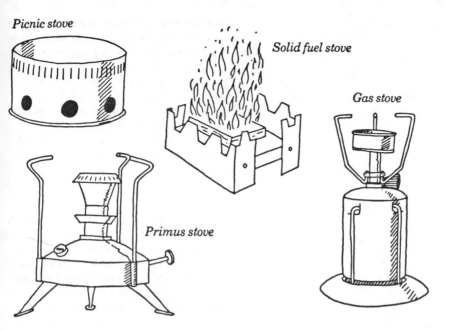

Picnic stove

Solid fuel stove

Gas stove

Primus stove

considerable time on one filling. However, it is a little more difficult to manage, needing some practice beforehand. It also needs priming to get going and for this you will need a second fuel such as methylated spirits or a solid fuel.

A petrol stove is also powerful, but it is a little risky to run and uses an expensive fuel.

There are several makes of lightweight stoves using camping gas. They are all easy to operate. You light them by simply turning on a valve and applying a match to the gas ring. When it is cold, below 1° C, butane gas liquifies and cannot be lit. There is no such problem, however, with propane.

Whatever type of cooking stove you use, do not run it inside your tent or too close to the canvas. Do not refuel it inside the tent either. Spare fuels should be kept outside,

away from the tent and away from the stove. A windshield will be necessary when using your stove unless it is one of those with the windshield built into it.

Cooking utensils

The absolute minimum you will need for lightweight camping is a frying pan and a pot. But there are some extremely practical and inexpensive camping canteens on the market which are well worth considering. Normally they consist of a number of aluminium cooking and eating utensils that nest compactly one inside another when packed. One of these canteens is illustrated. The handle of the frying pan is hinged and it is so constructed that it can be folded over the nest of pans to snap them tightly together. To lift the pot you will need a bulldog grip.

Pot

Frying pan

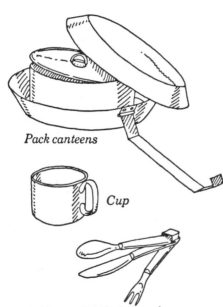

Pack canteens

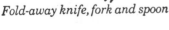

Cup

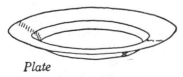

Fold-away knife, fork and spoon

Plate

A plastic mug is a must, and it is useful to have an extra plate, either plastic or aluminium. Make sure it is a fairly deep one that can hold soup or stew. Aluminium cutlery sets consisting of knife, fork and desert spoon that clip together neatly for packing purposes can be found in camping shops. Don't forget a can-opener and a box of matches.

Camp fires
Camp stoves are so efficient and reliable that it is not really necessary to light a fire. On the other hand a camp fire can be a great comfort in cold weather and will help to conserve the limited amount of stove fuel that you carry. You must remember that fire can spread and cause damage, so always be very careful and never leave the fire unguarded.

To make a fire you will need to collect some tinder – material that will ignite easily and burn long enough to enable the fire to catch the kindling wood. Suitable materials for tinder are dry fir cones, dry grass and weeds knotted into bundles and fallen tree bark.

Collect larger pieces of fuel for kindling and still larger pieces for the basis of the fire. The logs may be arranged in several different ways and there are many ways of supporting the pots and pans. It all depends on how quickly you wish to cook the food.

A *criss-cross fire* is a very good cooking fire because it supplies an even bed of coals and all the sticks burn uniformly. Make it by laying a row of sticks alongside each other on the ground. A second row

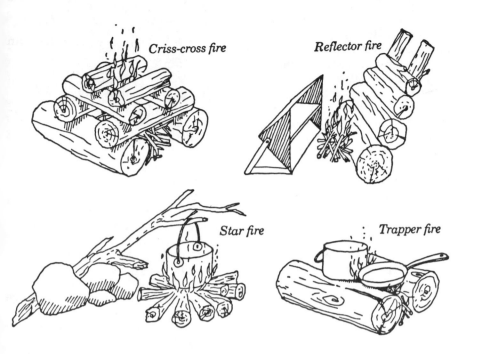

Criss-cross fire

Reflector fire

Star fire

Trapper fire

is placed crosswise on top of them, another row crosswise on top again until the pile is the desired height. When the sticks have burnt down there is a glowing bed of hot coals.

A *reflector fire* is often used to reflect heat into a bivouac or shelter. It is an ideal arrangement for baking. Drive two poles into the ground so that they slope backwards slightly. Stack several logs against them to form a wall. The fire is then built against this wall. The reflector oven is placed in front of it. As the bottom logs burn away the others drop down and the fire keeps burning. This is a good all-night fire. A reflector oven can be improvised by propping up a frying pan in front of the fire.

The star fire is a slow-burning fire which is very economical on fuel and which requires little attention. Make it by building up a small fire until you have a good blaze. Then place the ends of several long timbers into the blaze, igniting the ends one at a time. By the time you have finished the timbers radiate like the spokes of a wheel which burn only where the ends meet. As the ends burn away you push the logs inwards to keep the fire going steadily.

The trapper fire is another effective cooking fire. Place two green logs, or two long stones, just far apart enough to support your cooking pot. They should be laid so that one end catches the breeze and so fans the flames.

Canoeing

Canoeing has become a very popular sport. Both kayaks and canoes (in which the paddler kneels) are used in competition. The dimensions and weights of competitive craft are strictly regulated. Canoe competitions are divided into three main types: slalom, wild-water or down-river racing; long-distance racing; and sprint racing. Canoes vary in size, shape and construction according to their purpose. Most measure from about 3.5 to 6 m (11 to 20 ft) long and 90 to 100 cm (35 to 40 in) in beam (the width of the widest part). Their depth varies from 30 to 36 cm (12 to 14 in). The most common types of canoe are:

1 folding, with sectional framework and flexible skin,
2 rigid construction in plywood,
3 rigid construction in glass fibre,
4 rigid, with plasticized canvas skin,
5 Canadian, a wooden canoe modelled on Red Indian lines, sometimes with a plasticized skin.

Some canoes are open boats without a deck. Others have an enclosed deck and a small cockpit where the canoeist sits. A spray-cover is usually used to cover the cockpit except in calm waters. Decked canoes, resembling Eskimo kayaks, are used in rough water where an open canoe would quickly fill up with water. Most canoes are either single seaters or double seaters.

Paddles, which are usually of wood, vary greatly in length and width. A wide blade provides a powerful stroke but needs someone with both strength and skill to operate it. A narrow blade requires less strength but gives less power. Decked canoes are propelled by double-bladed paddles, open canoes by single-bladed paddles.

Some canoes have a keel which consists of a flat piece of wood or metal extending into the water from the bottom of the hull. A canoe with a keel can be steered easily on a straight course in still water (a lake, for example). On a fast-moving river, however, it is difficult to manoeuvre.

The size and shape of a canoe also affect its characteristics. A short hull gives manoeuvrability, a long one gives speed. A narrow hull is fast, but it has less stowage space than a wide one and is not seaworthy. The shape of the cross-section is another factor influencing a canoe's speed and stability.

Because a canoe has a draught of only 5 cm (2 in), it can be used to explore shallow waters inaccessible to most other craft. On some expeditions the craft may have to be carried overland, to take a short cut for example, or to avoid waterfalls or rapids. The canoeist may then use a padded yoke which enables him to carry the canoe upside down on his shoulders.

While many canoeists like to explore placid lakes and rivers, many enthusiasts prefer the open sea or fast-running mountain rivers where they can shoot the rapids.

An essential accessory for each person on a canoe trip is a life-jacket. Another important item is a bailer to empty out water from the bottom of the craft.

There is plenty of space in a canoe for stowing camping gear. Furthermore, considerable extra weight can be carried without a great difference in the power needed to propel the canoe. Anything that must be kept dry should be wrapped in waterproof bags. Goods stored in the canoe should be tied to cross-members or fittings so that in the event of a capsize they will not be washed out.

Caving (Potholing)

Caving is a pursuit devoted to the exploration of underground caverns and potholes. A pothole (or pitch) is a cylindrical shaft which descends from the surface of the ground or from levels inside caves. The shaft is climbed by using ladders and ropes. Ordinary mountaineering techniques usually cannot be employed in climbing a deep shaft because in most cases the smooth, water-polished vertical walls offer no holds at all.

The basic equipment for caving consists of a lamp and a wire ladder about 9 m (30 ft) long. A series of ladders can be clipped together for descending a long shaft. Security is provided by a nylon life-line.

Sometimes caving involves squeezing through damp, narrow holes – not many people's idea of having a good time. It can also involve swimming in cold underground rivers. But caving also has its rewards: there are beautiful underground caverns ornamented with stalactites, stalagmites and mineral encrustations of many colours. Total silence and total darkness are further experiences to be had by the caving enthusiast. Some people go caving for the team spirit to be found in the sport. Above all, there is the thrill of exploration, adventure and physical challenge.

Cycling

Touring by bicycle has long been a popular recreation. Some medical experts say that cycling is the healthiest of all sports. The touring bicycle, once heavy and fitted with balloon tyres, today looks more like a racing bike. When selecting a bicycle for touring, you should think more of distance and comfort than speed. Dropped handlebars or high handlebars are not suitable for touring.

Adjust the saddle so that your knees are very slightly bent when the pedals are at their lowest point. You should just be able to reach the ground with the tips of your toes when seated on the bike. Set the height of the handlebar grips at no more than 7.5 cm (3 in) above the saddle.

A variable gear is recommended. One or two low gears are more useful than high ones when you want to get up hills. If you want to go faster on a level stretch you can always pedal faster.

Fit your bike with a pump, lamps and a repair kit. If you are going to travel in isolated country take a spare inner tube with you. To travel in groups you need to be fit enough to keep up with the others. When you travel alone or

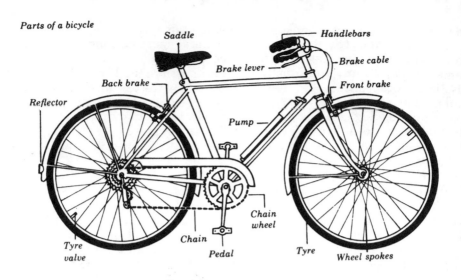

Parts of a bicycle

Saddle
Handlebars
Brake lever
Brake cable
Back brake
Front brake
Reflector
Pump
Chain wheel
Tyre valve
Chain
Pedal
Tyre
Wheel spokes

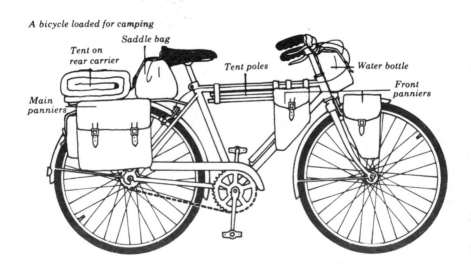

A bicycle loaded for camping

Saddle bag
Tent on rear carrier
Tent poles
Water bottle
Front panniers
Main panniers

in pairs you can set your own pace.
A cyclist who is a keen camper
can use his bicycle to carry
camping gear. The load should be
distributed as evenly as possible in
panniers and the saddle-bag. The
load should be kept low, otherwise
the bike will be difficult to handle.
Waterproof clothing should be
strapped on top of the saddle-bag
where it is easily accessible in bad
weather.

Hiking
Hiking is a popular recreational
activity for all ages. It is one of the
most economical pastimes because
it requires no special equipment.
Furthermore, hiking is an excellent
way of keeping fit.
A hike may last a few hours or be
spread over several days. Some
people walk alone, or in pairs.
Others join hiking or rambling
expeditions arranged by youth
clubs and other groups, generally
following a planned route. Skill in
reading a map and using a compass
is an asset in unfamiliar territory.
Youth hostels provide cheap
accommodation for walkers.
Backpackers (q.v.) take their
shelter with them in the form of a
lightweight tent.
The ability to walk considerable
distances without becoming
overtired is basic to many other
outdoor pursuits and is acquired
with practice. For example,
mountain climbers often have to
walk steadily hour after hour up
the lower mountain slopes before
making the final steep ascent, and
birdwatchers may do a considerable
amount of walking on field trips.
In fine weather no special

Clothes and equipment for hiking

Cagoule

Anorak

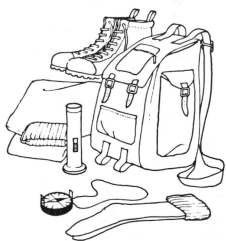

clothing is required for walking. A stout pair of shoes and garments suitable for the weather will suffice. Always be prepared, however, for a change in weather. In winter and on hill walks you need adequate protection against the cold. Wear two or three woollen shirts or thin sweaters rather than one very thick one. To keep out the wind and rain you should wear a garment such as a waterproof cagoule or a hooded anorak. The anorak should be large enough to cover your sweaters and long enough to come well down over your hips. As with a cagoule, the hood and hem of your anorak should be fitted with drawstrings and the sleeves should be elasticated. In bad weather, therefore, all the openings can be sealed up.

Using an ice-axe for braking

You should carry a change of clothes, maps, compass and your packed lunch in a small, frameless rucksack. Make sure that the straps, when adjusted, allow the load to be carried high on your back. Don't have it resting on your hips. For information about larger rucksacks used on extended hikes, see the section on backpacking. For hill walking you need special walking boots which are thick-soled and flexible. These will cushion your feet on stony ground and also support your ankles.

Mountain climbing (Mountaineering)

Why does anyone climb a mountain? One famous answer is 'because it's there'. For many people the pleasure of mountaineering lies mainly in the challenge of physical effort. For others, the impressive solitude and beauty of mountain peaks more than make up for the arduous labour of the ascent. Human comradeship is another important factor. In no other sport is so much co-operation necessary. Consideration for the other team members is essential for their safety, especially when climbing with ropes.

Accidents are usually caused by ignorance or inexperience. Nevertheless, mountain climbing always involves an element of risk from such hazards as falling stones or ice. Even very skilled climbers have lost their lives attempting challenging peaks.

Hill walking and rock scrambling are excellent ways to gain experience for the young person who wants to take up mountaineering. Some mountaineers may later branch into rock climbing (q.v.) and snow and ice climbing. It is advisable to have at least one companion with you when hill walking and scrambling, especially when there is snow and ice about. Never climb alone at any time.

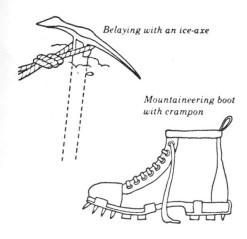

Belaying with an ice-axe

Mountaineering boot with crampon

Equipment essential for climbing on snow and ice includes:

1 vibram-soled footwear and crampons (spiked metal frames for walking on ice),
2 suitable clothing for the conditions,
3 a knapsack loaded with first-aid supplies, food and extra clothing,
4 an ice-axe,
5 slings (a sling is a loop of rope, usually 122–350 cm (4–10 ft) long, tied by a double fisherman's knot),
6 a nylon rope,
7 pitons, a piton hammer, nuts and karabiners.

A piton is a metal spike, with an eye or ring at one end, that can be driven into a crack in rock or ice. A karabiner, or snap-link, is a metal loop that can be snapped into a piton and through which a rope may be passed. Mountaineers' nuts are threaded on to ropes to wedge them in rock crevices. Climbers usually have a range of nuts to fit different types of fissure.

Perhaps the most versatile item in the mountaineer's array of equipment is his ice-axe. It is used as a firm point of support, for probing crevasses, to cut steps in the snow, for stopping a fall and emergency braking. Another important use is for belaying. 'Belaying' means securing the rope that is tied round a climber. When used for this purpose the ice-axe is plunged vertically in the snow up to its head. A figure of eight knot is tied in the main rope and placed over the head of the axe. A team of climbers, when roped up, should be belayed so that the fall of one person will not pull the others off as well. Normally every member is belayed while he is not moving.

If you wish to learn mountain climbing it is best to accompany older friends who are already experienced. Alternatively, you could join a local mountaineering club.

Orienteering
Orienteering is a competitive sport originating from Sweden. It combines cross-country running over rough and wooded terrain with map reading and direction-finding skills.

Participants use a compass and a map which they are given just before the race. They leave at timed intervals and must check in at control points shown on the map. The route between the control points is for them to choose, but the fastest to complete the course wins.

Orienteering does not depend on

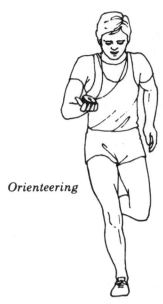

Orienteering

Punting

athletic ability alone. The fleet-footed are often left far behind by others whose map reading and selection of routes have been more shrewd. The shortest time-distance between two control points is not always a straight line. Considerations to be borne in mind when choosing a route include:

1 how severe are the obstacles (hills, cliffs, fences, etc.)?
2 what is the nature of the ground (thickly wooded, boggy, etc.)?
3 what useful landmarks are there (saving many time-consuming references to the map)?

Individual capacities must also be taken into account. A fast runner may prefer a long detour through open country or along paths. A slower one may gamble on a shorter but more complicated route, such as through a thick wood.

Punting
A punt is a narrow, flat-bottomed boat which is propelled by pushing a long pole against the river-bed. The punter must let the pole drop vertically to the bottom. Then he pushes against the river-bed, drawing the pole up again as the punt moves away. If the river has a muddy bottom the pole sometimes gets stuck in the mud. The punter then has the choice of letting the pole go, or to stay clinging to it as the punt moves away. Punting is easier on rivers with shingle beds.

Riding
Children and young people often learn to ride at a riding school. The most suitable mount for youngsters is a pony (a small kind of horse). There are several breeds of pony, including the hardy Shetland, the Dartmoor, the Exmoor, the grey Highland pony and the Welsh Cob. If you are lucky enough to have

your own pony, you will be responsible for all its needs and a friendship will quickly grow between you. Even at a riding school you may ride the same pony at each lesson and so build up a relationship with it.

A relatively inexpensive way of enjoying riding is pony trekking. Sure-footed ponies carry their riders over rough moorlands, forests and mountainsides. Pony-trekking holidays are arranged by a number of organizations. Groups of riders may spend up to six hours a day trekking. A different route is generally taken each day, and a break is taken for a picnic lunch. Trekking ponies rarely move faster than a walk and are therefore ideal for nervous and inexperienced riders. Experienced riders may in fact find the pace too slow. Pony-trekking holidays are not suitable for children under 12 even when accompanied by an adult.

Rock climbing

The techniques of rock climbing were originally developed by mountaineers in order to scale rock faces on the ascent to mountain peaks. They practised the techniques on crags and cliffs nearer home. Eventually, by the end of the 19th century, rock climbing had become a sport in its own right. Hill walking and rock scrambling are sound ways for a beginner to gain some experience. The difference between scrambling and rock climbing is only in the degree of difficulty.

Correct footwear is the most important equipment in rock climbing. The majority of rock climbers wear special boots for the purpose. These are less heavy and much more supple than stiff-soled mountaineering boots. Plimsolls, which are much cheaper, may be worn as long as they fit well and have smooth rubber or neoprene soles. Some climbers wear helmets to protect their heads from falling stones and to lessen injury should they happen to fall.

Ropes are crucial for safety. Most beginners use a single 11mm rope which is 36–45 m (118–147 ft) long. More experienced climbers use two ropes that are 45 m (147 ft) or

Before climbing starts, leader and second are tied to each end of the rope. The second anchors himself so that he is held in position if the leader falls. The leader fixes running belays, clipping them to his climbing rope with a karabiner. On reaching a ledge the leader then finds two or three anchors and belays himself so that the second can follow.

Rock climbing

50 m (164 ft) long. Normally, about
six slings are carried, as well as
pitons, nuts, karabiners, etc. (see
Mountaineering).

When using ropes, rock climbers
look first for safe natural anchor
(belay) points such as a spike on a
rock crag. If there is no good
natural anchor then a piton or a
nut must be used. The piton is
hammered into a suitably sized
crack in the rock and then the rope
is attached to it. Nuts threaded on
to a rope are used to firmly wedge
the rope in rock fissures.

The rowing stroke

Lift

Drop

Pull

Rowing and Sculling

Rowing as a general term means
propelling a boat by means of oars.
In racing terms 'rowing' is the use
of a single oar grasped in both
hands, while the use of two oars,
one in each hand, is called 'sculling'.

To row a dinghy, sit facing the
stern (the back end) and place the
oars in the rowlocks. To proceed
on a straight course, pull evenly on
the oars. At the beginning of the
stroke, push the ends of the oars
away from your chest, lifting the
blades out of the water behind you.
Then lower the blades into the water
and pull. At the end of the stroke,
raise the blades again and repeat
the process. The rhythm is therefore: lift, drop, pull, raise. To row
astern (backwards), lower the
blades in the water and push on
the oars instead of pulling.

To turn right, pull more steadily
on the left oar. Similarly, to turn
left, pull more strongly on the right
oar. For extra leverage, push on the
opposite oar while pulling on the
turning oar.

Sailing

Sailing boats are classified
according to their size and the way
their masts and sails are arranged.
There are many combinations of
sails and masts, including the
catboat, sloop, yawl, ketch and
schooner.

Most small sailing boats are
catboats or sloops. A type of catboat
that children and beginners often
learn to sail is called a sailing
dinghy. It is small enough to handle
and takes little looking after. You
learn to sail quickly in a dinghy
because it is very responsive to

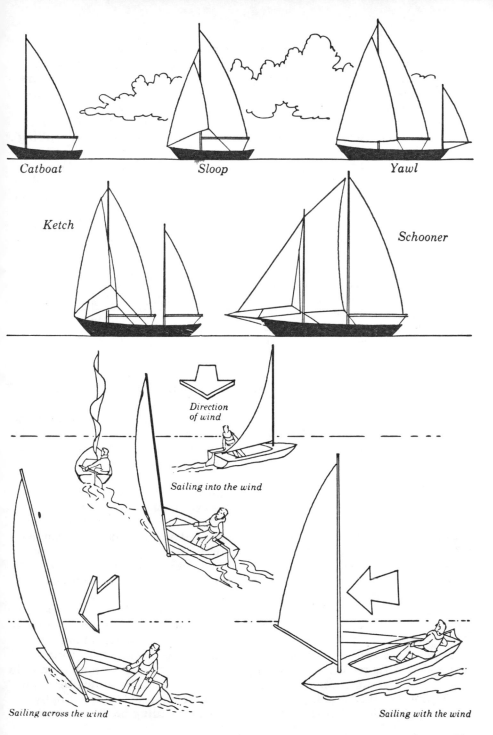

Catboat

Sloop

Yawl

Ketch

Schooner

Direction
of wind

Sailing into the wind

Sailing across the wind

Sailing with the wind

every movement of the wind, crew weight and sail adjustment. All movements are quicker than in a larger boat, so you have to make quick decisions.

A boat is designed to sail in all directions – across the wind, into the wind and with the wind. The sail has a deep curve down the leading edge, or *luff*, which gradually flattens at the after part, or *leach* edge. When the wind blows across the curved surface of the sail a difference in air pressure is set up between one side of the sail and the other. This tends to force the boat along. If there were no means of controlling the boat it would be driven downwind no matter in which direction its bow happened to be pointing.

Direction is partly controlled by the rudder. Also, to prevent the boat moving sideways when sailing across the wind, there must be something which offers a large area of lateral resistance to redirect the force into a forward movement. This is the function of the keel or centreboard under the hull. The same effect is achieved by the deep underwater shape of some boats.

Sailing with the wind is called *running before the wind*. The sail, almost at right angles to the direction of the wind, is simply pushed along by it. Because of the great wind resistance, running is the slowest of manoeuvres. Racing boats sometimes use a special triangular sail called a spinnaker when running before the wind. The spinnaker is rigged out on its own boom called a spinnaker pole.

Sailing into the wind is called *beating to windward* or sailing

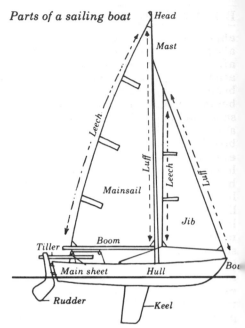

Parts of a sailing boat

close hauled. A boat cannot sail directly into the wind (the sail would just flap and be useless) but it can head to within 45 degrees of the direction from which the wind is blowing before the sail starts to luff (flap). Progress is made by following a zig-zag course at a 45-degree angle to the wind. This is known as *tacking*. When tacking, the sails should be trimmed as parallel as possible to the boat's direction.

Sailing across the wind, i.e. with the wind *abeam*, is called *reaching*. This is the fastest of manoeuvres. When the wind is brought abaft the beam the boat is said to be *broad reaching*. A good helmsman becomes finely attuned to his boat. He can anticipate a change in wind direction and trims the sails accordingly.

Small sailing boats can easily

BOATING TERMS

abaft Towards the aft of a boat
abeam On a line at right angles to a ship's length
aft Towards the stern of a boat
athwartships Anything that runs across a boat from side to side is athwartships
beam A boat's breadth
booms and gaffs The spars that extend at right angles to the masts and hold the sails straight out. Booms are fastened to the bottom of the sail, gaffs are fastened at the top
bow The front part of a boat
even keel A boat is on an even keel when it is level in the fore and aft line
halyards The ropes that hoist and lower the sails
heeled If a boat leans to the wind it is heeled
leeward Away from the wind
listing A boat which has a permanent lean through a leak or a shift in weight is listing
mainmast The mast that holds the largest sail. Some large sailing boats have a shorter mast towards the stern (the mizzenmast) or a shorter mast towards the bow (foremast)
making way A boat is making way when it is moving through the water
masts Upright poles that hold the sails
midships The middle of a boat
port The side of a boat that is on the left when you face forwards
rig The way a ship's masts, sails etc. are arranged
running rigging A collective term for the sheets and halyards
sheets The ropes that trim the sails
spars The poles that support the sails. They include masts, booms and gaffs
standing rigging The wires that hold the mast upright. They consist of a fore stay, a back stay and shrouds on either side
starboard The side of a boat that is on the right when you face forwards
stern The hind part of a boat
trimming Adjusting the sails to take full advantage of the wind
under way A boat is under way when it is not made fast to the shore, not at anchor, or not secured to a buoy
windward Into the wind

---

capsize if not handled correctly. Experienced sailors, however, know how to place their weight and will let the sails out (slacken off) when the pressure on them is so great that the boat tips too far. All crew members of sailing boats should wear a life-jacket. If the boat capsizes they should cling on to it until they are rescued. A small sailing boat that has gone over on its side in the water can usually be pulled upright again by its crew.

Scuba diving

Scuba diving is the sport of diving with the use of self-contained underwater breathing apparatus, from which it gets its name. One or more tanks of compressed air are strapped to the diver's back and are connected to an air hose. The flow of air is controlled by a device called a demand regulator which ensures that the air pressure in the diver's lungs is equal to that in the water. A diver using one tank can remain at a depth of 12 m (40 ft) for about an hour providing he does not exert himself too strenuously. An increase in depth would result in his oxygen supply being used more rapidly.

The diver's other equipment includes a face mask, a weighted belt, swim-fins and a snorkel (for conserving the air supply in the tanks when he swims near the surface). A flotation vest is worn so that he may return quickly to the surface in the event of an emergency – the vest is simply inflated with air.

Even in warm seas the temperature is low below 9.5 m (30 ft) because the Sun's rays cannot penetrate to that depth. To overcome the problem of having to spend prolonged periods in the cold, the diver wears a wet suit. The suit is made of a spongy rubber called neoprene which has a smooth outer surface. It is lined with nylon inside. A wet suit must be very close-fitting. When the diver is immersed, a thin layer of cold water creeps in between the suit and his skin. This layer is quickly warmed up to body temperature, but it would not be if there were large pools of water between his body and an ill-fitting suit.

Experienced divers may go to depths of about 40 m (130 ft). Those with less experience should not go deeper than 18 m (60 ft).

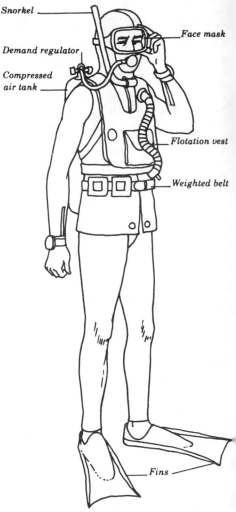

Snorkel

Face mask

Demand regulator

Compressed air tank

Flotation vest

Weighted belt

Fins

Skiing
There are two principal types of skiing: Alpine (downhill) and Nordic (cross-country and jumping). Skis are long, narrow runners curved up at the front ends (tips)

for travelling over snow. They are made of fibreglass, plastic, metal or wood. Alpine skis have bindings which clamp the ski-boot at the toe and heel. The bindings release the boot from the ski in the event of a fall, to help avoid injury. A safety strap prevents the released ski from hurtling down the slope where it might endanger other skiers.

Alpine ski-poles are usually

Downhill ski and boot

Cross-country ski and boot

metal. They are pointed at the bottom and have a ring called a *basket* about 8 cm (3 in) from the point. The baskets prevent the poles from sinking too deeply into the snow. The pole handle is usually rubber or plastic. It has a strap loop which fits around the skier's hand to prevent it slipping down the pole. Skiers carry a pole in each hand. These help them to maintain balance during manoeuvres.

Downhill skiing is both a popular recreation and a competitive sport. There are three basic manoeuvres to be learned. *Schussing* is skiing in a straight line without turning. *Traversing* is skiing across the slope at an angle. This manoeuvre can help skiers to control their speed. *Turning* is changing direction in a curving line when

skiing downhill.

To slow down or stop without changing direction, skiers may use the *snowplough* method. The legs are spread open with the skis in a V form from the tips. In a *snowplough turn*, skiers make the V and then complete the manoeuvre by putting their weight on one ski only. Parallel turns, with the skis close together, are much more difficult, although more elegant in appearance.

Cross-country skiing is ski-touring across undulating terrain. The skis are narrower and lighter than Alpine skis. The boots are lighter, flexible and usually cut below the ankle. They are clamped to the ski only at the toe, leaving the heel free so that the skier can lift it when moving forward. The most basic movement is a diagonal

Downhill skiing

Schussing   Snow-plough   Traversing

Snow-plough turn   Parallel turn

Cross-country skiing: diagonal stride

stride, rather like skating. To travel faster the skier pushes on his ski-poles.

Ski-jumping is from hills up to 90 m (294 ft) in height. After sliding down a track called an inrun, jumpers try to leap as high as possible, keeping a straight, forward-leaning position.

At ski resorts there is usually a variety of ski trails, from low, smooth 'nursery' slopes to steeper, more challenging ones for the experts. Ski lifts and ski tows bring skiers back to the top of a slope after their run.

Skin diving
Skin diving is an underwater sport in which the participant holds his breath. Diving with the aid of self-contained breathing apparatus, on the other hand, is known as scuba diving (q.v.).

Most skin divers wear a face mask and flippers, and a short J-shaped breathing tube called a snorkel. A wet suit is often worn in cold waters. One of the main interests in the sport is the exploration of marine life. The mask permits clear vision for this. It consists of a glass plate in a rubber frame that fits over the face. The rubber flippers or swim-fins help

even a mediocre swimmer to swim effortlessly through the water. Skin divers cannot descend very deeply because they must continuously return to the surface to breathe.

Surfing
Surfing is a thrilling water sport requiring good balance and split-second timing. It originated in Hawaii but is now enjoyed on open coastlines throughout the world.

The surfer stands on a long, narrow board which is borne towards the shore on the crest of a wave. Surfers sometimes train for surfboard riding by body surfing. A body surfer is swept along by the wave without using a board. He keeps his head down, his back arched and his hands at his sides. This sport helps a person to get used to the surf and to develop balance.

For a surfboard ride, the surfer lies on his board and paddles out beyond the breaking crests of waves to where the rollers rise up. As a wave approaches him, he paddles his board ahead of it. Then, as he coasts down the face of the wave, he rises to a standing position. The surfer rides the wave until it dies out near the beach. To increase

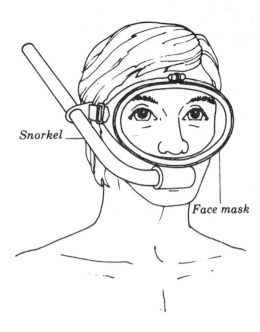

speed and distance, skilled surfers usually ride diagonally towards the shore.

The size of surfboards varies according to the size of the waves they are to ride. For light surf, flat boards 120–180 cm (4–6 ft) long and 30 cm (1 ft) wide are used. Where the waves are up to 6 m (20 ft) in height, surfers use a tapered, hollow board 3–3.7 m (10–12 ft) long and 60 cm (2 ft) wide with a stabilizing fin near the back.

Another kind of surfing, which can be performed on long, gentle beaches, is bellyboarding, using a kind of miniature surfboard. You must stand in the water waist-deep and wait for the biggest waves. Face the shore and, as the wave is almost on top of you, with a forward movement of your arms leap on to the board. You do not stand on it but simply lie on it prone. If your

Skin diving with the aid of a face mask and snorkel

Surfing

1. Paddling the board

2. Rising to the standing position

3. Riding the wave

iming is right you will be carried orwards on the wave towards the hore.

Tobogganing
A toboggan is a sled without runners used for sliding down snow-covered slopes and artificial ice-covered chutes. It is usually built of straight-grained boards fastened together by cross-pieces. The front end is curved back. The sled is usually about 1.8–2.4 m (6–8 ft) long and 46 cm (1½ ft) wide. Several people can ride on it at a time, either sitting or in the prone position. Sitting on a toboggan is called lugeing; lying on it is called cresta tobogganing. A toboggan team usually consists of four people. The one at the back does the steering. Steering is achieved by either twisting the front or by

dragging a foot in the snow.

An offshoot of tobogganing is bobsledding, which is a sport included in the Winter Olympics. Made of steel, bobsleds may weigh as much as 230 kg (500 lb). Speeds of 145 km/h (90 mph) can be reached. The bobsled run has sharp turns, but banked walls prevent the sleds from hurtling off course.

Water skiing
Water skiing originated in France in the 1920s. The water skier planes on the surface of the water, using one or two skis. (In trick riding, one ski may be used.) He is towed by a motor-boat which usually travels at speeds from 24 to 56 km/h (15 to 35 mph). There is a wooden handle attached to the towline for the skier to grip. The towline, which is often made of

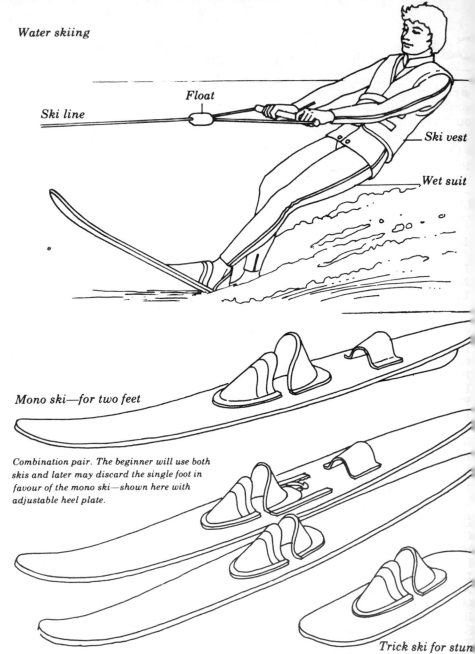

Water skiing

Ski line

Float

Ski vest

Wet suit

Mono ski—for two feet

Combination pair. The beginner will use both
skis and later may discard the single foot in
favour of the mono ski—shown here with
adjustable heel plate.

Trick ski for stun

nylon, is about 23 m (75 ft) long. A
typical water ski is of wood,
16.5 cm (6½ in) wide and 175 cm
(5 ft 9 in) long, with a stabilizing fin
near the heel. The skier uses tight-
fitting rubber foot bindings which
stretch, if he falls, and release his
feet without injury.

ar and Plane Spotting

ar spotting
ars travelling outside their
ountries of registration carry
ecial identification letters as well
s their normal number plates. In
e following list of national markings, countries bearing an asterisk (*) are those where the rule of the road is to drive on the left, while for the others it is to drive on the right. Among the most frequently seen are:

MARKING	COUNTRY
	Austria
DN	Yemen People's Democratic Republic*
L	Albania
ND	Andorra
US	Australia,* Norfolk Islands*
	Belgium
DS	Barbados*
G	Bulgaria
H	Belize*
L	Lesotho*
P	Botswana*
R	Brazil
RG	Guyana*
RN	Bahrain*
RU	Brunei*
S	Bahamas*
UR	Burma*
	Cuba
DN	Canada
GO	Congo
H	Switzerland
I	Ivory Coast
L	Sri Lanka
NB	Malaysia*
O	Colombia
R	Costa Rica
S	Czechoslovakia
Y	Cyprus*
	Germany (Federal Republic)
K	Denmark, Faroe Islands
OM	Dominican Republic

MARKING	COUNTRY
DY	Dahomey
DZ	Algeria
E	Spain, Balearic Islands, Canary Islands, Spanish Guinea
EAK	Kenya*
EAU	Uganda*
EAZ	Tanzania*
EC	Ecuador
EIR	Republic of Ireland*
ET	Egypt
F	France, and French overseas departments
FL	Liechtenstein
GB	Great Britain and Northern Ireland*
GBA	Alderney*
GBG	Guernsey*
GBJ	Jersey*
GBM	Isle of Man*
GBY	Malta, Gozo*
GBZ	Gibraltar
GCA	Guatemala
GH	Ghana*
GR	Greece, Crete, Dodecanese Islands
H	Hungary
HK	Hong Kong*
I	Italy, Sardinia, Sicily
IL	Israel
IND	India*
IR	Iran

MARKING	COUNTRY	MARKING	COUNTRY
IRQ	Iraq	RL	Lebanon
IS	Iceland*	RM	Madagascar
		RMM	Mali
J	Japan*	RNR	Zambia*
JA	Jamaica*, Cayman	RNY	Malawi*
	Islands*, Turks and	RSM	San Marino
	Caicos Islands*	RSR	Zimbabwe*
JOR	Jordan		
		S	Sweden
K	Kampuchea	SD	Swaziland*
KWT	Kuwait	SF	Finland
		SGP	Singapore*
L	Luxembourg	SK	Sarawak*
LAO	Laos	SME	Surinam
LT	Libya	SN	Senegal
		SU	USSR
MA	Morocco	SUD	Sudan
MC	Monaco	SWA	South West Africa*
MEX	Mexico	SY	Seychelles*
MS	Mauritius*	SYR	Syria
N	Norway	T	Thailand*
NA	Netherlands Antilles	TG	Togo
NGN	West Irian	TN	Tunisia
NIC	Nicaragua	TR	Turkey
NIG	Niger*	TT	Trinidad and Tobago*
NL	Netherlands	TZ	Tanzania*
NZ	New Zealand*		
		U	Uruguay
P	Portugal, the Azores,	USA	United States of
	Cape Verde Islands,		America
	Madeira, São João		
	Baptista de Ajuda	V	Vatican City
PA	Panama	VN	Vietnam
PAK	Pakistan*		
PE	Peru	WAG	Gambia*
PI	Philippine Islands	WAL	Sierra Leone*
PL	Poland	WAN	Nigeria*
PTM	Malaysia*	WD	Dominica*
PY	Paraguay	WG	Grenada
		WL	St Lucia
R	Romania	WS	Western Samoa*
RA	Argentina	WV	St Vincent*
RCB	Zaire		
RCH	Chile	YU	Yugoslavia
RH	Haiti	YV	Venezuela
RI	Indonesia		
RIM	Mauritania	ZA	South Africa*

IDENTIFYING CAR MAKES BY THEIR BADGES

Car badges are the manufacturers' means of making their products readily recognizable. Originally all that seemed necessary was a brass nameplate fixed to the front of the vehicle or on the dashboard. Later, trade marks were introduced. Once a trade mark was familiar there was no need for a passer-by to read the name plate because the car was instantly identifiable.

The trade mark was either in a special style of lettering or pictorial. Both types of car badge are used today.

BMW

Mercedes-Benz

Volvo

Volkswagen

Renault

Citroën

Ford

Aston Martin

MG

Jaguar

Plane spotting

As a means of transport, the aircraft offers many advantages over surface vehicles. The main one is that it has the freedom of the skies; it is able to use the extra dimension of height, unfettered by the limitations of over-populated land. Today, however, even this advantage is diminishing as more and more aircraft join the airways and crowd-holding patterns above their destinations, awaiting their turn to land.

Away from these crowded areas aircraft give us a wide choice of destination and direction. They can travel over land and sea, mountain and city, connecting countries, continents and islands. Some people fly their own aircraft on business, for pleasure or as farm machines, but most air travellers are chauffeured by airline pilots. A great deal of freight is also transported by air.

The many demands we make on flying machines have made it necessary to build a vast range of different aircraft: civil airliners, helicopters, military aircraft and so on. Each type is either specially designed for its purpose or adapted for use with special equipment. Many of these aircraft are common sights and are easily recognized. Others, although just as common, are less easily identified. In these pages you will be able to look at pictures of aircraft in use today, learn their names and some of the details of their specifications. Few people would not recognize Concorde, but do you know its wing span? On the other hand, can you name an aircraft made specially

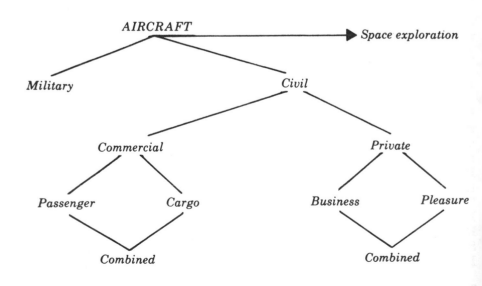

for long-range maritime patrol?
The two main categories are
military and civil, which can be
subdivided as shown in the diagram
on page 216.

Many countries in the world
have aircraft industries
producing aircraft of their own,
while some countries have joined
together to produce combined
efforts. Concorde, the Airbus and
the Jaguar fighter are products of
such co-operation. America
probably has the greatest number of
constructors but the USSR,
Germany, the Netherlands, France,
Britain, Poland, Italy, Switzerland,
Brazil, India, New Zealand, Spain,
Japan, Australia and many others
add their contributions to what is a
huge list of varied types of aircraft.
You are unlikely to see many of
these unless you make a special
study of aircraft. Plane spotting
can become a fascinating hobby.

PRIVATE, EXECUTIVE AND AGRICULTURAL AIRCRAFT

BAe HS 125

United Kingdom
Accommodation: crew 2; normal
seating for 8; alternative
arrangements for up to 14
Power: two 3,700 lb (1,678 kg)
thrust Garrett AiResearch TFE
731–3 turbofans
Performance: 495 mph (796 km/h)
Range: 2,705 miles (4,353 km)
Span: 47 ft (14.32 m)
Length: 50 ft 8½ in (15.4 m)

The HS 125 is a popular executive
jet, the current series (the 700)

having the specification listed
above. The 700 first flew on 28 June
1976 and production started on
8 November that year. The prototype
was built by De Havilland and was
designated the DH 125. It first flew
on 13 August 1962. Hawker Siddeley
continued the model as the HS 125
and produced civil, military and
hybrid versions. The series 1
through to the series 600 were
powered by turbojets. The 700, in
the interests of fuel economy, is
fitted with turbofans. Further
developments are planned.

BEECHCRAFT SKIPPER 77

USA
Accommodation: two-seat
primary trainer
Power: one 115 hp Avco Lycoming
four-cylinder horizontally opposed
engine
Performance: approx. 130 mph
(209 km/h)
Span: 30 ft (9.14 m)
Length: 23 ft 10¾ in (7.2 m)

Designed as a two-seater, side-by-
side trainer, the Skipper 77 is
intended to be economical in initial
cost and in running and maintenance. The prototype flew in 1975.
The first production prototype flew
in September 1978.

PIPER PA-44 SEMINOLE

USA
Accommodation: pilot and 3
passengers
Power: two 180 hp Avco Lycoming
0–360–EIAD four-cylinder
horizontally opposed engines
Performance: max. speed 192 mph
(309 km/h)

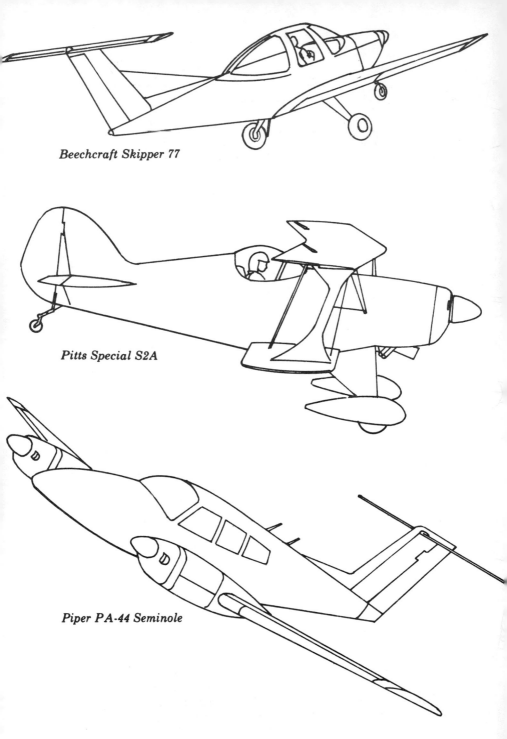

Beechcraft Skipper 77

Pitts Special S2A

Piper PA-44 Seminole

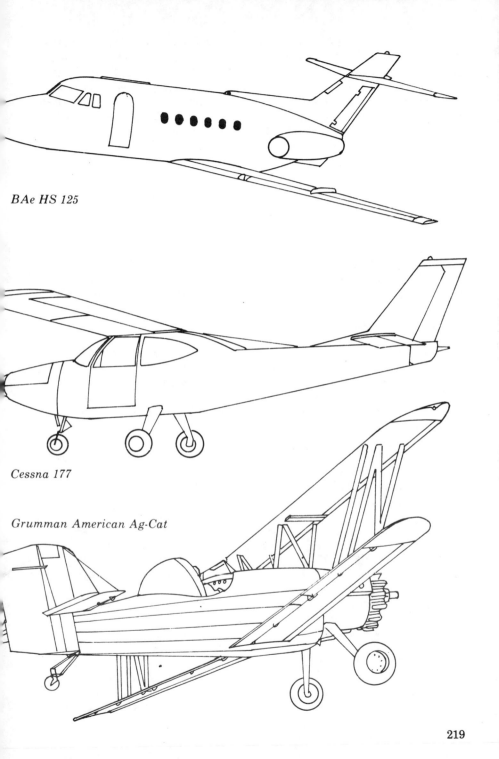

BAe HS 125

Cessna 177

Grumman American Ag-Cat

219

Range: max. 960 miles (1,544 km)
Span: 38 ft 6½ in (11.7 m)
Length: 27 ft 7 in (8.4 m)

The Seminole is a light cabin monoplane, one of the many manufactured by Piper. The prototype flew in May 1976 and production commenced in May 1978.

PITTS SPECIAL S2A

USA
Accommodation: pilot plus one
Power: 200 hp Lycoming
Performance: max. speed
140 mph (225 km/h)
Range: 450 miles (724 km)
Span: 20 ft (6 m)
Length: 18 ft 3 in (5.5 m)

Although the original Pitts Special flew as long ago as September 1944, these aircraft are still often seen in air displays performing aerobatics, the purpose for which they were built. Single- and two-seat models were produced. Power was increased from the original 90 hp to the present 200 hp. Its achievements include the 1972 US national team successes.

CESSNA MODEL 177

USA
Accommodation: 4 plus 2 children
Power: 180 hp Lycoming
Performance: 140–170 mph
(225–273 km/h)
Range: 785–1,005 miles (1,263–1,617 km)
Span: 35 ft 6 in (10.8 m)
Length: 27 ft 3 in (8.3 m)

The Cessna model 177 was introduced in 1971 and by the beginning of 1977 nearly 5,000 had been delivered. The 177 has a tricycle undercarriage and a cantilever wing, the latest model having a gull-wing shape to the leading edge. An extremely popular aircraft for private fliers, the 177 is part of the company's range of light planes.

GRUMMAN AMERICAN AG-CAT

USA
Crew: 1
Power: latest power units used are Pratt and Witney 450 or 600 hp
Performance: 80–100 mph
(128–160 km/h)
Span: 35 ft 11 in (10.9 m)
Length: 24 ft 3 in (7.4 m)

The Ag-cat is a single-seat agricultural crop-spraying biplane which was introduced in May 1967. It has an outstanding safety record.

COMMERCIAL AIRCRAFT

CONCORDE

United Kingdom and France
Accommodation: crew 3 or 4; passengers 128 or 144
Power: four 38,050 lb (17,259 kg) thrust reheat Rolls-Royce/SNECMA Olympus 593 Mk 602 turbojets
Performance: max. cruising speed Mach 2.02 (1,354 mph, 2,179 km/h) at 50,000 ft (15,240 m)
Range: 3,870 miles (6,228 km)
Span: 83 ft 10 in (25.6 m)
Length: 203 ft 9 in (62 m)

Concorde, first planned in 1955, is

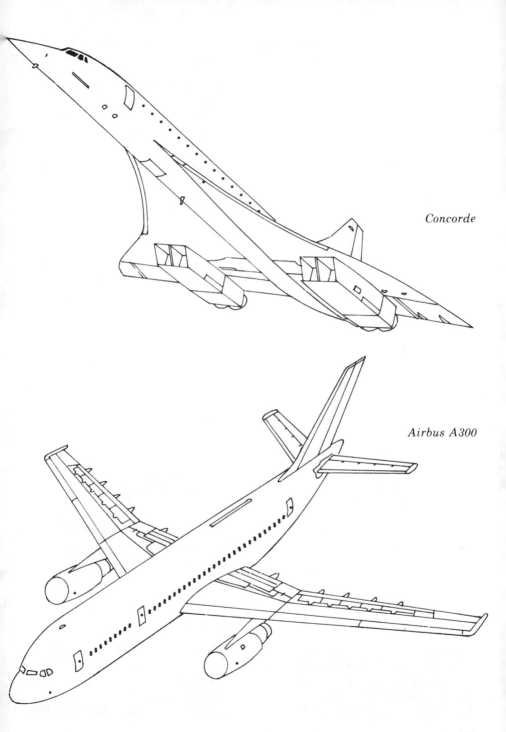

Concorde

Airbus A300

the world's first supersonic airliner to be used in regular passenger-carrying service. The combined resources of France's Aerospatiale and the British Aircraft Corporation achieved a first flight, with Concorde 001, on 2 March 1969 from Toulouse. Supersonic speed was achieved on 1 October 1969, and Mach 2 on 4 November 1970. The British Concorde, 002, flew from Filton on 9 April 1969. Production models, modified with a longer fuselage and revised wing leading-edge, made their maiden flights on 6 December 1973 and 13 February 1974. The first fare-paying passengers were carried on 21 January 1976. Accommodation is for 128 passengers in one-class luxury, or 144 in high-density loading.

Concorde has been received with mixed feelings. Some people are so enthusiastic that they have formed Concorde fan clubs and arrange outings to fly in it. Opposition is mainly on the grounds of noise. Because of this, Concorde is denied access to some airports and is not allowed to fly over some countries. The soaring cost of fuel has also caused problems. As a result, fewer orders have been taken than originally anticipated. However, Concorde continues to be very popular with trans-Atlantic passengers.

AIRBUS A300

United Kingdom, France, Germany, the Netherlands, Spain
Accommodation: flight crew 3; passengers 220–336
Power: two 51,000 lb (23,133 kg)

thrust General Electric CF6-50C turbofans
Performance: max. cruising speed 578 mph (930 km/h) at 28,000 ft (8,534 m)
Range: 2,618 miles (4,212 km)
Span: 147 ft (44.84 m)
Length: 175 ft 9 in (53.75 m)

The Airbus is built by a French/German/British/Dutch/Spanish consortium, with the final assembly being carried out at Aerospatiale in Toulouse. The plane is a wide-bodied, twin-engined 'jumbo' jet, built for short or medium distances. It is the quietest of the big jets because of the special design of the engines.

The project was started in 1965 and the first A300 Airbus entered service with Air France on 23 May 1974. There are several variations offering alternatives in seating and range. Further development work continues.

BAC ONE-ELEVEN

United Kingdom
Accommodation: minimum crew 2; passengers 119 max.
Power: two 12,550 lb (5,692 kg) thrust Rolls-Royce Spey turbofans
Performance: max. cruising speed 550 mph (885 km/h) at 21,000 ft (7,308 m)
Range: 1,440 miles (2,316 km)
Span: 93 ft 6 in (28.5 m)
Length: 93 ft 6 in (28.5 m)

From a project initiated in 1956 by Hunting Aircraft Ltd., the BAC One-Eleven first flew on 20 August 1963. Original plans had gone through several changes and the

resulting aircraft seated 79 people.
The standard version was the 200;
for the American market it was the
400; and an uprated engine
specification was given to the 300.
Certification was given on 6 April
1965 and BUA flew the first One-
Eleven service on 9 April. Later
variations have been the 500 (longer
fuselage) and the 475 with hotted-up
engines and low-pressure tyres. The
details above refer to the 670 which
started testing in April 1979.

BOEING 747

USA
Accommodation: flight crew 3;
first-class passengers 66; economy
class passengers 308; alternative:
447 or 490 (all economy)
Power: four 47,000 lb (21,319 kg)
thrust Pratt and Whitney JT 9D 7W
turbofans
Performance: max. speed 608 mph
(978 km/h)
Range: max. with special equipment 7,180 miles (11,552 km)
Span: 195 ft 8 in (59.64 m)
Length: 231 ft 4 in (70.51 m)

The details above refer to the 747-
200B. This is one of the many
variations of the 747 which, under
different series numbers, offers
alternatives in seating arrangements and capacities, cargo-
carrying facilities, and a choice of
engines. Some have an extended
flight range with reduced carrying
capacity, and there are smaller,
economy versions.

The 747 was developed from the
707; it is the world's largest airliner
and the first 'jumbo'. First flown on
9 February 1967, it entered service
with Pan Am on 22 January 1970.
By the beginning of 1979 over 400
had been ordered. The 747 is now in
service with airlines all over the
world. One interesting variation
has been used by NASA to carry the
space shuttle Orbiter on its air
launch.

FOKKER F28 FELLOWSHIP Mk 4000

Netherlands
Accommodation: flight crew 2;
passengers 85 single-class
Power: two 9,850 lb (4,468 kg) thrust
Rolls-Royce RB183-2 Spey
Mk 555-15 turbofans
Performance: max. cruising speed
523 mph (841 km/h) at 23,000 ft
(7,010 m)
Range: 2,566 miles (4,128 km)
Span: 82 ft 3 in (25.07 m)
Length: 97 ft 1¾ in (29.61 m)

The Fokker F28 Fellowship was
planned in early 1962 as a short-
haul jet airliner to complement the
F27 Friendship, which was later to
become the world's best-selling
turboprop airliner. The Fellowship
was originally designed as a 65-seat
one-class aircraft – the Mk 1000. A
version was made with a forward,
side cargo loading door for combined
cargo/passenger work. The Mk 2000
was longer and carried 79
passengers over shorter distances.

Currently in production are the
Mks 3000 and 4000, also the 6000
and the 6600 which is 87 in (221 cm)
longer. These later models have a
greater wing span than the originals
and better noise reduction. Plans
are in hand for the F29 series which
will seat 115.

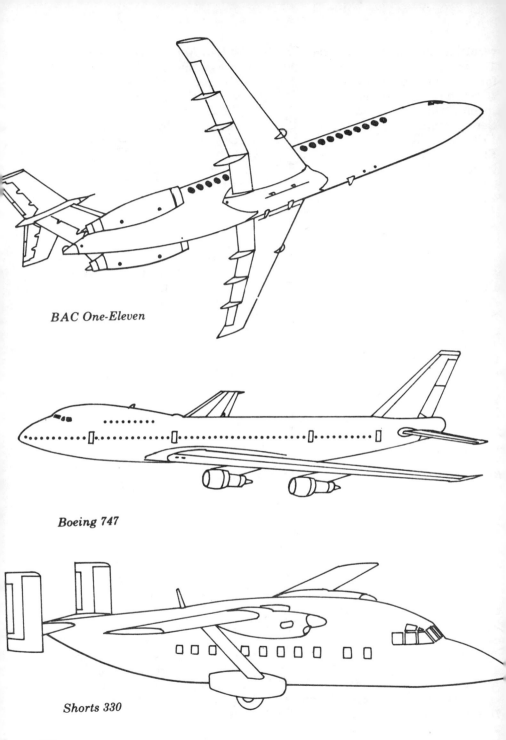

BAC One-Eleven

Boeing 747

Shorts 330

224

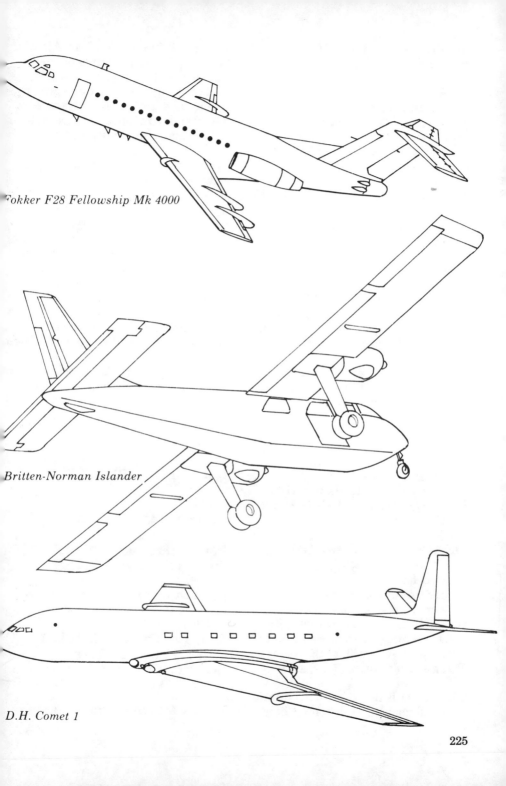

Fokker F28 Fellowship Mk 4000

Britten-Norman Islander

D.H. Comet 1

MCDONNELL DOUGLAS DC-10 SERIES 30

USA
Accommodation: flight crew 3+2; passengers 225–70 (max: 380+11 crew)
Power: three 52,500 lb (23,814 kg) thrust General Electric CF6-50CI turbofans
Performance: 594 mph (955 km/h) at 31,000 ft (9,449 m)
Range: 7,400 miles (11,906 km) at 540 mph (869 km/h)
Span: 165 ft 4 in (50 m)
Length: 181 ft 4 in (55 m)

Design work started in 1966 on an American Airlines specification for a 'jumbo' twin jet. The three-engine formula was later adopted. First flight of the series 10 was on 29 August 1970 and the first service flight was a year later. Alternative specifications of power, size and range have been provided by the series 30 and 40 variants. Initial orders from American and United airlines helped to give the three-jet jumbo market to the DC-10 over the Lockheed Tri-Star. Many airlines the world over have DC-10s in their fleets.

DE HAVILLAND COMET 1

United Kingdom
Accommodation: 36 passengers
Power: four 5,000 lb (2,268 kg) thrust D. H. Ghost turbojets
Performance: max. speed 480 mph (772 km/h) at 40,000 ft (12,192 m)
Range: 2,000 miles (3,218 km)

The Comet is not now in production in any form although some Comet 4s are still flying with Dan Air of London. The importance of the Comet 1 is that it was the world's first passenger airliner powered by jet engines. In 1952 it introduced a new standard of speed and passenger comfort previously unknown in commercial aircraft. In a pressurized cabin, passengers enjoyed smooth, almost silent travel at 40,000 ft, moving at 480 mph. Britain had made a very significant 'first', leaving the rest of the flying world behind – and below. Unfortunately, structural weakness, arising from the pressurization of the cabin, led to two disastrous crashes. All Comets were grounded except for testing. The development programme was held up for a time. Comet 2 was used by the RAF. Then came the Comet 3, built as a development airframe prototype for the Comet 4. The Comet 4 entered service in 1958 at the same time as the Boeing 707. As a transatlantic competitor the Comet 4 was outclassed.

LOCKHEED TRI-STAR

USA
Accommodation: flight crew 3; passengers 400
Power: three 48,000 lb (21,772 kg) thrust Rolls-Royce RB211-524 turbofans
Performance: max. cruise speed 608 mph (978 km/h) at 31,000 ft (9,449 m)
Range: 4,855 miles (7,811 km)
Span: 155 ft 4 in (47.24 m)
Length: 164 ft 2 in (50 m)

In 1966, following a four-year lull

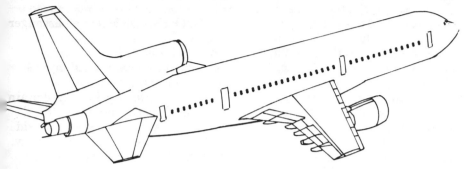

Lockheed Tri-Star

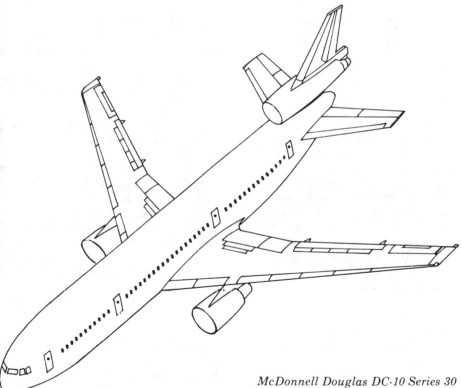

McDonnell Douglas DC-10 Series 30

after the ending of the production of the Electra, Lockheed took up the American Airlines specification enquiry and designed the model 385 Tri-Star. Using the three-engine format (one under each wing and one in the rear fuselage), the Tri-Star competed with the DC-10 for the American order – and lost. Other internal airlines in America placed orders and production started in 1968. The first flight was made on 16 November 1970 and deliveries began in April 1972. Various models have been built, a current one being the L-1011-500 whose specification is listed above. The Lockheed Tri-Star is powered by Rolls-Royce RB211 engines which currently rate as Rolls-Royce's most commercial engines.

SHORTS 330

United Kingdom
Accommodation: crew 2; up to 30 passengers and 1,000 lb (454 kg) baggage
Power: two 1,173 shp Pratt and Whitney PT6A-45A turboprops
Performance: max. cruise speed 221 mph (355 km/h) at 10,000 ft (3,048 m)
Range: 1,013 miles (1,630 km)
Span: 74 ft 9 in (22.78 m)
Length: 58 ft 0½ in (17.69 m)

The Shorts 330 is a third-level airliner and utility transport designed for commuter travel and local transportation. Directly developed from the Shorts Skyvan, the 330 is very boxlike in shape. It has the ability to take off and land on restricted airfields, and is used

worldwide by various operators. There is also a maritime surveillance version equipped with special radar equipment.

BRITTEN-NORMAN ISLANDER

United Kingdom
Accommodation: flight crew 1 or 2; up to 9 passengers
Power: two 260 hp Avco Lycoming six-cylinder engines
Performance: max. speed 180 mph (290 km/h) at sea level
Range: 700 miles (1,126 km)
Span: 49 ft (14.94 m)
Length: 35 ft 7¼ in (10.86 m)

The Islander is a light, twin-engined, passenger-carrying aircraft designed for short-haul work. It is able to take off and land in restricted space. Economy in cost and maintenance has added to its attraction and made it the best-selling multi-engined light commercial aircraft. By early 1978 sales had reached 750. It was first flown on 24 April 1967 and deliveries began on 13 August. It is now made under licence in Romania. Variations include crop sprayers, fire fighters and a turboprop version called the Turbo Islander.

MILITARY AIRCRAFT

GENERAL DYNAMICS F.16

USA
Crew: 1 pilot (F.16A); two-seat trainer (F.16B)
Power: one 25,000 lb (11,340 kg) thrust reheat Pratt and Witney turbofan
Performance: 1,255 mph

(2,019 km/h) at 36,000 ft (10,973 m)
Range: max. 340 miles (547 km)
tactical radius with 6 Mk-82 bombs
Armament: one 20mm cannon
plus 15,200 lb (6,795 kg) of bombs
and rockets
Span: 31 ft (9.45 m)
Length: 47 ft 7¾ in (14.5 m)

The F.16 is a lightweight fighter of
advanced aerodynamic design. It
attains stable flight only at supersonic speeds, when it is highly
manoeuvrable. The first prototypes
flew on 29 January 1974. It is now
operational in many countries.

BAe HARRIER G.R. Mk 3

United Kingdom
Crew: 1 pilot
Power: one 21,500 lb (9,752 kg)
thrust Rolls-Royce Bristol Pegasus
Mk 103 vectored-thrust turbofan
Performance: 720 mph (1,158 km/h)
Range: tactical radius 260 miles
(418 km)
Armament: two 30mm cannon
plus three 1,000-lb (454-kg) bombs
and 36 38mm rockets
Span: 25 ft 3 in (7.69 m)
Length: 45 ft 7¾ in (13.86 m)

The Harrier is the world's first
V/STOL strike and reconnaissance
fighter. The first pre-production
prototype flew on 31 August 1966.
It entered service with the RAF on
28 December 1967. Its vertical take-
off is achieved by deflecting the
engine thrust downwards through
rotating nozzles which turn to give
forward thrust for normal flight.
Naval and trainer versions have
also been built.

BAe NIMROD

United Kingdom
Crew: operating crew of 12 (2
pilots, 1 flight engineer, 9 navigators
and sensor operators)
Power: four 12,160 lb (5,516 kg)
thrust Rolls-Royce RB168–20 Spey
Mk 250 turbofans
Performance: max. speed 575 mph
(925 km/h)
Range: up to 5,755 miles (9,259 km),
12 hours endurance
Armament: homing torpedoes,
mines, depth charges, four AS 12
air/sea missiles
Span: 114 ft (35 m)
Length: 126 ft 9 in (38.4 m)

The Nimrod is a long-range
maritime patrol aircraft fully
equipped for sea search and attack
operations. In peacetime it is used
in air/sea search and rescue; its
extensive electronics and radar
equipment enable it to carry out
communications links and rescue
direction. The first Nimrods were
built on Comet 4C airframes and
the first one flew on 23 May 1967.
Development and improvement
work still continues.

DASSAULT-BREGUET
MIRAGE F1

France
Crew: 1 pilot
Power: one 15,873 lb (7,200 kg)
thrust SNECMA Atar 9K-50
turbojet
Performance: Mach 2.2 at 39,370 ft
(12,000 m)
Range: 560 miles (901 km) with
max. combat load
Armament: two 30mm cannon

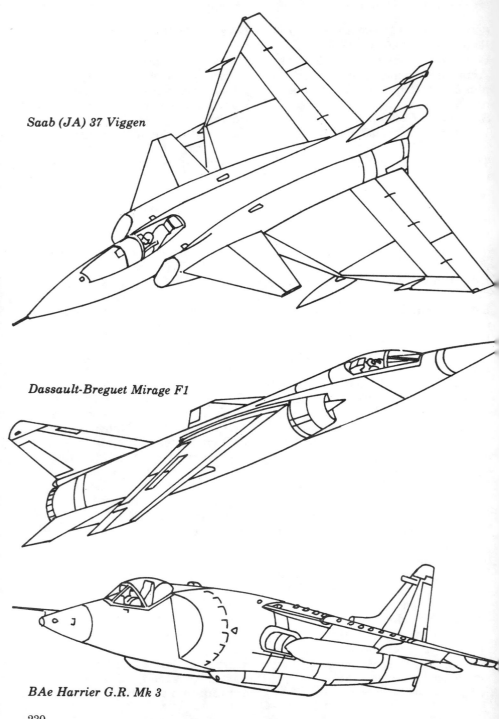

Saab (JA) 37 Viggen

Dassault-Breguet Mirage F1

BAe Harrier G.R. Mk 3

230

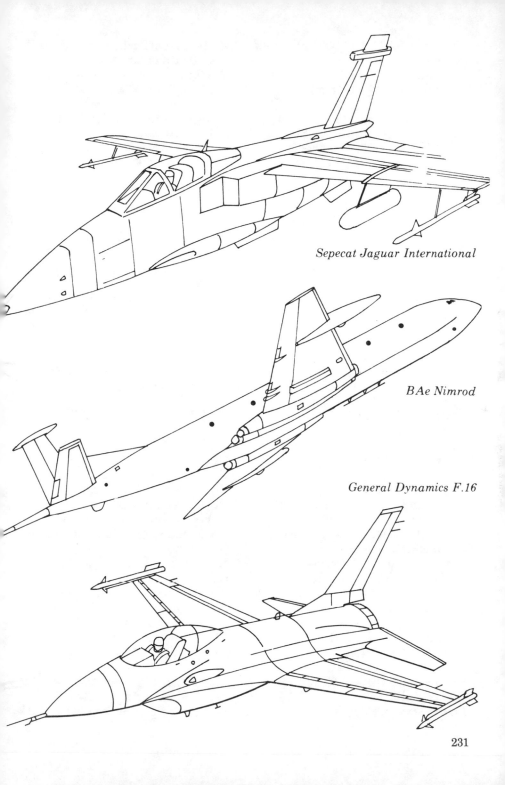

Sepecat Jaguar International

BAe Nimrod

General Dynamics F.16

plus up to 8,820 lb (4,000 kg) bombs and rockets
Span: 27 ft 6¾ in (8.38 m)
Length: 49 ft 2½ in (15 m)

The Mirage F1 single-seat multi-purpose fighter prototype flew on 23 December 1966. The first production plane flew on 15 February 1973. Currently about five are produced each month. Its primary use is for all-weather interception at any altitude but it is also suitable for ground attack. The two-seat version is used as a trainer.

MIG 25 FOXBAT

USSR
Crew: 1 pilot
Power: two 24,250 lb (11,000 kg) thrust afterburning turbofans
Performance: max. speed Mach 3.2
Range: 700 miles (1,126 km)
Armament: four AA6 Acrid air-to-air missiles
Span: 45 ft 11 in (14 m)
Length: 73 ft 2 in (22 m)

The MiG 25 entered service in 1970–1 and was recognized as the best interceptor aircraft in the world. It is used for interception and reconnaissance work and can operate at 80,000 ft (24,384 m). In 1975 the MiG 25 set a world record by climbing to 114,829 ft (35,000 m) in 251 seconds.

SEPECAT JAGUAR INTERNATIONAL

France and United Kingdom
Crew: 1 pilot
Power: two 5,368 lb (2,435 kg) thrust

Rolls-Royce/Turbomeca Adour Mk 102 turbofans
Performance: max. speed 1,057 mph (1,700 km/h) at 32,810 ft (10,000 m)
Range: tactical range 710 miles (1,142 km) max.
Armament: two 30mm cannon plus up to 10,000 lb (4,536 kg) bombs and rockets
Span: 28 ft 6 in (8.68 m)
Length: 50 ft 11 in (15 m)

The Jaguar was first flown as a prototype on 8 September 1968, and the first production flight took place on 2 November 1971. Jointly produced by Britain and France, the Jaguar is in service with their air forces and with other countries. The Jaguar is a single-seat strike aircraft. It is highly versatile and able to operate from forward, semi-prepared bases.

GRUMMAN TOMCAT F-14A

USA
Crew: 2
Power: two 20,900 lb (9,480 kg) thrust reheat Pratt and Witney TF30-P-412A turbofans
Performance: max. speed 1,545 mph (2,486 km/h) at 40,000 ft (12,192 m)
Range: tactical radius 450 miles (724 km)
Armament: one 20mm cannon plus air-to-air missiles or bombs
Span: 64 ft 1½ in (19.5 m) max. 37 ft 7 in (11.5 m) min.
Length: 61 ft 11¾ in (18.8 m)

The Tomcat is a swing-wing carrier-based fighter. Its multi-purpose role includes carrier task

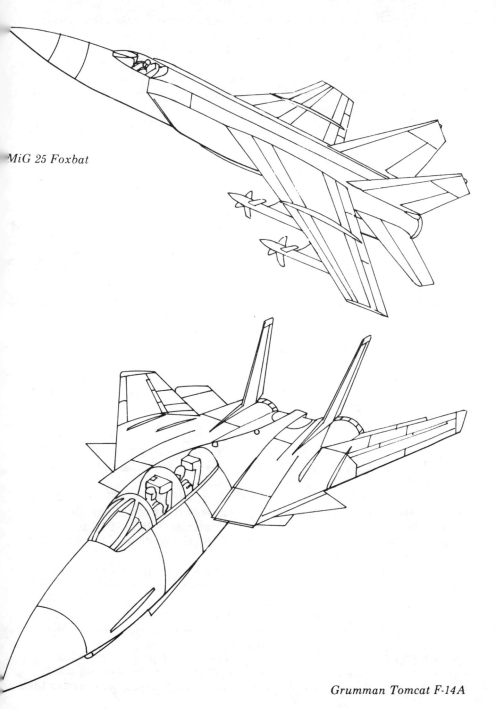

MiG 25 Foxbat

Grumman Tomcat F-14A

233

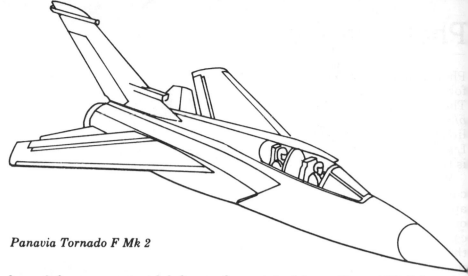

Panavia Tornado F Mk 2

force defence, escort and defence of attack aircraft, and ground target tactical attack. The first prototype flew on 21 December 1970.

PANAVIA TORNADO F Mk 2

United Kingdom
Crew: 2
Power: two 16,000 lb (7,257 kg) thrust reheat Turbo-union RB199 Mk 107 turbofans
Performance: max. speed 1,385 mph (2,229 km/h) at 36,000 ft (10,973 m)
Range: 450 miles (724 km) from base
Armament: one 27mm cannon plus rockets and bombs
Span: 45 ft 8 in (14 m)
Length: 58 ft 9 in (18 m)

The F Mk 2 is the United Kingdom's version of the original British/German/Italian project. It differs in engine power, radar equipment, length and fuel capacity. The Mk 2 has an air-to-air refuelling facility. This multipurpose fighter entered service in 1974 in its original form. Since 1979 it has been known as the Mk 2.

SAAB (JA) 37 VIGGEN

Sweden
Crew: 1 pilot
Power: one 28,108 lb (12,747 kg) thrust afterburning Volvo Flygmotor RM8B turbofan
Performance: max. speed 1,320 mph (2,124 km/h) above 36,000 ft (10, 973 m)
Range: 250 miles (402 km) tactical radius
Armament: one 30mm cannon plus two air-to-air missiles
Span: 34 ft 9¼ in (10.6 m)
Length: 50 ft 8¼ in (15.5 m)

The Viggen is a multipurpose combat aircraft used for ground attack, interception and reconnaissance, and training. Its unusual wing arrangement gives it extremely good take-off and landing characteristics. It was first flown in June 1974. Its predecessor, the AJ 37, originated in 1967.

Photography

Photography allows as much scope for creativity as any other art form. The word itself, from the Greek *photos* (light) and *graphos* (writing), literally means 'writing with light'. Light, with its infinite gradations, is the medium of the camera-artist.

When you press the shutter of a camera, light passes through the aperture and lens to strike a film, or a plate, at the back of the camera. The surface of the film or the plate is coated with light-sensitive chemicals. When the light strikes the surface, chemical changes occur so that when the film is developed and fixed, an image is clearly visible on the print or transparency. This, basically, is the way all cameras work.

The simplest model is the box camera. Provided that you make the best of its limitations, it is capable of producing good pictures. In more elaborate models, the size of the aperture (denoted by an f-number) can be controlled by a diaphragm.

The shutter, too, can be adjusted, to regulate the length of time the diaphragm will admit light through the lens. The lens itself will be bigger and of better quality than the lens in a simple box camera.

By manipulating the size of the aperture and the speed of the shutter, you can extend your range of subjects considerably. If you are photographing outdoors on a sunny day, for instance, when there is plenty of light, a small aperture and fast shutter speed will suffice. In the evening, when the daylight is fading, you will need to use a larger aperture and a slower shutter speed to admit more of the available light to activate the chemicals on the film. Some cameras have automatic exposure meters but it is great fun and good experience to work out your own exposure times and speeds until you can afford to buy an exposure meter of your own. When making exposures longer than 1/25 of a second, it is advisable to use a

How a box camera works

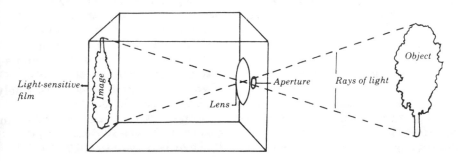

Light-sensitive film — Image — Lens — Aperture — Rays of light — Object

tripod, or to rest the camera on a stable object, since it is difficult to hold a camera steady for longer periods.

Whether you use black and white or colour, roll or cassette film, you will have to take into account the film speed (the light-sensitivity of the chemical emulsion on the film) when calculating your exposures. A fast film needs less light to activate the chemicals than a slow film. The speed is indicated on the packet; two gradings commonly used are DIN and ASA. Colour film is not generally available in the faster gradings. Ask the advice of your local photographic dealer (and tell him the type of camera you use) when you buy film. Remember to go indoors or into shadow when you load the camera. Otherwise, light may get into the edges of the film and ruin it by causing the chemical reactions to take place too soon.

There are many different kinds of camera available. The best advice is to buy as good a camera as you can afford – preferably under the guidance of a knowledgeable friend. A secondhand camera from a reputable dealer may be the ideal solution if your financial means are limited. The older-type folding cameras, for instance, often contain excellent lenses and give first-rate results.

Perhaps the best all-purpose model is the so-called miniature camera, which takes standard 35mm film with perforated edges. This camera has many advantages for the beginner. Being light, it is easily portable; the lenses are often interchangeable; and the film is comparatively inexpensive. It is an ideal camera, especially for 'human interest' and sports photography.

Other models include the single-lens reflex camera. The main advantage of this type is that you can view through the lens the exact scene you are about to photograph. The twin-lens reflex model has a viewing lens just above the 'taking' lens. The viewing lens enables you to see your subject as you take the picture. However, if a near object is being photographed, the image you see won't coincide exactly with the image on the film because of the different position of the two lenses. For all normal purposes, however, the twin-lens reflex model is perfectly satisfactory.

Let's assume you are about to take your first pictures. Why not start with a portrait of a member of the family? If using a box camera, do not move in close to the subject, or the resulting picture will be out of focus. Consider the background carefully – choose a setting that is pleasing to the eye but not obtrusive. The beginner's most common mistake is failing to notice in the background a tree or telegraph pole that appears to be growing out of the subject's head when the picture is developed!

Hazy sunlight generally gives better results in portraiture than brilliant sunlight, unless you wish particularly to emphasize the wrinkles on the face of an elderly sitter. Hands can be expressive; but if you pose your subject caressing a kitten or reading a book, for example, try to make the whole position of the sitter look natural. Take at least two or three photo-

The parts of a single-lens reflex camera

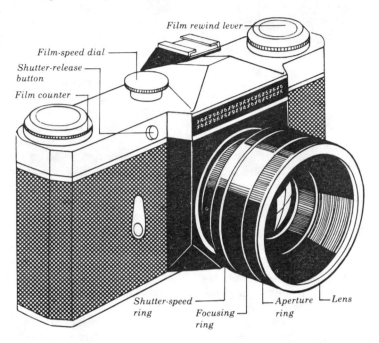

Film rewind lever

Film-speed dial

Shutter-release button

Film counter

Shutter-speed ring

Focusing ring

Aperture ring

Lens

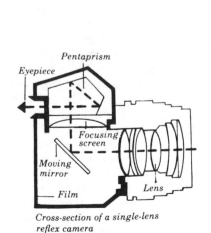

Pentaprism

Eyepiece

Focusing screen

Moving mirror

Film

Lens

Cross-section of a single-lens reflex camera

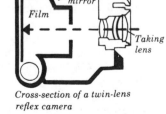

Focusing screen

Viewing lens

Fixed mirror

Film

Taking lens

Cross-section of a twin-lens reflex camera

Compose the elements of your pictures carefully. This composition would have been improved by placing the chair and bottle in slightly different positions.

graphs of the same pose, all slightly different, and choose the best for enlargement.

While landscapes present no real technical problems for the beginner, first attempts are often disappointing. Having checked from different angles to find the best vantage point, compose your picture very carefully. Different times of the day produce different lighting effects; for instance, shadows are longer in the late afternoon. You may need to introduce a sense of scale by including a near object, such as a cottage – or a gate, perhaps, with a friend leaning on it and looking away from you towards the view.

Action pictures with sharp images can be obtained only by giving very short exposures on fast film. If the minimum exposure possible on your camera has failed to produce a sharp image, try moving further back next time. The risk of movement visible on the photograph is lessened as the distance between camera and subject is increased. Alternatively, you can 'pan' the camera (move it round in the direction of, and at a speed relative to, the moving object) as you take the shot. This will produce a blurred background, which will add to the impression of speed in the photograph. Successful results have been secured with box cameras using this approach.

It is a good idea to keep your camera loaded and near to hand at all times, ready for the unexpected event or the chance of a candid shot. Try setting your focusing distance at one metre and keeping it at that setting when the camera is not in use. When shooting the unexpected, it is quicker to move to the set distance of one metre than to reset the camera. Pausing to reset every time will considerably lessen your chances of catching a good shot.

Collecting as a Hobby

Philately

Of all the collecting hobbies, stamp-collecting, or philately, is probably the greatest, measured by numbers of enthusiasts and worldwide coverage. The scope for stamp-collectors is enormous, and continues to grow every day as countries issue new sets in vast numbers. One big advantage for the beginner is that no great outlay is required when starting a stamp collection. You need basically only an album, some stamp hinges and tweezers, plus a suitable catalogue.

First you should decide what form your collection is going to take. You may wish to collect stamps of every kind from all over the world, or concentrate on specimens from a single country. You may also collect stamps from a group of nations such as the British Commonwealth, or stamps devoted to a particular subject e.g. sport, anniversaries, transport.

When you have obtained your first stamps, possibly by buying some at a local shop, you should place them in the album, as described in the catalogue, using the tweezers at all times. The stamp hinges, for mounting the stamps in the album, should be folded over 6 mm ($\frac{1}{4}$ inch) with the gummed side outwards. Moisten this fold slightly and fix it to the top of the stamp. Then moisten the other part of the hinge and stick it, together with the stamp, in place on your album leaf.

As your collection grows you will acquire duplicates of stamps. These can be set aside in a separate book or album for use as swaps. You may also need additional equipment such as a magnifying glass, watermark tray and perforation gauge.

Many collectors form groups or join stamp clubs to add to the hobby's interest and for the speedier development of their collections. In this way, catalogues and other books of reference can be shared, and the door is opened to the endless fascination and interest of philately. Stamps have historical associations and provide exciting background information on a range of subjects. Your collection will increase in value, particularly as you acquire rare specimens and complete older sets.

Over the years collecting hobbies have increased in number and range, and some of the leading ones are mentioned in the following summary.

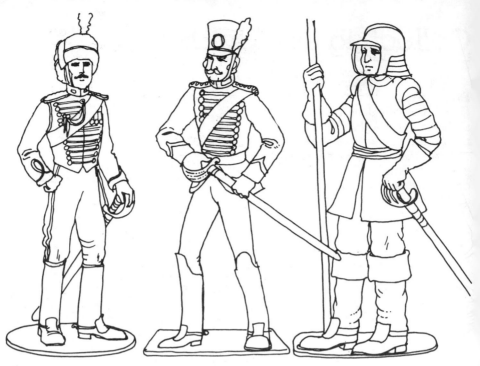

Phillumeny
Phillumeny is the collecting of matchbox labels. Like stamp-collecting, it offers worldwide scope. Some phillumenists gather all specimens, while others prefer to confine themselves to either box labels or book-matches. There are a great many varieties of both kinds. An interesting example of matchbox labels is provided by a modern Dutch series depicting veteran and vintage cars, and book-matches are issued by countless hotels and restaurants everywhere in order to advertise themselves.

There are worldwide collectors of cheese labels, beer mats (also issued by the producers of other drinks), tickets (covering transport by land, sea and air in every part of the world, and many other services and performances) and sports and theatre programmes.

Cigarette cards were widely collected in pre-World War II days but tobacco companies have now ceased to issue them. Opportunities for collecting these cards are restricted unless prospective collectors are prepared to pay considerable sums of money to acquire them. Similar series were distributed more recently by producers of tea and other commodities.

Models
The collection of models – particularly soldiers, but also many other metal miniatures – has become very popular indeed. Lead models produced from about 1890 until the time of World War II are avidly sought by keen collectors. There is a broad range of model soldiers representing the armies and

egiments of many nations, at
different periods in history. They
appear in both action and ceremonial dress and those in perfect
condition can command high prices.
Much prized are special items such
as models of the celebrated British
coronation coach, complete with
horses and riders, and the military
band of the Guards in their full-
dress uniforms.

Some collectors prefer to concen-
rate on civilians and lead models
of farm and zoo animals, or gardens
complete with beds and a variety
of flowers to slot into them. Rare
igures, such as the village curate,
can be valued highly. The range of
Dinky Toy vehicles presents another
nteresting opportunity for col-
ectors of models. Their value is
also rising. Other popular
collectors' items are model aircraft
which are built from kits.

Numismatology

The collecting of coins, numismatology, is another hobby which
provides great scope. Nations have
minted coins since the earliest
historically-recorded times. Designs
are changed frequently, particularly
when a new monarch or ruler takes
office.

In recent years many countries
have converted their currencies to
a decimal system, offering collectors
the opportunity to acquire the old,
outgoing coins. Inflation, too, often
causes a change of coinage, one
example being the introduction of
the new franc in France not long
after World War II. At that time
many comparatively short-lived
coins were minted as a result of
military actions and the political

changes that arose from them.

Closely associated with numismatology is the collection of paper money, which circulated in China as far back as AD 650. Collectors sometimes specialize by concentrating on notes from only one country, on artistic design, on associations with historical events, or on a particular theme. There is a great variety of notes from World War II, including military notes, occupation notes, and paper money issued by partisan forces or for prisoners of war.

Ordinary stamp albums can be used for a paper money collection if you use photo-corners for mounting, but banknote albums are also available. These are designed so that you can see both sides of the notes. The historical and geographical interest to be derived from collecting paper money is enormous, besides which there is every probability that the value of notes will increase as years go by.

Playing cards

Playing cards appeal to a growing number of people as collectors' items. Before the 16th century, playing cards were hand-made on a small scale and were often works of art in their own right. After that time they were printed in large quantities. Early examples are rare and valuable but in those manufactured nearer our own time the range and variety are enormous.

Specialization often takes place in this hobby, like so many others. Some enthusiasts are interested in only the back or front designs of cards; some adopt a particular theme or concentrate on jokers only. There are packs devoted to specific themes: artistic, comical, educational or political. Fashion also plays a part as, for instance, during the French Revolution, when court cards were designed without crowns and sceptre-heads, in deference to republicanism. Christian religious symbolism is to be seen on tarot cards, first issued in medieval times in Italy.

Postcards

Postcard-collecting is, perhaps, one of the simplest hobbies to take up because there are so many types of card available everywhere, generally at low cost. Ordinary view-cards, sent by people on holiday, may provide the foundation of a collection which can later be expanded or directed into special subjects. Old cards showing places, buildings, streets, vehicles and people of bygone days are interesting in themselves and can often be compared with modern cards depicting the same scenes as they appear today. Stamp shops, antique or bric-a-brac dealers and some market stalls are likely places to pick up such cards for a collection.

If and when you decide to start specializing in postcard-collecting, the following categories are suggested: art reproduction, art nouveau, aviation, railways, religious or romantic themes, royalty, shipping, sport, theatre, military, heraldic, political, novelty and fantasy.

Prints and maps

Purchasing original prints and maps, or copies of them, can be a rather expensive hobby but a great

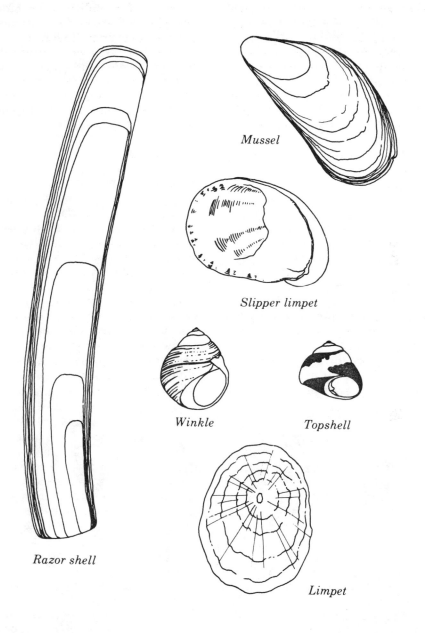

Mussel

Slipper limpet

Razor shell

Winkle

Topshell

Limpet

deal can be achieved without too great an outlay. Searching for prints and maps can provide pleasure and interest for a lifetime, and the results of the collector's efforts can be framed and displayed. There is great scope for specialization. You may wish, for example, to concentrate on the work of a particular artist or collect maps of a certain region showing changes that have taken place throughout two or three hundred years.

Natural history

A natural history collection offers special interest to ramblers and lovers of the outdoors. There are plenty of botanical and geological specimens awaiting the collector everywhere, but no collector should pick any protected flowers or plants. The seashore offers considerable scope, too, with a large variety of seashells and seaweeds obtainable in many places.

Frequently, however, natural history enthusiasts prefer to observe wildlife in its natural environment.

Instead of collecting specimens at random, they compile a large album of drawings, photographs, maps and notes of what they have seen, recording exactly when and where discoveries were made. All manner of relevant items can be included so that the collector builds up a comprehensive survey of a particular area, complete with all the necessary pictorial and textual information of what can be found there throughout the year. Sometimes items from the past come to light as well, adding a little archaeological and historical interest to the collection.

Nowadays, people are interested in making collections of almost anything, but particularly items which become increasingly rare as time goes on. Old bottles of every shape and size, tins of bygone days, wooden boxes, old-fashioned toys, utensils and ornaments, and gramophone records of past times are a few examples of objects which offer a great deal of interest to collectors.

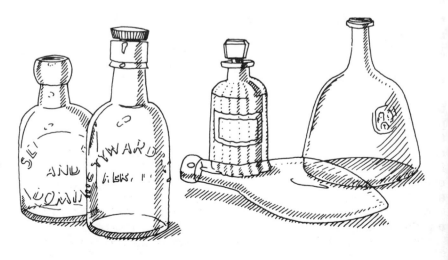

Crafts

Most handicrafts are based on very simple techniques and most of them date back to prehistoric times. When our ancestors first began to twist fibres together, to make ropes and nets, to spin hair and wool, and to combine these with knots or weaves to make fabric, they had very little to work with. You will find, often, that the most interesting things are produced with a few pieces of basic equipment and some scraps of material or yarn.

The next few pages will show how you can start to use some of the different techniques to make things yourself. You may know some of these techniques already, but there are always new ideas to try out and new ways of making a particular thing. Have you tried knitting a cushion cover? Or making an owl out of knots?

Equipment
The following items will be of use to you and some of them will be necessary for several techniques, so you should try to obtain or borrow:

a pair of scissors for material and a pair of scissors for paper and card
tape measure
pins, both large and small
tacks
cardboard
fine sewing needles
embroidery needles
a bodkin or large blunt needle, with a large hole
a piece of insulating board or fibreboard, about 18 inches square

beads, sequins and buttons of different sizes and colours
empty cotton reels
sticks – plant supporting cane, for example
as many scraps of different yarns (e.g. wool, cotton and silk)
scraps of different materials (used or unused)
sewing threads
embroidery threads
adhesive transparent plastic
paintbrush
blotting paper
pencil and paper
pair of compasses
ruler
crochet hook
pair of knitting needles
rubber solution glue
optional – rigid heddle and box loom
embroidery ring

ROPES AND CORDS
To make a length of twisted cord, take a strand of yarn (wool, cotton, string, etc.) and fasten one end to something secure, such as a drawer handle. Pull tautly on the yarn and begin to twist it in the direction of the twist already on it. When it begins to look very twisted, still holding it tautly, take hold of the middle of the yarn and bring the end you are holding to meet the other fastened end. Carefully allow the end you are holding to unravel into itself, undo the fastened end and tie the two ends together with an OVERHAND KNOT (*see* diagram).

You can vary the type of cord in

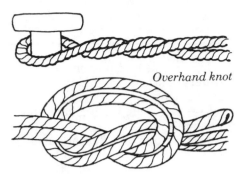

Overhand knot

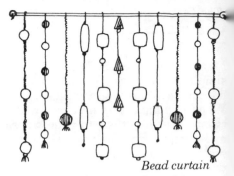

Bead curtain

these ways:
– use two or three yarns together, twisting them as if they were one;
– take two strands of yarn and twist each separately;
– put more or less twist in the yarn. Always remember to secure the ends with a knot. When measuring your strands make allowance for the twists, you will find that you need more than twice the cord's finished length in yarn.

PROJECT IDEA
bead curtain
You will need
lengths of coloured and/or natural yarn
beads with large holes
strong holding cord or string for the top of the curtain
With cords alone, you can make something extremely attractive and eye-catching to hang in front of a window or on a wall!

When you have decided on the size of the curtain and the colours you want to use (a mixture could be very effective), you will be ready to start. The strong holding cord or curtain cord, which is to be the top of the curtain, should be secured to a convenient working place such as between two drawer handles on a chest of drawers. Take the colour

you want to begin with and measure at least three times the length of the finished cord in your chosen yarn. Double it and place it around the holding cord. Now start twisting both strands of the yarn and let it unravel into itself. Thread some beads onto your new cord and secure each bead somewhere on the cord by tying a knot underneath it so that it won't slip down. Then tie a knot at the bottom of the cord, where the two ends are. Repeat until you have as many cords hanging from the holding cord as you wish. Vary the points at which you secure the beads on the cord. You can also thread beads on before you start twisting or tie beads into the knot, as well as leave the bead above the knot. Let some cords hang without beads or knots and some cords hang with a knot or two only. Finally, tidy the ends of the cords and the curtain is ready to hang up.

Macramé
The word macramé comes from the Arab word *mukharram* meaning trellis and the technique is based on a few knots which are repeated in various ways. All that is needed is the yarn to work with, a board to pin the work on (for example, an

The Larkshead

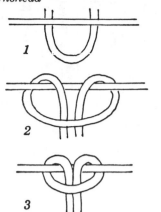

1

2

3

The Half-knot

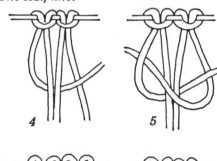

4

5

6

7

The Square-knot

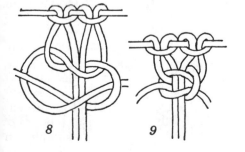

8

9

insulating board covered with cotton), large-headed pins or tacks, and scissors. The kinds of yarn to try are dishcloth cotton, crochet cotton, parcel string, rope, leather strips, nylon cord, piping cord, wool etc. but the easiest sort of yarn to work with is a medium-thick, smooth yarn with a good twist in it.

The square knot and the half knot

To start the work, tie a short length (20–30 cm/8–12 in) of any strong string or cord to two large pins, spaced 15 cm (6 in) or so apart on your working board. Cut four lengths of yarn, each about 1 m (40 in) long, and mount them onto the holding cord in the following way: fold each length in half and pass the loop formed behind the holding cord, pushing both long ends through the loop. This is known as the LARKSHEAD. (*See* diagrams 1, 2 and 3.) In the end, you should have eight strands hanging off the holding cord, on the board. Take the first four strands and pass the left-hand one of these behind the next two and over the fourth (diagram 4). Pass the right-hand strand over the centre two and through the loop formed by the left-hand strand (diagram 5). Pull the two outer strands up firmly. This is the HALF-KNOT (diag. 6).

Now continue with this knot to make the SQUARE KNOT. Take the right-hand strand (this was on the left-hand side originally) and pass it under the centre two and over the strand lying on the left-hand side (diagram 7). Next, take the left-hand strand and pass it over the centre two and through the loop on the right-hand side (diagram 8). Pull the two ends tightly. This is the completed square knot (diagram 9).

Work five square knots on both sets of four strands. Then take the centre four strands (so that there are two strands left over on either side) and make ten half knots. You will find that it tends to want to curl round in a spiral and this is part of its pattern. Now take the side pairs and make overhand knots (*see* previous section on ropes and cords) with them. On one side, use the same strand each time to tie the knot (diagram 1a or 1b) and on the other, alternate the strands (diagram 2). The second method gives a pretty bobbled effect and looks especially good in a fringe.

You have worked the square knot or flat knot (which is, in fact, similar to the reef knot), half knot, and overhand knot.
Practise these knots on the strands you have and try combining them in different ways. For example, use different groups of four for the knots, as well as repeating a knot on the same strands. Try to build up little patterns using these knots. One pattern you can try makes a kind of net effect (diagram 3) using the square knot. Another variation of it is shown in diagram 4.

Finally, you can use the square knot to make a PICOT edging. If you make one knot below another, using the same strands but leaving a space between them, and then push up the lower knot, you will find a little loop has formed

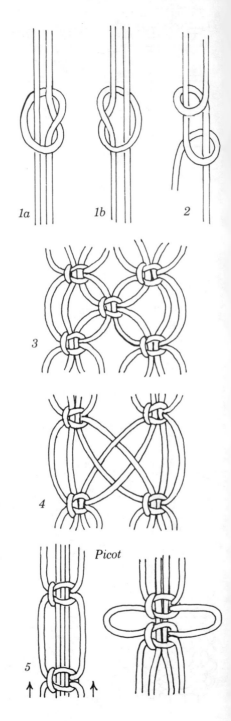

248

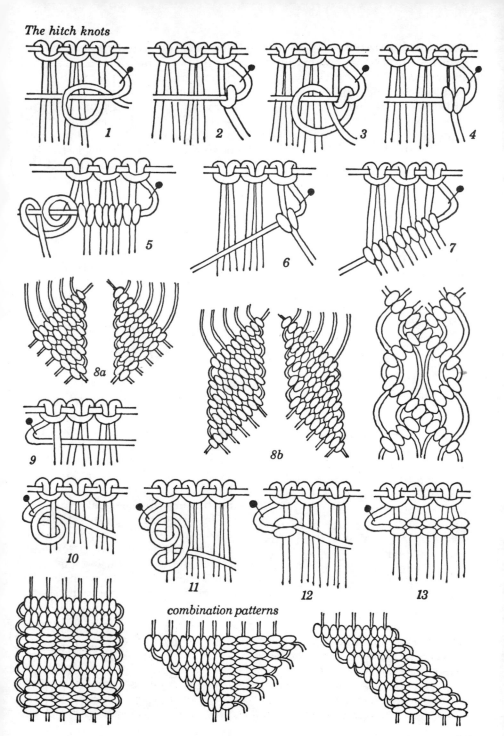

combination patterns

between the knots. This is a picot (diagram 5). Try some picots in different sizes.

Take this sample off the holding cord by sliding it off and keep it for reference.

The half hitch, the double half hitch or clove hitch

Cut four more lengths of yarn, a little longer this time. Mount them on the holding cord using the lark's heads as before. You are now going to try the other basic macramé knots – the HALF HITCH and the DOUBLE HALF HITCH. These knots can be worked upwards and downwards (vertically), or sideways (horizontally) or on a slant (diagonally).

Start at the very right-hand side and take the first strand as your 'knot-bearer'. Place the strand at a right-angle to the other strands as in diagram 1 and pick up the second strand from the right. Wind it clockwise round the horizontal strand and pull (diagram 2). This is one half hitch. Repeat this and you will have the double half hitch. (diagrams 3 and 4). Complete the row in this manner (diagram 5). Try several rows, starting at the right each time. You will find that the rows start coming in on a slant. If you then do a few rows working from left to right, you will find, the slant travels in the opposite direction.

Now try working the double half hitch on the diagonal as in diagrams 6 and 7. This is a little more tricky but, if you do a few rows, you will see that it is not as hard as it first seemed. The most important thing is to take care that

you pull the strands evenly. Now try a few of the patterns using the double half hitch diagonally (diagrams 8a and 8b).

Finally, try the double half hitch vertically. For this, each of the hanging strands becomes a 'knot-bearer', and the strand on the left or right of the work is the actual knotter. Start with your first strand underneath the next one as in diagram 9. Then make the clockwise knots as in diagrams 10 and 11 and continue along the row, remembering to place the knotting strand under the next strand each time (diagrams 12 and 13). And lastly, try a few of the patterns using combinations of horizontal and vertical double half hitches.

PROJECT IDEAS

If you liked trying out these knots and think that you would like to do something with them, why not try and make a little knotted picture? All you need is a stick or rod to hang your strand on, the yarn and extra beads or buttons as desired. You can use the diagonal double half hitch to make curved shapes for flowery and leaf patterns, adding beads onto the strands for extra interest. Another shape from nature that would suit macramé technique is an owl. Remember you don't have to use each single strand for a knot; you can take

groups of the strands and use them as one. This way you can bring two sides of a piece in towards the middle. You can leave the ends of strands hanging to make a fringe.

When you have a design in mind that you would like to try, draw it roughly on some paper. Think what texture you want – should it be rough, shiny, smooth etc.? And decide what colours you are using – are they natural, contrasting, toning? Finally, cut enough yarn for the work: square knots use up over half the length and double half hitches take up at least four to eight times as much! So allow for the types of knots you make.

A simpler project might be to make a small bag. You will need two wooden rings for the handles. Start by mounting at least 24 doubled strands of yarn onto each handle. Fasten the handle onto your working board or a door handle and work a few rows on each handle separately as in the pattern on page 48, diagram 3. This way you will have two slits at the top of the bag. Then take a piece of cardboard, roughly the size of your bag, or a cushion, or a block of foam, and work the knots all round until you have reached the length you want for your bag. A pair of strands from each side (two pairs) are then knotted together at the bottom of the bag with an overhand knot.

WRAPPING, TASSLES AND POM-POMS

There are several ways of making attractive finishes and extra decorations to add to what you are making. Tassels and pom-poms can also be used by themselves to make little dolls, furry animals, balls, bells etc.

WRAPPING is an excellent way of making ends look very neat (for example with a knotted curtain or bag). To wrap a group of ends, first smooth them out. Then, holding them firmly together, take a length of the yarn you are using for wrapping, make a loop as shown in diagram 1 and hold it against the group of ends. Start winding the yarn firmly over the loop and the group of ends (diagram 2). Work upwards, covering the loop, but leave a small part of the loop showing, and thread your wrapping yarn through this loop (diagram 3). Now pull the lower end of your wrapping yarn showing and you will see the top end of your wrapping yarn tuck under the wrapped section as the loop disappears. You can then cut the top end off and neaten the lower pulling end (diagram 4).

You can use wrapping to make TASSLES. Start by cutting off a group of threads the same length. A simple method for doing this is shown in diagram 5; just make sure that the width of the card you wind the yarn around is the length of the tassle you want. Cut another length longer than the tassle threads and tie it round the middle of the group with an overhand knot (diagram 6). Alternatively you could use a lark's head (*see* the

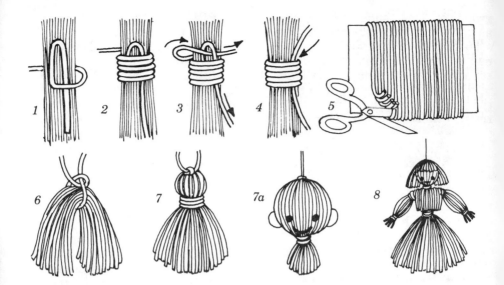

1 2 3 4 5

6 7 7a 8

section on macramé). If you wrap the threads firmly a little way down, you will make a neck as in diagram 7.

Now, if you try putting a bean, or a bead into the top part of the tassle, before you wrap it, you can make its head even rounder. The bigger the object you use for stuffing it, the more threads you will need for the tassle. Try using an empty cotton reel which you have covered with the same yarn as you have used for your tassle.

These little shapes can be used as Christmas tree figures or even presents. You can sew on sequins for eyes, use felt for ears or wings, extra wool for hair (7a), and you can combine more than one tassle to make a tassle doll (diagram 8).

To make POM-POMS, you will need some strongish cardboard and a pair of good cutting scissors, as well as the yarn you are using for your pom-pom. Draw out two discs on your card, each with a large hole in the middle (for example, use a saucer for the outer circle and a glass for the hole in the middle). The size of the pom-pom depends on the size of the disc. You then begin winding your yarn round the two discs together, as in ⁀iagram 1. You might need to use a thick-eyed blunt needle towards the end, but you can equally well do this with your fingers.

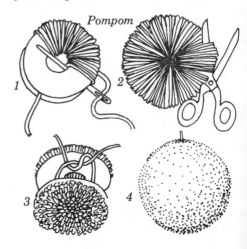

Pompom

1 2 3 4

Continue winding until the centre hole is completely filled and no more yarn can be pushed through, as in diagram 2. The yarn is then cut with sharp-pointed scissors, which you guide carefully between the outer edges of the two cardboard discs (diagram 2).

When the discs are free and all the yarn is cut, you push them apart slightly and tie a length of yarn round the cut threads between the discs, as in diagram 3. Fasten this thread securely. The ends of this length of yarn are left long so that the pom-pom can be attached to whatever you are making. The cardboard discs are then gently pulled off (diagram 4).

An attractive mobile

PROJECT IDEA
Try making a mobile out of different kinds of tassles and sizes of pom-poms.
You will need
either some light but firm wire or some gardening sticks
different coloured yarns
sequins, buttons, felt, and sewing things

It is better not to try and make a mobile that is too big and it is much easier if you start from the lower part, balancing each new section against the rest as you create your colourful mobile.

CROCHET
You may have done some crochet already and, if you have, you will know that all you need is a crochet hook and some wool. There are just a few basic stitches and, with these, you can make many things, for which there are plenty of patterns available. In a short time, with a bit of practice, you can also start to make things for yourself or others.

The first stitch
Make the first loop or slip knot as follows. Hold the end of your wool between the thumb and the second finger of your left hand while you pass the strand around your first finger, from the side nearest to you. Bring the wool round to the left of the circle this makes and hold the loop in place with your thumb. Pick up the crochet hook, as if you were going to write with it, slip it under the loop where it crosses the top of your first finger and draw the strand of wool through. Drop the loop off the finger and draw the wool up to the hook. (*See* diagrams 1 and 2.)

Keep the wool away from the work by looping the long thread round the little finger of your left

253

hand, across the palm and behind the first finger (diagram 2). You have now made one CHAIN-STITCH. Hold the end of this stitch between your thumb and first finger (diagram 3) close to the hook and pass the crochet hook under the wool behind the chain. Catch it from left to right (diagram 4) and draw it through the first stitch. Repeat this until you have a short length of chain (diagram 5). Try not to pull the stitches too tightly and keep them as even as possible. You have now made a foundation row.

Slip-stitch or single crochet
To make the second row, you can now do the basic crochet stitch – SLIP-STITCH. Pass the hook into the stitch below to the left of the hook, you now have two loops on your hook. Catch the wool again from left to right and draw it through both loops. When you turn to come back, make one chain and this counts as the first slip-stitch in the next row. The stitch makes a flat chain, which is useful for edges or for joining two edges together (diagrams 6 and 7).

Double crochet
Instead of making one chain extra at the end of your last row, make two. Put your hook into the next stitch, under both of its top loops, then under the wool from left to right and draw it through, which gives two loops on the hook (diagrams 1 and 2, p. 54). Pass the hook under the wool again and draw it through both loops (diagram 3). This leaves one loop on the hook. Continue along the row and start

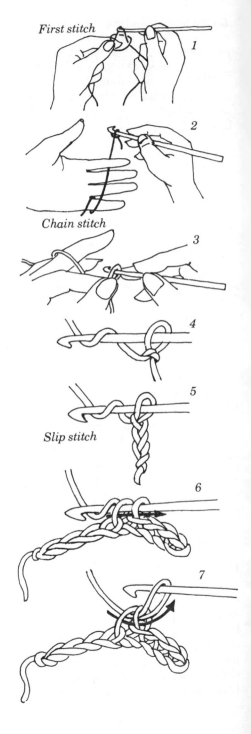

First stitch

Chain stitch

Slip stitch

1
2
3
4
5
6
7

Double Crochet

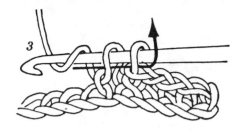

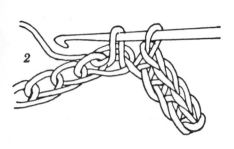

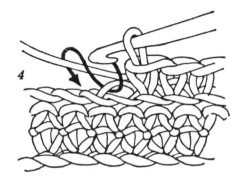

the second row of DOUBLE
CROCHET by making two chains
again. If you wish to have a ribbed
effect with this stitch, instead of
passing the hook under both loops
of the stitch below, just pass the
hook under one of these loops
(diagram 4). The other loop then
forms a little ridge and creates the
rib effect. This applies also for
single crochet.

Half treble
Begin the row with three extra
chains. Pass the hook under the wool
and then straight into the first stitch
below. This makes three loops on
the hook. Catch the wool once
more from left to right and draw it
through all loops on the hook,
leaving one loop (diagrams 5 and 6).

Treble crochet
Start by making three extra chains
at the end of the last row and pass
your hook under the wool from left
to right and then under the stitch
below, making three loops on the
hook. Pass the hook under the
wool again and draw it through
two of the loops (diagram 7), pass
the hook again under the wool and
draw it through the two remaining
loops (diagram 8). Remember to
make the extra chains at the ends.

Double treble
For this stitch, you make four
extra chains at the end of each
row. Pass the hook twice under the
wool, and then under the next
stitch. Pull the wool through to
make four loops on the hook. Pass

255

Half treble

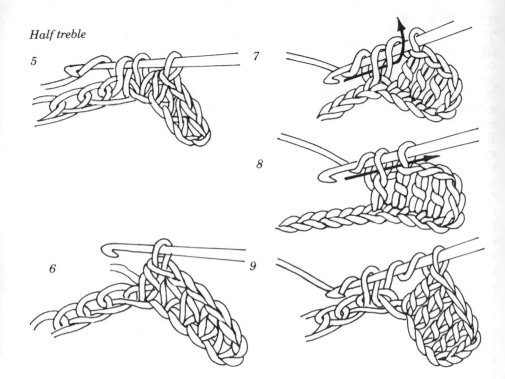

the hook under the wool and draw it through two of these loops. Put it under the wool again and draw through two more loops, again, and then through the remaining loops (diag. 9).

To complete crochet
Cut off the wool, leaving about 15 cm (6 in). Draw the wool through the last loop on the hook until it has all come through and tighten. Sew in the rest of the wool with a thick-eyed needle.
Note: For those who are left-handed, the instructions are reversed and the diagrams will be correct if seen in a mirror.

PROJECT IDEA
Once you feel more comfortable about the crochet stitches you have learnt, you can begin to make articles by following patterns or experimenting yourself. Here is a simple pattern for a crochet square that you can try. It is known as 'Old America'. It could be used for a baby blanket or a shawl, or even a rug, depending on the thickness of the wool you choose. Remember, you will need a larger crochet hook for thicker wool. When joining up the squares for the article you are making, oversew the edge loops of the sides of each square and be careful not to draw the stitches too tight. Use wool or silk to match your work and try not to stretch one edge more than another. Press the seams lightly with an iron on a damp cloth.

The pattern

This square is very effective if done in two contrasting colours but you could make it multi-coloured, or just plain, and vary the squares. Make 6 chains in a light colour and join into a ring with a slip-stitch.

Round 1: With the light colour, make two chains, two trebles and three chains, * three trebles, three chains into a ring and repeat from * twice, then slip-stitch to first two chains.

Round 2: With the dark colour, slip-stitch to first space, (two chains, two trebles, three chains, three trebles) into first three chain space, * (1 chain, 3 trebles, 3 chains, 3 trebles) into next 3 chain space, repeat from * twice, join with a slip-stitch.

Round 3: With the light colour, slip-stitch to first space (2 chains, 2 trebles, 3 chains, 3 trebles) into first 3 chain space, * 1 chain, 3 trebles into 1 chain space (1 chain, 3 trebles, 3 chains, 3 trebles) into each corner, repeat from * ending 1 chain, slip-stitch to join.

Round 4: With the dark colour, slip-stitch to first space (2 chains, 2 trebles, 3 chains, 3 trebles) into first 3 chain space * 1 chain, 3 trebles into each 1 chain space (1 chain, 3 trebles, 3 chains, 3 trebles) into each corner, repeat from * ending 1 chain, slip-stitch to join. Fasten off, leaving a thread long enough to join the squares later.

When making up the final article, you could add a little flower at each corner join. These are very simple to make and can of course be used in many other ways. For the flower you simply need some of the wool you are using and a pencil. Cut a length about the size of the pencil and another length two or three times longer. Hold the shorter length against the pencil and wind the other length of wool around the pencil and wool.

Tuck the beginning end under the next loop. When you have wound the wool around, hold the pencil firmly in one hand, taking care the wool does not unravel, and pull the two ends of the short length of wool up. Tie them together and when you have slipped the whole row of loops of the pencil, fasten the knot tightly. The loops will bunch out into a flower. Use the ends of the holding strand of wool for sewing the flower on.

If you wish, you can add an extra row of slip-stitch all the way around the finished article to make it even more attractive.

KNITTING

We shall only be dealing with knitting with two needles here. You can also do circular knitting, in tubes. If you have knitted before, you will have seen that, even more than with crochet, the size of the needles and the type of yarn affect the finished product. For the best results, use rigid knitting needles with good (not sharp) points made in a light metal alloy.

Wool is definitely the most common material used in knitting. It has great elasticity, unless this is spoilt by careless washing, and it is of course warm and, up to a point, weatherproof. Cotton does not stretch so much and may not

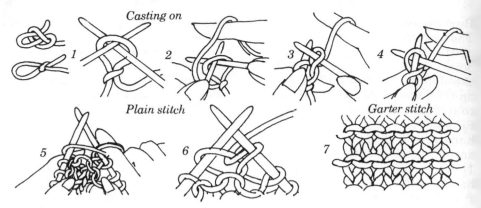

Casting on

1
2
3
4

Plain stitch

5
6
7

Garter stitch

keep its shape so well when knitted.

Try out different yarns to see how they look when knitted. What does parcel string do? However, when making something special, you should follow the pattern or try out the yarn on different needles until you get the required effect and the right amount of stitches per centimetre.

Holding the needles

In your left hand, the needle should be between your fingers and thumb and against the palm. In the right hand, the needle should rest on top of the hand between the thumb and the first finger. The wool lies across the top of the first finger of the right hand and is looped under the second finger to hold it firm.

Casting on

With your wool, make a loop 10 cm (4 in) from the end. (*See* section on crochet.) Hang it onto the left-hand needle and push the right-hand needle into the stitch (diagram 1). Pass the wool around the point of the right-hand needle in a clockwise direction (diagram 2).

Pull the wool through the stitch on the left-hand needle, using the point of the right-hand needle (diagram 3). Slip the new stitch from the right-hand to the left-hand needle (diagram 4). Repeat until you have the number of stitches you need on the left-hand needle.

Plain stitch

Push the point of the right-hand needle into the first stitch on the left-hand needle from left to right and pass the wool, from behind, clockwise around the right-hand needle (diagram 5). Pull the loop through the stitch on the left-hand needle (diagram 6) and slip the stitch off the left-hand needle, keeping the new stitch on the right-hand needle. The wool stays behind the needles when doing this stitch.

Garter stitch

This is a strip of knitting where every row is plain stitch. It is very stretchy and thick (diagram 7).

Note: At the end of a row, turn the right-hand needle round so that it becomes the left-hand needle.

Purl stitch

The wool is kept in front of the needle for this stitch. Push the point of the right-hand needle through the front of the first stitch on the left-hand needle from right to left (the opposite to plain stitch). Pass the wool around the right-hand needle from the front in an anti-clockwise direction (diagram 1). Keeping this loop on the right-hand needle, draw it through the stitch on the left-hand needle (diagram 2) and slip the stitch off the left-hand needle.

Stocking stitch

This is knitting where one row is purl and the next row is plain, and continuing in this way. It is often used in patterns (diagram 3).

Ribbing

This is made by knitting one purl stitch and one plain stitch repeatedly along the row and is worked with an even number of stitches, to give a rib effect (diagram 4). A variation is to knit two purl and two plain to give a wider rib (diagram 5).

Increasing

Knit the stitch as usual, but do not slip it off the left-hand needle. Instead, push the point of the right-hand needle through the back of the same stitch on the left-hand needle and knit it again. Slip the stitch off the left-hand needle, keeping the two new stitches made from it on the right-hand needle (diagram 6).

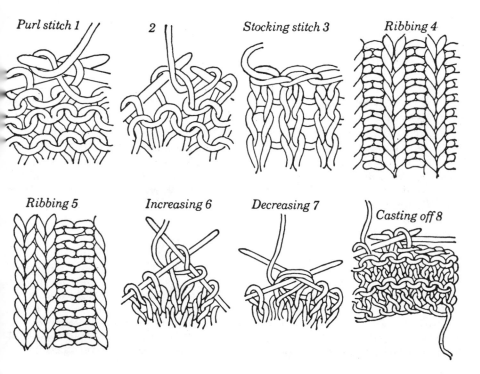

Purl stitch 1   *2*   *Stocking stitch 3*   *Ribbing 4*

Ribbing 5   *Increasing 6*   *Decreasing 7*   *Casting off 8*

Decreasing
Simply knit two stitches together (diagram 7).

Casting off
Knit two stitches and with the point of the left-hand needle, slip the first stitch on the right-hand needle over the second. Knit another stitch onto the right-hand needle and again slip the first over the second (diagram 8). Repeat until the row is finished, and one stitch remains. Break the wool and draw it through the last stitch, pulling firmly. The end is now ready to be sewn.

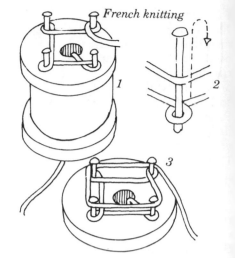

French knitting

PROJECT IDEA
There are so many patterns available for different kinds of knitted garments and objects that it would be worth trying out some ideas here which you might not find in a bought pattern. There is nothing to stop you knitting with strips of paper if you want and you can certainly include beads and sequins on to your yarn before you start knitting. You can also change your yarns in the middle of the knitting. Either knit the two yarns together for a section and then drop the old one behind, cutting it to leave about 10 cm (4 in), or leave 10 cm (4 in) straight away and sew the ends in later.

Try making four equal-sized patches or squares from as many different textures as you like, using both different stitches and different yarn for effect. You could try to make one diagonally, i.e. start from one or two stitches and increase at either end until you come to the centre diagonal and then start decreasing until you have a square.

Remember that a ribbed pattern will pull the knitting much more than a garter stitch or stocking stitch. You can join your squares with a crochet or embroidery stitch and use this as the front of a cushion.

French knitting
This is a basic form of circular knitting which is done on an empty cotton reel that has four small nails or tacks pushed into one end, equally spaced apart. The only other item you need apart from the yarn is a blunt needle. To begin, pull the yarn through the hole in the middle of the reel and loop it round the nails, going from right to left (diagram 1).

When all the loops have been made, pass the yarn right round the four nails (diagram 2) and hold in place. Take the needle and slip the first loop around the first nail and over the yarn held around the nail. You now have a new loop (diagram 3). This is the basic stitch

Four-stranded plaits

and it is repeated continuously.

Soon the knitted tube will appear at the lower end of the reel and will grow longer as you go on knitting. When the tube is long enough, break the working yarn, leaving enough to put into a needle and thread through the loops on the reel. Slip all the loops off and pull the yarn tight.

PROJECT IDEAS

The lengths of tube can be used to line clothes, oven cloths, added on to toys and used as cords for bags. You can also coil them around so that they look like a snail's shell and stitch them in this shape to make little mats. If you have used different colours in your knitting, the little mat will look bright and interestingly patterned.

FOUR-STRANDED PLAITS

These can also be used in many ways. Like the tube of French knitting, plaits can be used for edging on bags, jackets, tablecloths, and also coiled and stitched together to make mats and even baskets. Again, the colour of the yarns provides new patterns. The plaits shown here can be made with only your fingers and the yarn. If you have a board handy, one end can be pinned onto it, but you can also tie the end of your plait to a handle, or even your big toe, as the women in some tribes do.

To practise these plaits, start by using two contrasting colours only. Cut two lengths of the yarn, fold them in half and secure them. Arrange them first, as in diagram 1, in the order Light 1, Dark 1, Light 2, Dark 2. After you have tried this plait and worked a small length of it, arrange the strands as in diagram 2, in order Light 1, Light 2, Dark 1, Dark 2. The plaiting sequence is the same for both:

Left strand over middle two strands, right over left strand
New left strand over middle two strands, right over left strand
Repeat.

This plait is flat. You can also make a round plait from four strands. Take them in the order Light 1, Light 2, Dark 1, Dark 2, as in diagram 3. The plaiting sequence now is:

L1 behind L2 and D1, over D1, the order now is L2, L1, D1, D2
D2 behind D1 and L1, over L1, the order now is L2, L1, D2, D1
L2 behind L1 and D2, over D2, the order now is L1, L2, D2, D1
D1 behind D2 and L2, over L2, the order now is L1, L2, D1, D2
Repeat.

Once you see how the pattern is made you will find the plaiting becomes quite easy. Lastly, you can try a plait with a diagonal pattern running over it. Arrange your four strands in this order, as in diagram 4; Dark 1, Light 1, Light 2, Dark 2. The plait is made as follows:

Take the left strand over the one next to it
Take the right strand under the one next to it, and over the next strand
Repeat.

Now you have tried the plaits in light and dark contrasting colours, you can try to vary the colours, the thicknesses and the texture of the yarns, and see what effects you get.

FINGER WEAVING

If you tried making the plaits, you will have made narrow strips of cord or band, depending on whether it was a rounded or a flat plait. Plaits can be made wider, by adding more strands and continuing to cross the strands over and under each other. Wider plaits are, however, not always as firm and strong as braids and belts made by FINGER WEAVING. It is easier to pull the yarn tighter with the latter method. Mostly, you will find finger weaving used for straps, trimmings and belts, for daintier objects such as chokers or bracelets, and for softer bands such as neck-ties. Your hands can only

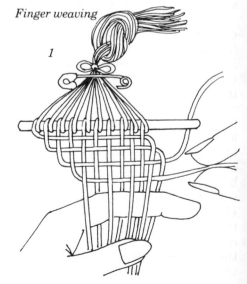

Finger weaving

1

control a certain number of strands at once! Plaiting and finger-weaving may look alike, but the difference between making plaits and finger weaving is that plaits are made with the threads being worked over and under each other diagonally, whereas in finger weaving you use the strands as warp threads and weft threads, as you do in all types of weaving. WARP threads are a set of vertical yarns (each length of yarn making the warp is called a WARP END). WEFT is the thread or threads that pass through the warp ends horizontally. In finger weaving, the warp and weft threads are actually the same threads, depending on how you are using them. This is not the case with most kinds of weaving.

You will need
a pencil
coloured yarns of about the same thickness
scissors

Cut 10 equal lengths of yarn. The finished article will be about $\frac{1}{3}$ the length of your cut yarn, if you want a fringe as well, and about $\frac{1}{2}$ if you do not want a fringe. Gather the ends of your yarn together and tie an overhand knot. Fasten this knot somewhere securely. Then, take a pencil and wind each strand of yarn around it, about 5 cm (2 in) below the knot. It is neater if you wind all the strands the same way. Now, working from left to right, take the first strand, weave it under the second strand, over the third, under the fourth and so on until you have come to the end of

the row. Pull the strand parallel to the pencil (this strand has now been used as a weft). Keep this strand pulled up towards the pencil until the next row is completed, when it will become another new warp end hanging downwards. Repeat from left to right, You can see how this works out in diagram 1, and note that you are using the same strands both downwards (as warp ends) and across (as wefts). It is not always easy at the beginning to keep your strands untangled and to keep the work firm. But after a few rows you will begin to see your band growing.

To finish, you can either leave the strands at an angle, or continue to weave each new row, leaving one strand spare at the end each time, until you have an edge at 90° from the sides. Then you can either tie overhand knots close to the last strand passed across to make a loose fringe, twist the strands together to make a corded fringe or plait a few of the strands at a time to make a plaited fringe. Finish cords and plaits off with another overhand knot. You can add beads onto the fringe or even onto the band itself but, for the latter, you must start by threading the beads on your strands.

For a hem, tie the strands in pairs with a square knot, trim the ends close to the knot and turn the ends over to the wrong side. Fold again 2·5 cm (1 in) from the edge. Using the same yarn as in the weaving, stitch right through the work to prevent the ends unfolding.

Patterns
Diagonal stripes Set the strands in colour groupings, e.g. 6 of green,

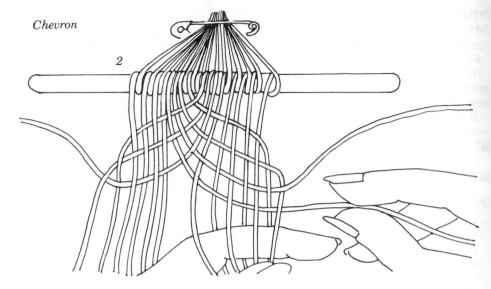

2

6 of cream, and 6 of rose.

Wavy lines Again use stripes of coloured strands, as with the diagonal stripes, but when you have used each strand once for the weft, working from left to right, begin taking your weft from right to left. Continue working from this direction, and when you want to change the angle of the stripes again, start working from the opposite side. You can make your own wavy pattern – large, small, or mixed.

Chevron Take an even number of colours and strands and divide into two groups, each with the same sequence of colours, Mount them on the pencil as shown in diagram 2. The colour sequence on one side reflects but does not repeat the colour sequence on the other side. Take the first warp end at the right of the left group and weave this end over to the very right. Pull it parallel to the pencil. Now take the first warp end on the left of your

right hand group and weave it over to the left hand side, again pulling it parallel to the pencil. Repeat. You will notice that you now have two different weft strands making new warp ends at either side. Using this pattern, the band does not slope out at an angle as it did with all of the previous examples in this section.

Diamond in chevron Mount the strands on the pencil in the same sequence as for the chevron pattern above, but start half way down. Tie one lot of warp ends in a loose knot to keep them out of the way. With the free strands, work the chevron pattern to the length you want. Then untie the loose knot, take the pencil out, turn the work round so the other half of the warp ends are hanging ready for you to work them, and continue the chevron pattern. You are now working in the opposite direction and forming a diamond in the centre of your band.

PROJECT

Make a colourful belt or headband for yourself, using any one of the patterns above. Remember to allow 2 to 3 times more yarn than the length of the finished article. Also try using different textures of yarn – fluffy, smooth, tightly twisted, wobbly – in a combination that you like.

NEEDLE WEAVING

You will need

a sheet of strong card the size of the article you are making (e.g. if it's a little bag, you will need a card twice the length of the bag and a little wider)
card-cutting scissors
a blunt needle with an eye thick enough for your chosen yarn
yarn (wool is easier to start with).

To prepare the card Make a set of holes at either end of the card, 1 cm (0·5 in) apart, with the point of the scissors. The holes should be parallel to one another (diag I).
To make the warp Thread your needle with a good length of yarn. Tie a double overhead knot at the end and thread it through the first hole on one side, down through the parallel hole on the other side, up through the next hole on the first side and so on until you have reached the last hole. Keep the yarn pulled firmly, but not too tight, and check that all the strands are at about the same tension. Make another double overhand knot on the wrong side (the right side is where the strands pass straight down the card). You are now ready to start weaving.
To weave Thread another length

Needle weaving

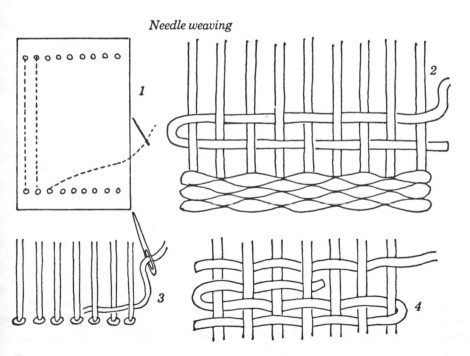

of yarn through your needle and pass your needle over and under a few warp ends near the edge as in diagram 2. This will keep the end in neatly. Then pass the needle alternately over and under each warp end until you come to the end of the row. If you are over this last warp end, you now go under it to start your next row, and vice versa. Push each row down with your fingers, so that it looks like the weaving in diagram 3. This is called PLAIN WEAVE.

To make a stripe Make at least two rows in another contrasting colour. Try and see what happens if you do just one row in a contrasting colour, the next row in your main colour, then another row in a contrasting colour and so on. Do you get some other stripes? What happens when you use weft yarns of different thicknesses? And what happens when you weave with strips of rag cloth? With a thicker weft, do you see more of the warp ends or less? Can you make new patterns using thick and thin wefts? Remember not to pull tight on your weft or you will find your weaving becoming narrower and narrower. If your warp ends need to be a little tauter, slide a ruler or a pencil underneath to give some extra tension. Begin a new weft by doubling over a few centimetres of the old weft, as in diagram 4.

To finish off When you have woven as much as you can up the front of the card, tuck your weft over and under a few warp ends as you did at the beginning. Turn the card over and cut the strands in the middle. The ends can now be finished as suggested in the sectio on finger weaving.

PROJECT IDEA
You will see that it is possible to make a scarf or a little runner using card and needle. But you ca also use needle weaving with finei threads and a smaller card, with the holes spaced closer together, t make tapestry pictures. These can be very delicate and can be left on the card to be framed as it is.

You have learnt to make stripe and different patterns through texture. You can also build up areas of colour without weaving right across all the warp ends.

In diagram 1 (p. 66) a method fo making a triangle shape is shown and diagram 2 shows a method for a zig-zag join between two differer wefts. You can also build up squai shapes, so that there is a little slit between them, and then bring the slit together by weaving right across, as shown in diagram 3. An you can weave curves, as shown ii diagram 4. Try and weave a circle.

It would be better to practise some of these shapes first on a sample warp and then design or paint a little picture you would like to weave. You could of course just try to build up a pattern as you go, but it might look more effective if you chose a theme, e.g. bricks using square shaped areas over each other.

In tapestry, there are many more wefts than in ordinary weaving. If you are patient, you can weave all the ends in, but this is not necessary, as the picture will be seen only from one side. Therefore you can just leave a few

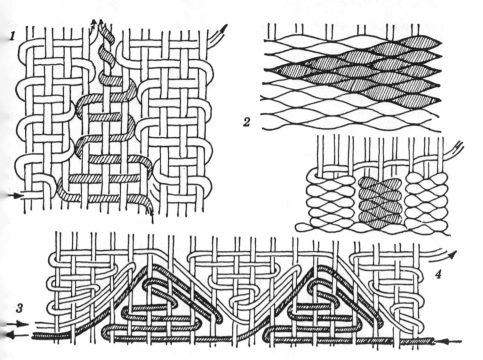

centimetres of weft tucked in at the back.

EMBROIDERY

You will need
needles of varying sizes to take thick and thin threads
embroidering threads and yarns

Embroidery can be used on any fabric, including knitting and crochet. Generally it is best done with a type of yarn similar or complementary to that of the fabric. If the fabric is fine, it is better to do the work using embroidery rings, which are two wooden rings, one completely enclosed, and the other open with a screw for adjusting the tension over the opening. The fabric is placed over the closed ring, the other ring is placed on top, the fabric is pulled gently to stretch it while the outer screw is tightened to keep the fabric taut.

Method: The embroidery thread can be fastened with a small overhand knot at the end, which stays on the wrong side of the fabric. However, knots can make bumps, so it is better to avoid them. Here are a few other ways to begin your work. Take a few running stitches toward the starting point and cover with the stitch you are using (diagram 1). Use half the length of thread at the beginning of a row and use the rest for your next row (diagram 2). Diagram 3 shows how to end by passing the thread under about three stitches before cutting it, and diagram 4 shows how to start a new thread by passing it under a few stitches to secure it.

Running stitch or darning stitch
This stitch should be regular in size, about twice the length above as it is below the fabric, as in diagram 5. It can also be whipped in a contrasting colour, as in diagram 6, or it can be threaded with one or two colours giving a wavy or circular pattern, as in diagram 7. Running stitch can be made in two rows and threaded to make a loopy pattern (diagram 8), or it can be made in two rows at right angles to each other (diagram 9).

Back stitch This stitch makes a continuous line. Working from left to right, take the thread up from the back and then make a backwards stitch. Bring the needle up a little way in front of the first

stitch and make another backward stitch, taking the needle through the point where it first came up (diagram 1, p. 68).

Pekinese stitch This is made on back stitch with a contrasting colour by looping the thread back into the previous stitch and taking it up and then under the next stitch along (diagram 2, p. 68).

Stem stitch This is used mainly for outlines, usually curvy, and stems. It is worked from left to right in diagram 3, p. 68. Make slightly slanting stitches along the line you are to stitch. The thread always comes up a little behind and to the left of the stitch you have made. This stitch can be whipped in a contrast colour, as in diagram 4, p. 68.

Satin stitch This stitch is used for filling in small areas. Take the

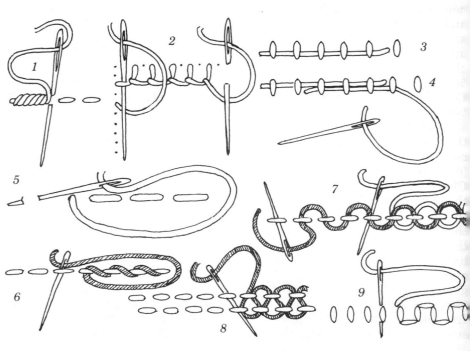

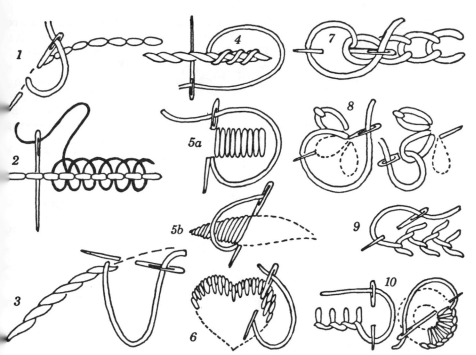

needle up at one edge of the design and draw it through to the back at an opposite point. Take the needle up again on the starting edge, very close to the first stitch (diagrams 5a and 5b).

Long and short stitch This is a type of satin stitch using long and short stitches that begin also inside the design area. Different colours can be used for shading or effect (diagram 6).

Chain stitch Bring the needle to the right side of the fabric and hold the thread down with your left thumb. Push the needle back through the point from where it has just come out and bring it up again a short distance away. Pull gently to make a loop and repeat (diagram 7).

Lazy daisy stitch The chain stitch is used to make little petals and leaves. Instead of continuing a second chain, the thread is passed back under, catching the loop down, and the needle is brought up at the starting point of the next leaf or petal (diagram 8).

Feather stitch The needle is taken up at the top of the line of stitches. Hold the thread down with the left thumb, push the needle through a little to the right on the same level and bring the needle up a little way down between these points. Keep the thread below the needle. Pull up the thread and you will have made an 'open chain'. Hold the thread with your thumb and push the needle through a point a little to the left of where it has just come up. Bring it up a little below, between these two new points. Pull the thread up, making a second 'open' chain.

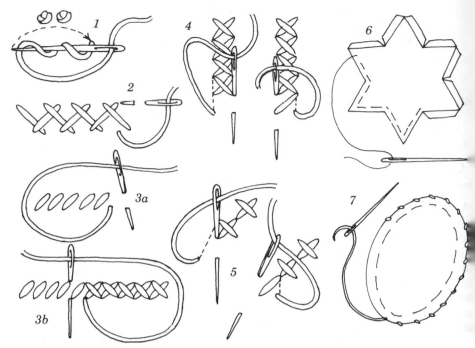

Repeat (*see* diagram 9.)

Blanket or buttonhole stitch For buttonholes, this stitch is worked closer together. Working from left to right, bring needle up on a lower level. Hold the thread down with the left thumb and push needle through a little to the right of the starting point, on the upper level. Bring up again directly below and pull through catching the loop of thread (diagram 10).

French knots Bring thread up at the place for the knot, hold the thread down with your left thumb and wind the thread twice (or more, as desired) round the needle. Holding the needle firmly, pull it through the twists and push them down to make a little 'knot' next to the fabric. Then push the needle back through at the point it came out (diagram 1).

Herringbone stitch Working from left to right, bring the needle up, make a diagonal stitch and take a very short stitch backwards behind the fabric. Bring needle up and over to form another diagonal stitch over the first one and continue, alternating from side to side, as in diagram 2.

Cross stitch The simplest method is for the horizontal row, as in diagram 3. Working from left to right, make half the cross with a diagonal stitch to the upper right corner, push through and bring up directly below. Keep the line even, and work the second half from right to left (diagrams 3a and 3b). A method for working a few vertical cross stitches at a time is shown in diagram 4, and for working diagonal cross stitches is clearly illustrated in diagram 5.

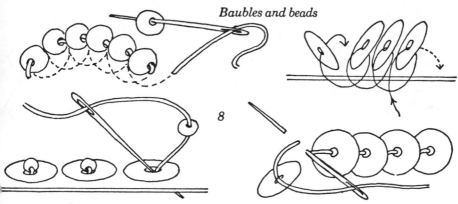

8

APPLIQUÉ

Embroidery is particularly useful for APPLIQUÉ work. Appliqué is simply the French for 'applied'. A smaller shape is applied to another larger area. It could be a patch on some old jeans or it could be a piece of felt cut into a motif and embroidered onto a cushion cover.

You will need

scraps of material and felt – avoid slippery and stretchy fabrics, and fabric that frays easily. Cotton is the most suitable.

background fabric for the motifs
needle, sewing cotton and embroidery threads
scissors – small and sharp are better
pins
pencil, tracing paper and rubber for designs

Draw your design onto a piece of tracing paper and pin it onto the scrap of material you are using for the appliqué. Cut out the shape, leaving 6 mm (0·2 in) for turning at the edge. With felt, no extra width is required and the motif can be stitched on as it is. If you want to

embroider extra details, do so now. Turn the edges under and baste the motif into place – using a long running stitch which can be pulled out easily later (diagram 6, p. 69). Stitch into place using a very fine slip-stitch (diagram 7, p. 69) or buttonhole stitch. If you want to raise the design, you can stuff it with a bit of wadding before finishing the stitching.

Motifs can also be stitched on top of other motifs, and so building up more interesting patterns. The work can be decorated with sequins and beads, some ways of applying these are shown in diagram 8.

PATCHWORK

This handicraft has been popular for centuries, particularly in Ireland and America. It has been used for home furnishing as well as for garments. Many types of fabric have been used for patches, but as with appliqué, cotton is the most suitable. It is generally better to start by taking the same type of fabric for all the patches in one piece of work, because otherwise the work will not lie flat. Small prints together can make lovely designs, whereas patches from bold stripes and checks can be very eye-catching. If you use a one-colour fabric, then you must be extra neat and careful when cutting the shape and stitching it, as these become more obvious.

You will need
card
scissors
pair of compasses
brown parcel paper
needle and sewing cotton
fabrics for patches
ruler, pencil and rubber

To make regular patches of the right size, you first need to make a template. This is the exact shape of your patch cut in card. The hexagon (six-sided) shape is not difficult and very pleasing to use (diagram 1). The hexagon shape is drawn out on cardboard. Take the pair of compasses, draw a circle roughly the size of your patch. Do not alter the compasses, and placing the leg on the drawn circle, mark off two points on the circle to either side of the point you are standing on. Repeat by putting the leg onto one of these marks. Repeat twice more and you should find 6 equidistant points on the circle. Join them up and you have a hexagon. Cut out the hexagon and use this to cut as many hexagons in brown paper as you need for your patchwork. You must have one for each patch. Cut the fabric about 6 mm (0·2 in) wider than the hexagon, place the paper lining on the wrong side in the middle and pin (diagram 2). Making a small tuck at each corner, fold the fabric

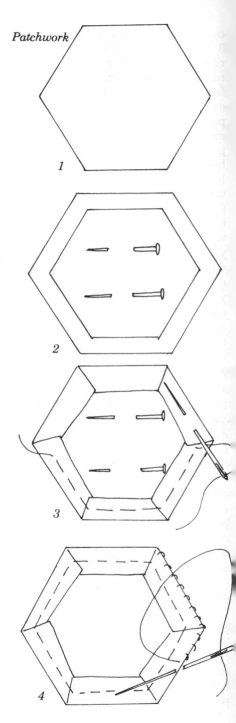

Patchwork

1

2

3

4

272

over and baste all around (diagram 3, p. 71). When all the patches are ready, you can begin to stitch them together. Hold two right sides facing together, and oversew one edge (diagram 4, p. 71). Avoid the paper lining and keep the corners exact. When you have joined all the patches together, take out the basting thread and the paper lining. Press the patchwork on the wrong side, so that the edges lie flat, pointing towards the centre of the patch. You can appliqué your work onto a larger piece of cloth or you can line it with a pre-shrunk washable fabric. Cut the lining material 1 cm (0·4 in) wider than your finished patchwork, turn the edges over and clip in places to adjust the corners. Oversew the edges all around (unless you are making a cushion) holding the wrong sides together.

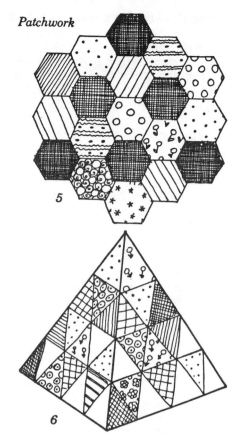

Patchwork

5

6

PROJECT IDEAS
You could make a patchwork table cloth or pram-cover by using appliqué to attach little sets of hexagons on to a plain-coloured, thicker cotton and edging the cover with patchwork squares. Use embroidery stitches to sew the patchwork on the cloth. Try making some of the patchwork motifs lighter, some darker, some with lighter patches outside and a darker one in the middle. An example is given in diagram 5.

If you are using felt for your patchwork, you might like to try 'Irish patchwork'. You do not have to cut extra seam allowance with felt but, to join the patches, you first blanket-stitch all around each patch and then double-crochet the

edges together, using the top of the blanket stitch as the foundation row of your crochet.

Patchwork does not need to be flat. You can of course use different thicknesses of material and different shapes and make something called 'crazy patchwork'. But you can also make three-dimensional objects with patches. Using triangles, you can make four triangular pieces, which can be joined together to make a tetrahedron (diagram 6), with six squares you can make a cube, and with twelve pentagons you could even make a little ball!

PRESSING FLOWERS

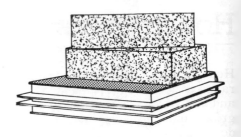

You will need
some sheets of white blotting paper
or thick absorbent sugar paper
large heavy books
bricks or other heavy weights

Flowers and leaves are best
gathered on a dry day, after the
dew has evaporated. A thick, fleshy
plant or a flower with many petals
are best separated carefully and
dried in pieces. Arrange the flowers
and leaves on the blotting paper as
soon as you can after picking,
remembering to include stems as
well. Smooth out the surfaces, so
that the pieces dry the way you
want to see them later. Cover with
another sheet of blotting paper and
place these sheets in a heavy book.
It is better to take a book with
paper that is glossy because the
moisture from the drying flowers
and leaves will not be absorbed by
shiny surfaces. Place bricks and
other heavy objects on top and
keep in a dry place for at least six
weeks. Peeping before that time
has passed is not allowed!
Remember NOT to overcrowd the
blotting paper and NOT to press
the sheets down so heavily that the
moisture cannot escape. You might
find, otherwise, that the plants
have gone mouldy.

MOUNTING

You will need
rubber solution glue
cards of different sorts
adhesive transparent plastic
scissors
paintbrush

The type of card you use depends
on what you are making. You can
use thin cards for greetings cards
or for covering match-boxes or for
making bookmarks, thicker card
for pictures to hang on the wall or
for mats. Cut the card to the size
required and first arrange your
dried petals, leaves and stems as
you wish for your design. Then,
using the tiniest dab of glue on the
back, stick the pieces down. A
paintbrush is useful here, because
you can push the petals or leaves
about with the brush end and dab
the glue on with the other end.
Now, cut the shape of the card in
the sticky backed plastic, and
mount the plastic on the card over
the dried arrangement, by tearing
off the backing of the plastic a
little at a time and smoothing the
plastic carefully down into place.
Trim off any uneven edges.

There are so many ways to use
dried flowers – you will probably
have lots of other ideas yourself.
You could try embedding them in
plastic to make paperweights,
using a 'Plasticraft' kit or other
similar type. You could mount
flowers on a strip of ribbon instead
of card for bookmarks. You could
even make an album of dried flower
arrangements and cover the front
with a special flower design.

274

House Plants

Houseplants come in a wonderful range of colours, shapes and sizes and many of them are easy to grow. So don't be deterred if you do not have green-fingers. You can have amazing success provided you stick to the basic rules.

Before dealing with plant care, however, you must decide whether you want a tall or trailing plant, one with or without flowers, a plant to occupy permanently a particular position or one just to provide a shorter-term deccration. Each type of plant must be cared for differently.

SELECT SOMETHING SIMPLE

A house plant is one which lives its entire life indoors. These fall into two groups: flowering and foliage plants, the latter are grown for their almost endless variety of leaf-shapes. Of course, an indoor collection can well include all sorts of pot plants. Often, these are given as gifts. They are, however, only temporary visitors which, after flowering, should be removed and, in some cases, planted in the garden.

Beginner's Guide
For any beginner deciding to buy a house plant, here are four simple-to-grow favourites.

Spider Plant (*Chlorophytum*)
Despite its creepy name, it is a very popular foliage plant with arching, striped, grass-like leaves. It is good value, too, because it produces plantlets at the end of long runners. You can plant each of these into a pot of compost. Once rooted, detach them from the mother plant. The Spider Plant is an ideal eye-catcher whether suspended or placed on a cupboard or table. Just remember it likes a well-lit position, though not in direct sunlight.

Swiss Cheese Plant (*Monstera Deliciosa*)
For a little extra cost, you can buy this big, climbing plant which brings a true touch of the tropical into your house. Its large, shiny leaves develop deep cuts and holes – hence, the plant's name. Again, this plant does not like direct sunlight. It prefers a medium light and a warm, draught-free, moist atmosphere.

Busy Lizzie (*Impatiens*)
If you like flowering house plants, this one provides pretty pink, red or white flowers and blooms for most of the year. Ideally, it should be placed in a sunny spot, this helps it to flower well.

Shrimp Plant (*Beloperone Guttata*)
Another plant that likes a sunny window-sill, this one takes its name from the shrimp-like flowers.

If you are searching for a tough, easy-to-keep trailer or climber, the Ivy (*Hedera*) family offers a superb choice. Spring flowers, for contrast, can be grown simply by planting bulbs or corms in pots to provide delightful, temporary indoor plants. Sunny Daffodils will cheer a room.

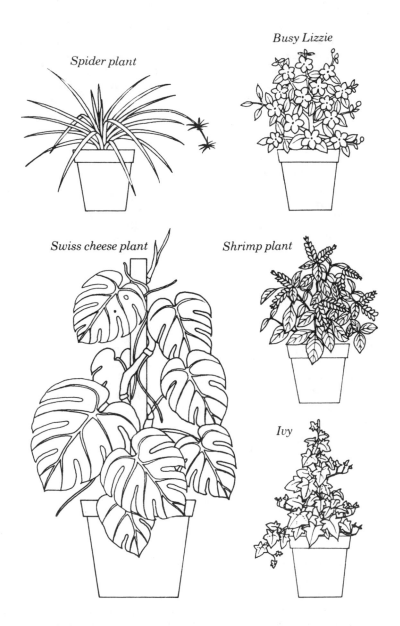

Spider plant

Busy Lizzie

Swiss cheese plant

Shrimp plant

Ivy

HOW TO KEEP YOUR PLANT HEALTHY

Plants are similar to people and have individual likes and dislikes. Some prefer sunny spots, others where there is good but indirect lighting. The two golden rules to help keep them healthy are never over-water or place them near draughts. These are the major killers.

There are five main points relating to plant care and growth: light, food, air, warmth and water. Get this balance right and you will see your plants flourish. In the garden, nature provides this. House plants, however, must rely on you.

Obviously, requirements vary from plant to plant. So when you buy one, study the recommended instructions carefully. Don't treat all plants the same and remember that winter provides a rest season when you should allow much longer intervals between watering. Never let the soil dry out completely or, on the other hand, become so sodden that the roots cannot survive.

As a general guide, water your plants two or three times a week in summer and only once a week or even less in winter.

Swift changes of temperature are harmful. Try to keep your plant in a room where it does not exceed 25°C (75°F) and where the temperature is normally moderate and constant. Usually, foliage plants prefer a little more warmth than do the flowering types.

Most plants do not like a very dry atmosphere. Central heating in a house can cause this. To compensate, stand plants in a dish of moist gravel or pebbles. Spray the leaves with water, too, or put your plant in the kitchen or bathroom, where steam increases the air's moisture content. When your plant is in its growing season, feed it with a fertilizer. Again, do not overdo this.

There are countless books available on the precise care and needs of particular house plants. So if in doubt, always check first.

Nonetheless, rest assured that provided you stick to the simpler plants, such as the few mentioned here, they will grow happily with only the basic care and attention.

WHAT TO WATCH FOR

There are all sorts of tell-tale signs to warn of trouble with your plant. If you keep a keen look out and act quickly when these signs appear, your plant will stay safe. It's rather like being a doctor who must identify the symptoms to apply a remedy. Here is a brief guide for some conditions.

Condition	Solution
Leaves turning yellow, and falling off	If several leaves are affected, watch for over-watering, dry air or draughts
Slow or no growth	If during the growing season, watch for over-watering, underfeeding, or perhaps the plant is becoming too pot-bound
Spindly plant with pale leaves	If during the growing season, watch for

	inadequate light or insufficient feeding
Mildew	Watch for poor conditions, over-watering
Leaf rot	Again, watch for poor conditions or over-watering in winter
Brown edges and marks on leaves	Watch for over-watering, draughts, sun-burn and hot, dry air.

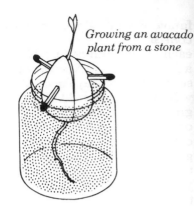

Growing an avacado plant from a stone

A bottle garden

WASTE NOT, WANT NOT

Creating something from nothing can add a little extra fun to raising house plants. Pips from everyday fruits like lemons, grapefruit and oranges can be grown quite easily. Germinate them in shallow, moist compost. Then move the young plants to bigger pots, as they develop. In the case of the lemon pip, you may even end up picking your own fruit, provided the plant gets plenty of sunshine.

Life from a stone

Watching an avocado pear stone grow into a plant can be very interesting. One method of starting the process is to suspend the stone, pierced with small cocktail sticks or matchsticks for support, in water. When roots appear, plant the stone in a pot of compost. You will be surprised with the final result.

SPECIAL HOUSE PLANT DISPLAYS

If you find that your interest in house plants really develops, there are many ways of making your plants appear even more attractive. Hanging baskets are popular. So, too, are miniature gardens, with smaller plants carefully designed in a shallow dish. The idea is to create a life-like garden complete with pool, path and even a model building. There are other suggestions, too.

The bottle garden

Use a large glass bottle or carboy which must be washed out and dried. Pour gravel into the bottom for drainage. Then add a layer of moss. Using a plastic or paper funnel, carefully pour in the soil, consisting of two parts loam to one each of peat and sand. Also, mix in a little charcoal. Now you are all set to arrange the plants.

It is best to use small, slow-growing plants and not too many or it will easily look over-crowded when the plants begin to grow. Use two slim pieces of wood to plant them. To make it easier, you can tie spoons to the ends of the sticks. Use a long-spouted can for watering and continue to water occasionally, unless you seal the bottle and let the plants create their own moisture.

A Dish Garden
As its title suggests, you simply use a shallow dish or container. Just make sure it is sufficiently deep to allow the plant roots to establish themselves properly. Add your soil to a layer of moss which lies on a bed of gravel. Then pick your plants – either foliage, flowering or both – to produce the design you want. You can even make a miniature jungle by carefully selecting and adding pieces of dead wood or stones of the right shape and size. Whenever a plant grows too large for the dish, simply replace it with a smaller one.

Dish gardens are especially attractive

SPORTS
AND GAMES

Equestrian Events

Show jumping

The earliest record of competition jumping is of a steeplechase held in Ireland in 1752. Show jumping or as it was then called 'leaping', began to appear in horse shows in England in the late 1870s although contests for high and wide leaps were included in the Royal Dublin Society's show in 1865. By the beginning of the 20th century show jumping had become a popular sport and three jumping events were included in the Paris Olympic Games of 1900. In 1907, at the first International Horse Show to be held at Olympia in London, competitors had the chance to enter 11 jumping events.

It was not until after 1948 that civilians began to take a major part in show jumping competitions as up until then they had been dominated by the army.

Despite the set-back of two world wars, show jumping has grown into a major world sport enjoyed by riders, horses and spectators alike.

Show jumping is an event where a horse and rider jump a course of fences designed and built specially for each competition. The rider with the least number of faults at the end is the winner.

The same rules apply to all show jumping competitions and a rider will be given:

Four faults for knocking down a fence;
Three faults for a refusal (this includes circling or swerving round the side of a jump);

Three faults for a second refusal of the same fence;
Eight faults if the rider or his horse falls (a horse is judged to have fallen if its shoulder touches the ground);
Four faults for a foot or feet in the water or on the landing tape;
A quarter of a fault for every second over the time set for jumping the course.

A rider will be eliminated if:

The horse refuses the same fence three times;
Does not pass the start or finish on his horse;
Takes the wrong course;
Receives unofficial help;
Starts before the bell.

If at the end of the first round two or more riders have an equal number of faults or no faults (a clear round), they will be asked to jump the course again. This is called a 'jump off'. If there is still a tie at the end of the first jump off there will either be a second jump off or the rider with the fastest time will be the winner.

The four basic fences are.

The upright is made from poles or planks in a vertical plane.

The parallel is usually made from two poles both at the same height and set apart from one another.

The pyramid has a central pole with a lower pole on either side.

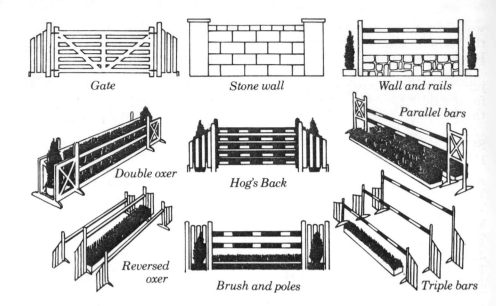

Gate

Stone wall

Wall and rails

Double oxer

Hog's Back

Parallel bars

Reversed oxer

Brush and poles

Triple bars

This can be jumped from either side.

Staircase or triple bar consists of three poles, each higher than the one in front.

Children under the age of 18 are not allowed to enter the major international competitions but a lot of small shows and gymkhanas will include classes for children. Many famous show jumpers start at these shows, working their way up through the various shows. At the small shows there will usually be three rings, with a different range of jumps in each. The classes will be divided into pony sizes; experience and previous winnings will also be taken into account.

The puissance is a competition to test a horse's jumping power. It starts with several fences and continues until the final

competitors are asked to jump only two fences, one spread and one upright, which are raised after each jump. Britain only allows three jump offs, because of the vast heights of the fences the horse is pushed to its limit. In 1949 Captain Alberto Larra-guibel Morales of Chile jumped the amazing height of 2·47 metres (8 ft 1¼ in). This is still the world record.

Shows and competitions
In Europe each country is allowed to hold one official international horse show each year; the USA is allowed to hold two. This will include a Nations Cup World Team Championship. Teams of four riders compete against teams from other countries. Each team jumps two rounds. The lowest score in the team is not counted. The six best scores from the various competitions held around the

world are added together to find the winning team of the prized President's Cup.

A special saddle is used for show jumping which has a special place for the rider's knee when he is in the forward jumping position.

SOME OF THE SHOWS HELD IN BRITAIN.

April
The Badminton Horse Trials
The Hickstead Spring Meeting

May
The Royal Windsor Horse Show

June
The Cardiff International Show Jumping Championships, Wales
The Royal Bath and West Show
The South of England show, Sussex
The Royal Show, Stoneleigh, Warwickshire

July
The Royal International Horse show, Wembley: since 1975 this has incorporated the July meeting at Hickstead enabling Nations Cup competitions to be held at Wembley.

September
Burghley Horse Trials

October
Horse of the Year Show, Wembley: this includes the competition for 'Leading Show Jumper of the Year' and 'Junior Show Jumper of the Year'.

December
The International Show Jumping Championships, Olympia, London

SOME OF THE OVERSEAS SHOWS

The Aachen International Show, Germany: this is one of the largest shows and has one of the toughest courses a horse and rider will have to face in the year's competitions.

The Rome Show in May: This has been described as one of the most beautiful shows of the year.

The Dublin Horse Show: held at Balls Bridge in early August.

Dressage

Dressage originated from the time when men trained their horses to survive against their enemies in battle. A horse would be trained to kick backwards with both legs to kill an enemy creeping up on him from behind. He was also taught to rear up on his back legs to ward off any attack on him or his rider from the front with a knife or a sword. He would even be trained to leap into the air to avoid or jump over an enemy concealed on the ground.

These movements can still be seen performed in the dressage exhibitions given by the famous Lippizzaner horses of the Spanish School of Riding in Vienna.

Most of the dressage seen today in competitions has been modified. Dressage was first included in the Olympic Games in 1912. Britain and America were late in taking dressage seriously, giving the experienced European riders a great advantage in earlier competitions. The dressage competitions were first held at Goodwood and have helped to promote dressage in Britain.

Dressage competitions are divided into standards of difficulty. These are Elementary, Medium, and Advanced (Prix St Georges). Dressage is a form of training to make a horse supple, calm, collected and keen to obey perfectly the commands the rider gives. These are given with the hands, legs and seat.

A special saddle is used for

dressage which is cut very straight and has a deep seat allowing the rider to sit well into the saddle. This gives the rider maximum use of his legs. A special girth is also used called a Lonsdale girth which buckles low down so that it is not felt through the sides of the saddle.

The official size for a dressage arena is 60 metres (198 ft) by 20 metres (66 ft). This may be smaller for Elementary dressage and small shows. Each competitor performs individually and has to memorize the programme before the show. The rectangular arena is marked with letters along the sides, in the corners and down the centre. The programme will have told the rider what pace he is to perform between the different letters. Each move is marked individually and marks are also given for general impression. Each movement is marked out of six. At large shows there are three judges (there may be only one at a small show). The three judges' total marks for a rider are added together and divided by three to give an average. This is then subtracted from the possible total score. If there are 15 movements the possible total would be 90. The competitors' final score is given as penalties so the rider with the lowest score is the winner or leader if it forms part of a competition. The movements are based on three movements. The trot, the walk and the canter.

The walk
The three paces used in the walk are the medium, collected and extended. A medium walk should contain four steps to one step of a relaxed walk. A collected walk is more springy than the medium walk with the horse collected up. The extended walk is when the horse is striding out as far as possible with even steps. This is the most difficult walk.

The trot
Collected, working, medium and extended are the four types of trot. The working trot is an ordinary trot, while in the medium trot the power comes from the horse's back legs. A collected trot is where the horse is gathered in and the extended trot is with a lengthened stride.

The canter
There are four types of canter, the same as for the trot. The stride is short in the collected canter and lengthened for the extended. All the movements should be carried out smoothly and with precise balance.

The three-day event
The three-day event started in Europe where it was used for cavalry endurance tests and training. This consisted of rides over long distances and varied in length. The winner needed to have speed as well as stamina. They took place on roads and tracks and were very dangerous. During one competition in 1902 in which the riders had to ride from Brussels to Ostend, 16 of the 29 horses which started, died.

France at this time used long distance cross-country riding for military training and not as a competition. As jumping was not

The walk

The trot

The canter

The gallop

popular until the late 18th century all these were ridden on the flat. Perhaps the first competition to include all aspects of riding was held in France in 1902 which was called the Championnat du Cheval d'Armes and included dressage, steeplechase, a 31-mile ride on roads and tracks, and show jumping. This became popular with other regiments in other parts of the world and was included in the Olympic Games of 1912 which were held in Stockholm.

The three-day event as we know it now is held, as the name implies, over three days. Dressage on the first day, speed and endurance tests on the second (this includes riding on roads and tracks, steeplechase, and cross-country) and show jumping on the final day.

By the second day the rider will have gained penalty points from the dressage tests. He now has to ride over roads and tracks for anything from 6 to 12 miles. This is to test the horse's endurance and is not ridden at a great speed but at a fast trot or a slow canter. The steeplechase which follows is ridden at a fast gallop. After this there is more road work and the rider may dismount and run with his horse to give it a rest. When this section is finished the rider has a compulsory ten minute break while the horse is checked by a veterinary surgeon to see that it is fit to take part in the cross-country event which follows. The cross-country event is held over a distance of three to five miles and the horse and rider will have to negotiate 30 to 40 fences. The rider will have walked the course beforehand.

This section is perhaps the most exciting requiring skill, speed and stamina.

The fences are varied and will

have been built to form a natural part of the countryside. They can include log piles, stiles, water troughs, stone walls, tree trunks and ditches. Some of them will require the horse to jump into water, down steep slopes or onto ground which is much lower than the take-off. At some of the jumps the rider will have the choice of taking the longer, but easier, route or the quicker, but more difficult, approach. A rider will be given penalty points for:
A first refusal, 20 faults;
A second refusal (at the same fence), 40 faults;
A fall of rider or horse in the zone around the jump, 60 faults.

The rider will be eliminated for:
A third refusal;
Taking the wrong course;
A second fall in the steeplechase;
A third fall of horse or rider in the cross-country section.

The horses which are still in the competition on the third day will again be checked by a veterinary surgeon. If they are passed fit they will enter the final stage which is show jumping. This will decide the winner of the gruelling three-day event.

Cross-country events are held in smaller forms than the big three-day events, in these smaller forms children are allowed to take part.

Outstanding Sportswomen

Adams, Sharon Sites Born USA, sailor. The first woman to cross the Pacific Ocean solo in a boat. She left Yokohama, Japan and took 75 days to reach San Diego, USA, 9,513 km (5,911 miles) away.

Blankers-Koen, Francina E. Born Netherlands 1918, athlete. Winner of four gold medals in the 1948 Olympics for 100 m and 200 m sprints, 80 m hurdles and 4 × 100 m relay.

Board, Lillian Born UK, athlete. Winner of 4 × 100 m relay in world record time of 3 min 30·8 sec at the European Games in Athens in 1969.

Comaneci, Nadia Born Romania 1961, gymnast. The only woman to gain seven perfect scores at the 1976 Olympics. She became the overall winner of the European section.

Connolly, Maureen ('Little Mo') Born USA 1934, tennis player. Won three successive US championships at Forest

Hills before she was 17. She won the Wimbledon championship at her first attempt in 1952 and held it for three years. In 1953 she won the Australian, French, Wimbledon and US titles and so became the first woman to hold the four major championships simultaneously.

Cook, Sylvia Born UK, sailor. She partnered John Fairfax in *Brittania II*, a 35 ft rowing boat, on their voyage across the Pacific in 1971–2. The journey took them nearly a year to complete.

Court, Margaret (née Smith) Born Australia 1942, tennis player. Won the 'grand slam' in 1970 by holding the US, French and Australian championships, and the Wimbledon title. In 1971 she retained the Australian title but lost Wimbledon and France to Yvonne Goolagong, and the US title to Billie Jean King, possibly the greatest woman tennis player, ever.

Davies, Sharron Born UK, swimmer. Won the 200 m freestyle in 2 min 4·11 sec in 1978 and the 400 m in 4 min 18·59 sec in 1979 at Coventry. These are British national long course records. She also won the 200 m individual medley in 2 min 17·55 sec at Amersfoot, Netherlands and the 400 m individual medley in 4 min 4·67 sec.

De la Huntey, Shirley, MBE (née Strickland) Born Australia 1925, athlete. The only woman ever to have won 7 medals (3 gold, 1 silver and 3 bronze) in the 1948, 1952 and 1956 Olympic Games. Unofficially she is thought to have deserved a further bronze.

Dod, Charlotte Born UK 1871, died 1960, a versatile all-round sportswoman. In 1887, at 15 years of age, she won Wimbledon. She won it another four times between 1887 and 1893. She also won the British Ladies Golf championship in 1904 and gained a silver medal for archery at the 1908 Olympics. She played hockey for England in 1899. She was also an excellent skater.

Earhart, Amelia Born USA 1898, died 1937(?), aviator. In 1917 Amelia decided that she wanted to fly, this was an extraordinary choice for a woman at that time. Her first airplane was a Kinner Canary. In 1928, with Bill Stultz, she crossed the Atlantic, the first woman to do so in an airplane. In 1932 she flew solo from America to Ireland – another first for a woman. Tragically, in an attempt to fly round the world she disappeared in 1937 and was never found.

Ederle, Gertrude Caroline Born USA 1906, swimmer. Swam the English Channel from Cap Gris-Nez to Deal on 6th August 1926. She took 14 hr 39 min and was the first woman to swim the Channel.

Ender, Cornelia Born East Germany 1958, swimmer. Winner in the 1976 Olympics of four gold medals (100 m and 200 m freestyle, 100 m butterfly and 4 × 100 m medley).

Evert-Lloyd, Chris (née Christine Marie Evert) Born USA 1954, tennis player. One of the world's most popular tennis stars, she has won three singles women championships at Wimbledon and six US championships.

Frazer, Dawn, OBE (now Mrs Ware) Born Australia 1937, swimmer. Australia's finest swimmer, she won four gold medals in the 100 m freestyle in 1956, 1960 and 1964, and in the 4 × 100 m freestyle in 1956. She also won four silvers.

Green, Lucinda (née Prior-Palmer) Born UK 1953, horse rider. Thought to be Britain's most consistent rider. Winner of the Badminton Three-day Event six times, on *Be Fair* in 1973, *Wide Awake* in 1976, *George* in 1977, *Killane* in 1979, *Regal Realm* in 1983 and *Beagle Bay* in 1984.

Hambleton, Kitty Born USA. Holder of the world land speed record driving the SMI *Motivator* (a 4,800 hp rocket-powered 3-wheeler) in the Alvard Desert, Oregon. She clocked up a recorded time of 524·016 mph.

Henie, Sonja Born Norway 1912, died 1969, ice skater. The only woman to win three gold medals in succession at the 1928, 1932 and 1936 Olympics for figure skating. She also held 10 world and 8 European titles. She later became a very popular Hollywood film star.

Heyhoe-Flint, Rachel, MBE Born UK 1939, cricketer. Captain of the English cricket team, she scored 1,594 runs between December 1960 and July 1979 in test matches.

James, Naomi Born New Zealand, sailor. Circumnavigated the world via Cape Horn in the Bermuda sloop *Express Crusader*. She left Dartmouth, England on the 9th September 1977 and rounded Cape Horn on 19th March 1978, arriving back in Dartmouth on 8th June 1978.

Kanetaka, Kaoru Born Japan, traveller, author, lecturer. She set the world commercial propellor-driven flight record for circumnavigation, Tokyo to Tokyo in 81 hours. The first Japanese woman to visit the South Pole, the first Japanese woman to parachute jump and the first Japanese woman to take a balloon over the Alps and to hang-glide.

Kim, Nelli Born USSR 1957, gymnast. The most gifted competitor in the Russian gymnastic team at the 1976 Olympics. Gained a perfect score twice and was second in both the European and World championships in 1975. Her grace and skill are considered perfection.

King, Billie Jean (née Moffitt) Born USA 1943, tennis player. Six times singles champion at Wimbledon with a total of 20 Wimbledon titles between 1961 and 1979. A player of incredible stamina and consistency, she has probably done more for young tennis players than any other champion.

Korbut, Olga Born USSR 1958, gymnast. Miss Korbut has probably done more to popularize gymnastics than any other gymnast. She was the first woman to perform a backward somersault on the beam. She won three gold medals and one silver at the 1972 Olympics.

Kulakova, Galina Born USSR 1942, skier. Won gold medals for the 5 km, 10 km and 3·5 km relay at the 1972 Olympics and the 4 × 5 km relay in the 1976 Olympics. She also won one silver and two bronze medals in 1968 and 1976.

Lacoste, Catherine Born France, golfer. The only woman to win the US Open, US Amateur and British and French Open championships (1965–9).

Latynina, Larissa Semyonovna Born USSR 1934, gymnast. She holds ten individual world titles and five team titles, she has also won six individual gold medals

and was a member of three winning teams. She also gained five silver and four bronze medals and therefore holds 18 medals in all. This is an Olympic record for any sport.

Lopez, Nancy Born USA, golfer. When Nancy Lopez turned professional she won nine tournaments in her first year, her winnings reached an all-time record.

Moser, Annemarie (née Proell) Born Austria 1953, skier. Probably the finest woman skier in the world. She won the Women's Alpine World Cup six times, in 1971–5 and 1979. She won 11 consecutive downhill races and between 1970 and 1979 won 62 individual events.

Mould, Marion (née Coakes) Born UK, showjumper. Winner of the Queen Elizabeth Cup three times on *Stroller* in 1965, 1971, and on *Elizabeth Ann* in 1976.

Navratilova, Martina Born Czechoslovakia 1956, tennis player. In 1983–4, she became the third woman (after Maureen Connolly and Margaret Court) to hold the Grand Slam – that is, to be champion at Wimbledon and in the Australian, French and US championships. In 1984 she became the highest paid woman athlete of all time, when her earnings passed $8 million.

Phillips, Fran Born Canada. On the 5th April 1971 she was the first woman to set foot on the North Pole.

Rand, Mary Denise MBE Born UK, athlete. Jumped an incredible 6·7 m (22 ft 2¼ in) at the 1964 Olympics.

Rodnina, Irina Born USSR 1949, ice skater. Winner of ten world pairs titles, gained the highest number of maximum marks in the 1974 European pairs title, considered to be the most graceful of all women skaters.

Smythe, Patricia, OBE Born UK 1928, horse rider. Winner of the British Women's Show Jumping Association championships eight times, 1952, 1953,

1955, 1957, 1958, 1959, 1961 and 1962. Riding *Flanagan* she won three of these, the only horse to have won three times.

Tabei, Junko Born Japan 1939, mountaineer. She started climbing when she was nine. On 16th May 1975 accompanied by Ang Tsering, her Sherpa guide, she conquered Mount Everest. She had already climbed Annapurna in 1970.

Torvill, Jayne Born UK 1957, ice skater. With her partner Christopher Dean (born UK 1958), Jayne Torvill won the Grand Slam with three titles for Ice Dance in the same year, 1984. These were the European, World and Olympic titles.

Wickham, Tracy, MBE Born Australia, swimmer. Holder of the 200 m, 400 m and 800 m freestyle world records.

Outstanding Sportsmen

ALEXEEV, Vasili Born USSR, 1942. Weightlifter, super-heavyweight class. Broke his 80th world record on 1 November 1977 by lifting 256 kg. He has broken more world records than any other sportsman.

ALI, Muhammad (Cassius Clay) Born USA, 1942. Boxer, heavyweight class. Won the World Heavyweight Championship three times, first by beating Sonny Liston (1964), secondly by beating George Foreman (1974) and thirdly in 1978 by beating Leon Spinks. The most highly paid of all boxers, he probably earned as much as $69 million between 1960 and 1981.

ASHE, Arthur Born USA, 1943. Tennis player. Wimbledon champion 1975, US Open champion 1968, World champion 1975.

'BABE' RUTH (Full name George Herman Ruth.) Born USA 1895, died 1948. Baseball player. Held world record for home runs (60 in a 164-game season). Left-handed pitcher and batter. Played with the Boston Red Sox, the New York Yankees and the Boston Braves. Became coach to the Brooklyn Dodgers in 1938.

BANNISTER, Sir Roger Gilbert Born UK, 1929. Doctor and athlete. He was the first man in the history of

sport to run a mile in under 4 minutes. On 6 May 1954, at Oxford, he ran 1 mile in 3 mins 59.4 secs.

BARRY, Rick Born USA, 1944. Basketball player. He led the Golden State Warriors to victory in the National Basketball Championship in 1975. Considered to be the most accurate free-throw shooter in the world.

BEST, George Born Northern Ireland 1946, soccer player. One of the most brilliant players of his generation, Best was the European and English Footballer of the Year in 1968, when he won a European Cup Medal with Manchester United. The premature end to his career was the result of off the field pressures.

BIKILA, Abebe Born in Ethiopia. Marathon runner. Won the gold at the 1960 Olympics with a time of 2 hrs 15 mins 16.2 secs, running barefooted. The marathon is run over a distance of 26 miles 385 yards (42.105 km).

BORG, Bjorn Born Sweden 1956. Tennis player, the only man ever to have won five consecutive Wimbledon championships (1976–80).

BOTHAM, Ian Terrence Born UK 1955, cricketer. One of the greatest all-rounders of all time, Botham was the first player to score 2,500 runs and take 250 wickets in Test cricket. At the start of the 1985 season, he had scored 4,159 Test runs and taken 312 wickets. Only the Australian Dennis Lillee and the Englishman Bob Willis had taken more Test wickets (355 and 325 respectively).

BROOME, David Born UK, 1940. Horseman. Winner of George V Gold Cup and Queen Elizabeth II Cup four times.

CAMPBELL, Sir Malcolm Born UK 1885, died 1948. Racing driver. Holder of the water speed record from 1937 until his death. His hydroplane *Bluebird* reached 141.75 mph on Coniston Water, England. Also held land speed record from 1924 to 1935, reaching 301.13 mph in his car *Bluebird*.

CAMPBELL, Donald Malcolm Born UK 1921, died 1967. Engineer and designer son of Sir Malcolm Campbell. Following in his father's footsteps, he set the world water speed record of 276.33 mph in 1959 and the world land speed record, in 1964, of 403.1 mph. He was killed in 1967 attempting to beat his own record in the jet powered boat *Bluebird*.

CHARLTON, Bobby, OBE Born UK, 1937. Soccer player. His long career as a member of the England team spanned the years 1958–70, during which he scored 49 goals.

CHICHESTER, Sir Francis Born UK 1901, died 1972. Yachtsman and aviator. The first to cross the Tasman Sea in an East/West direction flying solo. In 1966–7 he sailed single-handed round the world in *Gypsy Moth IV*.

CLARKE, Bobby Born USA, 1949. Ice hockey player. Captain of the Philadelphia Flyers (winners of the 1974–5 Stanley Cup). Although diabetic, he has consistently led his team to victory. One of the youngest captains in the National Hockey League.

COE, Sebastian Newbold Born UK 1956, athlete. A popular middle distance runner, Coe won the Olympic gold medal for the 1,500 metres and the silver for the 800 metres in both the 1980 and 1984 Games. His total of four Olympic medals is a British record. As of September 1984, he was the world record holder in the 800 and 1,000 metres and also the mile.

CONNORS, Jimmy Born USA, 1954. Left-handed tennis player. Won the US Open, Australian and Wimbledon championships in 1974 but was barred from the French Open by the Association of Tennis Professionals. Considered to be one of the most powerful players on the international circuit.

COOPER, Henry William, OBE Born UK, 1934. Boxer. British heavyweight champion 1959–69 and 1970–1. Winner of three Lonsdale Belts. He voluntarily relinquished his title in 1969 but fought again in 1970 and regained it.

CURRY, John Antony, OBE Born 1949, in the UK. Ice skater. Probably the world's most graceful male performer on ice. The only skater to have won all three major titles (World, Olympic and European) in a single year. His style is greatly influenced by his training in ballet.

DAVIS, Steve Born UK 1957, snooker player. The first millionaire of snooker, Davis won the World Professional Snooker Championship in 1981 and in 1983–4, but he lost the 1985 Championship in the final frame of the tournament to Irishman Dennis Taylor.

FAIRFAX, John Born UK. Soldier and adventurer. In 1969 he made the first solo East/West crossing of the Atlantic Ocean by rowing boat. He left Las Palmas in the Canary Islands on 20 January and took 180 days to reach Fort Lauderdale in Florida. His boat, the *Britannia*, was only 6.7 m (22 ft) long. He also made the first rowboat crossing of the Pacific Ocean from San Francisco to the Hayman Islands

(Australia). This took 362 days from 26 April 1970 to 22 April 1971. He was accompanied by Sylvia Cook in the 10.6 m (35 ft) *Britannia II*.

FANGIO, Juan Manuel Fangio y Cia Born Argentina, 1911. Racing driver. The only man to win the World Racing Drivers' Championship five times (between 1951 and 1957). He retired in 1958, having won 24 Grand Prix races.

FISCHER, Robert (Bobby) James Born USA, 1943. Chess Grand Master. Considered to be the greatest chess player alive. He won 20 grand master games in succession from 1970 to 1971.

FOSBURY, Richard Born USA. Athlete. The 'Fosbury flop', a new innovation in high jumping, was developed by this remarkable man. Before Fosbury's time, the high jump was made forwards but Dick Fosbury attained a height of 7 ft 4¼ in (2.2 m) with a backward flop over the bar.

GRACE, William Gilbert Born UK 1848, died 1915. Cricketer. Known as 'the father of modern batting'. He scored over 54,000 runs during his long career and took 2,876 wickets in first-class cricket.

HILL, Graham Born 1929 in the UK, died 1975. Engineer and racing driver. He won 14 Grand Prix races and competed in a total of 176 Grand Prix events. He raced for the Lotus team, 1950–9 and 1967–9, and for the British Racing Motors 1960–6. He won the Indianapolis 500 in 1966, driving a Lola 90 Ford. He was killed near Elstree, England, while trying to land a light aircraft in fog.

HILLARY, Sir Edmund Percival Born 1919, in Australia. He was initially a beekeeper but was always fascinated by exploration and mountaineering. In 1953 he and Tensing Norgay, a Sherpa, were the first men to reach the summit of Mount Everest, the highest mountain in the world. Hillary was also the first man

after Captain R. F. Scott to reach the South Pole overland (1958).

LEWIS, Carl Born USA 1961, athlete. The greatest sprinter/long jumper since Jesse Owens, Lewis won four gold medals in the 1984 Olympics.

LOUIS, Joseph Louis Barrow Born USA, 1914. Boxer, heavyweight class. The longest reigning heavyweight ever. He held the title from June 1937 until May 1949 when he announced his retirement. He defended his title 25 times.

MCENROE, John Born USA 1959, tennis player. One of the world's leading tennis players of the 1980s, McEnroe was the US singles champion in 1979–81 and 1984, and Wimbledon champion in 1981 and 1983–4. His sometimes disputatious behaviour on court has caused controversy.

MARCIANO, Rocky Born 1923 in the USA, died 1969. Boxer, heavyweight class. His career lasted from 1947 to 1956 and he was undefeated world champion from 1952 to 1956.

MERCKX, Eddie Born in Belgium, 1945. Cyclist. He won the Tour de France five times.

MOORE, Robert (Bobby) Frederick Born in the UK, 1941. Footballer. Played for England 108 times. Between 1962 and 1977 he played in 1,000 games for West Ham United, Fulham and England.

NICKLAUS, Jack Born USA, 1940. Golfer. Winner of the USA Masters Championship five times (1963, 1965, 1966, 1972, 1975). He also played on six winning teams in the World Cup (1963, 1964, 1966, 1967, 1971, 1973) and took the individual title three times. He has earned more than three million dollars and is the only man to have won the five major titles twice.

OVETT, Steven Michael James Born UK 1955, athlete. Identified in the minds of most people as the rival of

Sebastian Coe, Steve Ovett won the Gold for the 800 metres in the 1980 Olympic Games and, as of September 1984, was holder of the world record for the 1,500 metres.

OWENS, Jesse Born USA, 1913. Athlete. Probably the finest all-round athlete in Olympic history. On 25 May 1935, at the Intervarsity Athletics Meeting in Michigan, within one hour he set four world records (100 yards dash in 9.4 secs, 26 ft 8¼ in in the long jump, 220 yards low hurdles in 22.6 secs, 220 yards in 20.3 secs). In 1936 at the Berlin Olympics he won four gold medals.

PELE, Edson Arantes Do Nascimento Born in Brazil, 1940. Soccer player known as 'the king of soccer'. Played for Brazil and the Santos Football Club, and then the North American soccer league. When in Brazil, over his eighteen-year career, he scored 1,216 goals in 1,253 games. His estimated earnings at the height of his career were two million dollars.

RICHARDS, Sir Gordon Born UK, 1904. Jockey. He has won 4,870 races. He was champion jockey 26 times, and was knighted in 1963.

RICHARDS, Isaac Vivian Alexander Born Antigua 1952, cricketer. One of the greatest batsmen ever, Richards' Test career for the West Indies began in 1974. In 1976 his aggregate of 829 runs in a Test rubber against England was the highest ever by a West Indian, while his 189 not out made against

England in 1984 was the highest ever in a one-day International match. In 1985 he succeeded Clive Lloyd as captain of the West Indies.

SCHOCKEMOHLE, Alwin Born West Germany, 1937. Show jumper. In 1975, riding *Rex the Robber*, *Warwick Rex* and *Santa Monica*, he won the European Championship. He won a gold medal at the 1976 Olympics with no faults.

SIMPSON, Orenthal James (O.J.) Born USA 1947. Professional American football player. Plays running back position. Winner of the Superstars Competition held on US television.

SOBERS, Sir Garfield St Aubrun Born Barbados 1936. Cricketer. One-time captain of the Barbados team, Gary Sobers played for the West Indian team and Nottinghamshire. He has scored 8,032 runs in test cricket and has appeared in 85 consecutive tests between 1955 and 1972.

SPITZ, Mark Born USA, 1950. Swimmer. Most outstanding athlete of the 1972 Olympics. He won seven gold medals (100 and 200 m freestyle, 100 and 200 m butterfly, 4 × 100 m freestyle relay, 4 × 200 m freestyle relay, 4 × 100 m medley relay).

THOMPSON, Francis Morgan 'Daley' Born UK 1958, athlete. Winner of the 1984 Olympic gold medal for the Decathlon with 8,797 points, one less than the world record made by Jurgen Hingsen in West Germany in 1984.

The Olympic Games

Traditionally, the first Olympic Games were held in 776 BC at Olympia in the western Peloponnese, Greece. They continued to be held at four-year intervals until AD 393, when the Roman emperor Theodosius abolished them.

At first the games lasted for one day and consisted of only one race run the length of the stadium. Some time later other events were added. These included the discus, the javelin, the broad jump, boxing, chariot racing, wrestling and the pentathlon. When competitors from all the Greek colonies were allowed to enter, a sacred truce was declared to allow the competitors to travel to the games freely. Women were not allowed to compete or watch, except for the priestesses of Demeter who observed the proceedings. The The greatest honour was to win a branch of wild olive, and the games attained such importance that an 'Olympiad' or the four-year span between the games became an official measure of time.

In 1894 Baron Pierre de Coubertin called an international conference at the Sorbonne in Paris. He proposed the creation of a modern cycle of Olympic Games. The representatives of 12 nations agreed to his proposal, and the first modern games took place in 1896 in Athens, in a marble stadium built specially for the occasion. Thirteen nations sent a total of 311 participants and there were 43 events covering nine sports.

The Olympic movement is controlled by the International Olympic Committee (IOC) based in Lausanne, Switzerland. According to article 26 of the IOC rules and regulations, contestants must be amateurs: they must always have participated in sport as an avocation, without material gain of any kind. An athlete is eligible for the Olympic Games:
1 If he has a basic occupation designed to ensure his present and future livelihood;
2 if he does not receive, or has never received, any remuneration for participation in sport;
3 if he complies with the rules of the International Federation concerned, and the official interpretations of this article (26).

A person who complies with these conditions is considered an amateur from the Olympic point of view.

The opening ceremony
The opening ceremony of the Olympic Games does not vary. The head of state of the host country is welcomed to the stadium by the president of the IOC, the national anthem of the host country is played and then there is a parade of all the competitors. Greece

always heads the parade and the host country comes last. Between these two the competing countries march past in alphabetical order, each contingent carrying a shield bearing the name of their country and their national flag. The competitors march round the stadium and then line up in the centre.

The president of the Olympic committee which has organized the games gives a speech of welcome and asks the head of state to open the games. A fanfare of trumpets sounds and the Olympic flag, bearing its linked rings, is raised. Hundreds of doves are released and there is a gun salute. At this moment a runner arrives carrying the Olympic flame. The flame is kindled at Olympia in Greece and is carried by teams of runners to the stadium, where it burns throughout the games. The games are then blessed and the Olympic hymn is sung. A contestant from the host country steps forward and takes the Olympic oath on behalf of all the contestants:
'In the name of all competitors I promise that we will take part in these Olympic Games, respecting and abiding by the rules which govern them, in the true spirit of sportsmanship, for the glory of sport and the honour of our teams.'

The choir then sings the national anthem of the host country and the competitors leave the stadium.

Throughout the games, as each event is completed, award ceremonies take place. The winner and the second- and third-place competitors step on to a rostrum and are presented with gold, silver

and bronze medals respectively. The national flags of their countries are raised and the national anthem of the winning competitor is played.

At the completion of the games the president of the IOC draws the ceremonies to a close. He exhorts the youth of the world to gather again in four years for the next games:
'May they display cheerfulness and concord so that the Olympic torch may be carried on with ever greater eagerness, courage and honour for the good of humanity throughout the ages.'

With a last fanfare of trumpets, the Olympic flame dies down and the flag is lowered. There is a five-gun salute and the final anthem is sung. The games are over for another four years.

The events
From 1896 the main events in the Olympic Games consisted of track and field sports although from time to time other sports, from archery to yachting, were included. The 1896 Olympics covered nine sports with 43 events. By 1972, 23 sports with 205 events were covered.

Today, the Olympics contain some or all of the following events (but never less than 15 in any one games): Archery, Athletics, Badminton, Basketball, Boxing, Canoeing, Cycling, Diving, Equestrian sports, Fencing, Football (soccer), Gymnastics, Handball, Hockey, Judo, Tennis, Pentathlon (riding, fencing, shooting, swimming, running), Polo, Rowing, Shooting, Swimming, Track and Field Events (running, hurdling, relay, walking, high jump, long jump, shot put, pole vault, triple jump, discus, javelin, hammer, decathlon, steeplechase, marathon), Water polo, Weightlifting, Wrestling (Freestyle and Greco-Roman), Yachting.

The Winter Olympics contain these events: Figure skating, Speed skating, Ice hockey, Cross-country skiing, Ski relay, Ski jump, Biathlon, Slalom, Giant slalom, Bobsled, Luge.

LOCATIONS OF MODERN OLYMPIC GAMES

Year	Place	Country
1896	Athens	Greece
1900	Paris	France
1904	St Louis	USA
1908	London	UK
1912	Stockholm	Sweden
1916	No Games	
1920	Antwerp	Belgium
1924	Paris	France
1928	Amsterdam	The Nether-lands
1932	Los Angeles	USA
1936	Berlin	Germany
1940	No Games	
1944	No Games	
1948	London	UK
1952	Helsinki	Finland
1956	Melbourne	Australia
1960	Rome	Italy
1964	Tokyo	Japan
1968	Mexico City	Mexico
1972	Munich	West Germany
1976	Montreal	Canada
1980	Moscow	USSR
1984	Los Angeles	USA
1988	Seoul (scheduled)	S. Korea

LOCATIONS OF WINTER OLYMPIC GAMES

Year	Place	Country
1924	Chamonix	France
1928	St Moritz	Switzerland
1932	Lake Placid	USA
1936	Garmisch Parten-kirchen	Germany
1940	No Games	
1944	No Games	
1948	St Moritz	Switzerland
1952	Oslo	Norway
1956	Cortina d'Ampezzo	Italy
1960	Squaw Valley	USA
1964	Innsbruck	Austria
1968	Grenoble	France
1972	Sapporo	Japan
1976	Denver	USA
1980	Lake Placid	USA
1984	Sarajevo	Yugoslavia
1988	Calgary (scheduled)	Canada

THE OLYMPICS:
NUMBERS OF COMPETITORS AND SPORTS

Year	Where held	Number of sports	Number of competitors	Number of nations competing
1896	Athens	10	285	13
1900	Paris	13	1066	20
1904	St Louis	12	496	11
1908	London	20	2059	22
1912	Stockholm	14	2541	28
1920	Antwerp	19	2606	29
1924	Paris	19	3092	44
1928	Amsterdam	16	3015	46
1932	Los Angeles	16	1408	37
1936	Berlin	21	4069	49
1948	London	18	4468	59
1952	Helsinki	17	5867	69
1956	Melbourne	18	3183	67
1960	Rome	18	5396	84
1964	Tokyo	20	5558	94
1968	Mexico City	18	6059	112
1972	Munich	21	7147	122
1976	Montreal	21	6815	88
1980	Moscow	21	5923	81
1984	Los Angeles	21	7055	140

Besides the medals which are awarded during the games, the International Olympic Committee also makes the following awards:

The Olympic Diploma of Merit
This is awarded to an individual who has made an outstanding contribution to sport (amateur) or to the Olympic movement.

The Olympic Cup
Awarded to an organization which has contributed outstandingly to amateur or Olympic sport.

The Count Bonacossa Trophy
This is awarded annually to the national Olympic committee which has most furthered the Olympic movement.

The Mohammed Taher Trophy
Awarded to the most outstanding Olympic athlete.

The Fearnley Cup
Awarded to the most meritorious amateur sports club or local association.

The Tokyo Trophy
Awarded to the individual or group who have showed outstanding sportsmanship, whether or not medals have been won.

Olympic events

Long jump

Judo

Fencing

High jump

Boxing

Javelin

Discus

Running

Rowing

Diving

Gymnastics

This sport has gained unbelievably in popularity over the last few years. The inspiration to hundreds of young girl gymnasts came from a young girl gymnast from Russia called Olga Korbut and a young girl from Romania called Nadia Comaneci. It was at the 1972 Munich Olympic Games, that the tiny Olga Korbut thrilled the thousands of spectators with her energetic and daring performance. But perhaps the main reason for the crowd taking this tiny girl to their hearts was the sight of her crying with disappointment after she had made two mistakes on the beam. Despite her two mistakes she won three gold medals and one silver at Munich.

Olga became the star of gymnastics with a huge following. It came as a surprise when in 1975 at the Montreal Olympics a new girl emerged as the overall Olympic champion. This was Nadia Comaneci. Nadia gained full marks for seven of her exercises. The first time this has ever happened in the history of the Olympic Games. It is without doubt that these two young girls are responsible for the popularity of gymnastics today.

Since 1948 all gymnastics have been judged and marked in the same way throughout the world. The way of marking is laid down in a Code of Points.

In major competitions each gymnast has to perform on four pieces of apparatus. These are the broad horse, the asymmetric bars, the beam and the floor. Each girl has to perform a compulsory and a voluntary programme.

In the compulsory section the mark is out of ten and is given for rhythm, precision, correctness, and co-ordination. Marks will be lost for lack of control, requiring help, falling or faulty movements. The voluntary exercises are marked out of ten but these ten marks are divided between the different things the judges are looking for. The difficulty of the movement is marked out of three. There are two grades of difficulty in women's gymnastics, medium and superior, Seven medium and three superior exercises must be included in the gymnastics, medium and superior. will lose marks for leaving out a movement. Composition is marked out of 0·5 and is where a gymnast is judged for the way in which she puts her performance together. Execution and extent are marked out of four and the general impression made by the gymnast or the judges is marked out of one. Originality is marked out of 1·5 and it is here that a daring and exciting performance will gain marks.

A young girl interested in becoming a gymnast will probably start by joining a club. There may be one at school, if so it will probably be connected to the regional school's gymnastic association. The competitions organised through this association will enable a good gymnast to become a national champion.

If there is no club at school, the

gymnast will have to join a local gymnastics club. The club will probably have a fully qualified coach who will instruct the new member in the basics of gymnastics. A good gymnast may be asked to join a special group which will offer the opportunity for extra coaching. The training will be hard and require many hours of dedicated work. A gymnast who is a member of a leading club and who trains hard will be able to enter major competitions at national and international levels. But most gymnasts climb to the top through local championships. A gymnast entering any competition will need mental concentration as well as physical perfection.

In Britain probably the most sought after prize is the Champions Cup; a competition held at London at the Royal Albert Hall and which is held in January. This is where the six top girl gymnasts (men also) in the country compete against each other.

Training

The training to become a top gymnast is very hard, requiring hours of regular training. Ballet lessons will also be included in a young gymnast's training as this strengthens the legs as well as giving grace of movement.

Before performing on the apparatus or the floor a gymnast will warm up for at least half an hour to get the body ready for the physical extremes needed in gymnastics.

Vaulting

Women vault across the horse by placing their hands in the centre of the horse. In competitions women are allowed two vaults. A vault is divided into two parts when it is being judged. The first from when the gymnast starts her run up to the horse to when she touches the horse. This is judged on how the body is placed on the horse and for the flight through the air. The second part is from leaving the horse to the landing. This is marked on the distance the gymnast travels before landing and on the landing itself. This must be smooth and balanced. Marks will be lost for a fall or staggering.

In all vaults the gymnast's hands must touch the horse.

Some of the vaults a gymnast uses

The Horizontal Vault is the simplest vault and the body and the legs must be kept straight. The body should be in a horizontal position when it passes over the horse. The back is to the horse on landing.

In a Handspring Vault, the body, the arms and the legs are all kept straight when landing on the horse. The legs should be straight above the head as the gymnast moves through a handstand to land with the back to the horse.

A Yamashita Vault named after a Japanese male gymnast, Haruhiro Yamashita, is a variation on a basic handspring. On leaving the horse the body goes into a pike position, straightening out and landing with the back to the horse.

Turns can be added to handsprings. A half turn before landing on the horse, a handspring over the horse and then a full turn before landing facing the horse, is just one of the combinations which can be put together.

Somersaults can be incorporated with handsprings and cartwheels in a variety of different ways. It depends upon how daring the gymnast is and how advanced.

The beam

This consists of a beam of wood 1·2 metres (4 ft) from the ground, 4·9 metres (16 ft) in length and only 10 centimetres (4 in) wide. Balance and perfect line combined with deep concentration are needed for any work on the beam. In competitions, the gymnast will be expected to use the whole length of the beam and include in her programme walking, running, jumps, leaps, cartwheels, and if she is a top gymnast, acrobatic exercises. Her performance must be smooth and flowing, any hesitation will lose marks. She must also include three pauses of not more than three seconds each. This will show the judges that she has perfect balance. Before the gymnast can begin her exercises she has to get onto the beam. This is important as she must land on the beam with her body perfectly balanced in order to be able to move smoothly into her next movement. The gymnast does not think of the mount as merely a way of getting onto the beam but as the start of the exercise with which she has chosen to open her performance. This may be a handstand, a cartwheel or any of the other movements used in work on the beam. She can use a spring board to help her or she may walk or run up to the beam. Whatever she does she will be marked and timed from the moment her feet leave the ground. She will also lose marks if she falls from the beam and she must regain the beam within ten seconds.

Movements on the beam

A cat leap with a turn is where the gymnast raises one foot from the beam, followed by the other and turns through 360 degrees back to her original position.

There are various hold positions (pauses). A gymnast may choose to stand sideways on the beam with one leg straight on the beam and the other held to the side as high as it will go.

An arabesque hold is where the legs are in a full splits position with one foot on the beam and the other high in the air. The arms are held horizontally to the legs and the head is down.

The way the gymnast leaves the beam is important. She may choose any way of getting off the beam but as well as being perfectly executed it must be of a superior standard of difficulty. She must also land on her feet without falling or staggering.

Back support: Body in front of bar with upper thighs resting on bar. Supported by straight arms.

Cartwheel: Complete turn through 360 degrees sideways from feet to hands to feet.

Dismount: Final movement of an exercise descending from the apparatus being used.

Beam exercises demand perfect balance

Front handstand: Body vertical, supported on hands.

Front support: Body behind bar, hips resting on bar.

Hip circle: Rotation round bar with hips in contact throughout.

Hold position: Any position held for three seconds or more.

Kip: Usually performed on the bars. A swing over the bar, head and feet coming together. Continuing to front support.

Mount: Movement bringing gymnast onto apparatus.

Movement: One particular part of an exercise.

Overgrasp: Palms' downwards grasp of bars.

Pike: Body bent at waist with straight legs.

Rear lying hang: Uses high bar and low bar. Hands hold high bar, body straight supported by buttocks on low bar.

R.O.V.: Bonus factors taken into account when judging. Risk, originality and virtuosity.

Straddle: Legs straight and held apart.

Tuck: Body bent at waist with bent legs held up to the chest.

Undergrasp: Palms under bars, holding bar upwards.

Uprise: Arms straight, body straight, swinging to front support.

Walkover: 360 degree turn, forwards or backwards, rotating round shoulder.

Floor exercises
It is in this section of gymnastics that a gymnast's skills of self-

*Floor exercises are a combination of
gymnastic skill and musical interpretation*

expression, suppleness and agility are all put together. The one to one and a half minute performance is carried out on a 12 metre (39 ft) square mat. This is made of plywood with a layer of sponge in the centre. The exercise is performed to music which must be chosen with great care as the rhythm of the music and the gymnasts movements must complement each other. The arms, the hands and the head must be used with expression to fit with the powerful and quick movements across the mat. It is here that the gymnast's basic ballet training becomes apparent.

The gymnast must use the whole area of the mat, moving diagonally across it as well as from side to side. She will lose marks if she steps over the edge of the mat. She will also be judged on general posture, lightness, suppleness, turns, balances and relaxation; as well as for the way she interprets the music.

The routine will include springs, body waves, leaps, jumps, rolls, cartwheels, flic-flacs, somersaults, splits, pauses and variations on all these movements. It is perhaps the most exciting secton out of the competition.

Exercises on the parallel bars require strong arm and stomach muscles

Some of the movements used in floor exercises

A flic-flac is where the gymnast leaps forward from one foot with arms stretched forwards and upwards, while at the same time turning through 180 degrees. She then circles backwards onto her hands and pushes off again to do more flic-flacs across the mat.

Tinsicas are used to cross the mat using the arms as well as the legs. Using her first leg to push off with she bends so that one hand after the other touches the mat. This brings her legs into a straddle position above her head with her body straight. Her first foot touches the floor as her first hand leaves it. She then pushes off with her second hand which brings her back to the position she started in.

LOOKING
AFTER YOURSELF

How to Survive

Should you ever find yourself in a dangerous situation, you may need to use all your resourcefulness in order to cope. However, it is wise to be prepared in advance and to know what kinds of action you may have to take.

How to tackle a fire

If the fire is indoors, shut all doors and windows to prevent air currents fanning the flames. Throw water over the fire *except*:

When the water could hit live electric wires. A shock could flash back and electrocute you. Switch off the electricity at the mains. If the television set is on fire, pull out the plug first before dowsing with water.

When a pan of fat is burning. Burning oil floats on water, so you will merely succeed in scattering the flames round the room. Stifle the fire by covering it with a large lid.

If you need to extinguish a bonfire, throw water on to the centre of the blaze, or shovel sand or earth on the flames.

If a fire shows any sign of getting out of hand, call the fire brigade.

Escape from a building on fire

You may wake in the night smelling burning. If you then find that the door handle is too hot to turn, you know that the fire is right outside. If there is no alternative route to escape the fire, do *not* try to open the door by padding the handle

with a cloth. Smoke and fumes would instantly pour into the room. With luck, the fire would take some time to burn the door down and reach you. Until help comes, seal the bottom of the door with a carpet or rug to help keep out the fumes. If there is thick smoke, it is best to keep your head near the floor where the smoke is less dense. But first call for help at a window so that rescuers will know where you are.

It is always dangerous to jump from a height. However, if you are on the first floor you may have to do it. If necessary, break the window by throwing a chair through it. Then hang by your hands from the window-sill, thereby reducing the distance you have to jump by the length of your body. Let go and bend your knees when you hit the ground to take the shock. Another method of getting out of a burning building is to make a rope. Tear curtains, sheets or blankets and join the strips with reef knots. Tie one end securely to a heavy piece of furniture and lower the other end out of the window. Climb down the rope hand over hand – it won't be easy.

Safety on the water
The best safety precaution against drowning is to learn to swim. A non-swimmer will be lucky to survive a crisis in the water. Whether you swim or not, it is sensible to wear a life-jacket when out boating.

When a boat capsizes, even

Drownproofing

though you may be a swimmer, the rule is to *stay with the boat*. Not only will you be able to cling to it, you will be seen more easily by rescuers. If you try swimming towards the shore against a strong current you may never make it. If possible, make yourself more conspicuous by holding up a piece of brightly coloured clothing. In rough weather, when it is difficult to cling to the side of a rowing dinghy, swim underneath the hull and cling to the seats inside. There will be plenty of air to breathe underneath the boat.

When there is nothing to cling to, such as a boat or a lifebelt, the natural buoyancy of your body will keep you floating as long as you don't panic and throw your arms up in the air (the weight of your arms out of the water will make

you sink). If the water is calm, you can float on your back. If it is choppy, treading water is a good way of staying afloat for long periods. This uses very little energy. With your nose and mouth clear of the water, take up a vertical position and slowly pedal with your feet as if on a bicycle. Your hands should make circling movements just under the water.

When you tread water, you have to hold your head – which is quite heavy – out of the water. An even less tiring method of staying afloat is 'drownproofing'. After taking a deep breath, you float vertically, being completely submerged apart from the back of your head, with your arms spread out. Hold your breath for several seconds, then breathe out through the nostrils. To take a fresh breath, lift your

ead upwards and backwards, and
t the same time sweep your arms
ownwards. Your mouth should
hen clear the surface.

Avoid swimming where there are
trong currents or tides. However,
f you ever do have to battle against
current, swim across it diagonally.
wimming directly against it is
nore exhausting.

High winds in the mountains

A sudden upcurrent of air in a gale-
orce wind could fill your cagoule,
r anorak, like a balloon and lift
ou bodily, perhaps over a precipice.
o tuck your cagoule into your
rousers. When the wind gusts
iercely, flatten yourself against a
ock if you happen to be climbing.
f walking, fling yourself to the
ground.

Danger from lightning

One of the worst places to be in a
hunderstorm is under a tall,
solated tree. But in the midst of a
lense wood where all the trees are
bout the same height you are
comparatively safe. Avoid any high,
solated object such as a tower or a
pylon, and do not think you will be
safe in the middle of an open plain.
You will be standing higher than
anything else around and therefore
likely to attract lightning. When
caught in a wide-open space by a
thunderstorm, make yourself as low
as possible by lying on your
stomach.

Other places to avoid are
mountain crests, steep rock faces
and the mouths of caves (ionization
at a cave entrance can draw
lightning). A good spot to choose
would be a hollow in the ground, or

a few yards away from a solitary
tree. You can also safely shelter in
a car.

Danger from animals

Avoid the centres of fields where
there are horses or cattle. Although
such animals are usually harmless
they can be unpredictable. Should
you be unfortunate enough to be
charged at by a cow or a bull, throw
down whatever you happen to be
carrying, or any clothing you can
get off quickly as you run. The
animal will be temporarily dis-
tracted by them while you make
your getaway.

When confronted by an angry
dog, the best thing to do is to
freeze. Talk to it gently but on no
account run. If the dog does not
then leave you but starts to attack,
try hitting it on the nose and, as
soon as possible, grab it by the
scruff of the neck. If a dog grips
your arm or leg in its teeth do not
try to tug the limb away; you will
cause a nasty tear instead of a
clean wound. Try pushing your
limb towards the attacker's throat
and he may then let go. Afterwards,
wash the wound in cold water and
immediately go to a doctor for an
anti-rabies injection.

Cold can be a killer

It is important to be well prepared
for cold weather and to know what
to do in a crisis where it is essential
to stay warm until help comes. Even
on a hot summer's day temperatures
can be freezing on a high peak. If
you are hungry, wet, exhausted and
perhaps lost or injured, you can
easily succumb to cold even when
temperatures are not much below

During thunderstorms it is dangerous to shelter near cave mouths or tall, isolated trees. These attract lightning. If you are in an exposed place keep as close to the ground as possible.

provise a shelter if you are stranded in remote places.

Tin lid signalling. Hold the lid up to the sun. With your other arm outstretched, hold your hand up in front of your face so that it blots out whoever you are signalling to. Tilt the lid this way and that until you hit your hand with a reflection of the sun. Sight the person through the slits between your fingers while keeping the lid flashing on that hand. A mirror or a broken piece of glass can also be used for flashing by this method.

freezing point. Your body heat can leak away so that you are chilled to the very core. You will then be suffering from a dangerous condition known as 'exposure', more correctly termed 'hypothermia'.

To beat the cold it is wise to wear several loose-fitting layers of warm clothing rather than just one thick sweater. When hiking, carry some extra pullovers in your rucksack as a safety precaution. You must take care not to get wet, so have a waterproof jacket and trousers with you as well. To keep you going, take some quick-energy foods that you can eat as you walk along, such as barley sugar, nuts, raisins or chocolate.

Should you become stranded in remote places, you will need to improvise a shelter from whatever materials are available at the time. One of the simplest is a sloping roof standing against a solid support such as a stone wall or rock face, or even a large fallen tree trunk. It could be made of logs or branches, or it might be a sheet of plastic anchored by small rocks and secured by string. Make sure that the entrance faces away from the wind.

Snow, surprisingly, can help you keep warm in an emergency. It is a good insulator against cold and can be used to make a shelter. In a deep snow drift, for example, yo could dig a tunnel. For a shove., use an ice axe, a chunk of tree bark. a rock, or whatever you happen to have with you that will suffice. Don't make the tunnel too big or it will be less warm. When the tunnel is finished, block the entrance with snowballs, but not completely. It is essential to have adequate ventilation in a snow shelter. An alternative is to dig a fairly deep trench in the snow with hollowed-out chambers to sit in. The top can be covered with large snowballs pressed together. Leave one free so that it can be rolled away when you come in or out. Cover the place where you sleep or sit with evergreen branches. Do not sit on or lean directly on the snow.

Shortage of water

It is possible to go without food for several weeks, but one cannot go completely without water for many days, especially in hot weather. On a long trek it is essential to take some water with you.

When water is scarce, you can conserve what you already have in your body by reducing perspiration. Button up your clothing. Uncomfortable though this may be in the heat, it will prevent you sweating so much. If you have a fair distance to cover, rest in the shade while the sun is at its hottest and resume your journey later when it is cooler.

Signalling for help

You will have to act according to circumstances and improvise a means of attracting attention. For example, you may have a mirror or a tin lid which you could use to flash reflected sunlight as a signal. This is one way of signalling to an airplane or helicopter pilot who is trying to locate you from the air. Another way is to light fires. Three fires set several metres apart, making an equilateral triangle, are recognized by pilots the world over as a distress signal. If you have no

SOS bonfire signal

means of lighting a fire, a large SOS spelt out in white stones or snow will also serve the same purpose.

If you are in trouble in mountain country, remember that six blasts of a whistle blown during one minute, followed by a minute's silence, is the international mountain distress signal. Anyone hearing your signal for help should reply with three whistle blasts in a minute, followed by a minute's silence. If you have no whistle, or can't whistle yourself, use a flashlight. Flash the on/off switch in the same sequence.

The international Morse code distress signal is different. You make three short flashes (or whistle blasts), then three long ones, and end with three short ones again. In Morse code this spells out 'SOS'. Another signal for help that is recognized everywhere is a white flag flying.

First Aid and Home Remedies

It is important to stress that the following instructions provide only a brief introduction to the important subject of first aid. Readers are urged to contact their local first aid training centre if they wish to study first aid thoroughly.

There are other vital points to be kept in mind whenever presented with a serious accident or case. The first essential is to contact medical aid – a doctor, nurse or ambulance – and then to attend to the casualty. Remember that an injured person should not be moved. You should, however, take steps to guard the casualty from traffic or any other danger. If it is possible try to divert the traffic rather than move the patient.

Keep the person's head low and the body warm with any suitable covering. Do not give the casualty anything to drink while waiting for help to arrive. If there is severe bleeding or the person has stopped breathing, however, treatment should be given immediately (*see* appropriate entries).

Bleeding
When bleeding is severe, the following five steps should be taken at once:
1 Ensure that whatever caused the cut or cuts cannot inflict any further damage. Try not to move the casualty but to clear the area instead;
2 Using a clean cloth, towel or your fingers, if nothing else is available, press the wound's edges together. Continue doing this until the bleeding ceases. This can be anything up to 15 minutes;
3 As soon as possible, get the patient to lie down, raising the feet higher than the head;
4 When you are sure that the bleeding has stopped use any handy material, such as a sock or stocking, to bind round the wound;
5 Telephone for an ambulance, or doctor, if you think the patient's condition is serious enough.

In less serious cases, such as when the bleeding is slight, you should expose the wound and remove any foreign matter from it. Be very careful not to disturb any blood-clots. Gently wash away any dirt by pouring water freely over the wound. Apply an antiseptic and cover the wound with a dry dressing and then cotton-wool or lint, finally followed by a bandage. Support the injured part and make sure it is not moved. Treat for shock if there are any signs of it.

A nose-bleed should be treated in the following way. Sit the patient in an air-current from an open window. The head should be thrown slightly back. Loosen any tight clothing around the neck and chest. The patient must keep the mouth open to breathe through, and should on no account blow the nose. Applying something cold to the nose and the spine at collar level generally helps to stop the bleeding.

Shock
Accidents can cause a wide range

of injuries. They may be external or internal, such as broken bones or damaged organs. In all such cases, first aid must include treatment for shock.

Shock always occurs when there is a severe injury, blood loss or pain. It is caused by an insufficient supply of blood to the brain, which results in oxygen deficiency. The patient may feel faint, or cold and clammy, and possibly sick. Treatment should be carried out as follows:
1 Ensure that the casualty is not in danger of further injury. Never move the person unless it is *absolutely essential*. Just provide as much comfort as you can by using cushions for example;
2 Raise the patient's legs higher than the head if this can be done without affecting the injured part of the body. If you are unsure of the extent of the injuries move the patient as little as possible;
3 Make sure that warmth is maintained by covering the casualty with a light blanket. Never use hot water bottles or fires to provide artificial heat.

If the injured person shows any sign of the shock becoming worse, an ambulance should be called at once. This should be done anyway whenever a patient has been seriously injured. In the case of a heart attack, the casualty should be propped up, in order to aid breathing, before you call for an ambulance.

Burns, scalds and bruises
Dry heat, such as a fire or hot metal, causes burns; and moist heat, boiling water or steam,

causes scalds. Treatment is the same in both cases, except for the first step:
1 *Burns*: If the person's clothing is on fire, approach the casualty, holding a rug, blanket, coat or table-cover in front of you. Wrap it round the patient to smother the flames and lay the person on the floor as fast as possible.
Scalds: Remove soaked clothing and anything tight, such as bracelets, belts or boots;
2 Cool the burnt or scalded parts with cold water for at least ten minutes;
3 Do not move the patient if the burn or scald is serious, but do all you can to make the person comfortable;
4 Cover the burn or scald lightly with a pillowcase or sheet to prevent infection. Never touch the affected areas with your hands or prick any blisters;
5 For serious cases, call an ambulance.
N.B. The treatment for sunburn is the same as that for other burns.

Bruising can be eased by rubbing the affected area gently with olive oil or by applying something cold to it, such as ice or a cold compress

Choking
When somebody has something stuck in the throat, bend the person's head and shoulders forward and thump the back hard between the shoulder-blades. If this is not successful, try to make the person vomit. Pass two fingers right to the back of the throat. Should the choking continue – perhaps because a fishbone is lodged in the throat – call a doctor.

Foreign matter in the eye

Usually, grit or an eyelash can be removed simply by rolling the eyelid back from the eye and carefully applying a soft cloth or handkerchief. If, however, a quantity of sand, grit, or some chemical such as ammonia, is in the patient's eye, persuade the person to put her head into a basin of cool water and blink several times. Repeat the process after you have changed the water. Generally you will find the eye is clear of the foreign matter.

Poisoning

In cases of poisoning it is vital to telephone for an ambulance immediately. Only a hospital can cope properly with poisoning. Keep a sample of the poison, if possible, to show to the doctor so that the correct treatment can be given. While waiting for the ambulance to come, keep the patient as quiet as possible. Do not give her anything to drink or eat. In cases when the patient complains of a burning mouth or throat she has most certainly swallowed an acid. Give her plenty of water to drink in order to dilute the acid. Continue until the burning stops. Avoid making the patient sick as vomit may be inhaled and cause choking.

Squeezed fingers, splinters and stings

After squeezing the top of a finger, hold it in warm water for a few minutes. This causes the nail to expand and soften. The blood beneath it now has more room to flow, thus lessening the pain.

Splinters can be removed by nearly filling a wide-mouthed bottle with hot water, and then holding the injured part over this and pressing it down tightly. The suction acts as a poultice and draws the flesh down. The splinter will normally come out quite easily after this.

When a sting is still present it should be extracted, if possible, with the point of a sterilized needle. For bee stings, apply spirit, toilet water, sal volatile, a solution of baking soda or washing soda to relieve the pain. For wasp or hornet stings, use a weak acid such as vinegar or lemon juice. Then, put on a dry dressing and treat for shock.

Sprains

Place the affected limb in a comfortable position and prevent movement. Next, expose the sprained joint and apply a firm bandage. The bandage should be wetted with cold water and kept wet. Repeat this process, whenever necessary to provide relief. When in doubt, treat the injury as a break (fracture).

Sunstroke

In cases of sunstroke, get the patient to a cool and shady place. Strip the person to the waist and lay her down with the head and shoulders well raised. Fan the patient rigorously and also sponge the body with cold water all the time. Apply ice-bags or cold water to the head, neck and spine.

When the person is conscious, give her drinks of cold water. Do all you can to help the patient to become conscious and do not try to give her a drink until then.

The first step is to clear the person's airway because, once it is cleared, the casualty may start breathing again without further ado. Anything that you find in the mouth (blood, vomit, false teeth, etc.) must be instantly cleared out. It is also vital to tilt the casualty's head well back, as an unconscious person's tongue falls back and obstructs the airway.

Tilting the head extends the neck and moves the tongue clear of the airway.

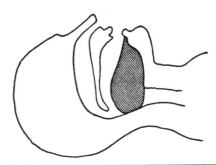

If you then breathe into the casualty's mouth and the person's chest rises and falls, you will know that the airway is clear; otherwise, you must immediately repeat the first step. Again clear the mouth of any obstruction and make sure that the head is tilted back far enough.

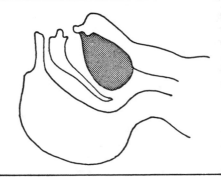

When applying mouth-to-mouth breathing remember to pinch the casualty's nostrils to close them. This will stop any of the air you are breathing in from escaping by way of the person's nose.

You are now ready to start mouth-to-mouth breathing. Begin with four quick breaths *in order to replenish the casualty's blood with a good supply of oxygen. There is a sufficient amount of oxygen in your breath when exhaled.*

Now settle down to a steady breathing at the normal rate of 10–15 breaths per minute. Remember to keep the casualty's nostrils pinched all the time. This must be kept up until medical help arrives, somebody takes over from you or, of course, the person starts breathing properly again without your help.

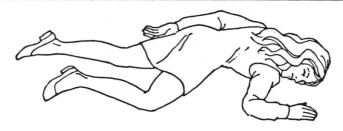

When a casualty does start breathing, place the person carefully in the recovery position shown in the illustration. This makes it possible for the casualty to

breathe easily without the tongue falling back across the airway or any further vomit being inhaled.

Should you have to deal with a heavy person, use the following method to turn her into the recovery position: kneel alongside the casualty; place the arms at the sides of the body; cross the far leg over the near one and then pull the person over by the clothes at the hip. After that, put the casualty's arms and legs into the proper recovery positions, as illustrated.

Finally, there are a few additional points to keep in mind for special cases. Gentle breathing is essential for young children and babies, and you may have to seal your lips over both the child's nose and mouth. When injury to the casualty's mouth makes it impossible to give breathing aid by the usual method, you must as an alternative apply mouth-to-nose breathing.

315

The correct treatment for convulsions

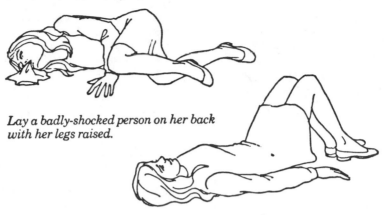

Lay a badly-shocked person on her back with her legs raised.

Convulsions

If a person is having convulsions (a fit) remove any objects nearby which can cause injuries. Protect the patient but do not restrain her in any way. If choking occurs, put a piece of cloth or anything soft into the mouth but *never* use force. Stay by the person after the convulsions have stopped as she may suffer from a temporary loss of memory and a headache.

Electric shock

Before any assistance can be given to the victim of an electric shock, the electric contact must be broken. Do this by switching off the appliance, turning off the current at the mains or pushing the person away with a piece of dry wood. Next see if the casualty is breathing. If she is not, give her mouth-to-mouth breathing (*see* below).

A badly shocked but conscious person should be laid on her back with the legs raised. If she is unconscious, she should be laid in the recovery position (*see* diagram on page 30).

MOUTH-TO-MOUTH BREATHING

It is very important that as many people as possible know how to apply 'mouth-to-mouth breathing' as it is the surest method of saving the life of a person who has ceased to breathe due to an accident, heart attack, drowning, electric shock or other reason.

Practice, after studying this form of first aid in the following description, is a very good idea. *Never* practise on another person but try to attend a proper class at which mouth-to-mouth breathing can be practised on dummies.

As soon as you are certain that the casualty is not breathing at all, start giving her mouth-to-mouth breathing. Delay can cause damage to the brain in three minutes!

Beauty and Health

Although your body has an amazing built-in ability to repair and renew itself, it can do this successfully only if you give it the proper basic care and attention. Proper care leads to good health, good health makes you feel and look your best, giving you the kind of vitality and confidence which enables you to tackle and enjoy all the experiences that come to you.

Eat your way to beauty and health

Mention diet and most people think of slimming. However, the word 'diet' really means 'a way of eating' and a normal diet means a way of eating which gives your body all the ingredients it needs to keep it in tip-top condition.

Meat, fish, cheese, eggs, nuts and pulses (various peas and beans) are full of protein. Protein is the material the body needs for growth, and for replacing parts like hair and nails. It also gives you energy.

Fruit and green vegetables provide you with roughage – the material that makes your digestion work efficiently. They are also full of mineral salts and vitamins. Vitamin C, found in citrus fruits and green vegetables is essential if you want glowing, healthy skin. As this vitamin cannot be stored in the body, you need a good supply every day.

Milk, cream and cheese supply you with calcium for your teeth, bones and nails. Milk and yoghurt also supply you with vitamins A and D – the vitamin which you also get from sunshine. These are also good for your skin and for your hair.

Wholemeal bread also provides roughage and is a valuable source of vitamin B.

The foods to avoid, if you want to stay slim and healthy, are the ones that are fattening without being very nutritious. These are white bread, cakes, sweets, biscuits, jams, fizzy drinks – everything, in fact, which contains lots of starch and sugar. Sugary foods are also very bad for the teeth (they are the main cause of decay) and for the skin (they cause spots).

If you are overweight, you are eating more food than you need. Eating less doesn't mean skipping meals and starving yourself; what it does mean is eating less of the wrong foods and more of the right ones. So concentrate on the proteins, vegetables and fruits, and cut out the sugars and starches.

The calorie value of most of the items is based on a sample weight of 28g (1oz). For special cases the amount is listed next to the item. Anything cooked in oil has a higher calorific value than it has when raw.

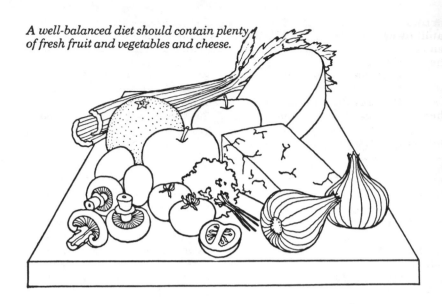

A well-balanced diet should contain plenty of fresh fruit and vegetables and cheese.

Food	Calories
All-Bran	69
Almonds	170
Anchovy fillets	40
Angel Delight	43
Apples, dried	50
fresh	10
Apricots, canned	30
dried	50
fresh	5
Artichokes, Globe	5
Jerusalem	5
Asparagus	5
Aubergines	5
Avocado pear	25
Bacon, fat	130
lean	115
Bagel, one	125
Baked beans and Frankfurters	37
Bananas	15
Bass, steamed	20
Bean sprouts, fresh	8
Beans, Baked	25
Broad (lima)	10
French	5
Haricot (navy)	75
Runner	5
Beef, fat	75
lean	50
Beefburger, one	155
Beetroot (beet), fresh	10
Bilberries, fresh	10
Biscuit, plain	110
sweet	140
Blackberries	10
Blackcurrants	10
Blueberries, *see* Bilberries	
Bread, white or brown large loaf, average slice	70
small loaf, average slice	80
small loaf, average slice	50
ginger	108
Broccoli	5
Brussels sprouts	10
Butter	225
Buttermilk, 600ml/1pt	235
Cabbage, red or white	5
Cake, plain	75
rich	105

Carrots	5	Gooseberries, fresh	10
Cauliflower	5	Grapefruit	8
Celery	3	Grapes	15
Cheese, Cheddar	120	Haddock, raw	20
Cottage	30	smoked	20
Edam	90	Hake fillets, raw	25
Processed	120	Halibut, raw	30
Cherries, fresh	10	Ham, lean	65
glace	60	fat	95
Chicken, flesh only,		Hamburger, *see*	
raw	35	Beefburger	
Chicory	3	Herrings, raw	65
Chives	10	Honey	80
Chocolate, milk	165	Ice Cream	55
plain	155	Jam and jellies	75
Chutney, average	50	Kidneys raw	35
Cocoa (half milk),		Kippers, raw	30
300ml/½pt	110	Lamb, lean	75
Cod, raw	20	Lard	260
Consommé, canned,		Leeks, fresh	10
300ml/½pt	40–65	Lemon, fresh	5
Corn, *see* Sweetcorn		Lentils, fresh	85
Cornflakes, and most		Lettuce, fresh	3
cereals	105	Liver, raw	45
Cornflour (Cornstarch)	100	Loganberries	5
Courgettes	2	Macaroni, boiled	30
Cranberry, fresh	4	Mackerel	30
sauce	35	Margarine	225
Cream, double	130	Marmalade	75
single	60	Marrow, boiled	2
soured (sour)	55	Melon	5
Cucumber	3	Milk, whole, 600ml/1pt	380
Currants	70	skimmed,	
Custard powder, made		600ml/1pt	190
up	30	Mushrooms, fresh	2
Damsons	10	Nuts, Almond	170
Dates, dried	85	Brazil	180
Doughnuts, jam filled	100	Chestnuts	50
Duck, meat only, raw	70	Peanuts, salted	180
Eggplant, *see*		Walnuts	155
Aubergines		Oil, Corn, 30ml/1fl oz	250
Eggs, whole, 1 small	70	Olive, 30ml/1fl oz	265
1 large	90	Olives	25
white	10	Onions, fresh	5
yolk	100	Orange, fresh	10
Fish finger, one	54	Parsnips, raw	5
Flour	100	Pasta, cooked	29
Fudge	100	Peaches, raw	10
Gelatine (Gelatin)		Pears, raw	10
powder	100	Peas, canned	20
Goose, meat only, raw	63	canned, processed	25

dried	30	Squash, *see* Marrow	
fresh, boiled	15	Stock cube, each	15
frozen	20	Strawberries, fresh	5
Peppers, red or green	10	Suet	260
Pineapple, canned	20	Sugar, white or brown	110
fresh	15	Sweetcorn, canned or	
Plaice, raw	15	frozen	25
Plums, fresh	10	on the cob	35
Pork, fat	110	Syrup	85
lean	55	Tangerines	5
Potatoes, boiled, two		Tomatoes, ketchup	
medium	95	(catsup) 30ml/1fl oz	28
fried, two medium	270	puree	40
Rabbit, meat only, raw	50	raw	5
Radishes, fresh	5	Tongue	85
Raspberries, fresh	5	Trout, raw	25
Redcurrants, fresh	5	Tuna, canned in oil	75
Rhubarb, fresh	2	Turbot, steamed	30
Rice, boiled	35	Turkey, meat only,	
Salmon, canned	40	raw	35
raw	55	Turnips, raw	5
smoked	45	Veal fillet, raw	30
Sardines, canned	85	Vinegar, 30ml/1fl oz	1
Sausages, average,		Waffles, one	216
raw	100	Water chestnuts	23
Sole, raw	15	Watercress	5
Soup, consommé,		Watermelon	5
300ml/½pt	40–65	Whiting, raw	15
thin, e.g. chicken		Yogurt, natural low	
noodle, 300ml/½pt	65–100	fat, 30ml/1fl oz	15
thick, 300ml/½pt	90–200	fruit flavoured,	
Spaghetti, boiled	35	30ml/1fl oz	25
Spinach	5	Zucchini, *see*	
Spring greens	3	Courgettes	
Spring onions	10		

SOFT DRINKS	Portion	Calories
Apple juice, unsweetened	small glass	50
Blackcurrant concentrate	1 × 15ml spoon	35
Grapefruit juice, unsweetened	small glass	55
Lemonade	600ml/1pt	120
Orange juice, unsweetened	small glass	60
Tomato juice	small glass	25
Low-calorie Minerals		0
Low-calorie Orange Squash	30ml/1fl oz	5
Low-calorie Lemon Squash	30ml/1fl oz	2

EXERCISE

Many people think of exercising only when they are overweight. This is a great pity. Regular exercise keeps your body supple and strong so that it can do everything you ask of it with ease and grace, after practice, of course.

Try to take part in some active sport at least once a week: tennis, squash, or hockey if you enjoy playing with a team or a partner; skating, riding, running or jogging if you are a loner. Swimming is especially good because it exercises just about every muscle in your body. If you do not care for any of these activities, have you considered dancing or walking?

If lack of exercise has made you feel a bit stiff and awkward or if you have a few extra inches you would like to lose, try these exercises and see how beautifully you begin to move, and how unwanted bumps and bulges begin to melt away as you strengthen and firm the flabby muscles that cause them.

Fast roll

1 Sit cross-legged on the floor.

2 Take hold of your left foot with your right hand and your right foot with your left hand.

3 Bend slightly forward and tuck your head in towards your knees.

4 Pull on your feet and let yourself roll backwards on to your shoulders, allowing your momentum to bring you back up again.

You can do this up to ten times. It will massage your spine and all your back muscles, and it is marvellous for improving your posture. Be sure to do this exercise on a rug or a folded blanket, never on a hard floor.

The butterfly

This one is good for firming flabby thighs and removing surplus fat from the hips and bottom.

1 Sit on the floor (against a wall if you want to make sure your back is straight).

The fast roll

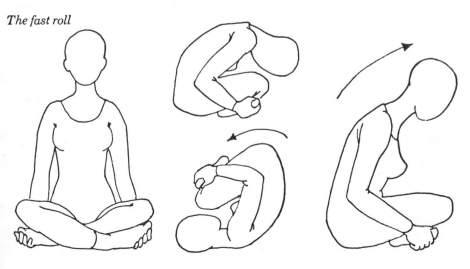

2 Bend both knees and bring the soles of the feet together.

3 Clasp the feet firmly with both hands.

4 Breathing in, raise the knees up and hold them there for a second or two.

5 Breathing out, lower the knees as far as they will go without strain. Repeat two or three times.

6 Now, with your legs in the open position, gently move them up and down, making very tiny movements, like trembling butterfly wings.

7 Finally, keeping your knees in the open position, rock your bottom from side to side.

The scissors

This is an excellent exercise for flattening your tummy and strengthening your legs and lower back muscles.

1 Lie flat on your back, arms at your sides.

2 Raise one leg until it is as near 90° from the floor as it will comfortably go. Lower it. Repeat with the other leg.

If you do this very fast, it is quite easy. What you have to work towards is raising your leg as slowly as possible.

3 Repeat the exercise, this time pausing for a count of five when your leg reaches an angle of 45°.

4 Now repeat the whole exercise, raising both legs together.

When your stomach muscles have become strong enough to do this without strain (and not until then) add this next stage to the exercise.

5 Raise both legs until they are 45° from the floor.

6 Now sweep them apart and together again, letting one leg cross over the other; sweep them apart and together, letting the other leg cross over. Make the movement as flowing and rhythmical as you can.

Do this exercise just once or twice at first, increasing the number of times gradually as your muscles get stronger.

The scissors

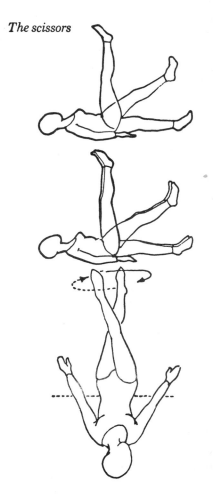

Neck roll

Neck, shoulder and back muscles tense up when they get tired; especially when you have been hunched over a table or desk for some time. These and the following exercises will help to rest and to relax them.

1 Sit comfortably on a chair, or kneel on the floor and sit back on your heels. Let your head drop forward, very gently, as far as can.

2 Slowly roll your head round to the right shoulder and hold it there for three seconds.

3 Continue rolling the head slowly back through another 90° and hold it there for three seconds.

4 Roll the head slowly to the left shoulder and hold it for three seconds.

5 Roll the head forward again and hold for three seconds.

6 Now repeat the exercise, rolling the head in the other direction. This exercise should never be done quickly. The object is very gently to stretch and then relax all the neck muscles, and to do it with smoothness and grace.

Shoulder loosener

1 Sit erect, arms hanging loosely by your sides.

2 Close your eyes.

3 Very slowly, circle the right shoulder backwards three or four times and then forwards three or four times. Make the circle as big as you can, without straining.

4 Repeat the exercise with the left shoulder.

5 Now circle both together.

Waist trimmer

1 Stand with your legs comfortably apart.

2 Breathing in, raise your arms to shoulder level, palms facing downward.

3 Holding your breath in and keeping your arms on a line with your shoulders, bend as far as you can to the left.

4 Breathing out, return to the upright position and lower your arms.

5 Repeat the exercise, bending to the right.

6 When you become supple enough to grasp your ankle, raise your other arm over your head until it is parallel with the floor.

The waist trimmer

Chest expander

1 Stand with your heels together, arms at your sides.

2 Breathing in, bring your hands up in front of you until your fingertips are together and your thumbs are touching your chest.

3 Stretch your arms straight out in front of you, the backs of your hands facing each other.

4 Now take them behind you, keeping them as high as you can, until you can interlace your fingers.

5 Holding your breath in, bend very slightly backwards.

6 Now begin to breathe out, bending slowly and gracefully forward as you do.

7 Hold this position for a few seconds, breathing normally and keeping your neck and head completely relaxed.

8 Straighten up slowly and let your arms fall back to your sides.

The tree

Finally, an exercise which will improve your balance and help you to stand and move gracefully.

1 Stand up straight. Bend your right leg and place the sole of your foot, flat against the inner thigh of your left leg.

2 Breathing in, slowly raise both arms to shoulder level.

3 Breathing out, raise your arms over your head and bring the palms together.

4 Breathing normally, stretch

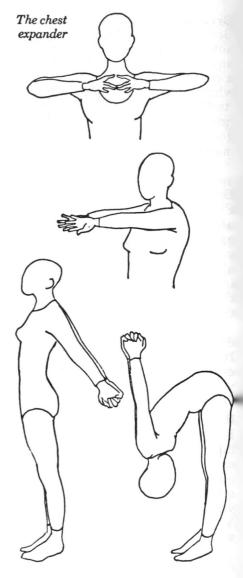

The chest expander

gently upward once or twice.

5 Breathing in, lower the arms to shoulder level.

6 Breathing out, lower your arms to your sides and your right leg to the floor.

7 Repeat with the other leg.

324

Breathing

Because our breathing goes on automatically, we very seldom pay any attention to it. The body needs a continual supply of oxygen with which to repair and re-energize itself, so giving it an extra supply now and then, by taking a few good deep breaths, has a marvellous effect.

Try this. Stand, feet slightly apart, near an open window. Breathe only through your nose. First, breathe out until there is no air at all left in your lungs. This expels all the stale air and allows your lungs to take in as much fresh air as they will hold. Now breathe in to the count of seven and out to the count of seven, three or four times.

Breathing deeply and slowly doesn't only give you more energy. It also has a calming, relaxing effect – so it's worth trying if you're in a situation that makes you feel nervous.

Relaxing

Knowing how to relax is just as important as knowing how to exercise. Try it for ten minutes after you've been doing something strenuous or for ten minutes before you go out on an important date. You'll be surprised how good it will make you feel.

Lie flat on the floor, preferably on a rug or folded blanket. Cover yourself with a blanket, too, if the room is at all chilly. Have your arms stretched out a little way away from your sides, and your legs slightly apart. Close your eyes.

Turn your attention to your feet, and for a moment tense all the muscles in your feet as tight as you can – then let them go, and be aware of your feet feeling relaxed and heavy. Gradually work up your body, doing the same thing with your legs, your bottom, your stomach, your chest, your back and shoulders, your hands and arms, your neck, your head and your face. Imagine yourself feeling heavy, like a sack of potatoes, and be conscious of the floor pushing up underneath you. When you feel completely heavy all over, turn your mind to something pleasant – a beautiful place you enjoy being in, for example.

When you feel you've relaxed for long enough, turn your attention back to your feet and give them a little wriggle. Then work up your body, wriggling each bit in turn, until you've got every bit of it moving again. Then sit up, take a deep breath, and you'll be ready for anything.

The perfect position for relaxation

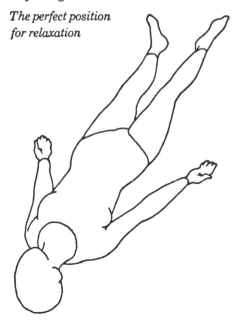

THE ARTS

Who Wrote That?

General Literature

Are You There God, It's Me Margaret, Judy Blume
Anne of Green Gables, Lucy M. Montgomery (1874–1942)
Ballet Shoes, Noel Streatfield (b. 1895)
Blue Boat, The, William Mayne (b. 1928)
Boney was a Warrior, Rosemary Manning (b. 1911)
Borrowers, The, Mary Norton (b. 1900)
Christmas Carol, A, Charles Dickens (1812–70)
Circus Boy, Ruth Manning-Saunders (b. 1895)
Clunie, Hugh Charteris
Danny Champion of the World, Roald Dahl
David Copperfield, Charles Dickens (1812–70)
Family From One End Street, The, Eve Garnett
Famous Five, The (Secret Seven etc.), Enid Blyton (1897–1968)
Gemma, Noel Streatfield (b. 1895)
Grass Rope, A, William Mayne (b. 1928)
Green Knowe series, Lucy M. Boston
Good Wives, Louisa M. Alcott (1832–88)
Hardy Boys books, Franklin W. Dixon
Heidi, Johanna Spyri (1827–1901)
House in Turner Square, Ann Thwaite (b. 1932)
Iggy's House, Judy Blume
Jeremy stories, Sir Hugh Walpole (1884–1941)
Jo's Boys, Louisa M. Alcott (1832–88)
Judy Blume books, Judy Blume
Just William books, Richmal Crompton (1890–1969)
Little House on the Prairie, Laura Ingalls Wilder (1867–1957)
Little Lord Fauntleroy, Frances Hodgson Burnett (1849– 1924)
Little Princess, A, Frances Hodgson Burnett (1849–1924)
Little Tim and the Brave Sea Captain, Edward Ardizzone (1900–79)
Little Women, Louisa M. Alcott (1832–1888)
Lorna Doone, R. D. Blackmore (1825–1900)
Marianne Dreams, Catherine Storr (b. 1913)
Marmalade Atkins books, Andrew Danes
Martin Pippin in the Daisy Field, Eleanor Farjeon (1882–1965)
Milly-Molly-Mandy books, Joyce Lankester Brisley (b. 1896)
Mystery at Witchend, Malcolm Saville (b. 1901)
Not Scarlet but Gold, Malcolm Saville (b. 1901)
Our Exploits at West Poley, Thomas Hardy (1840–1928)
Paddington Bear books, Michael Bond (b. 1926)
Pigeon Post, Arthur Ransome (1884–1967)
Pinnochio, Carlo Collidi (1826–1890)
Pippi Longstocking, Astrid Lindgren

Railway Children, The, E. Nesbit (1858–1924)
Rebecca of Sunnybrook Farm, Kate Douglas Wiggin (1856–1923)
Secret Garden, The, Frances Hodgson Burnett (1849–1924)
Silver Curlew, The, Eleanor Farjeon (1882–1965)
Stalky and Co., Rudyard Kipling (1865–1936)
Stig of the Dump, Clive King (b. 1924)
Sue Barton books, Helen Dore Boylston (b. 1895)
Susan and Bill books, Malcolm Saville (b. 1901)
Swallows and Amazons Forever, Arthur Ransome (1884–1967)
Swish of the Curtain, The, Pamela Brown (b. 1924)
Tales From Shakespeare, Charles and Mary Lamb (c. 1775–1834/1847)
Then Again, Maybe I Won't, Judy Blume
Thumbstick, The, William Mayne (b. 1928)
We Didn't Mean to Go to Sea, Arthur Ransome (1884–1967)
What Katy Did books, Susan Coolidge (1835–1905)
White Boots, Noel Streatfield (b. 1895)
Wintle's Wonders, Noel Streatfield (b. 1897)

Animal Stories
At the Back of the North Wind, George MacDonald (1824–1905)
Bambi, Felix Salten (1869–1945)
Battle of Bubble and Squeak, Phillipa Pearce (b. 1920)
Black Beauty, Anna Sewell (1820–78)
Born Free, Joy Adamson (1910–80)
Call of the Wild, Jack London (1876–1916)
Dog Crusoe, R. M. Ballantyne (1825–94)
Dog So Small, A, Phillippa Pearce (b. 1920)
Follyfoot, Monica Dickens
I Wanted a Pony, Diana Pullein-Thompson
Jungle Book, The, Rudyard Kipling (1865–1936)
Just So Stories, Rudyard Kipling (1865–1936)
Mousewife, The, Rumer Godden (b. 1907)
National Velvet, Enid Bagnold (b. 1889)
One Hundred and One Dalmations, Dodie Smith
Orlando books, Kathleen Hale (b. 1898)
Rufty Tufty books, Ruth Ainsworth (b. 1908)
Shardik, Richard Adams (b. 1920)
Snow Goose, The, Paul Gallico (1897–1976)
Tarka the Otter, Henry Williamson (b. 1897)
Watership Down, Richard Adams (b. 1920)
White Fang, Jack London (1876–1916)
Wind in the Willows, The, Kenneth Grahame (1859–1932)
Wish for a Pony, Monica Edwards (b. 1912)
Yearling, The, Marjorie Kinnan Rawlings

School Stories
Abbey Girls, The, Elsie Oxenham (d. 1960)

Autumn Term, Antonia Forest
Beyond the Blue Mountains, L.-T. Meade (1854–1914)
Billy Bunter books, C. H. St John Hamilton (1875–1961)
End of Term, Antonia Frost
Exciting Term, An, Angela Brazil (1869–1947)
Grange Hill books, Robert Leeson
Jeanette's First Term, Alice Lunt
Jennings books, Anthony Buckridge
Manor House School, The, Angela Brazil (1869–1947)
Rebel of the School, L. T. Meade (1854–1914)
School on the Lock, The, Angela Brazil (1869–1947)
School under Snowdon, Mabel Esther Allan (b. 1915)

Fantasy and Fairy Stories
Alice's Adventures in Wonderland, Lewis Carrol (1832–98)
Blue Fairy Book, The, Andrew Lang (1844–1912)
Book of Discoveries, A, John Masefield (1878–1967)
Box of Delights, The, John Masefield (1878–1967)
Catweazle, Richard Carpenter
Charlie and the Chocolate Factory, Roald Dahl (b. 1916)
Enchanted Castle, The, E. Nesbit (1858–1924)
English Fairy Tales, Joseph Jacobs (1854–1916)
Five Children and It, E. Nesbit (1858–1924)
Happy Prince and Other Stories, The, Oscar Wilde (1854–1900)
Hobbit, The, J. R. R. Tolkien (1892–1973)
Invisible Man, The, H. G. Wells (1866–1946)
Iron Man, The, Ted Hughes
James and the Giant Peach, Roald Dahl (b. 1916)
Kingdom Under the Sea, The, Joan Aiken
King of the Golden River, John Ruskin (1819–1900)
Lion, the Witch and the Wardrobe, The, C. S. Lewis (1898–1963)
Lord of the Rings, The, J. R. R. Tolkien (1892–1973)
Lost World, The, Sir Arthur Conan Doyle (1859–1930)
Magic City, The, E. Nesbit (1858–1924)
Magic Finger, The, Roald Dahl (b. 1916)
Mary Poppins Books, Pamela L. Travers (b. 1906)
Midnight Folk, The, John Masefield (1878–1967)
Moon of Gomrath, The, Alan Garner (b. 1934)
Mouse and His Child, The, Russell Hoban
Mrs Pepperpot, Alf Proysen
Princess and the Curdie, The, George MacDonald (1824–1905)
Oz books, L. Frank Baum (1856–1919)
Peter Pan and Wendy, Sir James Barrie (1860–1937)
Phoenix and the Carpet, The, George MacDonald (1824–1905)
Prince Caspian, C. S. Lewis (1898–1963)*
Puck of Pook's Hill, Rudyard Kipling (1865–1936)
Shadow-Cage, The, Phillippa Pearce (b. 1920)

Story of the Amulet, The, Walter de la Mare (1873–1956)
Super Gran is Magic, Forrest Wilson
Through the Looking Glass, Lewis Carroll (1832–98)
Tom's Midnight Garden, Phillippa Pearce (b. 1920)
Tulku, Peter Dickinson
Tripods, The, John Christopher
Weirdstone of Brisingamen, The, Alan Garner (b. 1934)
Warrior Scarlet, Rosemary Sutcliffe (b. 1920)
Witch's Daughter, The, Nina Bawden

Adventure Stories
Adventures of Huckleberry Finn, The, Mark Twain (1835–1910)
Adventures of Tom Sawyer, The, Mark Twain (1835–1910)
Around the World in 80 Days, Jules Verne (1828–1905)
Carrie's War, Nina Bawden
Coral Island, The, R. M. Ballantyne (1825–94)
Dark is Rising, The, Susan Cooper
Hornblower books, C. S. Forester (1899–1966)
Kidnapped, Robert Louis Stevenson (1850–94)
King Solomon's Mines, Sir Henry Rider Haggard (1856–1925)
Moby Dick, Herman Melville (1819–91)
Moonfleet, J. Meade Falkner
Prisoner of Zenda, The, Anthony Hope (1863–1933)
Robinson Crusoe, Daniel Defoe (1660–1731)
Scarlet Pimpernel, The, Baroness Orczy (1865–1947)
Silver Sword, The, Ian Serraillier
Swiss Family Robinson, W. H. G. Kinston (1814–80)
Treasure Island, Robert Louis Stevenson (1850–94)
Twenty Thousand Leagues Under the Sea, Jules Verne (1828–1905)
Uncle Tom's Cabin, Harriet Beecher Stowe (1811–96)

Humorous Stories
Bad Child's Book of Beasts, Hilaire Belloc (1870–1953)
Book of Nonsense, A, Edward Lear (1812–88)
Charlie and the Chocolate Factory, Roald Dahl (b. 1916)
Dr Doolittle books, Hugh Lofting (1886–1947)
Father Christmas, Raymond Briggs (b. 1934)
Nonsense Novels, Stephen Leacock (1869–1944)
Now We are Six, A. A. Milne (1882–1956)
Old Possum's Book of Practical Cats, T. S. Eliot (1888–1965)
Professor Branestawn books, Norman Hunter (b. 1899)
Three Men in a Boat, Jerome K. Jerome (1859–1927)
Wind on the Moon, The, Eric Linklater (1899–1974)
Winnie-the-Pooh, A. A. Milne (1882–1956)
Wombles Books, Elizabeth Beresford (b. circa 1890)
Worst Witch, The, Jill Murphy
Worzel Gummidge books, Barbara E. Todd (d. 1976)

Historical Stories
Children of the New Forest, The, Captain Marryat (1792–1848)
Eagle of the Ninth, The, Rosemary Sutcliffe (b. 1920)
Fearless Treasure, The, Noel Streatfeild (b. 1897)
Ghost of Thomas Kempe, The, Penelope Lively
Hereward the Wake, Charles Kingsley (1819–75)
House of Arden, The, E. Nesbit (1858–1924)
Land the Ravens Found, The, Naomi Mitchison (b. 1897)
Lantern Bearers, The, Rosemary Sutcliff (b. 1920)
Men of the Hills, Henry Treece (1911–66)
Smith, Leon Garfield
Stone Book quartet, The, Alan Garner
Traveller in Time, A, Alison Uttley (1884–1976)
Wolves of Willoughby Chase, The, Joan Aiken
Wool-pack, The, Cynthia Harnett (b. 1893)
Word to Caesar, Geoffrey Trease (b. 1909)
Viking's Dawn, Henry Treece (1911–66)

Myths and Legends
Heroes of Greece and Troy, Roger Lancelyn Green (b. 1918)
Sword in the Stone, The, T. H. White (1906–64)
Tanglewood Tales, Nathaniel Hawthorne (1804–64)

Music

SYMPHONIES, CONCERTOS, INSTRUMENTS AND ORCHESTRAS

The word symphony is derived from the ancient Greek word *symphonia*, literally meaning 'harmonious sound'. In musical terms it has come to mean a composition for full orchestra. Traditionally a symphony consisted of four contrasting but closely related movements.

Until the time when Haydn and Mozart began to dominate the musical world, that is, prior to the middle of the 18th century, symphony still retained its archaic meaning of 'harmony' or 'consonance of sounds' (sounding together). A variety of compositions, termed symphonies, were then written to be performed by a number of musical instruments. Haydn and Mozart were largely responsible, by their innovations, for altering the meaning of the word symphony, and from then on it was used to describe an orchestral sonata.

Beethoven, in the early years of the 19th century, broke the rules which had developed to turn the design of symphonies into a set formula. He raised the standard of classical symphonies to new heights of perfection. As generally happens to innovators, he was derided in many quarters for these changes.

The next stage in the development of the symphony came with the rise in popularity of the romantic composers – first Berlioz and then Liszt. Berlioz introduced a specific idea, making his symphonies relate a musical tale and contain a theme throughout. The *Fantastic Symphony* is a typical example of his style. Liszt enlarged on this development to a greater extent. In his *Faust* symphony, for example, we are presented with a symphonic poem rather than the generally accepted form of the 'classical' symphony.

Further developments occurred when Franck and Tchaikovsky, during the second half of the 19th century, used the symphony to express their own particular philosophies in musical form.

Since the late 19th century, composers such as Borodin and Sibelius have usually based their works on an initial theme, letting a symphony or movement develop from it naturally. This was a far cry from the concepts of the classical originators of the symphony. Nevertheless, during the last century, the original approach to the composition of symphonies was maintained, with excellent results, by Mendelssohn and Brahms. The latter based his four symphonic works on the styles of Beethoven and Mendelssohn.

Concertos, overtures and symphonic poems

In the first instance, there was not a great deal of difference between a symphony and a concerto. Both were performed by playing several instruments together. Concertos for

The positions of the instruments in a symphony orchestra

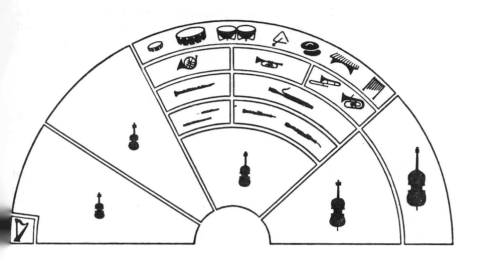

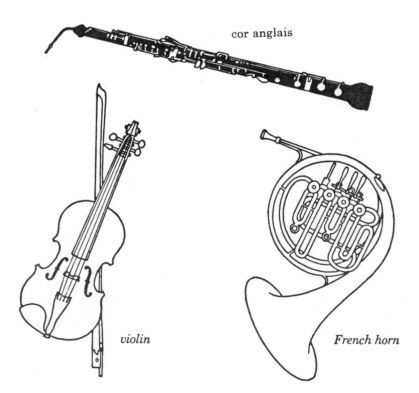

cor anglais

violin

French horn

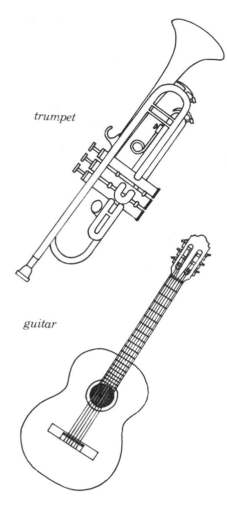

trumpet

guitar

Accordian

string orchestras were composed by Corelli, Bach and Handel in the first part of the 18th century.

Nowadays, a concerto is described as a composition designed for one or more solo instruments accompanied by an orchestra. More often than not, however, it concentrates on just one solo instrument and there are usually three movements.

An overture generally follows the design of a symphony's first movement. It is an orchestral form which frequently acts as the introduction to an opera. Sometimes an overture is performed as a concert piece. Beethoven's *Coriolan* is a good example.

Symphonic poems date from the mid-19th century, when this new musical form was introduced by Liszt. Liszt tried to convey a sequence of ideas or emotional moods, suggested in the music by transformations of the principal theme that he had chosen.

Instruments

A summary of the instruments used in an orchestra ought to start with the piano. It is probably more popular than any other instrument because of its outstanding ability to reproduce not only melody but also wide-ranging harmony without any accompaniment.

Before the appearance of the earliest kind of piano, the virginal, spinet, clavichord and harpsichord had been in use as keyboard instruments. Despite the fact that the first pianos date back to the start of the 18th century, it was not until the end of the century that they began to become popular. More often than not, to the regret of some people, music composed for the earlier instruments is nowadays frequently played on a modern piano.

Beethoven, who had a deep understanding of a piano's flexibility, wrote many sonatas and concertos for it. The instrument's popularity increased further as, in succession, Schubert, Chopin, Schumann, Brahms and Liszt all composed for the piano. As a result of these composers' works and the advances in technique they made, the piano's mechanism was perfected by the end of the 19th century, presenting the modern pianist with the fine instrument we all know today.

Another instrument which deserves special mention is the violin. A great quantity of music has been specially written for it by famous composers. This stringed instrument, a smaller form of the even older viol, has been in use since remote times, and the modern version is virtually the same as that played in the 16th century. During the 17th century, violin construction was perfected to a degree never since equalled, and Antonio Stradivari (1644–1730), of Cremona, is regarded as the supreme master of all time in the art of making violins. His instruments are worth vast sums of money today.

Other orchestral musical instruments, listed alphabetically, are as follows:

Bassoon Uses a double reed, and is the lowest in pitch of the woodwind instruments.

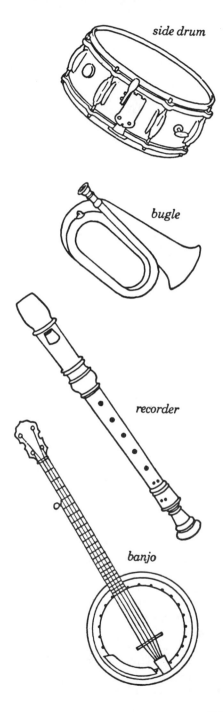

side drum

bugle

recorder

banjo

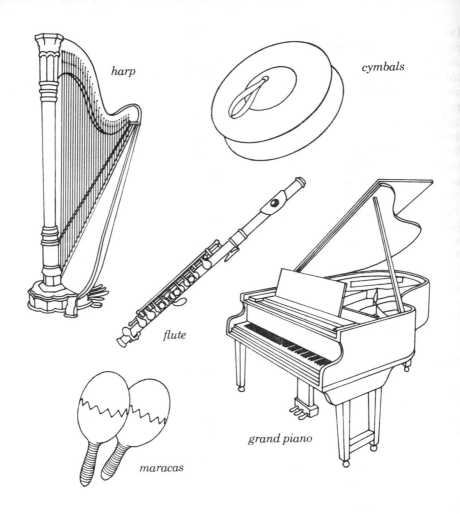

harp

cymbals

flute

grand piano

maracas

Cello Placed between the viola and double bass, this four-stringed instrument has a bass range and is played with a bow.
Clarinet In use since the mid-18th century, this woodwind instrument has a single reed.
Cymbal A brass percussion instrument shaped rather like a plate. Two cymbals are struck together.
Double bass Played with a bow,

this is the largest member and has the lowest pitch of the violin family.
Drums Percussion instruments. Sound is produced by hitting a skin tightly stretched across a hemisphere or hollow cylinder. The largest, the bass drum, is placed upright and hit on its side. The kettledrum can be tuned by turning handles on its rim to tighten or relax the skin. The person who

...lays the kettle drums in an orchestra is known as the timpanist.

English horn Otherwise known as the *cor anglais*, this is a woodwind instrument with the double reed of the oboe family.

Flute Blown sideways, this woodwind instrument is played through a hole and not a reed. Some modern flutes are manufactured with metal.

French horn This is a brass instrument with coiled tubes. Valves were introduced during the 19th century.

Harp An ancient instrument, the harp is played by plucking strings that are stretched, parallel, across its frame. A set of pedals is used to alter the instrument's basic scale, C flat major.

Oboe This woodwind instrument is a descendant of the old hautboy. It has a double reed. It has been in use for some 400 years and has had its present form since the 18th century.

Trombone A brass instrument which has a slide to adjust the length of its tube and thereby alter the pitch.

Trumpet Another ancient instrument, the trumpet is made of metal and has three valves.

Piccolo A small flute. It is an octave higher than the ordinary flute.

Tuba Equipped with three or four valves, the tuba is the deepest-pitched brass instrument.

Viola This is slightly larger than a violin and is tuned a 5th below.

Xylophone Consisting of a series of wooden bars, this percussion instrument is played with sticks.

MUSICAL TERMS

Accelerando increasing in tempo
Adagio at a slow pace
Ad lib (*ad libitum*) strict time need not be observed
Affettuoso affectionately, with tenderness
Agitato in agitated manner
Allegretto rather less fast than Allegro
Allegro at a quick pace
Andante fairly slow pace
Animato lively
Calando becoming quieter and slower
Cantabile in a singing manner
Con brio with spirit, dash
Con fuoco with fire
Crescendo getting louder
Da capo return to the beginning of the first section
Diminuendo getting softer
Dolce sweet
Forte strong, loud
Fortissimo very loud
Fugato in the manner of a fugue
Grave slow tempo
Grazioso gracefully
Largamente spaciously
Largo slow
Legato with notes smoothly connected
Lento slowly
Maestoso stately
Marcato with each note strongly marked
Molto much, e.g. Allegro Molto, very quickly
Piano soft
Pianissimo very soft
Piu more, e.g. Piu Lento, more slowly
Presto quick
Rallentando getting slower
Rubato performing a piece without strict rhythm for purposes of expression
Scherzando in a jesting manner
Sforzando forced, strongly accented
Tremolando tremulously
Tremolo tremulous effect in singing or in playing bowed instruments
Vivace in a lively manner

Composers and Their Works

ADAM, Adolphe Charles (1803–56), French. Composed light operas. He is best known today for the classical ballet *Giselle*.

ALBÉNIZ, Isaac (1860–1909), Spanish. Best-known composition is *Iberia*. Also wrote operas and songs.

ALBINONI, Tommaso (1671–1750), Italian. Operas and instrumental music.

ARNE, Thomas (1710–78), English. Best-known works are his songs, including 'Rule Britannia' and 'Where the Bee Sucks'.

ARNOLD, Malcolm (b. 1921), English. Compositions include incidental music to Shakespeare's *The Tempest*, the overture *Beckus the Dandipratt*, symphony for strings, and concertos for horn, clarinet and oboe.

BACH, Johann Christian (1735–82), German. He composed many operas and cantatas, and much orchestral music, chamber music and keyboard music.

BACH, Johann Sebastian (1685–1750), German. Composed an enormous amount of sacred choral music, including 200 cantatas, the St Matthew and St John Passions and the Mass in B Minor. Bach's orchestral music includes the six Brandenberg Concertos, a number of concertos for violin and clavier, and four orchestral suites. There is a number of important keyboard works for clavier and organ including the collection of 48 preludes and fugues known as *The Well-tempered Clavier*.

BACH, Karl Philipp Emanuel (1714–88), German. Composed about 200 pieces for clavier. His church music includes the oratorio *The Israelites in the Wilderness*, a Magnificat and 22 Passions. Also symphonies, concertos, organ sonatas, chamber music and songs.

BALAKIREV, Mily Alexeievich (1837–1910), Russian. Works include two symphonies, incidental music to Shakespeare's *King Lear*, overtures, piano music and songs.

BALFE, Michael (1808–70), Irish. Works include 29 operas, such as *The Bohemian Girl,* the ballet *La Pérouse*, three cantatas and many songs.

Bach

Beethoven

BARBER, Samuel (b. 1910), American. Operas *Antony and Cleopatra, Vanessa,* and *A Hand of Bridge*. Two symphonies, concertos for piano, violin and cello, *Capricorn* Concerto for flute, oboe, trumpet and strings. Chamber music and songs.

BARTÓK, Béla (1881–1945), Hungarian. His numerous works include violin and piano concertos, orchestral suites, the Concerto for Orchestra, the opera *Bluebeard's Castle* and string quartets.

BEETHOVEN, Ludwig van (1770–1827), German. Works include two masses (in C Major and *Missa Solemnis*), the *Choral Fantasia*, the opera *Fidelio*, nine symphonies, five piano concertos, one violin concerto, a concerto for piano, violin and cello, and several concert overtures such as *Egmont*. Beethoven's chamber music includes a septet, a string quintet, 16 string quartets, six piano trios, four string trios, ten violin sonatas and five cello sonatas. His piano music includes 32 sonatas, 22 sets of variations, and three sets of bagatelles.

BELLINI, Vincenzo (1801–35), Italian. Operas, including *Norma* and *La Somnambula*.

BERG, Alban (1885–1935), Austrian. A well-known work is his opera *Wozzeck*. He also wrote one violin concerto and several instrumental pieces and songs.

BERLIOZ, Hector (1803–69), French. Works include the operas *Benvenuto Cellini, Les Troyens* and *Béatrice et Bénédict*; programme symphonies *Symphonie Fantastique, Harold in Italy* and *Roméo et Juliette* (with voices); *Symphonie Funèbre et Triomphale*; six concert overtures; choral works including a Requiem, *La Damnation de Faust, Te Deum* and *L'Enfance du Christ*; as well as several songs.

BIZET, Georges (1838–75), French. Operas include *Carmen, The Pearl Fishers, The Fair Maid of Perth* and *Djamileh*. Orchestral works include Symphony in C, the suite *Jeux d'Enfants* (Children's Games) and incidental music to Daudet's *L'Arlésienne*.

BOCCHERINI, Luigi (1743–1805), Italian. His works include oratorios, a mass, cantatas, motets, 20 symphonies, four cello concertos, concertos for flute, violin, harpsichord, much chamber music and one opera.

BOITO, Arrigo (1842–1918), Italian. Operas *Mefistofele* and *Nerone*.

BORODIN, Alexander (1833-87), Russian. Opera *Prince Igor* (unfinished). Orchestral works include *In the Steppes of Central Asia, Scherzo* for orchestra, an three symphonies. Chamber music and songs.

BOULEZ, Pierre (b. 1925), French. Avant-garde compositions include *Le Martea sans Maitre* for alto and six instruments, *Sonatine* for flute, and *Structures* for two pianos.

BRAHMS, Johannes (1833-97), German. Orchestral works include four symphonies, two piano concertos, a concerto for violin and a concerto for violin and cello, *Academic Festival Overture, Tragic Overture,* and the *St Anthony Chorale (Variations on a Theme by Haydn).* The best known of Brahms's choral works is the *German Requiem.* His chamber music includes three string quartets, two string quintets, a clarinet quintet, two string sextets, five piano trios (one with clarinet, one with horn), three piano quartets and a piano quintet.

BRIDGE, Frank (1879-1941), English. Works include the orchestral suite *The Sea,* a symphonic poem *Isabella,* rhapsody *Enter Spring,* and tone poem *Summer,* as well as chamber music.

BRITTEN, Sir Benjamin (1913-77), English. Works include three symphonies, two piano concertos, *War Requiem, Hymn to St Cecilia, Young Person's Guide to the Orchestra, Variations on a Theme of Frank Bridge, Serenade for Tenor, Horn and Strings, Sinfonia da Requiem,* and two string quartets. Operas include *Peter Grimes, The Rape of Lucretia, Albert Herring, Billy Budd, Gloriana* and *Noye's Fludde.*

BRUCH, Max (1838-1920), German. Works include three symphonies, two violin concertos, *Scottish Fantasia,* and the *Serenade* for violin, harp and orchestra.

BRUCKNER, Anton (1824-96), Austrian. Works include nine symphonies (the last unfinished), four masses, a Requiem and a Te Deum.

BUSONI, Ferruccio Benvenuto (1866-1924), Italian. Composed mostly piano music but also several operas, the *Fantasia Contrappuntistica* on an unfinished fugue by Bach, and an immense piano concerto with chorale finale.

BUTTERWORTH, George (1885-1916), English. Works include the rhapsody *A Shropshire Lad,* an idyll *The Banks of Green Willow,* and two song cycles on Housman's *A Shropshire Lad.*

BUXTEHUDE, Dietrich (1637-1707), Danish. Church cantatas, sonatas for strings, organ music including chorale preludes, and suites for harpsichord.

BYRD, William (1543-1623), English. Church music, madrigals, virginal pieces, etc.

CAGE, John (b. 1912), American. Music for 'prepared piano', i.e. where different objects are inserted between the strings to alter the tone; electronic music.

CAVALLI, Pietro Francesco (1602-76), Italian. Many operas, masses, motets, psalms, vespers, a Requiem, etc.

CHABRIER, Alexis Emmanuel (1841-94), French. His works include the operas *Le Roi Malgré Lui,* the rhapsody *España* and *Marche Joyeuse.*

CHERUBINI, Luigi (1760–1842), Italian. Operas include *The Water Carrier, Médée* and *Les Deux Journées*. Church music includes Mass in F and Requiem in D Minor.

CHOPIN, Frédéric (1810–49), Polish. Piano music includes three sonatas, 14 waltzes, 26 preludes, 27 études, 19 nocturnes, four ballades, four impromptus, four scherzos, three rondos, 16 polonaises and 50 mazurkas. Chopin also composed two piano concertos.

COPLAND, Aaron (b. 1900), American. Ballets *Billy the Kid, Rodeo* and *Appalachian Spring*. Orchestral works include three symphonies, *El Salon Mexico* and *Danzon Cubano*. Also some chamber music.

CORELLI, Arcangelo (1653–1713), Italian. Works include violin sonatas and a set of concerti grossi.

COUPERIN, François (1668–1733), French. Over 200 harpsichord pieces, 42 organ pieces, several works for chamber orchestra, church music, motets, etc.

CZERNY, Karl (1791–1857), Austrian. Czerny's best-known works today are his piano studies.

DEBUSSY, Claude (1862–1918), French. Numerous piano pieces, chamber music, songs and ballet music. Opera *Pelléas et Mélisande*. Orchestral pieces include *L'Après-midi d'un Faune, La Mer*, three *Images, Printemps*, and *Danse Sacré et Danse Profane* for harp and strings.

DELIBES, Léo (1836–91), French. Ballets include *Coppélia* and *La Source*. Also comic operas such as *Le Roi l'a Dit* and *Lakmé*.

DELIUS, Frederick (1862–1934), English. Operas such as *Irmelin, Koanga, A Village Romeo and Juliet* and *Fennemore and Gerda*. Choral works include *Sea Drift, Song of the High Hills, Appalachia, Songs of Sunset* and *Requiem*. Orchestral works include *Brigg Fair, In a Summer Garden, Over the Hills and Far Away, On Hearing the First Cuckoo in Spring* and *A Song Before Sunrise*. Delius also composed chamber music and songs.

DONIZETTI, Gaetano (1797–1848), Italian. Many operas, the best-known being *Lucrezia Borgia, Lucia di Lammermoor, La Fille du Régiment, La Favorita* and *Don Pasquale*.

DUKAS, Paul (1865–1935), French. Works include the popular orchestral piece *The Sorcerer's Apprentice*, and a successful opera *Ariane et Barbe-Bleue*.

DVOŘÁK, Antonin (1841–1904), Czech. Nine symphonies, including *From The New World* (the 9th), one piano concerto, one violin concerto, one cello concerto. Five concert overtures include *Carnival, Amid Nature* and *Othello*. Other orchestral works include *Scherzo Capriccioso*, two sets of Slavonic dances, Slavonic rhapsodies and five symphonic poems: *The Water Sprite, The Noon-Day Witch, The Golden Spinning Wheel, The Wood-Dove* and *Hero's Song*. Ten operas, including *Rusalka*; a Mass in D Major, Requiem, *Te Deum*, chamber music and many songs.

ELGAR, Sir Edward (1857–1934), English. Works include two symphonies, one violin and one cello concerto, concert overtures *Froissart, Cockaigne, In the South*,

Chopin

Dvořák

Polonia. Orchestral pieces include *Enigma Variations, Introduction and Allegro for Strings,* symphonic study *Falstaff,* and the five *Pomp and Circumstance* marches. His four oratorios include *The Dream of Gerontius.*

FALLA, Manuel de (1876–1946), Spanish. Opera *La Vida Breve;* ballets *El Amor Brujo* and *The Three-cornered Hat;* orchestral piece *Nights in the Gardens of Spain,* and *Master Peter's Puppet Show* (with solo voice). Also several songs and works for piano and guitar.

FAURÉ, Gabriel (1845–1924), French. Orchestral works include *Pavane* and suite *Masques et Bergamasques;* incidental music *Pelléas et Mélisande;* Requiem for solo voices, chorus and orchestra. Songs and chamber music.

FINZI, Gerald (1901–56), English. Works include cantata *Dies Natalis,* festival anthem *Intimations of Immortality,* and *For St Cecilia* for chorus and orchestra.

FRANCK, César (1822–90), Belgian. Symphony in D Minor, *Symphonic Variations* for piano and orchestra; oratorios, organ pieces, church music and songs.

GABRIELI, Andrea (c. 1520–86), Italian. Works include masses, madrigals, motets and church music.

GABRIELI, Giovanni (c. 1555–1612), Italian. Works include church music for voices and instruments, organ music and various instrumental pieces.

GERSHWIN, George (1898–1937), American. Popular songs and musical comedies. More serious music includes *Rhapsody in Blue,* the opera *Porgy and Bess* and a piano concerto.

GESUALDO, Carlo (c. 1560–1613), Italian. Works include madrigals and church music for voices.

GLAZUNOV, Alexander Constantinovich (1865–1936), Russian. Works include eight symphonies, two piano concertos, a violin concerto, a concerto for saxophone, flute and strings, ballets *Raymonda, Ruses d'Amour* and *Les Saisons,* and some chamber music.

GLIÈRE, Reinhold (1875–1956), Russian of Belgian descent. Three symphonies, three symphonic poems, several operas and patriotic songs. Ballets include *The Red Poppy.*

GLINKA, Mikhail (1804–57), Russian. Two operas: *A Life for the Tsar* and *Russlan and Ludmilla.* Orchestral pieces include *Kamarinskaya* and *Festival Polonaise.*

GLUCK, Christoph (1714–87), German. Several operas including *Orfeo, Alceste, Iphigénie en Aulide* and *Iphigénie en Tauride.*

GOUNOD, Charles (1818–93), French. Sacred songs, masses and an oratorio *The Redemption.* Operas include *Sappho, Faust, Philémon et Baucis, Mireille* and *Roméo et Juliette.*

GRÉTRY, André Ernest Modeste (1741–1813), French. His many operas include *Richard Coeur-de-Lion* and *Zémire et Azor.*

GRIEG, Edvard (1843–1907), Norwegian. Works include a piano concerto, incidental music for *Peer Gynt* and *Sigurd Jorsalfar, Holberg Suite* for string orchestra, concert overture *In Autumn,* chamber music and songs. Grieg's piano music includes the collection of Lyric Pieces.

HANDEL, George Frideric (1685–1759), German. About 40 operas, including *Rinaldo.* Oratorios include *Messiah, Samson, Belshazzar,* the *Occasional Oratorio, Israel in Egypt, Judas Maccabaeus* and *Jephtha.* Secular choral works include *Alexander's Feast, Acis and Galatea, Ode for St Cecilia's Day* and *L'Allegro.* The *Water Music* and *Music for the Royal Fireworks* are among Handel's most popular works.

HARTY, Sir Hamilton (1879–1941), Irish. Works include the tone poem *With the Wild Geese* and *Irish Symphony,* together with many songs.

HAYDN, Franz Joseph (1732–1809), Austrian. A prolific composer of 104 symphonies, chamber music including 84 string quartets, piano sonatas, operas, church music and oratorios. *The Creation* and *The Seasons* are among his best-known works.

HENZE, Hans Werner (b. 1926), German. Works include several operas, six symphonies, concertos for piano and violin, an oratorio and chamber music.

HINDEMITH, Paul (1897–1963), German. Several operas, including *Mathis der Maler,* a violin concerto, a cello concerto, the *Sinfonia Serena, Symphonic Metamorphosis on a Theme by Weber* and chamber music.

HOLST, Gustav (1874–1934), English. Best-known work is the orchestral suite *The Planets.* Choral works include *Hymns from the Rig-Veda* and *The Hymn of Jesus.* Operas include *Savitri* and *The Perfect Fool.* Two more popular works are *St Paul's Suite* for strings and the orchestral piece *Egdon Heath.*

HONEGGER, Arthur (1892–1955), Swiss. Operas, such as *Antigone;* five symphonies, a cello concerto, symphonic poems, ballets *Skating Rink* and *Sémiramis,* orchestral pieces *Pacific 231* and *Pastorale d'été;* stage oratorios including *King David* and *Judith,* and chamber music.

HUMMEL, Johann Nepomuk (1778–1837), German. Most important compositions are piano works consisting of trios, sonatas, rondos and six concertanti.

HUMPERDINCK, Engelbert (1854–1921), German. Best-known opera is *Hansel and Gretel.*

d'INDY, Vincent (1851–1931), French. Works include symphonies, chamber music, symphonic variations, *Istar*, operas such as *Fervaal* and *Le Chant de la Cloche*, *Quintette* suite for flute, string trio and harp and arrangements for hundred of songs.

IPPOLITOV-IVANOV, Mikhail (1859–1935), Russian. Most popular work is *Caucasian Sketches*.

IRELAND, John (1879–1962), English. One piano concerto; choral work *These Things Shall Be*; orchestral works including *The Forgotten Rite* and *Mai-Dun*; songs, such as the setting of Masefield's 'Sea Fever', and Songs Sacred and Profane

IVES, Charles (1874–1954), American. Orchestral work includes five symphonies *Three Places in New England* and *July 4th*. Also chamber music and over 200 songs.

JANÁČEK, Leoš (1854–1928), Czech. Several operas including *Jenufa, Katya Kabanova* and *The Cunning Little Vixen*. A popular orchestral work is *Sinfonietta*. Janáček also composed numerous choral works, some chamber music and organ pieces.

KABALEVSKY, Dmitri Borisovich (b. 1904), Russian. Works include several operas, four symphonies, three piano concertos, a violin concerto, chamber music, piano music and songs.

KHACHATURIAN, Aram (b. 1903), Russian of Armenian descent. Works include ballets *Happiness* and *Gayaneh*, two symphonies, concertos for piano, violin, cello, and violin and cello, and incidental music such as that for *Macbeth*.

KODÁLY, Zoltán (1882–1967), Hungarian. Much chamber and instrumental music. Comic opera *Háry János*. Orchestral works include *Dances of Galánta* and *Dances of Marosszék*, and Symphony in C Major. Choral works include *Psalmus Hungaricus* and *Missa Brevis*.

LALO, Edouard (1823–92), French. Operas, including *Le Roi d'Ys*, Symphony in G Minor, *Symphonie Espagnole*, concertos for piano, violin and cello, the ballet *Namouna* and several chamber works.

LAMBERT, Constant (1905–51), English. Ballet music *Romeo and Juliet, Pomona* and *Horoscope*; cantata *Summer's Last Will and Testament*, a piano concerto, *Music for Orchestra*, and song setting for Sacheverell Sitwell's poem 'The Rio Grande'.

LEONCAVALLO, Ruggiero (1858–1919), Italian. Operas, the most successful being *Pagliacci*.

LIADOV, Anatol (1855–1914), Russian. Works include symphonic poems *Baba Yaga*, *The Enchanted Lake* and *Kikimora*, two orchestral scherzos and a number of piano pieces.

LIGETI, György (b. 1923), Hungarian. Electronic music such as *Artikulation* and other avant-garde music, including *Poème Symphonique* for 100 metronomes, *Apparitions, Atmospheres* and *Aventures* for orchestra.

LISZT, Franz (1811–86), Hungarian. *Faust* and *Dante* symphonies. Several masses and oratorios. Numerous songs and piano pieces, including Liebesträume

Mendelssohn

Mozart

and Hungarian Rhapsodies. Orchestral music includes symphonic poems such as *Mazeppa* and *Totentanz (Dance of Death)*.

LULLY, Jean-Baptiste (1632–87), French. Sacred music, including the famous *Miserere*, 49 ballets and 15 operas including *Les Fêtes de l'Amour et de Bacchus*.

MAHLER, Gustav (1860–1911), Austrian. Ten symphonies and *Song of the Earth* (six songs with orchestra). Various song cycles, such as *Songs of a Wayfarer*.

MARTINU, Bohuslav (1890–1959), Czech. Numerous works include ballet *Istar*, symphonic poem *Vanishing Midnight*, concerto grossó for chamber orchestra and the Double Concerto for two string orchestras.

MASCAGNI, Pietro (1863–1945), Italian. Best-known of his several operas is *Cavalleria Rusticana*.

MASSENET, Jules (1842–1912), French. Many operas including *Hérodiade (Salomé), Manon, Le Cid*, and *Thaïs*. Incidental music including *The Furies*. Massenet also composed over 200 songs, a piano concerto and several orchestral suites and oratorios.

MENDELSSOHN, Felix (1809–47), German. Incidental music to *A Midsummer Night's Dream*, five symphonies, six concert overtures including *The Hebrides (Fingal's Cave)*, a violin concerto and two piano concertos. Oratorios: *St Paul* and *Elijah*. Chamber music includes seven string quartets, three piano quartets, two string quintets, two piano trios, an octet and a sextet. Piano pieces include *Songs without Words* and *Rondo Capriccioso*. Also wrote numerous songs.

MESSIAEN, Olivier (b. 1908), French. Much religious music. Orchestral works include *Turangalila Symphony, Chronochromie* and *The Awakening of the Birds*.

MEYERBEER, Giacomo (1791–1864), German. Many operas, including *Robert the Devil, The Huguenots, The North Star, The Prophet*, and *L'Africaine*. Meyerbeer also wrote an oratorio, church music and songs.

MIASKOVSKY, Nikolai (1881–1950), Russian. Works include the oratorio *Kirov Is With Us*, 27 symphonies, a violin concerto, symphonic poems, chamber music and songs.

MILHAUD, Darius (1892–1974), French. Operas, such as *Bolivar*; the oratorio *Christopher Columbus*; ballets *The Creation of the World* and *The Nothing-doing*

Bar; orchestral works *Suite Provençale* and *Saudades do Brazil*; piano duet *Scaramouche*, chamber music and songs.

MONTEVERDI, Claudio (1567–1643), Italian. Operas such as *The Coronation of Poppea*, sacred and secular madrigals, masses, magnificats and psalms.

MOZART, Wolfgang Amadeus (1756–91), Austrian. Orchestral works include 49 symphonies, *Sinfonia Concertante*, 25 piano concertos, five violin concertos, concertos for flute, horn, clarinet, etc. Chamber music includes 25 string quartets and 40 violin sonatas. Operas include *Idomeneo, Il Seraglio, The Marriage of Figaro, Don Giovanni, Cosi fan tutte* and *The Magic Flute*. Mozart's *Requiem* was left unfinished.

MUSSORGSKY, Modest Petrovich (1839–81), Russian. Orchestral pieces: *Pictures at an Exhibition; Night on the Bare Mountain*. Operas: *Boris Godunov, Khovanshtchina* and *Sorochintsy Fair*. Many songs.

NICOLAI, Otto (1810–49), German. Mainly operas, including *The Merry Wives of Windsor*.

NIELSEN, Carl (1865–1931), Danish. Six symphonies, one violin concerto and concertos for flute and clarinet, several overtures, such as *Helios*, and various instrumental works. Chamber music includes four string quartets. Operas: *Saul and David; Maskarade*.

OFFENBACH, Jacques (1819–80), German-French. Light operas, the best-known being *Orpheus in the Underworld, La Belle Hélène* and *La Vie Parisienne*. One grand opera: *Tales of Hoffmann* (unfinished). A popular orchestral work, *Gaité Parisienne*, a suite of Offenbach's music, was arranged by Manuel Rosenthal.

ORFF, Carl (b. 1895), German. Mainly operas and dramatic works. The secular oratorio *Carmina Burana* has achieved great popularity.

PAGANINI, Niccolo (1782–1840), Italian. Two violin concertos, three string quartets with a guitar part, 12 sonatas for violin or guitar and 24 *capricci* for violin.

PALESTRINA, Giovanni Pierluigi de (1525–94), Italian. Masses, motets, hymns, litanies and magnificats.

PERGOLESI, Giovanni Battista (1710–36), Italian. Several operas, oratorios, masses and other church music.

POULENC, Francis (1899–1963), French. Three operas, including *Les Dialogues des Carmélites*, ballets *Les Biches (The House Party)* and *Les Animaux Modèles*, several religious works and over 100 songs. Orchestral works include *Concert Champêtre* for harpsichord and orchestra, concerto for two pianos and orchestra and an organ concerto.

PROKOFIEV, Sergei (1891–1953), Russian. Seven symphonies, including the Classical (No. 1), five piano concertos, two violin concertos and two cello concertos. Six ballets and music for films. Operas such as *The Love for Three Oranges*. Orchestral works, *Scythian Suite* and *Peter and the Wolf*. Chamber music includes two string quartets, two violin sonatas and nine piano sonatas.

PUCCINI, Giacomo (1858–1924), Italian. Operas, including *Manon Lescaut, La Bohème, Madame Butterfly, Tosca* and *Turandot* (unfinished).

PURCELL, Henry (1659–95), English. Opera *Dido and Aeneas*, 62 settings for anthems and much incidental music.

RACHMANINOFF, Sergei (1873–1943), Russian. Three operas, including *Francesca da Rimini*, three symphonies, four published piano concertos, a number of piano and chamber works, and *Rhapsody on a Theme by Paganini* for orchestra.

RAMEAU, Jean-Philippe (1683–1764), French. Operas and opera-ballets. Best-known today is Rameau's music for harpsichord.

RAVEL, Maurice (1875–1937), French. Works include two piano concertos (one for the left hand) orchestral pieces *Rapsodie Espagnole* and *Boléro*; an opera *L'Heure Espagnole*; an opera-ballet *L'Enfant et les Sortilèges*, and the ballet *Daphnis and Chloé*. Chamber music includes a string quartet, a piano trio and three violin sonatas. Piano works include *Gaspard de la Nuit*, five *Miroirs*, and the suite *Le Tombeau de Couperin*.

RESPIGHI, Ottorino (1879–1936), Italian. Several operas. Orchestral works include *The Fountains of Rome, The Pines of Rome* and the suite *The Birds*.

RIMSKY-KORSAKOV, Nikolai (1844–1908), Russian. Operas include *The Maid of Pskov, The Snow Maiden* and *The Golden Cockerel*. Orchestral pieces include *Sheherazade, Easter Festival* Overture and *Capriccio Espagnol*.

ROSSINI, Gioacchino (1792–1868), Italian. Operas *Tancredi, The Barber of Seville, William Tell, Semiramide, Cinderella, The Italian Girl in Algiers* and *The Thieving Magpie*.

ROUSSEL, Albert (1869–1937), French. Works include four symphonies, chamber music, songs and choral works. Stage works include the opera *Padmâvatî* and the ballet *The Spider's Feast*. Orchestral works include *For a Festival of Spring*.

SAINT-SAËNS, Camille (1835–1921), French. Three symphonies, five piano concertos, three violin concertos. Operas include *Samson et Dalila*. Four symphonic poems, including *La Danse Macabre*. *Carnival of Animals* for small orchestra. Chamber music, church music and many songs.

SALIERI, Antonio (1750–1825), Italian. About 40 operas, some orchestral and church music.

SARASATE, Pablo (1844–1908), Spanish. Works include romances, fantasies and Spanish dances for violin.

SATIE, Erik (1866–1925), French. Works include the symphonic drama *Socrate*, ballets, including *Parade* scored for typewriters, sirens, airplane propellers, ticker tape and a lottery wheel. Several piano pieces and songs.

SCARLATTI, Alessandro (1660–1725), Italian. Works include 115 operas, over 600 chamber cantatas, and church music.

SCARLATTI, Domenico (1685–1757), Italian. Best-known works today are his keyboard sonatas.

SCHOENBERG, Arnold (1874–1951), Austrian. Two symphonies, one piano concerto, one violin concerto and chamber music. Other works include the symphonic poem *Pelleas und Melisande; Five Orchestral Pieces*. Drama with

Sibelius

Strauss

music: *The Hand of Fate*. Vocal music: *Gurrelieder; Pierrot Lunaire* for voice and chamber orchestra.

SCHUBERT, Franz (1797–1828), Austrian. Nine symphonies including the *Unfinished* (No. 8), and seven masses. Incidental music to *Rosamunde*. He wrote over 600 songs, including three great song cycles. Chamber music includes an octet, a piano quintet (*The Trout*), a string quintet, 15 string quartets and two piano trios. Piano music includes *Moments Musicaux*.

SCHUMANN, Robert (1810–56), German. Works include four symphonies, concertos for piano, violin and cello, incidental music to Byron's *Manfred*, much chamber music (piano sonatas 11 and 22 are particularly famous), and songs.

SCRIABIN, Alexander Nicolas (1871–1915), Russian. Three symphonies, tone poems *Prometheus*, etc., *Rêverie* and *Poem of Ecstasy* for orchestra. A piano concerto and many works for piano.

SHOSTAKOVICH, Dmitri (1906–75), Russian. Works include 15 symphonies, two piano concertos, two violin concertos and two cello concertos. Operas include *The Nose*, and ballets include *The Golden Age*. Shostakovich also composed a good deal of chamber music.

SIBELIUS, Jean (1865–1957), Finnish. Seven symphonies including the *Kullervo* Symphony. Symphonic tone poems: *En Saga, The Swan of Tuonela, Finlandia, Pohjola's Daughter, The Bard* and *Tapiola*. Other orchestral pieces include *Valse Triste*, the *Karelia Suite*, violin concerto, and incidental music *Pelléas et Mélisande* and *The Tempest*.

SMETANA, Bedřich (1824–84), Czech. Symphonic suite *Ma Vlast (My Country)*. Operas include *The Bartered Bride* and *Dalibor*. He also wrote the quartet *From My Life*.

SOUSA, John Philip (1854–1932), American. Many marches for brass bands, such as *Washington Post* and *The Stars and Stripes Forever*.

SPOHR, Ludwig (1784–1859), German. Works include nine symphonies, 17 violin concertos, four clarinet concertos and several operas. Oratorios: *Calvary* and *The Last Judgement*. Chamber music, piano music and songs.

STOCKHAUSEN, Karlheinz (b. 1928), German. Rather unusual works include

Stravinsky

Wagner

Kontakte for electronic sounds, *Gruppen* for three orchestras and *Kontrapunkt* for ten instruments.

STRAUSS, Johann (1804–49), Austrian. Over 150 waltzes and other dance music.

STRAUSS, Johann (1825–99), Austrian. Operettas, such as *Die Fledermaus* and *The Gypsy Baron*. Many well-known waltzes such as *The Blue Danube*, *Morgenblatten (Morning Leaves)*, *Wine, Women and Song* and *Tales from the Vienna Woods*.

STRAUSS, Richard (1864–1949), German. Symphonic tone poems include *Don Juan, Death and Transfiguration, Till Eulenspiegel, Don Quixote, Also Sprach Zarathustra* and *Ein Heldenleben*. Operas include *Salome, Elektra, Der Rosenkavalier, Ariadne auf Naxos, Arabella* and *Die Schweigsame Frau*.

STRAVINSKY, Igor (1882–1971), Russian. Many and varied works include the ballets *The Firebird, Petrushka, Pulcinella* and *The Rite of Spring*. Operas include *The Rake's Progress*. Orchestral works include four symphonies, concertos for piano and violin, concerto for 16 instruments (Dumbarton Oaks), and *Symphony of Psalms* for chorus and orchestra.

SUK, Josef (1874–1935), Czech. Orchestral works include symphonic poems *Prague* and *Maturity*, two symphonies, chamber music and piano pieces.

SULLIVAN, Sir Arthur (1842–1900), English. Light operas written in collaboration with Sir W. S. Gilbert, include *HMS Pinafore, The Pirates of Penzance, Patience, The Mikado, The Yeomen of the Guard, The Gondoliers, Ruddigore, Iolanthe* and *Princess Ida*. One serious opera: *Ivanhoe*. The ballad *The Lost Chord* and other songs.

SUPPÉ, Franz von (1819–95), Austrian. Operettas include *Light Cavalry, Fatinitza* and *Boccaccio*. Ballets include *Poet and Peasant* and *Wallensteins Lager*. Also more than 200 stage works.

SZYMANOWSKY, Karol (1883–1937), Polish. Three symphonies, two operas, ballets, choral music, chamber music and songs.

TALLIS, Thomas (*c.* 1505–85), English. Masses, anthems and other church music.

TCHAIKOVSKY, Peter Ilyich (1840–93), Russian. Six symphonies, three piano con~~certos~~ (the third unfinished), one violin concerto, four suites for orchestra, two serenades for strings, fantasy overture *Romeo and Juliet*, orchestral fantasies *Francesca da Rimini* and *Hamlet*, *Variations on a Rococo Theme* for cello and orchestra, *1812 Overture*, *Italian Caprice* and *Marche Slav*. Ballet music: *Swan Lake*, *The Sleeping Beauty* and the *Nutcracker*. Operas include *Eugene Onegin* and *The Queen of Spades*. Tchaikovsky's chamber music includes three string quartets, one trio and one sextet.

TELEMANN, George Philipp (1681–1767), German. His works include 46 operas, choral works, instrumental music and church music.

TIPPETT, Michael (b. 1905), English. Orchestral works include two symphonies. An oratorio: *A Child of Our Time*. Operas: *The Midsummer Marriage*, *King Priam* and *The Knot Garden*. Also chamber music and songs.

VAUGHAN WILLIAMS, Ralph (1872–1958), English. Operas, including *Hugh the Drover*. Orchestral works include nine symphonies, the *Fantasia on a Theme by Tallis*, concertos for piano, oboe and tuba, fantasy on *Greensleeves*, *The Lark Ascending*, and overture *The Wasps*. *On Wenlock Edge* for tenor, string quartet and piano.

VERDI, Giuseppe (1813–1901), Italian. Operas include *Rigoletto*, *Il Trovatore*, *La Traviata*, *Don Carlos*, *Aïda*, *Otello* and *Falstaff*. Religious music includes Verdi's *Requiem*.

VILLA-LOBOS, Heitor (1887–1959), Brazilian. Operas, ballets, 12 symphonies, symphonic suites and chamber music. A characteristic work is *Bachianas Brasileiras* (nine pieces for various instrumental and vocal groups).

VIVALDI, Antonio (1678–1741), Italian. Many operas and at least 450 concertos for various instruments, the best-known being *The Four Seasons*.

WAGNER, Richard (1813–83), German. Best known for his operatic works including *Rienzi*, *The Flying Dutchman*, *The Mastersingers*, *Tannhäuser*, *Lohengrin*, *Tristan and Isolde*, *The Ring of the Nibelungs* and *Parsifal*. A well-known piece for small orchestra is *Siegfried Idyll*.

WALTON, Sir William (b. 1902), English. Works include two operas, two symphonies, concertos for violin, viola and cello, overtures including *Doctor Syntax* and *Portsmouth Point*, a ballet *Façade*, music for the films *Henry V* and *Hamlet*, marches *Crown Imperial* and *Orb and Sceptre*, chamber music and songs.

WEBER, Carl Maria von (1786–1826), German. Romantic operas: *Abu Hassan*, *Der Freischütz*, *Euryanthe* and *Oberon*. Also symphonies, concertos, chamber music, piano music and masses.

WEBERN, Anton von (1883–1945), Austrian. One symphony, choral works, chamber music and instrumental pieces.

WEILL, Kurt (1900–50), German. Operas and operettas, such as *Mahagonny*. Orchestral music includes two symphonies and a concerto for violin and wind band.

WOLF, Hugo (1860–1903), Austrian. Many songs. Orchestral works include *Italian Serenade*. An opera: *Der Corregidor*.

Glossary of Styles in Art and Architecture

Abstract art A term usually applied to 20th-century art in which form and colour are all-important, being independent of any recognizable form of reality.

Baroque The flamboyant art style of the period *c.* 1600–1720. A characteristic of Baroque painting and sculpture is its strong drama and appeal to the emotions. Architecture in the Baroque style is heavily ornate.

Classicism A form of art which emphasizes the characteristic qualities of Greek and Roman art, such as restraint, simplicity of form and harmony. The paintings of Ingres (1780–1867) are examples of Classicism. *See* neo-Classicism.

Cubism A movement created in the years 1907–9 by the painters Picasso (1881–1973) and Braque (1882–1963). Natural subjects were reduced to several interlocking planes, often seen from different perspectives.

Dadaism A forerunner of Surrealism, Dadaism was born of the disillusion induced by World War I. The Dadaists aimed to overthrow all standards and traditions in art and set out to outrage and scandalize. An example is a painting by Duchamp (1887–1968) of the Mona Lisa with a moustache.

Expressionism A 20th-century style of painting which does not imitate nature but tries to convey what the artist feels about a subject. The movement was influenced by the work of van Gogh and Munch. Important expressionist painters include Klee, Kandinsky and Kokoschka.

Fauvism An art movement originating in Paris when a number of artists, including Matisse (1869–1954), exhibited their works in one room. The paintings were full of flat patterns, distortion and brilliant colour. A critic contemptuously described the artists collectively as *les fauves*, meaning 'the wild beasts'.

Gothic The predominant style of church architecture in northern Europe from the 12th to the 15th century. It is characterized by tall, pointed arches and pillars with fan vaulting, and flying buttresses supporting the building on the outside. Wall space was reduced to a minimum, giving a feeling of space and of striving upwards. The Gothic style was revived in Europe and the USA during the 18th and 19th centuries.

Impressionism A movement originating in France in the 1860s. Artists such as Monet, Manet, Sisley and Pissarro sought to capture the fleeting play of light, particularly in landscapes. The impressionists did not mix their paints but dabbed them side by side in the pure state on the canvas. The shadows of objects were represented in the complementary colours. For example, an orange object would have a purple shadow. In the widest sense, Turner and Constable were impressionists, and in fact the French impressionists were much inspired by these artists. The artists Cézanne, van Gogh and Gauguin, once associated with impressionism, were later labelled 'post-impressionists'.

Mannerism The art style of the period 1530–1600, principally in Italy. A characteristic of mannerist paintings is the emphasis on the human figure, often frenziedly twisted and gesticulating. Emotional effects were heightened by vivid and sometimes harsh colours. Tintoretto and El Greco painted in this style.

Neo-Classicism A movement which originated in Rome in the middle of the 18th century and then spread rapidly in Europe. Painters and architects consciously

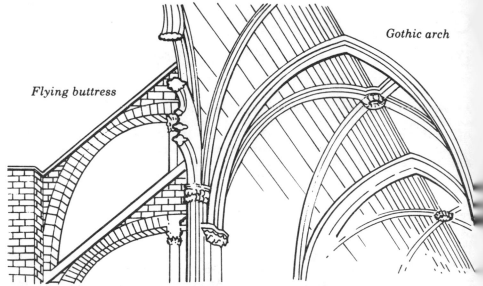

Gothic arch

Flying buttress

imitated antique art in style and subject matter. A notable painter in the neo-Classic style was the French artist David (1748–1825).

Pre-Raphaelites In 1848 a number of English artists revolted against the art of their time. They wished to make a return to the simple naturalism of the pre-Raphael Italian painters such as Botticelli, Fra Angelico and Filippo Lippi. The Pre-Raphaelite brotherhood used bright colour and great detail. The three founding members of the brotherhood were Dante Gabriel Rossetti, J. E. Millais and W. Holman Hunt.

Realism The frank and vigorous representation of the actuality of everyday life. The first Realist painter was Courbet (1819–77) who rejected idealized art and romanticism in the mid-19th century.

Renaissance The word means 'rebirth'. During the Renaissance (14th to early 16th century), art in Italy was revived or 'reborn' under the influence of Greek and Roman models. The Renaissance spread all over western Europe. At its height, c. 1600, the Renaissance produced artists of supreme skill including Leonardo da Vinci, Michelangelo and Raphael.

Rococo A style of architecture and decoration prevailing in France during the period 1720–70. The name comes from the French word *rocaille*, meaning 'shell-shaped'. The shell was a favourite motif in Rococo ornamentation. The style was more dainty and graceful than that of the more robust Baroque from which it grew. Paintings of the period, such as the works of Watteau (1684–1721), Boucher (1703–70) and Fragonard (1732–1806), show the same light-hearted vitality.

Romanticism A movement that began in France in 1830 as a reaction to Classicism. Romanticism put imagination before reason, expressing unbridled passion and a love for the exotic. A painter in the Romantic style was Delacroix (1798–1863).

Surrealism An art movement which developed from Dadaism in the 1920s. Surrealist painters aimed to create from the depths of the subconscious mind, free from the dictates of reason. Their works depict the weird and fantastic, such as Salvador Dali's trees with limp watches draped over their branches.

The Seven Wonders of the Ancient World

The pyramids of Egypt	The biggest, the Great Pyramid of Cheops, was originally 147 m (481 ft) high and 230 m (756 ft) square at the base. The oldest pyramid is that of Zoser, at Saggara, built about 3000 BC.
The Hanging Gardens of Babylon	These were terraced gardens adjoining the palace of Nebuchadnezzar near Bagdad. They were irrigated by means of large storage tanks on the uppermost terraces.
The tomb of Mausolus	This was built by the king's widow at Halicarnassus, in Asia Minor, about 350 BC. Our word 'mausoleum' is derived from it.
The temple of Diana at Ephesus	This was a great marble temple erected about 480 BC.
The Colossus of Rhodes	Set up about 280 BC, this bronze statue of Apollo, around 32 m (105 ft) high, stood with legs astride the harbour entrance at Rhodes.
The statue of Zeus at Olympia	Made of marble inlaid with ivory and gold, this statue was made by the sculptor Phidias about 430 BC.
The Pharos of Alexandria	Built about 250 BC, this was a marble watchtower and lighthouse on the island of Pharos in Alexandria Harbour.

Famous Buildings

People in ancient times talked of the Seven Wonders of the World. Of these, only the pyramids of Egypt have survived.

Many other ancient buildings could be classed as wonders of the world. In Egypt, in particular, there are many magnificent temples, the best known of which are those at Abu Simbel in the far south.

Abu Simbel The temples of Re-Harakhte and Hathor now overlook Lake Nasser, a man-made lake which has formed behind the Aswan High Dam on the River Nile. In the 1960s the temples would have disappeared under the lake had it not been for a great engineering project. The temples, which had originally been carved into a sandstone cliff, were cut into 1,050 blocks which were raised to a new site 210 metres (689 ft) higher up and rebuilt. The operation cost $42 million. The temples were built in the reign of Ramses II (1290–1244 BC). The Temple of Harakhte has four seated statues of Ramses, each 20 metres (66 ft) high, on either side of the entrance. Outside the smaller Temple of Hathor are large standing figures of Ramses and his wife Nefertari.

Pyramids were built not only in Egypt, but also in Central America. However, nearly all the Central American pyramids were temples, not tombs as in Egypt.

Tepanapa Pyramid at Cholula, near Puebla in central Mexico, covers more than 16 hectares (40 acres) and is 70 metres (230 ft) high. It is the world's largest pyramid in terms of its volume. It was built in stages between 1600 and 500 BC.

Other major civilizations, including ancient Greece and Rome, produced many famous buildings.

The Acropolis is a steep-sided, flat-topped hill in Athens, capital of Greece On it stand the remains of three great buildings, the Propylaea, the Erechtheum and the Parthenon, a temple which is probably the world's best known and most beautiful ruin.

The Romans also constructed many famous buildings throughout the western world. Some of the best known are in Rome itself.

The Colosseum, the world's largest amphitheatre, was 187 metres (614 ft) long and 49 metres (161 ft) high. Early Christians were martyred here to entertain crowds of about 50,000.

The Pantheon in Rome is a superb example of a Roman temple. Started in 27 BC, it was later modified. Its most impressive feature is a central circular rotunda, which measures 43.3 metres (142.5 ft) across. Above it is a huge 43.3-metre (142-ft) high dome with a window cut in the top. This window is the temple's only source of light.

Christianity inspired many great buildings which were designed in several distinctive styles.

St. Sophia, in Istanbul, Turkey, is a superb example of a Byzantine church. It was built between AD 532 and 537, but a new dome had to be built between

558 and 563, after an earthquake had
damaged an earlier one. The dome is
56.3 metres (185 ft) high and 32.6 metres
(107 ft) across.

The Basilica of St. Mark, in Venice,
Italy, is often rated as the finest
example of Byzantine architecture after
St. Sophia in Istanbul. Work began on
this church in about 1050. It was once
the private chapel of the Doge, Venice's
ruler, whose Gothic palace stands next
to it.

St. Basil's Church, Moscow, was
inspired by Byzantine architecture,
though it was built in the mid-16th
century. This impressive church is
crowned by eight onion-shaped, highly
coloured domes.

The Cathedral of Notre-Dame, in
Paris, is an example of Gothic
architecture. Consecrated in 1182, its
walls are supported by beautiful flying
buttresses.

The Cathedral of Florence, in Italy,
is a magnificent church that combines
Gothic and classical features. Its dome
was designed by the Renaissance
architect Filippo Brunelleschi (1377-1446).

St. Peter's Basilica, in Vatican City,
is the world's largest Christian church.
It was built during the Renaissance.
Several architects worked on it, the
most famous of whom was
Michelangelo, who designed its superb
dome.

St. Paul's Cathedral, London, uses
the Renaissance style. It was designed
by Sir Christopher Wren (1632–1723). In
the Whispering Gallery, which runs
around the inside of the dome, you can
clearly hear the whisper of someone on
the far side of the dome.

Other religions, including Islam,
have also inspired great buildings, such
as mosques, palaces and tombs.

Taj Mahal, Agra, in northern India, is
a tomb built by the Muslim ruler Shah
Jahan for his wife, who was called
Mumtaz Mahal, which means 'pride of
the palace'. Built between 1632 and
1653 of white marble inlaid with semi-
precious stones, it has a magnificent
dome. The bodies of the loving couple
lie in a vault beneath the dome.

The Alhambra, in Granada, in
southern Spain, is a Moorish palace,
with fountains set in finely decorated
courtyards and gardens. Built between
1248 and 1354, it is Europe's finest
example of Arab art.

Angkor Wat is a great temple once
lost in the forests of Kampuchea. It is
near Angkor, capital of the Khmer
Empire, a Hindu civilization which
flourished from 802 to 1413.

Famous palaces include:

The Imperial Palace, Peking, China,
is the world's largest palace. It covers
72 hectares (178 acres). It is in the
'Forbidden City', a part of Peking
where once only members of the royal

household could enter. It is now open to the public.

The Palace of Versailles, near Paris, was completed in 1682. It has hundreds of beautiful rooms, including the large Hall of Mirrors where the Treaty of Versailles, which officially ended World War I, was signed on 28 June, 1919.

Buckingham Palace, London, is the largest palace in Britain which is used by the Royal Family. Hampton Court Palace, about 24 km (15 miles) south-west of central London, is larger, but the last monarch to live there was George II.

London has many other famous buildings, including:

The Tower of London is a fortress where many people, including Ann Boleyn, Catherine Howard and Thomas More, were imprisoned and executed. The White Tower, the oldest building here, was erected between 1078 and 1098. The Tower of London is now a museum. Its many exhibits include the priceless Crown Jewels.

The Palace of Westminster contains the House of Commons and the House of Lords. A fire destroyed the original building, except for Westminster Hall, in 1834. But the Palace was rebuilt between 1840 and 1867 in the Gothic style.

Other famous government buildings include:

The Capitol in Washington DC, with its large white dome, houses the US Senate and House of Representatives. British troops burned down the first Capitol in 1814, but it was rebuilt in 1819, though it has been enlarged and modernized several times.

The White House in Washington DC is the home of the President of the USA. It was burned down in 1814, but it was rebuilt between 1814 and 1818.

The Kremlin is the main seat of government in the USSR. The Kremlin is a walled enclosure, measuring 2.4 km (1.5 miles) around. Besides government buildings, it also contains palaces, three cathedrals and other buildings.

The Spasskaya Tower, on one of its gateways, has chimes that are known throughout the USSR, because they are used to ring the hours on the radio.

Of the world's many famous towers, probably the two most famous are:

The Leaning Tower of Pisa, in Italy, is a 54.6-,metre (179-ft) high, marble bell tower built between 1174 and 1350. Soon after it was built, the ground beneath it began to sink and this handsome tower began to lean. It is now about 5 metres (16.4 ft) out of true.

The Eiffel Tower, in Paris, was built as a demonstration of what could be done in building with metal, in this case, wrought-iron. Completed in 1889, it was the world's highest structure, standing 300.5 metres (985.9 ft) high, with 1,792 steps. A television aerial has now increased its height to 320.75 metres (1,052.3 ft).

Many modern buildings have attracted much attention for their exceptional height, their design or some other feature. Examples include:

The Sears Tower, in Chicago in the USA, was completed in 1974. The world's highest office building, it rises 443 metres (1,454 ft). Chicago was also the site of the world's first skyscraper – a 10-storey building completed in 1884.

The United Nations Secretariat Building, in New York City, USA, is one of the most familiar skyscrapers on the city's eastern skyline. New York City also contains three of the world's six tallest buildings: the World Trade Center (1973) and the older Empire State Building and the Chrysler Building.

The Strahov Stadium in Prague, Czechoslovakia, is the world's largest stadium. Completed in 1934, it can hold 240,000 spectators.

The Superdrome in New Orleans, USA, is the world's largest indoor stadium. Completed in 1975, it covers 5.26 hectares (13 acres) and is 83.2 metres (273 ft) high.

The Radio City Music Hall, New York City, is the world's largest cinema. Opened in 1932, it now has 5,882 seats. It is also famous for its spectacular stage shows.

The Sydney Opera House in Australia was completed in 1973. It is famous for the unusual design (by the Dane Joern Utzon) of its shell-like roofs which, from a distance, resemble the sails of yachts in Sydney Harbour.

Drawing and Painting

Drawing

When you first started drawing you probably derived great satisfaction and enjoyment from drawing matchstick figures. Simple lines represented a body and limbs, while dots for eyes and a line for the mouth transformed a plain circle into a face. By experimenting you probably soon realised it was possible to give your little matchstick-man feelings. To show happiness or sadness you merely curved the mouthline up or down.

This ability to transform simple lines into works of art is the whole secret of drawing. From the intriguing half-smile of the celebrated Mona Lisa to the cheeky grin of your favourite cartoon character, all are achieved by mastery of the drawn line. As well as a representation of real objects, drawing is also an expression of the imagination.

Broken lines can suggest rain; wavy lines water. To appreciate fully the art of drawing, you must learn to enjoy lines! Study the linework of past masters of draughtsmanship, such as Leonardo da Vinci, Holbein, Rembrandt and Dürer. If you are unable to visit art galleries, search in your local library for books containing reproductions of the works of these artists.

Train yourself to look at things with a critical eye. Constantly remind yourself to analyse what you are seeing. When you look at a box, for instance, you do not see lines but edges (such as where the box ends and the background begins). Although you do not literally see lines you can depict exactly what you do see by using lines. Light and shade can be represented by the skilful use of lines. Known as *chiaroscuro*, this technique gives form and depth to the drawing, which, though only two-dimensional, appears to the eye to be in relief (that is, standing out from the surface).

An important element, if your drawing is to be convincing, is the ability to suggest foreshortening. A famous and very effective World War I recruitment poster, captioned 'Your Country Needs You!' shows Lord Kitchener pointing a finger directly ahead. No matter how far to either side of the poster the viewer moves, that commanding finger still points directly at the viewer! This dramatic effect is achieved by making the arm appear shorter and the hand bigger in relation to the head – just as it would if Lord Kitchener was really standing before the viewer and pointing at the viewer in person.

Foreshortening is really part of the principle of perspective, which is the art of representing objects as they appear to the eye from different viewpoints. You must have noticed, when standing on a bridge and looking along railway lines or a motorway, that the tracks or carriageways appear to meet in the distance? While you know perfectly well that telegraph poles in a line are really the same size, your eye persists in telling you that the pole nearest to you is both taller and fatter than those farther away!

These everyday examples underline the importance of an awareness of perspective. Develop the technique of perspective drawing by practising constantly. One simple and very useful exercise is to draw a box from as many different angles as possible.

Figure-drawing demands a basic knowledge of anatomy (the structure of the human body). It is well worth buying a good anatomy book, which will repay study and remain a useful source of reference.

Draw from life as much as possible. Try sketching the model in different poses and observe how muscles are thrown into relief when under tension.

The need for discipline in your drawing cannot be too strongly stressed. Indeed, until you have mastered the technique of drawing it is unwise to take the next step to painting. Many effects – clouds and seascapes, for instance – will be wholly dependent on the skill and ability to handle perspective you have acquired while learning to draw.

It is an excellent idea to keep a sketchbook permanently with you, not only to record figures, objects and places but also to note details you may need when later incorporating sketches into finished illustrations or paintings.

Water-colour painting
Whatever your first choice of subject – simple still life (fruit,

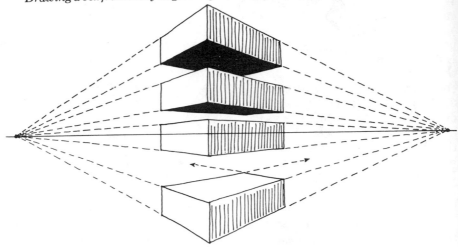

flowers, even vegetables) or that most popular of all water-colour subjects, landscape painting – you will need to equip yourself with a few basic items. The most essential are:

drawing board (size A3 or A4)
block paints (good quality, in box or tin with mixing trays)
water-colour paints in tubes
water-colour brushes
water-colour paper (experiment to find which type suits you best)
charcoal or soft pencils (2B, 3B or 4B)
soft rubber
sponge
blotting-paper
two bottles of water
drawing-pins or clips

For landscape painting, you will need also an easel, folding or telescopic, and a stool or folding camp-seat.

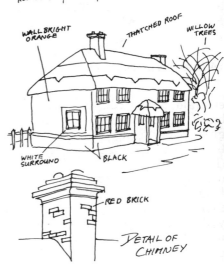

A typical sketchbook page

Your supply of paints (contents of paint-box plus tubes) should include the following colours: light yellow, middle cadmium, yellow ochre, orange madder, vermilion, light red, crimson lake, Indian red, ultramarine, cobalt, Prussian blue,

360

A home-made brush case

emerald, pale green, raw umber, burnt umber, and black or dark grey. Experiment with mixing these basic colours for a greater range. (For example: ultramarine + crimson lake = violet; Prussian blue + emerald = viridian.) Remember that, in general, red and yellow shades give a warm effect while blues and greens convey a cool quality.

Brushes should be carefully looked after. They are best kept in a case, or in a home-made wallet (flaps at both ends will protect the points and elastic bands can be used to hold the brushes in position).

It is generally accepted that the best time of day for painting outdoors is the afternoon, when the sun is past its height and the view is broken up into areas of light and shading. Many landscape artists prefer the daylight of spring, autumn or winter to that of high summer, which is often garish, flat and lacking in atmosphere.

The easel should be capable of being tilted horizontally (to prevent uncontrolled running of colour-washes), and should be adjustable in height to a sitting or standing working position. Your paper should be securely fixed to the board by means of drawing pins or clips. Charcoal and pencils are used to sketch in essential outlines in the first stages but do learn to draw with the brush, too.

Once you are comfortably settled, with the right equipment, try to construct your picture in the following sequence:

1 **Lightly indicate the outlines;**
2 **Begin with the dark colours;**
3 **Add the middle tones;**
4 **Add the light tones;**
5 **Pull the picture together by adding light or dark, washing away or pushing back areas, as necessary.**

Perhaps the most essential requirement in all water-colour painting is the ability to lay a flat wash successfully. You can practise this technique by mixing a pale colour (say, for the sky) with plenty of water and quickly sweeping a brushful from left to right across the top of your paper: this allows the colour to settle gently downwards. (Do not slope the board too steeply or the wash will run down too quickly.) While the first wash is still wet, mix a stronger tone of the same colour using slightly less water (it should still be very fluid) and run a brushful across under the first wash. This allows the colours to merge naturally.

Continue with washes, varying the strength of the colours, until you have a satisfactory sky. Let the final wash almost dry, then run in the first of a darker colour for mountains or distant landscape, with peaks or church spire piercing the lowest sky-wash.

This is the basic technique of water-colour painting. Practice will soon teach you how to achieve the exact effect you desire. All kinds of satisfying effect are possible, from the gentle haze of a misty landscape to the spectacular industrial scene, with belching chimneys and the red glow of furnaces. Dramatic results can be obtained by sweeping a sponge across part of a wet wash. The sponge can also be used to remove washes, or to spot out unsatisfactory patches. Blotting-paper, too, is effective when dabbed gently on a wet wash. And you might experiment with wetting the paper before you start work and allowing it nearly to dry before you apply the first colour-wash.

The secret is restraint: don't overwork the washes or attempt to touch up here and there. Do less, rather than more, to gain the desired result: for example, it is enough to let the paper show through, when you want to show white clouds, or snow. The overall effect should be clean, translucent and fresh – so remember to use clean water and to clean your brushes between colour-washes.

A final thought: painting that lacks the touch of emotion and individual creativity is not art. Never attempt to imitate the photographer – try, instead, to put something of yourself into the picture. (Though remember, with painting as with any other art, only when you have learned the rules can you break them!)

Anything worth doing brings its share of disappointment and frustration. If you persevere with your technique and practise your art, however, you will soon find yourself doing just what the title of this article suggests – drawing and painting for pleasure!

The Cinema

Academy of Motion Picture Arts
and Sciences Awards (Oscars)
The *Academy Awards* or *Oscars* are
given each spring for outstanding
merit in filmmaking during the
preceding year. Winners receive a
statuette made of bronze covered
with gold plate. The statuette was
named in 1931 after an Academy
librarian said it reminded her of
her Uncle Oscar.

AWARD FOR BEST ACTOR

1927–28 Emil Jannings (*The Way of All Flesh, The Last Command*)
1928–29 Warner Baxter (*In Old Arizona*)
1929–30 George Arliss (*Disraeli*)
1930–31 Lionel Barrymore (*A Free Soul*)
1931–32 Fredric March (*Dr Jekyll and Mr Hyde*), Wallace Beery (*The Champ*)
1932–33 Charles Laughton (*The Private Life of Henry VIII*)
1934 Clark Gable (*It Happened One Night*)
1935 Victor McLaglen (*The Informer*)
1936 Paul Muni (*The Story of Louis Pasteur*)
1937 Spencer Tracy (*Captains Courageous*)
1938 Spencer Tracy (*Boys Town*)
1939 Robert Donat (*Goodbye, Mr Chips*)
1940 James Stewart (*The Philadelphia Story*)
1941 Gary Cooper (*Sergeant York*)
1942 James Cagney (*Yankee Doodle Dandy*)
1943 Paul Lukas (*Watch on the Rhine*)
1944 Bing Crosby (*Going My Way*)

1945 Ray Milland (*The Lost Weekend*)
1946 Fredric March (*The Best Years of Our Lives*)
1947 Ronald Colman (*A Double Life*)
1948 Laurence Olivier (*Hamlet*)
1949 Broderick Crawford (*All the King's Men*)
1950 José Ferrer (*Cyrano de Bergerac*)
1951 Humphrey Bogart (*The African Queen*)
1952 Gary Cooper (*High Noon*)
1953 William Holden (*Stalag 17*)
1954 Marlon Brando (*On the Waterfront*)
1955 Ernest Borgnine (*Marty*)
1956 Yul Brynner (*The King and I*)
1957 Alec Guinness (*The Bridge on the River Kwai*)
1958 David Niven (*Separate Tables*)
1959 Charlton Heston (*Ben-Hur*)
1960 Burt Lancaster (*Elmer Gantry*)
1961 Maximilian Schell (*Judgment at Nuremberg*)
1962 Gregory Peck (*To Kill a Mockingbird*)
1963 Sidney Poitier (*Lilies of the Field*)
1964 Rex Harrison (*My Fair Lady*)

1965	Lee Marvin (*Cat Ballou*)	1941	Joan Fontaine (*Suspicion*)
1966	Paul Scofield (*A Man for All Seasons*)	1942	Greer Garson (*Mrs Miniver*)
1967	Rod Steiger (*In the Heat of the Night*)	1943	Jennifer Jones (*The Song of Bernadette*)
1968	Cliff Robertson (*Charly*)	1944	Ingrid Bergman (*Gaslight*)
1969	John Wayne (*True Grit*)	1945	Joan Crawford (*Mildred Pierce*)

1965   Lee Marvin (*Cat Ballou*)
1966   Paul Scofield (*A Man for All
        Seasons*)
1967   Rod Steiger (*In the Heat of the
        Night*)
1968   Cliff Robertson (*Charly*)
1969   John Wayne (*True Grit*)
1970   George C. Scott (*Patton*)
1971   Gene Hackman (*The French
        Connection*)
1972   Marlon Brando (*The
        Godfather*)
1973   Jack Lemmon (*Save the Tiger*)
1974   Art Carney (*Harry and Tonto*)
1975   Jack Nicholson (*One Flew
        Over the Cuckoo's Nest*)
1976   Peter Finch (*Network*)
1977   Richard Dreyfuss (*The
        Goodbye Girl*)
1978   Jon Voight (*Coming Home*)
1979   Dustin Hoffman (*Kramer* vs
        Kramer)
1980   Robert De Niro (*Raging Bull*)
1981   Henry Fonda (*On Golden
        Pond*)
1982   Ben Kingsley (*Gandhi*)
1983   Robert Duvall (*Tender Mercies*)
1984   F. Murray Abraham
        (*Amadeus*)

AWARD FOR BEST ACTRESS

1927–28   Janet Gaynor (*Seventh Heaven,
          Street Angel, Sunrise*)
1928–29   Mary Pickford (*Coquette*)
1929–30   Norma Shearer (*The Divorcee*)
1930–31   Marie Dressler (*Min and Bill*)
1931–32   Helen Hayes (*The Sin of
          Madelon Claudet*)
1932–33   Katharine Hepburn (*Morning
          Glory*)
1934   Claudette Colbert (*It
          Happened One Night*)
1935   Bette Davis (*Dangerous*)
1936   Luise Rainer (*The Great
          Ziegfeld*)
1937   Luise Rainer (*The Good Earth*)
1938   Bette Davis (*Jezebel*)
1939   Vivien Leigh (*Gone with the
          Wind*)
1940   Ginger Rogers (*Kitty Foyle*)

1941   Joan Fontaine (*Suspicion*)
1942   Greer Garson (*Mrs Miniver*)
1943   Jennifer Jones (*The Song of
        Bernadette*)
1944   Ingrid Bergman (*Gaslight*)
1945   Joan Crawford (*Mildred
        Pierce*)
1946   Olivia de Havilland (*To Each
        His Own*)
1947   Loretta Young (*The Farmer's
        Daughter*)
1948   Jane Wyman (*Johnny Belinda*)
1949   Olivia de Havilland (*The
        Heiress*)
1950   Judy Holliday (*Born
        Yesterday*)
1951   Vivien Leigh (*A Streetcar
        Named Desire*)
1952   Shirley Booth (*Come Back,
        Little Sheba*)
1953   Audrey Hepburn (*Roman
        Holiday*)
1954   Grace Kelly (*The Country Girl*)
1955   Anna Magnani (*The Rose
        Tattoo*)
1956   Ingrid Bergman (*Anastasia*)
1957   Joanne Woodward (*The Three
        Faces of Eve*)
1958   Susan Hayward (*I Want to
        Live!*)
1959   Simone Signoret (*Room at the
        Top*)
1960   Elizabeth Taylor (*Butterfield 8*)
1961   Sophia Loren (*Two Women*)
1962   Anne Bancroft (*The Miracle
        Worker*)
1963   Patricia Neal (*Hud*)
1964   Julie Andrews (*Mary Poppins*)
1965   Julie Christie (*Darling*)
1966   Elizabeth Taylor (*Who's
        Afraid of Virginia Woolf?*)
1967   Katharine Hepburn (*Guess
        Who's Coming to Dinner*)
1968   Katharine Hepburn (*The Lion
        in Winter*), Barbra Streisand
        (*Funny Girl*)
1969   Maggie Smith (*The Prime of
        Miss Jean Brodie*)
1970   Glenda Jackson (*Women in
        Love*)
1971   Jane Fonda (*Klute*)

1972	Liza Minnelli (*Cabaret*)
1973	Glenda Jackson (*A Touch of Class*)
1974	Ellen Burstyn (*Alice Doesn't Live Here Anymore*)
1975	Louise Fletcher (*One Flew Over the Cuckoo's Nest*)
1976	Faye Dunaway (*Network*)
1977	Diane Keaton (*Annie Hall*)
1978	Jane Fonda (*Coming Home*)
1979	Sally Field (*Norma Rae*)
1980	Sissy Spacek (*Coal Miner's Daughter*)
1981	Katherine Hepburn (*On Golden Pond*)
1982	Meryl Street (*Sophie's Choice*)
1983	Shirley Maclaine (*Terms of Endearment*)
1984	Sally Field (*Places in the Heart*)

AWARD FOR BEST SUPPORTING ACTOR

1936	Walter Brennan (*Come and Get It*)
1937	Joseph Schildkraut (*The Life of Émile Zola*)
1938	Walter Brennan (*Kentucky*)
1939	Thomas Mitchell (*Stagecoach*)
1940	Walter Brennan (*The Westerner*)
1941	Donald Crisp (*How Green Was My Valley*)
1942	Van Heflin (*Johnny Eager*)
1943	Charles Coburn (*The More the Merrier*)
1944	Barry Fitzgerald (*Going My Way*)
1945	James Dunn (*A Tree Grows in Brooklyn*)
1946	Harold Russell (*The Best Years of Our Lives*)
1947	Edmund Gwenn (*Miracle on 34th Street*)
1948	Walter Huston (*The Treasure of Sierre Madre*)
1949	Dean Jagger (*Twelve O'Clock High*)
1950	George Sanders (*All About Eve*)
1951	Karl Malden (*A Streetcar Named Desire*)
1952	Anthony Quinn (*Viva Zapata!*)
1953	Frank Sinatra (*From Here to Eternity*)
1954	Edmond O'Brien (*The Barefoot Contessa*)
1955	Jack Lemmon (*Mister Roberts*)
1956	Anthony Quinn (*Lust for Life*)
1957	Red Buttons (*Sayonara*)
1958	Burl Ives (*The Big Country*)
1959	Hugh Griffith (*Ben-Hur*)
1960	Peter Ustinov (*Spartacus*)
1961	George Chakiris (*West Side Story*)
1962	Ed Begley (*Sweet Bird of Youth*)
1963	Melvyn Douglas (*Hud*)
1964	Peter Ustinov (*Topkapi*)
1965	Martin Balsam (*A Thousand Clowns*)
1966	Walter Matthau (*The Fortune Cookie*)
1967	George Kennedy (*Cool Hand Luke*)
1968	Jack Albertson (*The Subject Was Roses*)
1969	Gig Young (*They Shoot Horses, Don't They?*)
1970	John Mills (*Ryan's Daughter*)
1971	Ben Johnson (*The Last Picture Show*)
1972	Joel Grey (*Cabaret*)
1973	John Houseman (*The Paper Chase*)
1974	Robert De Niro (*The Godfather, Part II*)
1975	George Burns (*The Sunshine Boys*)
1976	Jason Robards (*All the President's Men*)
1977	Jason Robards (*Julia*)
1978	Christopher Walken (*The Deer Hunter*)
1979	Melvyn Douglas (*Being There*)
1980	Timothy Hutton (*Ordinary People*)
1981	John Gielgud (*Arthur*)
1982	Louis Gossett Jnr. (*An Officer and a Gentleman*)
1983	Jack Nicholson (*Terms of Endearment*)

1984   Haing S. Ngor (*The Killing Fields*)

AWARD FOR BEST SUPPORTING ACTRESS

1936   Gale Sondergaard (*Anthony Adverse*)
1937   Alice Brady (*In Old Chicago*)
1938   Fay Bainter (*Jezebel*)
1939   Hattie McDaniel (*Gone with the Wind*)
1940   Jane Darwell (*The Grapes of Wrath*)
1941   Mary Astor (*The Great Lie*)
1942   Teresa Wright (*Mrs. Miniver*)
1943   Katina Paxinou (*For Whom the Bell Tolls*)
1944   Ethel Barrymore (*None But the Lonely Heart*)
1945   Anne Revere (*National Velvet*)
1946   Anne Baxter (*The Razor's Edge*)
1947   Celeste Holm (*Gentleman's Agreement*)
1948   Claire Trevor (*Key Largo*)
1949   Mercedes McCambridge (*All the King's Men*)
1950   Josephine Hull (*Harvey*)
1951   Kim Hunter (*A Streetcar Named Desire*)
1952   Gloria Grahame (*The Bad and the Beautiful*)
1953   Donna Reed (*From Here to Eternity*)
1954   Eva Marie Saint (*On the Waterfront*)
1955   Jo Van Fleet (*East of Eden*)
1956   Dorothy Malone (*Written on the Wind*)
1957   Miyoshi Umeki (*Sayonara*)
1958   Wendy Hiller (*Separate Tables*)
1959   Shelley Winters (*The Diary of Anne Frank*)
1960   Shirley Jones (*Elmer Gantry*)
1961   Rita Moreno (*West Side Story*)
1962   Patty Duke (*The Miracle Worker*)
1963   Margaret Rutherford (*The V.I.P.'s*)
1964   Lila Kedrova (*Zorba the Greek*)

1965   Shelley Winters (*A Patch of Blue*)
1966   Sandy Dennis (*Who's Afraid of Virginia Woolf?*)
1967   Estelle Parsons (*Bonnie and Clyde*)
1968   Ruth Gordon (*Rosemary's Baby*)
1969   Goldie Hawn (*Cactus Flower*)
1970   Helen Hayes (*Airport*)
1971   Cloris Leachman (*The Last Picture Show*)
1972   Eileen Heckart (*Butterflies Are Free*)
1973   Tatum O'Neal (*Paper Moon*)
1974   Ingrid Bergman (*Murder on the Orient Express*)
1975   Lee Grant (*Shampoo*)
1976   Beatrice Straight (*Network*)
1977   Vanessa Redgrave (*Julia*)
1978   Maggie Smith (*California Suite*)
1979   Meryl Streep (*Kramer vs Kramer*)
1980   Mary Steenburgen (*Melvin and Howard*)
1981   Maureen Stapleton (*Reds*)
1982   Jessica Lange (*Tootsie*)
1983   Linda Hunt (*The Year of Living Dangerously*)
1984   Peggy Ashcroft (*A Passage to India*)

AWARD FOR BEST PICTURE

1927–28   *Wings*, Paramount
1928–29   *Broadway Melody*, MGM
1929–30   *All Quiet on the Western Front*, Universal
1930–31   *Cimarron*, RKO
1931–32   *Grand Hotel*, MGM
          Special: *Mickey Mouse*, Walt Disney
1932–33   *Cavalcade*, 20th Century-Fox
1934   *It Happened One Night*, Columbia
1935   *Mutiny on the Bounty*, MGM
1936   *The Great Ziegfeld*, MGM
1937   *Life of Emile Zola*, Warner
1938   *You Can't Take It With You*, Columbia

1939	*Gone With the Wind*, Selznick International	1970	*Patton*, 20th Century-Fox

1939   *Gone With the Wind*, Selznick International
1940   *Rebecca*, Selznick International
1941   *How Green Was My Valley*, 20th Century-Fox
1942   *Mrs Miniver*, MGM
1943   *Casablanca*, Warner
1944   *Going My Way*, Paramount
1945   *The Lost Weekend*, Paramount
1946   *The Best Years of Our Lives*, Goldwyn, RKO
1947   *Gentleman's Agreement*, 20th Century-Fox
1948   *Hamlet*, Two Cities Film, Universal International
1949   *All the King's Men*, Columbia
1950   *All About Eve*, 20th Century-Fox
1951   *An American in Paris*, MGM
1952   *Greatest Show on Earth*, Cecil B. De Mille, Paramount
1953   *From Here to Eternity*, Columbia
1954   *On the Waterfront*, Horizon-American Corp. Columbia
1955   *Marty*, Hecht and Lancaster's Steven Productions UA
1956   *Around the World in 80 Days*, Michael Todd Co. UA
1957   *The Bridge on the River Kwai*, Columbia
1958   *Gigi*, Arthur Freed Production, MGM
1959   *Ben-Hur*, MGM
1960   *The Apartment*, Mirisch Co. UA
1961   *West Side Story*, United Artists
1962   *Lawrence of Arabia*, Columbia
1963   *Tom Jones*, Woodfall Prod. UA-Lopert Pictures
1964   *My Fair Lady*, Warner Bros.
1965   *The Sound of Music*, 20th Century-Fox
1966   *A Man for All Seasons*, Columbia
1967   *In the Heat of the Night*, United Artists
1968   *Oliver*, Columbia
1969   *Midnight Cowboy*, United Artists

1970   *Patton*, 20th Century-Fox
1971   *The French Connection*, 20th Century-Fox
1972   *The Godfather*, Paramount
1973   *The Sting*, Universal
1974   *The Godfather, Part II*, Paramount
1975   *One Flew Over the Cuckoo's Nest*, United Artists
1976   *Rocky*, United Artists
1977   *Annie Hall*, United Artists
1978   *The Deer Hunter*, EMI
1979   *Kramer vs Kramer*, Columbia
1980   *Ordinary People*, Paramount
1981   *Chariots of Fire*, The Ladd Company/Warner Brothers
1982   *Ghandi*, Indo-British Films, Columbia
1983   *Terms of Endearment*, Paramount-UIP
1984   *Amadeus*, Orion

AWARD FOR BEST DIRECTOR

1927–28 Frank Borzage, *Seventh Heaven*, Lewis Milestone, *Two Arabian Knights*
1928–29 Frank Lloyd, *The Divine Lady*
1929–30 Lewis Milestone, *All Quiet on the Western Front*
1930–31 Norman Taurog, *Skippy*
1931–32 Frank Borzage, *Bad Girl*
1932–33 Frank Lloyd, *Cavalcade*
1934   Frank Capra, *It Happened One Night*
1935   John Ford, *The Informer*
1936   Frank Capra, *Mr Deeds Goes to Town*
1937   Leo McCarey, *The Awful Truth*
1938   Frank Capra, *You Can't Take It With You*
1939   Victor Fleming, *Gone with the Wind*
1940   John Ford, *The Grapes of Wrath*
1941   John Ford, *How Green Was My Valley*
1942   William Wyler, *Mrs Miniver*
1943   Michael Curtiz, *Casablanca*
1944   Leo McCarey, *Going My Way*

1945	Billy Wilder, *The Lost Weekend*	1965	Robert Wise, *Sound of Music*
1946	William Wyler, *The Best Years of Our Lives*	1966	Fred Zinnemann, *A Man for All Seasons*
1947	Elia Kazan, *Gentleman's Agreement*	1967	Mike Nichols, *The Graduate*
1948	John Huston, *Treasure of Sierra Madre*	1968	Sir Carol Reed, *Oliver*
1949	Joseph L. Mankiewicz, *A Letter to Three Wives*	1969	John Schlesinger, *Midnight Cowboy*
1950	Joseph L. Mankiewicz, *All About Eve*	1970	Franklin J. Schaffner, *Patton*
1951	George Stevens, *A Place in the Sun*	1971	William Friedkin, *The French Connection*
1952	John Ford, *The Quiet Man*	1972	Bob Fosse, *Cabaret*
1953	Fred Zinnemann, *From Here to Eternity*	1973	George Roy Hill, *The Sting*
1954	Elia Kazan, *On the Waterfront*	1974	Francis Ford Coppola, *The Godfather, Part II*
1955	Delbert Mann, *Marty*	1975	Milos Forman, *One Flew Over the Cuckoo's Nest*
1956	George Stevens, *Giant*	1976	John Avildsen, *Rocky*
1957	Sir David Lean, *The Bridge on the River Kwai*	1977	Woody Allen, *Annie Hall*
1958	Vincente Minnelli, *Gigi*	1978	Michael Cimino, *The Deer Hunter*
1959	William Wyler, *Ben-Hur*	1979	Robert Benton, *Kramer vs Kramer*
1960	Billy Wilder, *The Apartment*	1980	Robert Redford, *Ordinary People*
1961	Jerome Robbins, Robert Wise, *West Side Story*	1981	Warren Beatty, *Reds*
1962	Sir David Lean, *Lawrence of Arabia*	1982	Sir Richard Attenborough, *Ghandi*
1963	Tony Richardson, *Tom Jones*	1983	James L. Brooks, *Terms of Endearment*
1964	George Cukor, *My Fair Lady*	1984	Milos Forman, *Amadeus*

MATHEMATICS

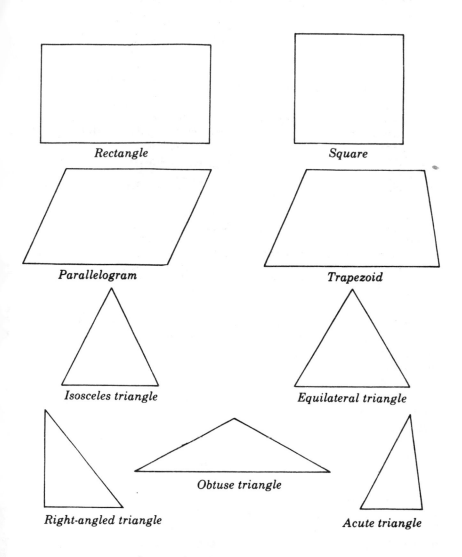

Rectangle

Square

Parallelogram

Trapezoid

Isosceles triangle

Equilateral triangle

Obtuse triangle

Right-angled triangle

Acute triangle

Mathematics is the science of space and number. Pure mathematics includes arithmetic, algebra, geometry, calculus and trigonometry. Applied mathematics is used in various sciences such as mechanics, physics and astronomy.

Very early peoples learned to count, measure and calculate for practical, everyday purposes. The pyramids of Egypt, built about 4,500 years ago, are miracles of precise measurement. Algebra was developed by astronomers in ancient Egypt, Babylon and India.

One of the earliest theoretical mathematicians was a Greek, Thales of Miletus (624–565 BC). He gave us the first theorems in plane geometry. His pupil, Pythagoras, established geometry as a science among his fellow Greeks. This paved the way for the school of Alexandrian mathematicians which produced Euclid and Archimedes in the 4th and 3rd centuries BC.

Euclid wrote 13 books called the *Elements*, nine of which were devoted to plane and solid geometry and four to arithmetic. Euclid's geometry books remained as standard textbooks until the present century.

The numerals we use today reached Europe about AD 1000. They came from the Arabs whose knowledge of mathematics was sought by European scholars. From the 15th century onwards mathematics began a continuous development in the West. Descartes connected algebra with geometry in 1637. Napier invented logarithms (published 1614) and the modern notation of fractions. Isaac Newton and Gottfried Leibnitz inde-

pendently invented the differential and integral calculus in the 17th century. The Russian mathematician Lobachevski (1793–1856) rejected Euclid's basic assumption and developed a non-Euclidian geometry; Einstein followed in the 20th century.

MATHEMATICAL SIGNS

equal to =
not equal to ≠
approximately equal to ≐ or ≏
identical to ≡
greater than >
not greater than ≯
less than <
not less than ≮
plus +
minus −
plus or minus ±
multiplication (times) ×
division ÷
brackets indicating that the quantities enclosed are to be treated together as forming a single term expression ( ), [ ], { }
varies as ∝
infinity ∞
square root √
per cent %
therefore ∴
because ∵
the difference between ∼
the sum of ∑
parallel to ∥
angle ∠
triangle △
perpendicular to ⊥
integration sign ∫

Algebra

Algebra is the branch of mathematics in which quantities are indicated by symbols in the solving problems. A quantity represented by a symbol is called a *variable*. Any collection of symbols, or numbers and symbols, combined by operations such as addition, subtraction, multiplication or division is an *expression*, e.g. 3a, x + y. An *equation* is a mathematical sentence saying that two expressions are equal, e.g. a + b^2 = 2(y). *Factors* are two or more expressions, the product of which is a given expression. A *term* is part of an expression connected to the rest by + or −, e.g. 3ab^2 + x − ay has three terms. An *exponent* is a number placed at the upper right of a number or variable indicating how many times it is to be used as a factor, e.g. a^2.

SOME ALGEBRAIC EQUATIONS

$$a(b + c) = ab + ac$$
$$a(b - c) = ab - ac$$
$$(a + b)(c + d) = ac + bc + ad + bd$$
$$(a - b)(c - d) = ac - bc - ad + bd$$
$$(a + b)^2 = a^2 + 2ab + b^2$$
$$(a - b)^2 = a^2 - 2ab + b^2$$
$$(a + b)(a - b) = a^2 - b^2$$
$$x^m \times x^n = x^{m+n}$$
$$x^m \div x^n = x^{m-n}$$
$$(x^m)^n = x^{mn}$$

Trigonometry

Trigonometry is a branch of mathematics whose principles are based on the fixed proportion of angles and sides in a right-angled triangle. The three principal ratios are:

$$\text{The sine (sin) of an angle} = \frac{\text{side opposite angle}}{\text{hypotenuse}}$$

$$\text{The cosine (cos) of an angle} = \frac{\text{side adjacent to angle}}{\text{hypotenuse}}$$

$$\text{The tangent (tan) of an angle} = \frac{\text{side opposite angle}}{\text{side adjacent to angle}}$$

Three further definitions are:

$$\frac{1}{\text{sine}} = \text{cosecant (cosec)}$$

$$\frac{1}{\text{cosine}} = \text{secant (sec)}$$

$$\frac{1}{\text{tangent}} = \text{cotangent (cot)}$$

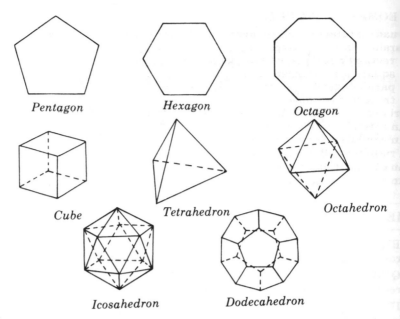

Pentagon   Hexagon   Octagon

Cube   Tetrahedron   Octahedron

Icosahedron   Dodecahedron

Geometry

Geometry is the branch of mathematics which deals with the properties of space. Kinds of geometry are:

Plane geometry is concerned with points, lines, circles and polygons on a flat surface. One can use it to prove that two triangles have the same shape or are of the same size; that two angles are equal or two lines are equal; and that two lines are parallel.

Solid geometry is the study of points, lines and planes in space. One can use it to find the dimensions of cubes, rectangular boxes, pyramids, spheres, cones, cylinders and prisms. Spherical geometry is particularly useful in navigation because the Earth is almost spherical in shape.

Analytic geometry solves problems by algebraical methods. To understand analytic geometry one needs to be able to understand graphs. Graphs can make an exact picture of an algebraic equation describing many kinds of lines and curves.

Non-Euclidian geometry breaks away from the basic assumptions of the Greek mathematician Euclid. Euclid's geometry describes the world as we see it and is useful for most practical purposes.

POLYGONS

A **pentagon** is a five-sided figure.
A **hexagon** is a six-sided figure.
An **octagon** is an eight-sided figure.

THE PLATONIC SOLIDS

These are any of the following regular polyhedra: **tetrahedron; cube; octahedron; icosahedron and dodecahedron.**

GEOMETRIC FIGURES

Quadrilaterals are closed figures with four straight sides. Squares, rectangles, parallelograms and trapezoids are all quadrilaterals.

A **rectangle** is a quadrilateral with four right angles and adjacent sides unequal.

A **square** is a quadrilateral with four right angles and equal sides.

A **parallelogram** is a quadrilateral whose opposite sides are parallel.

A **trapezoid** is a quadrilateral with one pair of sides parallel.

Triangles are closed figures with three straight sides.

An **isosceles** triangle has two sides the same length, also two equal angles.

An **equilateral** triangle has all sides equal, and all angles equal.

A **right-angled** triangle has one angle of 90°.

An **obtuse** triangle has one angle larger than 90°.

An **acute** triangle has all angles less than 90°.

MEASUREMENTS

TRIANGLE
Area $= \frac{1}{2}$ ah

SQUARE
Area $= a^2$

CIRCLE
Diameter (d) $= 2r$
Circumference $= 2\pi r$
Area $= \pi r^2$
(N.B. the constant $\pi = 3.1415$)

TRAPEZOID
Area $= \frac{1}{2}(m + n)h$

CUBE
Surface area $= 6a^2$
Volume $= a^3$

SPHERE
Surface area $= 4\pi r^2$
Volume $= \frac{4}{3}\pi r^3$

CONE
Curved surface area $= \pi r l$
Volume $= \frac{1}{3}\pi r^2 h$
Total surface area $= \pi r l + 2\pi r$
$\quad\quad\quad\quad\quad\quad = \pi r(l + r)$

CYLINDER
Curved surface area $= 2\pi r h$
Total surface area $= 2\pi r h + 2\pi r^2$
$\quad\quad\quad\quad\quad\quad = 2\pi r(h + r)$

PYRAMID
Surface area $= a^2 + 2la$
Volume $= \frac{1}{3}a^2 h$

ELLIPSE
Area $= \pi ab$

Triangle

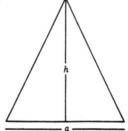

Square

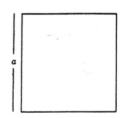

Circle

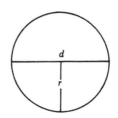

373

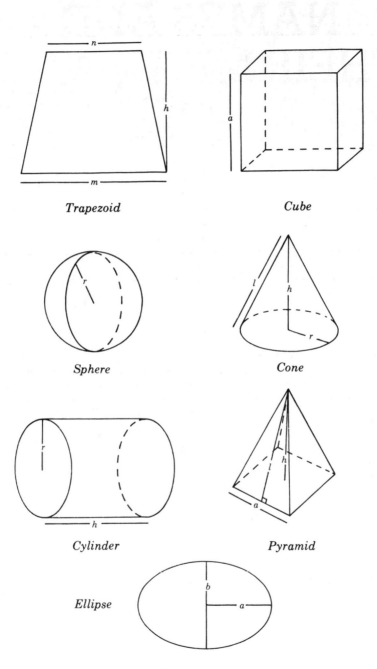

Trapezoid

Cube

Sphere

Cone

Cylinder

Pyramid

Ellipse

NAMES AND THEIR MEANINGS

NAME	MEANING
Barbara	Strange, foreign (Greek)
Beatrice, Beatrix	Bringer of joy (Latin)
Belinda	Snake
Bella	Beautiful (Italian) (pet form of names such as Isobel or Arabella)
Berenice	Bringer of Victory (Greek)
Bertha	Bright (Teutonic)
Beverley	Beaver stream (from an English surname derived from a place name
Brenda	Sword (Irish)
Bridget	The high one (Old Irish)
Bronwen	White breast (Welsh)
Candida	White (Latin)
Carol, Caroline	feminine forms of Charles, 'Man'
Catherine – see Katharine	
Cecilia, Cecily, Cicely	Blind (from the Roman family name, *Caecilius*, from the root *caecum*)
Celia	Heavenly (Latin)
Charlotte	feminine form of Charles, 'Man'
Charmian	A little joy (Greek)
Chloe	A green shoot (Greek)
Christina, Christine	Of Christ
Clara, Clare, Clarice, Clarinda, Clarissa	Bright, clear (Latin)
Colette – see Nicole	
Constance	Constancy
Cynthia	Of Cynthus (Mount Cynthus in Greece)
Daphne	Bay or laurel (Greek)
Deborah	Bee (Hebrew)
Deirdre	The raging one or the broken-hearted one (Irish)
Denise	from the Greek Dionysos, god of wine (French)
Diana	Roman Moon goddess
Dilys	Certain, perfect, genuine (Welsh)
Dinah	Dedicated (Hebrew)
Dolores	Sorrows (Spanish)
Dora – see Dorothy	
Dorcas	Roe or gazelle (Greek)
Doreen	probably an Irish version of Dorothy
Doris	A Dorian girl (from a region in Greece)
Dorothy, Dorothea	Gift of God (Greek)
Dulcie	Sweet (Latin)
Edith	Rich, happy (Anglo-Saxon)
Edna	possibly from a Hebrew word meaning rejuvenation
Eileen, Aileen	Irish equivalent of Helen or possibly Evelyn
Eithne, Aine	Fire (Celtic)
Elaine	Old French form of Helen
Eleanor, Leonora, Ellen, Ella	forms of Helen

NAME	MEANING
Elfreda	Elf, and strength (Anglo-Saxon)
Elizabeth, Elisabeth, Elsa	My God is satisfaction (Hebrew)
Elspeth	Scottish form of Elizabeth
Emily	from *Aemilus*, a Roman family name
Emma	Whole (Teutonic)
Ena	Fire (Irish)
Enid	Life, soul (Welsh)
Erica	female form of Eric, 'Kingly'
Esmé	Loved (a Scottish name derived from the French *Aimé*)
Esmeralda	Emerald (Spanish)
Estelle	Star (French)
Esther	Star (Persian) from the goddess Astarte
Ethel	Noble (Anglo-Saxon)
Eunice	Well and victory (Greek)
Eva, Eve	Life (Hebrew)
Evelyn, Evelina	from the surnames Aveline, Eveling and Evelyn
Fay	an abbreviation of Faith
Felicity	Happiness (Latin)
Fenella	White shoulder (Gaelic)
Fiona	Fair (Gaelic)
Flora	Roman goddess of Flowers
Florence	from the city, also Blooming (Latin)
Frances	feminine form of Francis, 'Frenchman'
Freda – *see* Winifred	
Gail	diminitive of Abigail
Gemma	Gem (Latin)
Gertrude	Spear, and strength (Teutonic)
Gillian	English form of Julian (a)
Gladys	Welsh form of Claudia, 'Lame'
Gloria	Glory (Latin)
Glennis, Glynis	Valley
Greta	Swedish abbreviation of Margaret
Gwendolen, Gwendolyn, Gwenda	White (Welsh)
Gwyneth	Blessed, happy (Welsh)
Hannah	God has favoured me (Hebrew)
Harriet	English form of the French Henrietta
Helen, Helena	The bright one (Greek)
Henrietta	female form of Henry, 'Ruler'
Hester – *see* Esther	
Hilary	Cheerful (Latin)
Hilda	War, battle (Teutonic)
Honor	Reputation (Anglo-Norman)
Ida	Labour (Teutonic)
Imogen	Daughter, girl (Old English)
Irene	from Eirene, the Greek goddess of peace
Isabel, Isabella Isobel	French and Spanish forms of Elizabeth
Ita	Irish form of Ida

NAME	MEANING
Jacqueline	the feminine form of Jacques (James), 'Follower' (French)
Jane	feminine form of John, 'Jehovah has favoured'
Janet, Jean	derived from Jane
Jemima	Dove (Hebrew)
Jennifer	from Guenevere King Arthur's wife (Welsh)
Jessica	He beholds (Hebrew)
Jessie	Scottish diminutive of Janet
Jill	pet form of Gillian
Joan, Joanna, Johanna	derived from Jane
Jocelyn, Joscelin	derived from surnames based on the folk name Goth
Josephine	feminine form of Joseph, 'Jehovah added'
Joyce	derived from the Breton saint, Jodoc
Judith	Jewess (Hebrew)
Julia	feminine form of Julius
June	the name of the month
Karen	Danish form of Katharine
Katharine, Katherine	Pure (Greek)
Kathleen – see Katharine	
Kay, Kitty	pet forms of Katharine
Laura	Laurel tree (Latin)
Leah	Cow (Hebrew)
Lena – see Helen	
Lesley	from a Scottish surname
Lettice	Gladness (Latin)
Linda	Serpent (Teutonic)
Lindsay	from a Scottish surname
Lois	the name of the grandmother of Timothy, meaning unknown (Greek)
Lola	diminutive of Dolores
Lorna	name invented by R. D. Blackmore in his novel *Lorna Doon*
Louisa, Louise	feminine form of Louis
Lucia, Lucy	Light (Latin)
Lydia	Woman of Lydia (Greek)
Lynn	Lake (Celtic)
Mabel	form of Amabel
Madeline, Madeleine	Woman of Magdala (Hebrew)
Madge – see Margaret	
Maire	Irish form of Mary
Marcia	feminine form of Mark, Marcus
Margaret	Pearl (Greek)
Margery, Marjorie	forms of Margaret
Marie	French form of Mary
Marilyn	American form of Mary
Marina	Of the sea (Latin)
Marion, Marian	diminutive of Mary or Mary + Ann
Martha	Lady (Aramaic)

NAME	MEANING
Mary	Wished-for child (Hebrew)
Matilda, Maud, Maude	Might, strength and battle (Teutonic)
Maureen	Irish diminutive of Maire (Mary)
Mavis	Song-thrush (Anglo-Saxon)
Maxine	feminine form of Maximilian (French)
May	pet form of Margaret or Mary, or the name of the month
Meg – *see* Margaret	
Melanie	Black or dark complexioned (Greek)
Melissa	Bee (Greek)
Merle	Blackbird (French)
Michelle	feminine form of the French Michel (Michael)
Mildred	Mild and strength (Anglo-Saxon)
Millicent	Work and strong (Anglo-Saxon)
Minnie	diminutive of Wilhelmina
Mirabel	Wonderful, glorious (Latin)
Miranda	Worthy of admiration (Latin)
Miriam	Longed-for, desired (Hebrew)
Moira, Moyra	forms of Maire, Irish for Mary
Molly – *see* Mary	
Mona	Noble (Irish)
Monica	from mother of St Augustine
Morag	Great (Gaelic)
Muriel, Meriel	Sea and bright (Celtic)
Naomi	Pleasant (Hebrew)
Natalie	Birth (French, German, Russian and other European countries form is Natasha)
Nelly	pet form of Ellen, Eleanor and Helen
Nessie, Nesta	Welsh diminutive of Agnes
Nicola, Nicolette, Nicole	feminine forms of Nicholas, 'Victory of the people'
Nona	Ninth (Latin)
Nora, Norah	abbreviated form of Honora (Irish)
Noreen	Irish diminutive of Nora
Norma	Precept, pattern (Latin)
Olga	Holy (a Russian name of Norse origin)
Olivia, Olive	from the tree
Olwen	White track (Welsh)
Oonagh – *see* Una	
Pamela	a name invented in a classic novel by Sir Philip Sidney
Patricia	feminine form of Patrick, 'Noble'
Pauline	feminine form of Paul, 'Small'
Peggy – *see* Margaret	
Penelope	Bobbin or weaver, faithful wife of Odysseus (Greek)
Philippa	feminine form of Philip, 'Lover of horses'
Phoebe	The shining one (Greek)
Phyllis	Leafy (Greek)
Polly – *see* Mary	

NAME	MEANING
Priscilla	feminine form of the Roman family name *Priscus* (*priscus*, meaning former or old)
Rachel	Ewe (Hebrew)
Rebecca	Heifer (Hebrew)
Rhoda	Rose (Greek)
Rita – *see* Margaret	
Roma	the name of the city
Rosalind	Horse and serpent (Teutonic)
Rosamund, Rosamond	Horse and protection (Teutonic)
Ruth	Vision of beauty or friend (Hebrew)
Sadie – *see* Sarah	
Sally – *see* Sarah	
Sandra	diminutive of Alessandra (Alexandra)
Sarah, Sara	Princess (Hebrew)
Selina	The Moon (Greek) or Heaven (Latin)
Sharon	biblical place name
Sheena	Gaelic form of Jane
Sheila	Irish form of Celia, from Cecilia
Shirley	surname derived from a place name
Sibyl, Sybil	a prophetess in ancient Greece
Sonia, Sonya	Russian diminutive of Sophia
Sophia, Sophie	Wisdom (Greek)
Stella	Star (Latin)
Susan, Susanna,	Lily (Hebrew)
Tabitha	Roe or Gazelle, Aramaic equivalent of Dorcas
Teresa, Theresa	Reaper (Greek) or from the name of an island near Crete (Greek)
Tess, Tessa	pet forms of Theresa
Thelma	an invented name in a novel by Marie Corelli
Tina	pet form of names such as Christina
Tracy	diminutive of Theresa
Trixie – *see* Beatrice	
Una, Oona	probably based on the Irish word for lamb
Ursula	She-bear (Latin)
Valerie	from Roman family name *Valerius*, probably derived from the word for strong
Vanessa	a name invented by Jonathan Swift
Vera	Faith (Russian)
Veronica	Of a true image (Latin)
Victoria	Victory (Latin)
Viola	Violet (Latin)
Virginia	from the Roman family name *Virginius*
Vivien	Alive (Latin) or derived from Ninian, an Irish saint
Wanda	Stem or stock (Teutonic)
Wendy	first used by J. M. Barrie in his play *Peter Pan*
Winifred	White wave or stream (Celtic)
Yvonne	feminine form of Yvon, 'Yew'
Zoë	Life (Greek)

BOYS' NAMES

NAME	MEANING
Abraham	Father of a multitude (Hebrew)
Adam	Red (from colour of skin) or Man of earth (Hebrew)
Adrian	Of the Adriatic (Latin)
Allan, Allen, Alan	Harmony, cheerful (Celtic)
Alastair – *see* **Alexander**	
Albert	Noble and bright (German)
Alec – *see* **Alexander**	
Alexander	Protector of men (Greek)
Alexis	Helper, defender (Greek)
Alfred	Elf counsel (Anglo-Saxon)
Algernon	With whiskers (Norman-French)
Alick – *see* **Alexander**	
Ambrose	Pertaining to the Immortals (Latin)
Andrew	Manly (Latin)
Angel	Messenger (Latin)
Angus	One choice (Scottish)
Anthony, Antony	Worthy, strong (Latin)
Archibald	Genuine, simple and bold (Teutonic)
Arnold	Eagle power (Teutonic)
Arthur	Bear (Celtic) or from Roman family name, *Artorius*
Aubrey	Elf ruler (from French form of the Old German Alberich)
Augustus	Venerable, consecrated (Latin)
Barnabas	Son of exhortation or consolation (Hebrew)
Barry	Spear (Irish)
Bartholomew	Son of Talmi (Hebrew)
Basil	Kingly (Greek)
Benedict	Blessed (Latin)
Benjamin	Son of good fortune (Hebrew)
Bernard	Bear and hard.(Teutonic)
Bertram	Bright raven (Teutonic)
Beverley	Beaver stream (from an English place name)
Brendan	Stinking hair (Irish)
Brian	Hill or strong, powerful (Celtic)
Bruce	surname of Robert the Bruce, King of Scotland
Bruno	Brown (Teutonic)
Caleb	Bold, impetuous (Hebrew)
Cecil	from the Roman family name *Caecilius* (the root *caecus* means blind)
Cedric	name first used by Sir Walter Scott in his novel *Ivanhoe*
Charles	Man (Teutonic)
Christian	Belonging to Christ
Christopher	Christ-bearer (Greek)

NAME	MEANING
Claud, Claude	from a Roman family name, probably derived from *claudus*, lame
Clement	Mild, merciful (Latin)
Clifford	derived from a place name
Clive	surname of Robert Clive of India
Colin	derived from Nicholas (French)
Conrad	Bold counsel (Teutonic)
Cornelius	from a Roman family name, probably derived from *cornu*, horn
Craig	Crag, stony hill (Celtic)
Cyril	Lord, master (Greek)
Daniel	God has judged (Hebrew)
David	Beloved (Hebrew)
Denis, Dennis	Of Dionysos, god of wine (Greek)
Derek	The people's ruler (Teutonic)
Desmond	Worldly, sophisticated (Celtic)
Dick – *see* Richard	
Dominic	Belonging to God (Latin)
Donald	World mighty or proud chief (Celtic)
Dougal	Black stranger (Celtic)
Douglas	Dark blue (Celtic river name)
Duncan	Brown warrior (Old Irish)
Ebenezer	Stone of help (Hebrew)
Edgar	Happy, rich and spear (Anglo-Saxon)
Edmund, Edmond	Happy, rich and protection (Anglo-Saxon)
Edward	Happy, rich and guardian (Anglo-Saxon)
Edwin	Happy, rich and friend (Anglo-Saxon)
Egbert	Sword bright (Anglo-Saxon)
Emanuel	God is with us (Hebrew)
Enoch	Skilled (Hebrew)
Erasmus	Beloved, desired (Greek)
Eric	Kingly (Teutonic)
Ernest	Sincere, earnest (Teutonic)
Esmond	Grace, beauty and protection (Anglo-Saxon)
Eugene	Noble, well-born (Greek)
Eustace	Tranquil or fruitful (Greek)
Everard	Boar and hard (Teutonic)
Ewen	Well born (Celtic)
Ezra	Help (Hebrew)
Felix	Happy (Latin)
Ferdinand	Journey and venture, risk (Teutonic)
Fergus	Man and choice (Old Irish)
Francis	Frenchman or free
Frank	diminutive of Francis
Frederick	Peace and ruler (Teutonic)
Gabriel	Strong man of God (Hebrew)
Gareth	first used by Tennyson in his *Gareth and Lynnet*
Gary	Mighty spear (Anglo-Saxon)
Gavin	White hawk (Welsh or Teutonic)

NAME	MEANING
Gene – *see* **Eugene**	
Geoffrey	Land and peace (Teutonic)
George	Farmer, tiller of the soil (Greek)
Gerald	Spear and rule (Teutonic)
Gerard	Spear and hard (Teutonic)
Gilbert	Pledge and bright (Teutonic)
Giles	Kid (Latin)
Glyn	Valley (Welsh)
Godfrey	God's peace (Teutonic)
Godwin	God's friend (Anglo-Saxon)
Gordon	From the cornered hill (Scottish family name)
Graham	From the grey home (Scottish family name)
Gregory	Watchful (Greek)
Guy	Guide, leader (French)
Hamish	Scottish form of James
Harold	Host, army and power (Anglo-Saxon)
Hector	Holding fast (Greek)
Henry	House, home and ruler (Teutonic)
Herbert	Host, army and bright (Teutonic)
Hew – *see* **Hugh'**	
Horace	Roman family name
Howard	probably from the surname, meaning heart, soul and protection
Hubert	Heart, soul and bright (Teutonic)
Hugh, Hugo	Heart, mind
Humphrey, Humphry	Giant and peace (Teutonic)
Ian	Gaelic form of John
Isaac	God may laugh (Hebrew)
Ivor, Ifor	meaning uncertain (Old Norse)
Jack	pet name for John
Jacob	God supplanted (Hebrew)
James	form of Jacob
Jeremiah, Jeremy	May Jehovah raise up, exhalt (Hebrew)
Jerome	Sacred name (Greek)
Jesse	Jehovah exists (Hebrew)
Job	Pious and persecuted (Hebrew)
Jocelyn, Joscelin	derived from surnames based on the folk name Goth
Joel	Jehovah is God (Hebrew)
John	Jehovah has favoured (Hebrew)
Jolyon – *see* **Julian**	
Jonah, Jonas	Dove (Hebrew)
Jonathan	Jehovah has given (Hebrew)
Joseph	Jehovah added (Hebrew)
Joshua	Jehovah is generous (Hebrew)
Julian	a derivative of Julius
Julius	a Roman family name, the most famous member being Julius Caesar
Justin	Just (Latin)

NAME	MEANING
Keith	Place (a Scottish surname derived from a place name)
Kenneth	Handsome (Celtic)
Kevin	Comely birth (Celtic)
Laurence, Lawrence	Laurel or bay tree (Latin)
Lee	Meadow (derived from the surname)
Leo	Lion (Latin)
Leonard	Lion and hardy, bold (Teutonic)
Leopold	People and bold (Teutonic)
Leslie	from a Scottish surname
Lionel	Young lion (French)
Luke, Lucas	Of Lucania (Latin)
Magnus	Great (Latin)
Malcolm	Servant or disciple of Columba (Celtic)
Mark, Marcus	derived from the Roman god Mars
Martin	Of Mars (Latin)
Matthew	Gift from God (Hebrew)
Maurice	Dark, a Moor (Latin)
Maximilian	a combination of two Roman names, *Maximus* and *Aemilianus* (German)
Mervyn	probably derived from the surname
Michael	Who is like God (Hebrew)
Miles	Merciful (Slavonic, Norman-French)
Montague	from the Norman surname
Morris – *see* Maurice	
Mortimer	from the Norman surname
Nathan	Gift (Hebrew)
Nathaniel	God has given (Hebrew)
Ned – *see* Edward	
Neil – *see* Nigel	
Neville	from the Norman surname
Nicholas	Victory of the people (Greek)
Nigel	Black (Latin) or Champion (Irish)
Noel	Birthday (Old French)
Norman	Northman
Oliver	Elf host (Anglo-Saxon) and from olive tree
Oscar	A god and spear (Teutonic)
Oswald	A god and power (Teutonic)
Patrick	Nobleman (Latin)
Paul	Small (Latin)
Percival	Pierce the valley (French)
Percy	Norman family surname, taken from the village of Perci
Peregrine	Stranger, a traveller, a pilgrim (Latin)
Peter	Rock (Greek)
Philip	Lover of horses (Greek)
Quentin, Quintin	a derivative of Latin word *quintus*, meaning fifth
Ralph	Counsel and wolf (Anglo-Saxon)
Randolph	Shield and wolf (Anglo-Saxon)

NAME	MEANING
Ray	derivative of Raymond
Raymond	Wise protection (Teutonic)
Reginald	Counsel, might and hard (Teutonic)
Rex	King (Latin)
Richard	Ruler and hard (Teutonic)
Robert	Fame and bright (Teutonic)
Robin – *see* **Robert**	
Roderick	Fame and rule (Teutonic)
Rodney	Renowned (Teutonic)
Roger	Fame and spear (Teutonic)
Roland	Fame of the land (Teutonic)
Rolf	Fame and wolf (Teutonic)
Rollo – *see* **Rolf**	
Rory	Red (Irish)
Roy	Red (Gaelic)
Rufus	Red-haired (Latin)
Rupert	a form of Robert
Samuel	Name of God (Hebrew)
Sean	Irish form of John
Sebastian	Man of Sebastia (a city, meaning venerable, in Greece)
Selwyn	House and friend (an old English surname)
Sidney	from the surname of an English family
Simon	Hearkening or little hyena (Hebrew)
Solomon	Little man of peace (Hebrew)
Stanley	surname derived from a place name
Stewart, Stuart	name of the royal house of Scotland and an extensive clan originating in the office of steward, the manager of a large household
Teddy – *see* **Edward**	
Terence	from the Roman family name
Theodore	God's gift (Greek)
Theophilus	beloved of God
Thomas	Twin (Aramaic)
Timothy	Honour, respect and god (Greek)
Tobias, Toby	God is good (Hebrew)
Tony – *see* **Anthony**	
Trevor	from the surname
Tristram	Tumult, din (Celtic)
Valentine	Strong, healthy (Latin)
Vernon	a surname and a place name in France
Victor	Conqueror (Latin)
Vincent	Conquering (Latin)
Vivian	Alive (Latin)
Wallace	a Scottish surname equivalent to the English and Welsh, Walsh
Walter	Rule and folk (Teutonic)
Wilfred	Will and peace (Anglo-Saxon)
William	Will and helmet (Teutonic)

FORTUNE-
TELLING

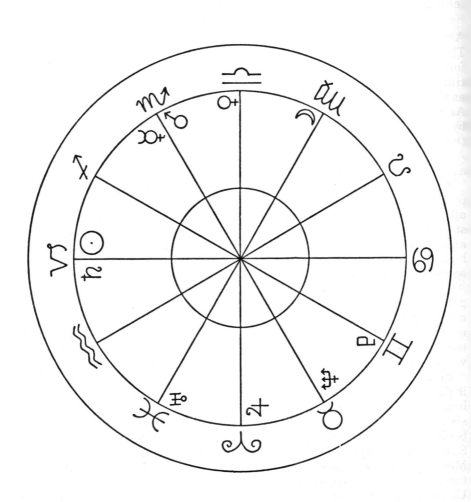

Most people at some time in their lives are interested in fortune-telling. The time-honoured art of foretelling the future is, broadly speaking, called divination. Its methods include all magical and supernatural means – anything outside the bounds of strict reason'. Despite the advance of science, some means of fortune-telling are still seriously regarded.

Astrology

This is probably one of the oldest forms of fortune-telling. In ancient times it included what is now known as the science of astronomy. Astrology was probably originated by the ancient Babylonians and then spread to Greece, Egypt and Arabia. India also has been claimed as an original source.

Astrologers believe that a person's characteristics and life are affected by the alignment of the stars and planets at the exact time and place of her birth. Here, however, fortune-tellers and serious astrologers disagree. Astrologers regard it more as a genuine science rather than as a means of foretelling exact future events. It studies the probable trend of the conditions a person will experience in her life.

In astrology the celestial sphere is divided into 12 parts called houses, six above the horizon and six below. The seven heavenly bodies known to the ancients, the Sun, Saturn, Jupiter, Mars, Venus, Mercury and the Moon, and the three recently discovered planets, Uranus, Neptune and Pluto are used. The zodiac is the belt of the celestial sphere, representing the path taken by the Sun as it appears to circle the Earth. It is divided into 12 sections, each with its own sign and name and each ruling one part of the human body. For this reason, in the past, astronomy was also linked with medicine, and even today astrology is used to indicate health trends. The word zodiac is linked with zoology, and several of the names are those of animals. The houses of astrology are quite distinct from the 12 divisions of the zodiac, though these too are sometimes termed 'houses'. The astrological reading of the heavenly bodies in relation to the divisions of the zodiac at the time of someone's birth is known as that person's horoscope.

Cartomancy

This is fortune-telling by means of cards. Ordinary playing cards are very commonly used. Hearts traditionally represent the emotions and affairs of the heart; Clubs friendship; Diamonds financial and home affairs; Spades matters of duty and will-power. The cards are laid out in a pattern and then a reading is taken. Several variations of pattern exist including the 'cross', 'wheel of fortune' and the 'mystic star'.

A more famous pack of cards used for cartomancy is the traditional tarot pack. These cards were introduced into Europe in the 14th century by gypsies, to whom the 78 cards have a particular significance. Fifty-six of the cards are the same as those found in a normal pack, except that the suits have different names; Cups instead of Hearts, Wands instead of Clubs,

Pentacles instead of Diamonds and Swords instead of Spades. The remaining 22 cards are trumps. Each trump has a picture such as the Devil, the Tower, the Hanged Man, and so on. The origin of these symbols and their meaning is unknown. The readings generally follow a set convention though variations exist.

Crystal-gazing (Scrying)

Scrying is seeing into the future by means of the traditional crystal ball but a mirror, pool of ink or water, or any shiny or reflecting surface can be used as well. These help the fortune-teller to concentrate. Imagination plays a great part as pictures are conjured up much in the same way as one might see images in the flames of a fire. Self-hypnotism also cannot be ruled out. In rural districts, particularly in the recent past, girls would gaze into a mirror in order to 'see' the face of her future husband-to-be, the wish probably being father to the thought. There are few records of great accuracy and in general crystal-gazing is more a part of fairground fun than a serious pursuit.

Dreams

These have been used throughout the ages to divine the future and in olden days dream 'interpreters' were highly paid. It could be a rather precarious occupation if one happened to be 'interpreter' to an emperor or king, for anyone who made a wrong interpretation would fall from favour. Classical literature gives many examples of dreams foretelling the future, though there have also been some

historically recorded instances of surprisingly accurate forecasts. It is said, for example, that by a dream Abraham Lincoln foresaw his own assassination. Many book: have been written about the interpretation of dreams, certain symbols being taken as a warning or sign of coming events. Unfortunately, these symbols are not always given single meanings; for instance, at least three possible interpretations arise from a dream about snakes. Different countries tend to have different conventions and the meaning of a symbol may differ from one area to another. In psychoanalysis dreams are regarded more seriously but on a very different basis. In this case dreams are used to explore a person's subconscious. The two approaches should not be confused.

Palmistry

Again a very ancient art, palmistry was used centuries ago by Indians, Greeks, Egyptians and Chinese. Gypsies in particular are famed for it. Some people regard it as a serious science, making claims which their opponents equally hotly deny.

A palmist reads a person's character and the main events of her life from the lines and general contour of the hand. Different parts of the hand are linked with the planets: the thumb with Venus, the first finger with Jupiter, the second with Saturn, the third with Apollo (Sun) and the fourth with Mercury. The 'mounts' are the slight swellings on the palm and are named after the Moon and Mars. The chief lines are those of Life,

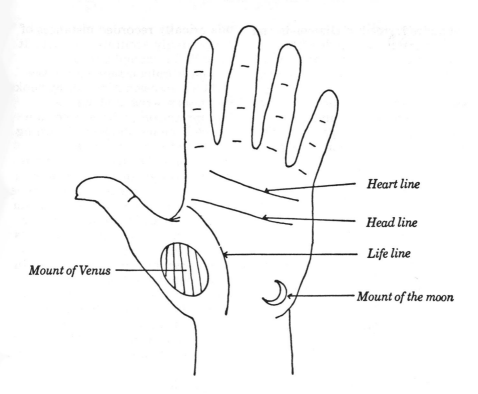

Heart line

Head line

Life line

Mount of the moon

Mount of Venus

Heart and Head, but other minor marks are taken into consideration. A full reading is very complicated. The left hand is usually read but the right is also studied, in some cases.

Palmistry was once regarded very seriously but it later fell into disrepute because of the way unscrupulous and often inept palmists used it to exploit believers, preying on fear and superstition. A law was brought in to prevent this and a palmist could be charged as a vagrant. Various interesting legal cases are on record.

Necromancy
This, often regarded as a 'black art', was a way of divining the future by calling up the spirits of the dead. The Bible gives one well-quoted example, that of Saul and the Witch of Endor. In England, particularly, this art was employed to reveal the whereabouts of hidden treasure and the diviner would sometimes end up in the pillory, accused of fraud. If it was thought that the Devil had assisted the diviner, the matter was regarded more seriously and cases are mentioned in old witch-hunt trials, though strangely enough the witches were never punished too severely. It seems to have been a slightly more acceptable form of black magic, probably because the hunt for buried treasure was a

motive very easily understood and even approved of. In a different context the 'witch' would have had a much rougher time.

Numerology
This is the 'science' of lucky numbers and lucky days. Numerical values are attached to the letters of the alphabet and the name of the fortune-seeker is then translated into figures. The method is shown below. The lucky number is obtained by adding all the numbers together until only a single digit remains. The numbers of a birth date can also be added. Today numerology is more a form of amusement than serious fortune-telling.

Omens
They were regarded as signs of coming events. Signs such as the flight of birds, movement of insects, certain trees, plants and the behaviour of certain animals were thought to be warnings of future happenings. Traditionally a family would adopt one standard omen which was always associated with a coming event or disaster. You may even know of some yourself, though not regard them too seriously. They are generally passed down and many have become quite famous. Norse mythology contains numerous references to omens.

Some people still tell fortunes by means of tea-leaves left in cups. The shapes formed by the leaves in the bottom of the cup are interpreted as symbols or omens. Again, it is chiefly a form of amusement today, though not all omens have been regarded lightly.

Oracle
The most famous oracle was at Delphi in Greece. The oracle was in a chasm near the temple of the Sun god, Apollo, where a priestess sat on a three-legged stool called a tripod. After going into an ecstatic trance, she answered questions asked by those seeking guidance for the future. The answers were deliberately ambiguous (allowing for several interpretations), which rather let the priestess off the hook if she made a mistake. This kind of 'insurance policy' has been used by many diviners.

The powers of the priestess were said to come from fumes and the strange atmospheric conditions arising from a river running at the foot of the chasm. Before the priestess was installed there, several people had committed suicide by casting themselves down the chasm, having been affected in some way by these fumes. Other diviners have similarly used a trancelike state to relate messages and visions relating to the future.

NUMEROLOGY

1	2	3	4	5	6	7	8	9
A	B	C	D	E	F	G	H	I
J	K	L	M	N	O	P	Q	R
S	T	U	V	W	X	Y	Z	

Working from the above, Tom Smith would have the numbers
$2+6+4+1+4+9+2+8=36$.
$36 = 3+6 = 9$ (the final total and thus the lucky number)

The final result must always be a single digit, numerals always being added together until this is arrived at. The Christian name used is the one by which the person is generally known, being Tom rather than Thomas in the above example. The answer would have been different for Thomas.

ASTROLOGICAL MEANING OF THE PLANETS

Jupiter	♃	Wisdom
Saturn	♄	Responsibility
Sun	☉	Vitality
Mercury	☿	Intelligence
Venus	♀	Love
Mars	♂	Energy
Moon	☽	Feeling
Uranus	♅	Change
Neptune	♆	Imagination
Pluto	♇	Power

DISTANCES BETWEEN PLANETS ALSO SHOWN BY SYMBOLS

0°	☌	Conjunction
30°	⚺	Semi-sextile
60°	⚹	Sextile
90°	□	Square
120°	△	Trine
150°	⚻	Quincunx
180°	☍	Opposition

SIGNS OF THE ZODIAC AND RELATION WITH HUMAN BODY

Sign	Symbol	Body Part	Date
Aries	♈	Head	March 20
Taurus	♉	Throat	April 20
Gemini	♊	Lungs	May 21
Cancer	♋	Stomach	June 21
Leo	♌	Heart	July 22
Virgo	♍	Bowels	August 23
Libra	♎	Kidneys	September 23
Scorpio	♏	Bladder	October 23
Sagittarius	♐	Thighs	November 22
Capricorn	♑	Knees	December 21
Aquarius	♒	Ankles	January 21
Pisces	♓	Feet	February 19

The Sun enters the signs of the zodiac on approximately the above dates throughout the year.

GENERAL
INFORMATION

Knots

The reef knot is used for tying together two ropes of equal size. It tends to slip if the ropes are of unequal diameter. These should be tied with a sheet bend.

The sheet bend is used for tying together two ropes of different diameters. If the end is passed round again the result is a double sheet bend.

The clove hitch is a knot by which a rope is secured around another rope or a rod that it crosses. When fastened it will slip neither up nor down.

A bowline makes a fixed loop at the end of a rope that will never slip. It can be used for making fast to a ring, post, bollard or cleat.

The sheepshank is used for shortening a rope.

The figure of eight is a knot used for stopping a rope running through a block.

The half-hitch is used to tie a rope to a ring or post.

The round turn and two half-hitches holds a rope to a ring or post even more securely than a simple half-hitch.

The timber hitch is used for dragging things along, such as a piece of wood.

The wall knot is used to finish off a rope that is unravelling.

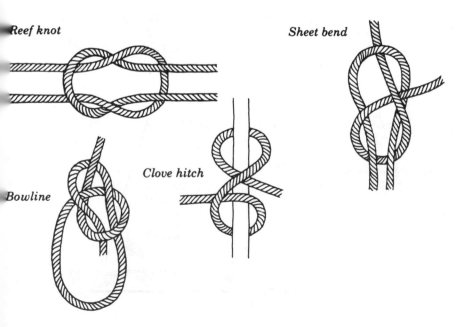

Reef knot

Sheet bend

Bowline

Clove hitch

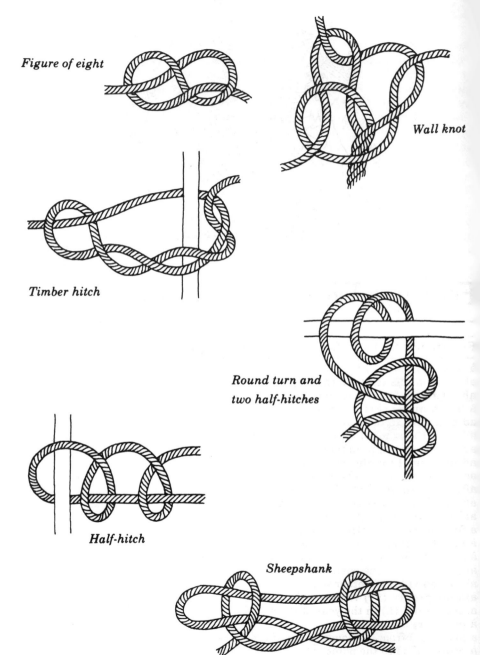

Figure of eight

Wall knot

Timber hitch

Round turn and two half-hitches

Half-hitch

Sheepshank

394

Foreign Words and Phrases

Fr = French L = Latin Ger = German It = Italian

à bas **(Fr)** down with
ab incunabilis **(L)** from the cradle
ab initio **(L)** from the beginning
à bon marché **(Fr)** cheap; a good bargain
ad astra **(L)** to the stars
ad hoc **(L)** arranged for this purpose; special
ad infinitum **(L)** to infinity
ad interim **(L)** in the meantime
ad nauseam **(L)** to disgust, satiety
affaire d'amour **(Fr)** a love affair
affaire de coeur **(Fr)** an affair of the heart
affaire d'honneur **(Fr)** an affair of honour; a duel
a fortiori **(L)** with stronger reason
à la belle étoile **(Fr)** under the stars
à la mode **(Fr)** according to the fashion, custom
al fresco **(It)** in the open air
alter ego **(L)** one's other self
amour-propre **(Fr)** vanity; self-love
anno mundi **(L)** in the year of the world
à pied **(Fr)** on foot
a priori **(L)** from the cause to the effect (in reasoning)
à propos **(Fr)** to the point
au contraire **(Fr)** on the contrary

au courant (Fr) fully acquainted with
au fait (Fr) well acquainted with
au fond (Fr) at bottom
auf wiedersehen (Ger) goodbye till we meet again
au revoir (Fr) goodbye till we meet again
à votre santé (Fr) to your health
bel esprit (Fr) a wit
ben trovato (It) cleverly invented
bête noire (Fr) a black beast; one's abomination
billet doux (Fr) a love letter
bona fide (L) genuine
bonhomie (Fr) good nature
bon mot (Fr) witty saying
bonne bouche (Fr) a tasty titbit
bon vivant (Fr) a good liver; gourmand
carte blanche (Fr) a blank paper; full discretionary powers
casus belli (L) that which causes or justifies a war
causa sine qua non (L) an indispensible cause or condition
cause célèbre (Fr) a law-suit that excites much attention
ceteris paribus (L) other things being equal
chacun son goût (Fr) everyone to his taste
comme il faut (Fr) as it should be; well-bred
compos mentis (L) in right mind
contretemps (Fr) an unlucky accident or hitch
corrigenda (L) things to be corrected
coup de grâce (Fr) a finishing stroke
coup d'état (Fr) a violent or illegal change in the government of a country
de facto (L) in point of fact, actual
dei gratia (L) by God's grace
de jure (L) rightful by law
de profundis (L) out of the depths
de rigueur (Fr) required by etiquette
deus ex machina (L) providential intervention at a critical moment
en bloc (Fr) in a lump; wholesale
en famille (Fr) at home, among one's family
enfant terrible (Fr) a terrible child, who asks awkward questions for example
en masse (Fr) all together
en passant (Fr) in passing; by the way
en rapport (Fr) in harmony, sympathy
entre nous (Fr) between ourselves
erratum, errata (L) error, errors (especially those noted in list attached to book)
esprit de corps (Fr) the animating spirit of a group or collective body of people
ex cathedra (L) from the chair (of high authority)
ex officio (L) in virtue of one's office
fait accompli (Fr) a thing already done
faux pas (Fr) a false step; mistake in behaviour
genius loci (L) the guardian spirit of a place
honi soit qui mal y pense (Old Fr) evil to him who evil thinks
hors de combat (Fr) out of the fight; disabled
hors-d'oeuvre (Fr) an extra dish served at the beginning of a meal
ich dien (Ger) I serve

tet (L) let it stand; do not delete
ub judice (L) under judicial consideration
ummum bonum (L) the principal good
ant mieux (Fr) so much the better
ant pis (Fr) so much the worse
ice versa (L) the other way round; the reverse
iva voce (L) orally
oilà (Fr) behold; there is
ox populi (L) the voice of the people; public opinion
eitgeist (Ger) spirit of the times

The Greek Alphabet

NAME	CAPITAL	LOWER CASE	ENGLISH EQUIVALENT
Alpha	A	α	a
Beta	B	β	b
Gamma	Γ	γ	g
Delta	Δ	δ	d
Epsilon	E	ε	ĕ
Zeta	Z	ζ	z
Eta	H	η	ē
Theta	Θ	θ	th
Iota	I	i	i
Kappa	K	κ	k
Lambda	Λ	λ	l
Mu	M	μ	m
Nu	N	ν	n
Xi	Ξ	ξ	x
Omicron	O	o	ō
Pi	Π	π	p
Rho	P	ρ	r
Sigma	Σ	σ ς	s
Tau	T	τ	t
Upsilon	Y	υ	u *or* y
Phi	Φ	ϕ	ph
Chi	X	χ	ch
Psi	Ψ	ψ	ps
Omega	Ω	ω	o

Roman Numerals

I	1	XVII	17	DC	600	MV̄	4,000
II	2	XVIII	18	DCC	700	V̄	5,000
III	3	XIX	19	DCCC	800	X̄	10,000
IV	4	XX	20	CM	900	L̄	50,000
V	5	XXX	30	M	1,000	C̄	100,000
VI	6	XL	40	MM	2,000	D̄	500,000
VII	7	L	50	MMM	3,000	M̄	1,000,000
VIII	8	LX	60				
IX	9	LXX	70				
X	10	LXXX	80				
XI	11	XC	90				
XII	12	C	100	**EXAMPLES**			
XIII	13	CC	200				
XIV	14	CCC	300	**1980**	MCMLXXX		
XV	15	CD	400	**1981**	MCMLXXXI		
XVI	16	D	500	**1979**	MCMLXXIX		

Latin Abbreviations

AD = *anno Domini* (in the year of the Lord)

ad lib. = *ad libitum* (at pleasure)

a.m. = *ante meridiem* (before noon)

c. = *circa* (about)

do. = *ditto* (the same)

et al. = *et alii* (and others)

etc. = *et cetera* (and the rest, and so on)

et seq. = *et sequens* (and the following)

ex lib. = *ex libris* (from the books of)

fl. = *floruit* (flourished)

ibid. = *ibidem* (in the same place)

id. = *idem* (the same)

i.e. = *id est* (that is)

ign. = *ignotus* (unknown)

incog. = *incognito* (unknown, unrecognized)

in loc. = *in loco* (in its place)

loc. cit. = *loco citato* (in the place cited)

N.B. = *nota bene* (note well)

nem. con. = *nemine contradicente* (nobody contradicting, unanimously)

no. = *numero* (number)

non seq. = *non sequitur* (it does not follow)

ob. = *obiit* (died)

op. = *opus* (work)

op. cit. = *opere citato* (in the work cited)

pinx. = *pinxit* (he painted)

p.m. = *post meridiem* (afternoon)

p.p. = *per procurationem* (by proxy)

pro tem. = *pro tempore* (for the time being)

rox.	= *proximo* (of the next month)	**sqq.**	= *sequentes, sequentia* (the following)
.s.	= *post scriptum* (postscript)	**ult.**	= *ultimo* (in the last month)
Q.E.D.	= *quod erat demonstrandum* (which was to be demonstrated)	**v.**	= *vide* (see); *versus* (against)
		verb. sap.	= *verbum sapienti sat est* (a word to the wise is enough)
q.v.	= *quod vide* (which see)		
R.I.P.	= *requiescat in pace* (rest in peace)	**viz.**	= *videlicet* (namely, that is to say)

Morse Code

The Morse code is a system of dots and dashes named after its inventor, an American called Samuel F. B. Morse (1791–1872). It is used for conveying messages by wireless, telegraph, etc. The dot is a signal of short duration, the dash is three times this length. A gap equal to one dot is left between each symbol, and twice as much is left between each letter. There is a longer break between words.

Morse code can be sent on a hand key, a skilled operator being able to tap out up to 25 words a minute. Automatic transmitters can exceed this speed many times.

The international Morse code is as follows:

Full stop · − · − · −
Semicolon − · − · − ·
Comma − − · · − −
Colon − − − · · ·
Question mark · · − − · −
Apostrophe · − − − − ·
Hyphen − · · · · −
Bracket − · − − · −
Inverted commas · − · · − ·
Invitation to transmit − · −
Wait · − · · ·
Break − · · · −
Understood · · · − ·
Error · · · · · · · ·
Received · − ·
Position report − · − ·
End of message · − · − ·
Finish of transmission · · · − · −

A · −	**K** − · −	**U** · · −	**1** · − − − −
B − · · ·	**L** · − · ·	**V** · · · −	**2** · · − − −
C − · − ·	**M** − −	**W** · − −	**3** · · · − −
D − · ·	**N** − ·	**X** − · · −	**4** · · · · −
E ·	**O** − − −	**Y** − · − −	**5** · · · · ·
F · · − ·	**P** · − − ·	**Z** − − · ·	**6** − · · · ·
G − − ·	**Q** − − · −		**7** − − · · ·
H · · · ·	**R** · − ·		**8** − − − · ·
I · ·	**S** · · ·		**9** − − − − ·
J · − − −	**T** −		**0** − − − − −

Weights and Measures

AVOIRDUPOIS WEIGHT

16 drams (dr)	= 1 ounce (oz)
16 ounces	= 1 pound (lb)
14 pounds	= 1 stone (st)
28 pounds (US: 25 pounds)	= 1 quart (qr)
4 quarters	= 1 hundredweight (cwt)
20 hundredweight	= 1 ton

METRIC WEIGHT

1,000 milligrams (mg)	= 1 gram (g)
1,000 grams	= 1 kilogram (kg)
1,000 kilograms	= 1 tonne

LENGTH

12 inches (in)	= 1 foot (ft)
3 feet	= 1 yard (yd)
5½ yards	= 1 rod, pole or perch
40 poles	= 1 furlong (fur)
8 furlongs	= 1 mile
1,760 yards	= 1 mile
3 miles	= 1 league

METRIC LENGTH

10 millimetres (mm)	= 1 centimetre (cm)
100 centimetres	= 1 metre (m)
1,000 metres	= 1 kilometre

LIQUID MEASURE

4 gills	= 1 pint (pt)
2 pints	= 1 quart (qt)
4 quarts	= 1 gallon (gal)
8 gallons	= 1 bushel

METRIC LIQUID MEASURE

1,000 millilitres (ml)	= 1 litre (l)
1,000 cubic centimetres (cc)	= 1 litre

MEASURES OF AREA

144 square inches	= 1 square foot
9 square feet	= 1 square yard
30¼ square yards	= 1 square rod, pole or perch
40 square poles	= 1 rood
4 roods	= 1 acre
640 acres	= 1 square mile

METRIC MEASURES OF AREA

100 square metres	= 1 are
100 ares	= 1 hectare
100 hectares	= 1 square kilometre

MEASURES OF VOLUME

1,728 cubic inches	= 1 cubic foot
27 cubic feet	= 1 cubic yard

METRIC MEASURES OF VOLUME

1,000 cubic centimetres	= 1 cubic decimetre
1,000 cubic decimetres	= 1 cubic metre

NAUTICAL MEASURE

6 feet	= 1 fathom
100 fathoms	= 1 cable
10 cables	= 1 nautical mile
6,080 feet	= 1 nautical mile
3 nautical miles	= 1 league

CONVERSION TABLE

WEIGHT

1 ounce	= 28.350 grams	**1 kilogram**	= 2.205 pounds
1 pound	= 0.454 kilogram	**1,000 kilograms**	= 0.984 ton
1 ton	= 1.016 tonnes		

LIQUID MEASURE

1 Imperial pint	= 0.568 litre	**1 litre**	= 0.220 Imperial gallon
1 American pint	= 0.473 litre	**1 litre**	= 0.264 American gallon
1 Imperial gallon	= 4.546 litres		
1 American gallon	= 3.785 litres		

SURFACE MEASURE

1 square foot	= 0.093 square metre	**1 square metre**	= 1.196 square yards
1 square yard	= 0.836 square metre	**1 are**	= 119.599 square yards
1 acre	= 4,046.850 square metres	**1 hectare**	= 2.471 acres
1 square mile	= 258.998 hectares	**1 square kilometre**	= 0.386 square mile

LENGTH

1 inch	= 2.540 centimetres	1 centimetre	= 0.394 inch
1 foot	= 30.480 centimetres	1 metre	= 3.281 feet
1 yard	= 0.914 metre	1 metre	= 1.094 yards
1 mile	= 1.609 kilometres	1 kilometre	= 0.621 mile

MEASURE OF VOLUME

1 cubic inch	= 16.387 cubic centimetres	1 cubic centimetre	= 0.061 cubic inch
1 cubic yard	= 0.765 cubic metre	1 cubic metre	= 1.308 cubic yards

TEMPERATURE

To convert degrees Fahrenheit (°F) to degrees Centigrade (°C), use the following formula: $3 = \frac{5}{9}(F - 32)$.

To convert Centigrade to Fahrenheit, the formula is: $F = \frac{9}{5}C + 32$.

To convert Centigrade to degrees Kelvin (°K) or absolute, the formula is: $K = C + 273$.

INDEX

Moses, 147
Mountain climbing, 196
Mountain peaks, notable, 22
Mountain ranges, 21
Mozart, Wolfgang Amadeus, 346
Music, 332
Mussorgsky, Modest Petrovich, 346
Mythology, 170

Namib desert, 22
Natural history, 244
Navratilova, Martina, 288
Needle weaving, 265
Nefertiti, 163
Neptune, 16
   satellites, 18
Newton, Isaac, 370
Nicklaus, Jack, 291
Nile, 25
North Atlantic Treaty Organization
   (NATO), 82
Northern line, 89
Numismatology, 241
Nymphs, 177

Oates, Lawrence Edward, 167
Oceans, 20
Odysseus, 178
Oedipus, 178
Offenbach, Jacques, 346
Olympic Cup, 296
Olympus, 178
Opal, 34
Organization for Economic
   Co-operation and Development
   (OECD), 81
Organization of African Unity
   (OAU), 80
Organization of American States
   (OAS), 80
Organization of Petroleum Exporting
   Countries (OPEC), 82
Orienteering, 197
Orion, 178
Orpheus, 178
Ovett, Steven, 291
Owens, Jesse, 292

Pacific Ocean, 20
Paganini, Niccolo, 346
Painting, 358

Palace of Westminster, 356
Palaeontology, 36
Pantheon, 354
Park, Mungo, 167
Passover, 145
Patchwork, 271
Peary, Robert Edwin, 168
Pegasus, 178
Pele, Edson, 292
Philately, 239
Phillumeny, 240
Photography, 235–238
Piano, 336
Piper aircraft, 214
Piton, 197
Plane spotting, 211
Planets, 16
   satellites, 16
Platonic solids, 372
Playing cards, 242
Pluto, 16
Poisoning, 313
Pollux, 12
Polo, Marco, 168
Polygons, 372
Population, 75
Pre-Raphaelites, 352
Pressing flowers, 274
Print collecting, 242
Prokofiev, Sergei, 346
Proxima Centauri, 13
Ptolemy, 13
Punting, 198
Purcell, Henry, 341
Pyramid, 374

Quartz-crystal clock, 121
Quebec bridge, 87

Ra, 172
Rachmaninoff, Sergei, 347
Radio City Music Hall, 357
Rail tunnels, longest, 89
Raleigh, Sir Walter, 168
Rand, Mary Denise, 288
Ravel, Maurice, 347
Reef knot, 393
Renaissance, 352
Richards, Viv, 292
Riding, 198
Rigel, 12

NOTES

NOTES

NOTES

NOTES

NOTES

NOTES

NOTES